COVENANT:

The Blood Is The Life

Tracing the River of Blood
from the Tree of Knowledge
to the Tree of Life

James Lindemann

RFLindemann & Son, Publisher
2011

James (Jim) Lindemann
Webpage: lindespirit.com
email: jim@lindespirit.com
Blog: CovenantMusings.lindespirit.com

©Copyright 2011 James Lindemann. All rights reserved
ISBN 978-0-9877280-0-5

Other titles by the author:
Creation's Ballet for Jesus
Celebration! - Holy Communion: A Love Story
In the Image of God: Male and Female He Created Them
Living Waters – Baptism: From His Heart Through Ours
The Mystery of Suffering: Freedom From or Presence Within Suffering

RFLindemann & Son, Publisher
541 33 Street South
Lethbridge, Alberta, Canada T1J 3V7
*1503

Flyleaf

Blood-Covenant spans the globe in such traditions as the Native American Blood-Brother bond. No mere contract variation, Covenant is a powerful relationship of a deep, unbreakable Love; yet when God does break it *once*, He pays the consequences *He designed* it to have. Throughout the 'Old' Covenant, certain elements of Covenant are declared, yet are not 'real' – until the 'New' Covenant comes, which is not a 'what' but a 'Who.' Everything changes when God literally comes to have Blood Himself, the result of which profoundly affects the 'Old' Covenant. This relationship is eternal and does not become obsolete on the Last Day.

If the Bible is written within a Covenant environment, what does the modern Western reader miss which the ancient hearer would naturally recognize? Living in a culture which only has vestiges of Covenant, there is no easy or perfect answer. But the question can be very stimulating.

The Author

The author, a pastor himself, is the recipient of perspectives, concerns and interests handed down from a long line of pastors in the Lutheran Church, hence his interest and background in such things as the Sacraments, the Covenant, and even the Star of Bethlehem. His Bible Study groups have also contributed greatly in developing these various themes, and now as retirement approaches, this is a good time to gather these thoughts into a more finished form.

Born and raised in New York City, he has come to also value the life in the smaller communities. With his deeply appreciated companion (his wife), their family bulges at the seams with four natural, two adopted, a variety of foster children, and now grandchildren – there is no end to the usually delightful competition for his attention. Perhaps in the coming years there may even be time to pursue his Master's interest in carpentry.

Table of Contents

Preface

I. Covenant Overview — 1
    Vestiges of Covenant in our Culture ... Covenant ... Love Must Give Itself ... The New and Old Covenants ... The Trigger and a Source ... The Premise of This Study

II. The Basics of Covenant
    A. Based on the Nature of God Himself — 5
        God's Steadfast Love (*HESED; AGAPE*)
        The Glory of God
        God's Grace
            Jehovah Initiates ... God's Autonomy ... Not Unusual for a "Greater" to Approach a "Lesser" ... "No One Greater Than Himself"
    B. Based on Life [נֶפֶשׁ (*NEPHESH*) Soul] — 10
        נֶפֶשׁ (*NEPHESH*) Soul, Life
        The Distinctive Human
            Respect for the Life/Soul ... The Breath of God ... Re-Creation
        The Extraordinary Power of Covenant
    C. Based on Blood (Life) — 14
        The Blood = The Life [Soul]
        The Cutting of Covenant
        One Blood = One Life [Soul]
        Substitute Blood
            The Red Stew ... The Blood of the Grape
            Living Water (Remedy Against the Contagion of Death: The Red Heifer ... "Living Waters" ... "Flowing Water" and Unsolved Murder)
            Shall I Drink The Blood Of These Men With Their Lives/Souls ... The Golden Drink ... The Anointing Oil
        Consuming the Blood / Life / Soul
            Respecting Life ... The Vehicle of Salvation ... The Shock of Jesus' Blood
        "That You Abstain from ... Blood"
            Where is the First Church's Council Coming From? ... A Lesson from Menstruation ... Transfusions ... So Then What About Blutwurst (Blood Sausage)?
    D. The Essence of Covenant — 25

III. Covenant Ramifications
    A. "You in Me and I in You" — 27
        What Is Mine Is Yours, for Am I Not in You? ... My Authority is in You ... My Life is Your Life ... Obliged ... But a Difference in

        Jehovah's Involvement ... Violating the Character of the Person ... My Covenant-Brother's Keeper
   B. Selflessness   33
        Jonathan ... Jehoshaphat
   C. Subsequent Covenants   35
        Affirmation, Assurance and Commitment – the Confirming Covenants
        The New Covenant Supplants Which Old Covenant?
            Is it the Sinai Covenant? ... There is an Older Covenant ... There is a Most Ancient Covenant ... Choosing the Covenant
   D. Posterity   37
        Covenants – Logically – Include the Whole Family
        Sex is Not an Element
   E. The Great Link   39
   F. Not to be Broken!   41
        Covenants are Deadly
            Divided We Die ... All or Literally Nothing ... Cut Off
        Covenants were Permanent
            Jehovah is the Basis of the Permanency ... Not Even for Deceit ... In or Out

IV. The Covenant Mosaic
   A. The Oath – To "Seven" Oneself   47
        An Unique Number ... Subliminal Messaging (A Surprising Discovery ... The Case Study of Jericho) ... Obligation Even after Centuries ... Other Vows
   B. The SIGN of Covenant ('OTH – אוֹת)   50
        The Scar ... "To Consent, Agree" ... The 'OTHs: More Than *Symbols* of Presence and Power ... ZIKARON and ANAMNESIS ... The "Mighty Hand and Outstretched Arm" ... The 'Mighty Hand' of Blessing
        "A Sign On Your Hand, Frontlets Between Your Eyes" (The Amulet/Phylactery ... The Ring ... Superstition)
        Monumental Reminders
        Not-So-Monumental Reminders (The Seven Lambs ... The Scarlet Cord ... The Robe)
        "*The Tent of Witness*" and "*The Ark of Witness*" ... Marriage Imagery ... Negative Side to 'OTHs ... Other 'OTHs?
   C. The 'OTH <u>YOU</u> Do, But is <u>GOD'S</u> SIGN!   64
   D. The New Name – The New Identity   65
   E. The Covenant Feast   66
        The Communal Meal ... *The Peace/Fellowship Offering*
   F. Covenant in Odd Situations   69
        The "Anti-Covenant"
        The "Squeeze-Play" Covenant
   G. The Live-r of Glory   69
        The Sump of Life ... The Glory ... The Cleanser ... The Appendage of the Liver

V. Restoring Lost Life/Blood
- A. No Guarantee of Faithfulness — 73
- B. Life/Blood is Precious — 74
- C. The *GO'EL* [גאל] – The Blood-Balancer — 75

  The Cry for Justice ... The Office ... **SHALOM** [שלם] ... The Example of Ruth ... The Example of David ... Redemption for Broken Covenant

- D. *KAPHAR* [כפר] – The Ransom, the Redeeming from Sin — 80

  The *GO'EL* Established the Pattern

  Atonement (Ransom ... Pour Out the Blood Before the Altar ... The Day of Atonement/Redemption – Yom Kippur ... פדה (*PADAH*) – ransom, redeem, rescue)

  The Ransom Cover ... The *Red* Tent ... Ransoming a Broken Oath/Seven ... The 'Atonement' of Salvation – Noah ... A Sense of Futility

VI. The Old Testament: THE Foundational Covenant
- A. Based on the Nature of God Himself — 89

  Grace: The First Move is Always God's
- B. The Creation Covenant

  Part 1: MANKIND IS GOD'S AMBASSADOR — 89

  Blood(Life)-Likeness ... The First Covenant (The Proto-Covenant)

  The *'OTH*/Sign (THE IMAGE OF GOD ... A Trinity! ... The High Priest of Creation)

  Part 2: MARRIAGE — 92

  The Man – the Cutting ... The Woman – Representing God to Each Other ... Common Tasks, Different Methods ... The Voluntary Servant – Blood-Likeness with God ... The "Pointman" (Headship) ... The Purpose ... Covenant vs Divorce

- C. Covenant (Flow of Life/Blood) is Broken — 98

  The Temptation – Genesis 3

  Rebellion's Beginning...Life is Sought Outside of Jehovah

  The *GO'EL* Restores Lost Life

  God's Glory:Promises! and Discipline

  The Pattern and Way to Restore Lost Life

- D. So It Continues — 101

  Cain

  The Heritage of Rebellion ... The Voice of the Blood – the *GO'EL* Must Act ... Justice and Mercy for the Unjust

  Noah: Hope Despite Judgment

  The Rebellion Deepens ... The *GO'EL* Restores ... Flesh vs. Blood

VII. Abraham Enters Covenant
- A. The Call to Covenant — 105
- B. the Land I WILL show you — 105

Learning Covenant with Jehovah 2
Advanced Studies in Covenant
C. I WILL Make You into a Great Nation; I WILL bless you   106
"And Abram Believed Jehovah"
God Cuts Covenant *Almost as a Human*
    But Only a Half Covenant–GRACE! ... Jehovah Under a Curse ... Abram Just Has Not Got It Yet
NOW the Other Half – Circumcision
    In Your Flesh ... The Pivot of Circumcision is GRACE ... Militant Grace in the Household of Faith
The Major Weakness in Jehovah's Covenant with Abraham
D. I WILL Make Your Name Great; YOU Will be a Blessing   112
The Shared Nature
Jehovah Found His Intercessor
E. All the Nations of the Earth will be Blessed Through You   113
"Laughter" – The Covenant Made Visible
A Father's Grief
THE Father's Grief
F. "Throughout Your Generations"   115
Jacob
    "We have turned each to his own way" ... Covenant Chases Jacob ... Returning To Covenant ... Settling, But Not Settled
Joseph
    Hard Lessons ... On to Egypt – as Promised

VIII. Moses – Living With Covenant

A. The Call of Moses   121
As Promised, On Schedule
The Call of Covenant (Chosen by God ... 'OTHs [SIGNs] ... 'Throw-away Lines')
B. The Call of Israel   124
I WILL Bring You Out From Egypt's Yoke; I WILL Free You   124
    'OTHs (SIGNs) of Judgment
    'OTHs (SIGNs) for Repentance
I WILL Redeem You With an Outstretched Arm, Mighty Acts;   125
    The Passover (Life for All Who Would Take It ... The Passover Lamb – the Portal to Life ... The Feast of Salvation ... In Remembrance of)
    Mercy, Grace and *HESED*
    The Outstretched Hand (Crossing the Red Sea: The Call to Confidence ... The Covenant-Partner Fights)
    The Wilderness of "Sin" ... The Raised Hand Conquers
I WILL Redeem You...; I WILL Take You as My Own People   130
    Mount Sinai (My Own People ... At the Feet of Jehovah ... The Covenant Environment – Ten "Words" Or Commandments... Israel's Re-Covenant)
    The Tent of Meeting

       The Grit of Covenant (The Golden Calf – 'Have a [god] Your Way' ... The Mediator Between Jehovah and Sinful Mankind ... Betrayed, Yet Intercedes Again ... Working Covenant)
The Fire of God's Presence ... Unclean – The Contrast Between Death And Life ... Punishment
   Acceptance At Last   138
   Give It to You as a Possession   139
       The Land ... Struggling with Covenant ... Even Moses Trips ... As Moses Lifted Up The Serpent
  C. A New Attitude Surfaces   143
   Balaam Meets Israel's Covenant   144
       "The LORD Your God turned Curse into Blessing"
Subterfuge, the Blood-Debt and the *GO'EL*
The Covenant of Peace
   Final Preparations   147
       Passing on the Leadership ... Dividing the Covenant Land ... Looking Behind Before Looking Ahead
  D. Deuteronomy – Moses' Last Will and Testament   149
       The Prologue ... The Sinai Covenant ... A Unique People! ... Moses' Song ... Moses' Farewell And Patriarchal Blessing ... The Death Of Moses

IX. Time with Jehovah – Israel's Worship
  A. The Priests   159
   The Priests ... Aaron the High Priest
  B. The Sacrifices
   All Life Is Mine!   160
   The Main Sacrifices – The Cost of Restored Communion   161
       The Sin Offering ... The Whole Burnt Offering ... The Peace/Fellowship Offering ... Special Differences for the Priest
   Still Needs Atonement   164
   Other Sacrifices   164
       Numbers 19 – The Water of Impurity (The Red Heifer)
Leviticus 2 – The Grain Offering
Leviticus 5:14-6:7 – The Trespass/Guilt Offering
  C. The Festivals
   The Three Important Festivals   165
   The Feasts   166
       Redeeming the Time (Daily, Weekly, Monthly)
The Sabbath, the Sabbath Year and the Year of Jubilee
The Passover (Feast of the Unleavened Bread)
The Festival of First Fruits
The Festival of Weeks (Harvest – Pentecost)
The Festival of Trumpets (Rosh Hashanah)
The Day of Atonement/Redemption (Leviticus 16) – Yom Kippur
The Festival of Tabernacles (Booths; Ingathering)

X. Different Circumstances, Same Covenant
A. Settling the Land
    Joshua – The Six Hundred Year Dream Becomes Real   171
        Preparations ... "I Claim This Land in the Name of" ... Jericho ... Joint Accountability ... Deceived ... Settling Down in the Land ... The Solemn Re-Commitment of Covenant

    Judges – Accountability for Spiritual Ownership of Covenant Land   177
        Progress and Regress
        Gideon
        Jephthah and Samson
        What Has Light To Do With Darkness? [II Corinthians 7:14-16]

B. A King! A King!
  Samuel   182
        A Nazirite for Life ... Eli ... Samuel, Meet Jehovah ... "Ichabod"

  Saul   184
        "A King! A King!" ... Saul - What Could Have Been ... "He Must Increase, I Must Decrease" ... "What Have You Done?" ... The Test of Amelek

  David – I & II Samuel   188
        The LORD's Anointed ... Goliath ... Jonathan ... "On the Lam" ... The End of Saul ... Winning the Kingdom ... A Home and a House ... Covenant Obligations ... Great Faith Falters, "But There is Forgiveness with Thee"... The Census and the LORD's House

  Solomon   196
        The LORD's Anointed ... The Course Set With Wisdom and Knowledge from Jehovah ... *The Temple* At Last! ... The Foolishness of the Wise

  The Split Kingdom   198
        Rebellion (that is, 'Transgression') and "the Sin of Jeroboam"
        Meanwhile, the Fall of the South
        Yet the Spiritual Southern Cross Does Shine Through
        If You Thought the South was a Problem, Just Try the North!

  Elijah   202
        Why Do You Go On Limping? ... I'm So Alone! ... King Ahab of the North ... Naboth's Vineyard ... Ahab's Death ... Jehoshaphat of the South ... The Short Life of Ahaziah (North) ... Elijah, NOW It is Time to Go Home

  Elisha   207
        Elisha is Established as Prophet of Jehovah ... After Such Righteousness, Such Treachery ... Naaman Learns of Jehovah's Grace ... The Covenant-Partner's Sense of Humor – and Mercy ... Ben-Hadad's Invasion of the North ... A Pause for the *HESED* of Jehovah ... Hazael and Jehu – Jehovah's Word to Elijah Took Shape ... Joash /Jehoash...Amaziah's Rule ... Meanwhile in the North ... The Death of Elisha

        The Final Spiral   214
            Back to the South ... The North's Final Descent ... Hezekiah Clings to Jehovah ... Sennacherib Meets Israel's Covenant-Partner ... Hezekiah's Illness – Physical and Spiritual ... Manasseh ... Josiah ... The Final Slide into Captivity ... Epitaph of the South
   C. Exile and the Return
      Ezra   222
            The Covenant-Partner Makes His Move ... "The People Gathered As One Man To Jerusalem" ... Rejoicing with a Broken Heart ... If You Cannot Beat 'Em, Distract 'Em! ... The New Beginning ... Ezra Leaves Babylon ... *TORAH* ... "So We Fasted and Petitioned Our God" ... "I Sat Horrified"
      Nehemiah   228
            The Heart Breaks ... "They Made Their Hands Strong for Good" ... Selfishness ... "But I Prayed, 'Now Strengthen My Hands'" ... "Do Not be Sorry, for the Joy of Jehovah is Your Stronghold!" ... "Leaning on the Everlasting Arms" ... Recommitment and Repopulating the "Holy City" ... Dedication Celebration ... 13:1-47 – How Hard It Is to Put the LORD First
      Esther   234

XI. Poetry
   A. Job   235
      What Is That All About??
      A Gritty Look at Covenant Yet Covenant None the Less
      "Jehovah turned Job's captivity, when he prayed for his friends"
   B. The Psalms   239
      Why? How Long? ... Broken Covenant ... Helper ... *GO'EL* ... Yearning for the Covenant-Partner ... Exuberance of Covenant ... Psalm 119 ... A Final Important Thought
   C. Proverbs   246
      Distancing From Covenant ... Striking Hands ... Friend ... The Seven Pillars ... No Irresponsibility
   D. Ecclesiastes   250
   E. Song of Solomon   250

XII. The Prophets
   A. Isaiah   251
      In Search of a *GO'EL* and Intercessor ... That Which is No God ... The Filthy Rags ... The Hand and the Arm of Jehovah ... Jehovah, Our *GO'EL* ... The Redeemed ... *You* are a Covenant
   B. Jeremiah   262
      No Intercession ... False Religion ... The Reoccurring Note of Justice ... The Loyalty That Should Have Been There ... Jehovah vs. Jehovah ... "And You Would Not!"... So Judgment will Descend ... Yet the Grief of God ... Holding Fast to Hope ... The *GO'EL* to 'Balance the Blood' ... And an Even Greater Hope ... Lamentations

   C. Ezekiel   276
      "Behold, It Has Come … The End Has Come … Behold, It Has Come"
      "The Land Is Filled With Crimes Of Blood" … "Sacrificed Their Sons Whom They Bore To Me" … "His Idols in His Heart" … The Watchman: "Why Should You Die?" … No Longer Could Any Human "Stand in the Gap" … Discarded Love and Covenant … The Remnant … My Holy Name's Sake … Recompense to the Nations … Even the Land had a Special Promise … The New Order
   D. The Minor Prophets
     Daniel   293
      Helpless to Help … Seven and the Messiah … 'Epimanes' and Covenant
     Hosea   296
      Ignored … Ichabod, "The Glory Has Departed From Israel!" … "My Heart Churns Within Me" … "Love a Woman Who is Loved By a Lover"
     Joel   302
     Amos   304
     Obadiah   306
     Jonah   307
     Micah   308
     Nahum   310
     Habakkuk   311
     Zephaniah   313
     Haggai   315
     Zechariah   316
      Warning From the Past For the Present … Hope – for All Nations … Joshua … Zerubbabel … Breaking the Covenant … Which Covenant? … What Does Broken Mean? … Love and Discipline in Tension … You Prisoners of Hope
     Malachi   326

XIII. The 'New' Covenant of God
   A. Two Covenants, One Blood   329
   B. What's So New About the 'New' Covenant?   330
     Love (*HESED*) *Must* Give Itself … Actually Really Real? … The "I Am" Statements … Covenant's New Name is: Jesus!
   C. Circumcision
     The New Bond of Blood   334
      GOD HAS BLOOD! … The Blood Flows *Both* Ways … The Enduring Relationship of *the Heart* … The Foundation of All 'Circumcision' is still Grace
     Circumcision and St Paul   338
      Law and Paul
        The Two Layers to the Old Testament … Blameless?? … What the Law Really Means

  Circumcision's Place
    The Privilege ... The Promise and the Environment of Faith ... Physical vs Spiritual ... The New Creation
 D. The Blood and the Water
  Covenant Incongruity   343
  From Jesus' Heart   343
  Witnesses   344
    The Three Witnesses ... Water and Blood
  The Witness of the Spirit   346
  The Witness of the Water   347
   From His Heart to Ours   347
    'Living Water' ... Born of the Water – Baptism ... "How Can These Things Be?"
   A Word about Faith and Baptism   350
    What Faith Is ... What Makes Spiritual Faith Different ... Faith Does Not Initiate the Promise ... The Problem of Which Comes First ... The Promise's Center is the *HESED* of Jehovah ... Concerning Infants Placed Within the Promise ... Baptism and Faith in Colossians ... The Role of Faith in Infant Baptism
   "The Right to Become Children of God"   359
    Birth of Privileged Ones ... "Baptized Into Christ Have Put On Christ" ... "Adoption as Sons" ... My Father ... Same Ol' Me?
  The Witness of the Blood   364
   God's Purchased People   364
    The People ... The *GO'EL* ... In the Name of Jesus ... All the Life of God in One Sip ... This is a Sacrament of Love ... The Calling Continues from 'Old' to 'New' ... What of Israel, Now that Jehovah Broke the Old Covenant?
   The Body of Christ – Covenant, New Testament Style   371
    One Body ... "Participation" ... *KOINONIA* ... "A *Living Sacrifice*"
    "With/All the Company" (from the Liturgy's "Preface")
    "With/All the Company *of Heaven*" (from the "Preface")
   The Living Bread   380
    From Living Water to Living Bread ... Outgrowing Jesus?
   All that I Am   383
    The Bridegroom and His Bride ... Covenant within Covenant, Demonstrating the Image of God ... The Unbreakable One ... Maintaining the Unity

XIV. The New Testament and the 'New' Covenant
 A. The Synoptic Gospels, John and Acts   387
  The Synoptics ... Luke's Prologue to the New Testament ... Covenant's Invisible Presence ... The Kingdom of God ... The Transfiguration ... John's Covenant Setting

B. St Paul's Writings 391
      The Glory ... *GO'EL* ... The Riches of the Mystery in the 'New' Covenant
   C. Hebrews 395
      The Will and the Way ... The Need for a Better Covenant ... The Better High Priest/*GO'EL* ... The Better Sacrifice
   D. The Minor Letters 400
      James
      Peter
      John's Letters
      Jude
   E. Revelation 403
      Numbers ... Blood and Judgment ... Blood and Salvation ... The Living Waters and Salvation

XV. Epilogue 407
   The Panorama of Blood-Covenant
   The Tension over Covenant
   What's in *Your* Veins?

Endnotes 409

PREFACE

It has been fun. It has been grueling. It has been a delight. It has been puzzling. It has been filled with wonder. It has been frustratingly slow. But most of all, it has been worth it.

And it is all my Dad's fault. Throughout especially his last years, he had always been intrigued by the Covenant. He would often refer to it in sermons, Bible studies, and even in our conversations. When he died, since he had never been a writer, I promised my Mom that I would put what I could into some kind of document. That was the beginning of a most wonderful journey for me. Sadly, neither he nor my Mom will see the result of what his interest has led to. I think they both would have gotten a kick out of it.

Unfortunately most of what my Dad had learned died with him. Most of what was in written form really only hinted as to what he saw. However, within his library he had a reprint of *The Blood Covenant* by H. Clay Trumbull. That did it. I was hooked.

What Trumbull had done was to research Covenant in its various forms worldwide. By the time of his last printing, he had included more material as contributed by quite a number of missionaries from their field experience. The picture startled me. I began to realize that Covenant is very ancient. It seemed as though every culture around the world, even on the islands of the Pacific, knew and understood Covenant (or what we might call "Blood-Brother"). It therefore must be an event/relationship that goes back to the very earliest days of humanity.

The Bible did not create Covenant, but rather was written in an atmosphere permeated by Covenant already well understood. I believe there are many things in the Bible that assumed this atmosphere and therefore never needed to define this connection/relationship explicitly.

It reminds me of a situation where a woman newly from Korea once asked me to explain what Christianity was about. As I tried to explain many different concepts, I found that she didn't understand what I was talking about. I began to realize how heavily I relied on my culture as the foundation and common starting point for my explanations – something we all do naturally. But since her culture was very different, the explanations didn't make sense the way I had hoped. The experience made me respect all the more the task a missionary is faced with.

Because culture is in the background of a written document and often economizes its descriptions, it made me curious in regard to the Bible. Given a culture which is permeated with an understanding of Covenant, how would the Bible look to such a person? What would he intuitively recognize, "because, *of course*, that would be Covenant"?

We westerners are far removed from this unique relationship, although we still have vestiges of it in our culture. In effect, Covenant must now intrude into our consciousness to make itself known. But many indigenous peoples, who have practiced Covenant at least up until recent times, may be better equipped to understand this basic theme that runs throughout the Bible. For instance, the Native American, who has practiced the "Blood-Brother" pact, has a much better concept of Covenant than most people with a European background.[1] Since most commentators are of European influence, what have they been missing?

So I embarked on a journey through the Bible with that question in mind, although I realize that with that European influence in my own background, I proceed at the risk of not fully capturing or understanding what is there. Still, some common events in the Bible are now seen with a different slant. And such common phrases as "the mighty Hand and the outstretched Arm of God" – although very plain and understandable – now raise a question for me: the hand and the arm are often the locations where a Blood Covenant might be cut and performed. Since the scar from such a joining was a treasured symbol, would this phrase also have an implicit underlying connection to Covenant? For someone steeped in a Covenant culture, would that part of the conversation take on added significance to the hearer? I can only ask.

I have been fascinated in doing this study, because I would get stumped at a certain place. I would struggle with the problem, in one case for a number of years. Then a passage would catch my eye, make me stop to realize what it actually said, and I would be rocked back on my heels in wonder. Other times, it would simply be a point of view turned inside out. Still other times I would be rewriting the same point for the umpteenth time only to discover I was saying something I didn't realize.

Thanks, Lord!

In writing this book, I am reminded of one of my favorite stories. At a clergy conference somewhere, the main speaker was at the podium, shuffling his papers and murmuring aloud to himself, "where to begin, where to begin…" A voice in the back of the room piped up, "As close to the end as possible!" Although that is part of the difficulty of this presentation, even more difficult is "what to include."

There have been many false starts in writing this book because as each progressed, it was realized that the end product would be of monumental size. The effect would be an anchor submerging the reader under what some might perceive as a floodwater of tedium. Whether this revision will achieve a balance between challenging thought and just enough information remains to be seen.

I realize that I do not have the resources for as thorough a research as I would like, so all I can do at this time is to record my observations and the possibilities of what I see. After all, I am only a European descendant who has had to have Covenant imposed into my way of thinking. Even so, the walk through the Bible with different glasses has been interesting and a delight.

Thanks, Dad.

Thanks particularly to my daughter Rachel who suffered through the manuscript to give me some readability pointers and to Jane Pollock for her grammar and other writing discipline.

James Lindemann
August 18, 2011

Postscript: some notes

Bible passage locations are in square brackets.

Double quote marks are basically used when an actual quotation is employed, single quotes when a generalized statement is used.

Likely with varying degrees of accuracy, the Bible quote translations are mine, however there is a heavy dependence on:

The Interlinear Hebrew/Greek English Bible, 4 volumes
Jay Green, ed., (Lafayette, IN: Associated Publishers and Authors, 1979)

As well as
The Online Bible computer program (http://www.onlinebible.net)
Copyright in Canada
by Larry Pierce
(11 Holmwood St., Winterbourne, Ontario, N0B 2V0)

and particularly its modules for

The Authorized or King James (1769) Version

American King James Version
Michael Peter (Stone) Engelbrite (True Grace Ministries)
Placed into the public domain on November 8, 1999.

also its dictionary linking to *Strong's Concordance* numbers and to

R Laird Harris, *Theological Wordbook of the Old Testament* (Chicago: Moody Press, 1981)

Gerhard Kittel and Gerhard Friedrich, ed., *Theological Dictionary of the New Testament*, (Grand Rapids, MI: Wm. B. Eerdmans Publishing Co., 1966).

Also to reduce confusion, various Hebrew word groups are discussed at the beginning of this study, as the framework of Covenant is identified. Later, when these words appear in the Bible texts, simply the word group heading will be indicated, rather than the form of the word as it is used in the text.

I. Covenant Overview

Vestiges of Covenant in Our Culture

Two men conclude a deal, then 'shake on it.' Why? From where does the idea come that once 'shaken on,' the pact is considered unbreakable, even when no one else witnesses it (if they are men of integrity, of course)? Why do people shake hands upon greeting each other? And what of the 'high five' and the clasping of forearms to show solidarity of one with another? Why do these have such significance?

Sadly these are but fuzzy images of Covenant which still remain in our society. But step back in time, perhaps by visiting a culture which has only recently been infected by modern attitudes (such as an aboriginal culture), and Covenant is still alive and well, usually in the form one might call 'Blood-Brother.' Might such cultures actually be better equipped to understand this great Biblical theme than modern Western culture, removed as it is from a lifestyle which incorporates such an extraordinary relationship?

Covenant

Covenant – what is it? Is it a contract or a treaty? Neither. Why? Because in a contract or a treaty, one really does not *have to* care about the other – all he would be concerned with is the benefit to himself. In fact, it probably would be best in some instances that he *does not care* about the other, because it might cost him too much.

But what is the pivot for Covenant? I Samuel 18:3 identifies it clearly: "Then Jonathan and David cut a Covenant, *because he loved him as his own Soul.*" Later, aware that David would be the next king rather than himself, Jonathan still risks his Life to protect David, fully realizing that to do so probably signs his own death warrant. Such Love is the pivotal element of Covenant, an intense Love that reaches down into the Soul, willingly *giving its own Life (that is, Soul)* in order to advance the other. This definitely is no 'contract' or some business relationship based on benefit to one's self. Yes, there are benefits to be had, but not as the prime motivator.

He Who is all-sufficient in Himself does not enter Covenant for some sort of benefit to Himself. He does not borrow it from a human institution (in fact, it is mankind that gets 'good ideas' from God, not the other way around). What Jehovah desires, designs, and initiates at the very creation of humanity arises entirely out of Love:

> Behold, to Jehovah your God belong the heavens, the heaven of heavens, the earth, with all that is in it; yet Jehovah determined to Love your fathers and chose their descendants after them, you out of all peoples, as at this day.   Deuteronomy 10:14-15

> In this is Love, not that we loved God but that He loved us and sent His Son to be the full compensation for our sins.... So we have known and believed the Love God has in us. God is Love, and he who dwells in Love dwells in God, and God dwells in him.
>   I John 4:10, 16

Love Must Give Itself

This is indeed an extraordinary Love (in the Hebrew, *HESED;* in the Greek, *AGAPE*) and has an important characteristic:

> What does love always desire? Love does not ask for gifts. Love asks for love. "I don't want your gifts" says the maid to the lover, "I want you." Why this? Because love must always give itself to and for the beloved. If love were to give anything else but love, it would not be real love. Now this little baby in Bethlehem is God. It is love, it is God giving Himself.
>   ... When we realize that God is Love, Bethlehem *must* follow.... Because God is Love, Love had to give itself. It did give itself. The Child in Bethlehem was born because God loved the world.
>   Berthold von Schenk[2]

God *must* give *Himself.* So often the concept of Covenant, when defined from the human perspective as a bundle of obligations and benefits, misses that compelling motivation which brings *Jehovah* to earth, to humanity, to give Himself, not as a response to or a reward for mankind's agreeableness. Rather, not dependent on human reaction for or against, He simply gives Himself even to death. This is what grace is all about. This is the foundation of Covenant.

God's compelling desire of the heart culminates finally on the Last Day with "Behold, the dwelling of God is with men" – note: not vice versa! – "and He will dwell with them ... God Himself will dwell with them" [Revelation 20:3; also Ezekiel 37:27], where we have had a foretaste of this in Jesus, "Immanuel ... 'God with us'" [Matthew 1:23]. Covenant then is not so much how mankind can become close to Jehovah, but rather how *He* desires to become close to us.

The New and the Old Covenants

Is the Covenant of grace, mercy, Love and Life only in the New Testament? Is Covenant in the Old Testament designed simply to be 'Law,' and therefore death [I Corinthians 5:56; Galatians 3:10-13], in which God knows full well that this relationship's only outcome is for condemnation? Both Jesus and Paul declare that the Covenant of Circumcision came long before the Law [John 7:22; Galatians 3:17] – so if the origin of *this* Covenant does not lie in Law, then upon what is it founded? Indeed, if God is the same and His compelling Love is the same, then the focus and intent of His Covenants must be consistent between both Testaments.

The Trigger and a Source

It is with deep appreciation that H. Clay Trumbull's *THE BLOOD COVENANT: A Primitive Rite and Its Bearing on Scripture* [3] came into our hands. His research shows how Covenant is not localized to the Bible and to the Biblical lands. Ancient / primitive cultures around the world, even on islands, have had a Blood (or originally a Blood-based) relationship which would be the strongest and closest of all unions, broken only with cultural horror and the direst of consequences. The fact that Covenant in some form or another occurs in every corner of the earth suggests a common ancestry.

The Premise of This Study

With all of the above in mind, Trumbull's argument invites us to consider Covenant not as a vehicle for the Law and predominantly legal obligations, but rather as a vehicle of deep Love and of the willing obligations as would occur, for example, in a marriage, as well as for *the same reasons* as in a marriage. (Yes, the legal is even there, but it hopefully is not the essence of the relationship.)

Imagine, then, a culture where this kind of Covenant is indeed a strong part of its existence – where the people know it and understand it because it is part of their common life. They know the pitfalls and the powerful commitment when they "cut Covenant." Then imagine how God identifies that *this* relationship is the one *He* designed for *His* relationship with humans. Already from Creation, deeply ingrained in their consciousness, He does not need to explain it, yet by using it these people will recognize the extraordinary things He declares.

Consider then what the ancient *listener* hears which the modern reader, especially from a western civilization so far removed from this concept and dependent on translation, would never recognize.

The premise for this study then is that Covenant does NOT come out of the Bible but the Bible comes out of a Covenant-environment, based on a Love extraordinaire that is as old as before the creation of human beings. The task is to identify what an ancient listener would understand as especially the Old Testament is read aloud within such a culture.

II. The Basics of Covenant

A. Based on the Nature of God Himself

God's Steadfast Love (*HESED* – חסד; *AGAPE* – αγαπη)

> Know therefore that Jehovah your God is God, the faithful God Who keeps Covenant and steadfast Love to those who love Him and keep His commandments, to a thousand generations.   Deuteronomy 7:9

> God is not only able to perform what He pledged to do, He could be counted on to also *want* to do so. The Old Testament word, occurring more than two-hundred times which epitomizes His fidelity to keep His covenants is *HESED*, translated variously as mercy, lovingkindness, steadfast love. The divine attribute, described by this term, is liable to change as little as His omnipotence is in danger of running out of power. The believer is assured that "it endureth forever" and "is from everlasting to everlasting" [Ps 103:17; also the refrain in Ps 136:1-26].   Walter R. Roehrs[4]

The Covenant between Jonathan and David is pivotally important to tell us that the root of Covenant lies in Love:

> When David had finished speaking to Saul, the Soul of Jonathan was knit to the Soul of David, and Jonathan loved him as his own Soul/Life. ... Then Jonathan and David cut a Covenant, *because he loved him as his own Soul/Life*.   I Samuel 18:1, 3

However, as strong as this human Love is, Jehovah's steadfast Love is far greater and is "unbreakable." Only as we recognize this essential element of God's Covenant can we grasp the depth of Jehovah Himself reaching down to touch mankind in its creation and then in its need. What should call for utter amazement is that we see Almighty Creator Jehovah God personally cutting Covenant with a creature, a man, Abraham [Genesis 15:12-21], binding *God* in an absolute way to a human, years before the man is required to reciprocate! Despite mankind's abuse, sabotage, even apathy, despite having every most compelling reason to throw Covenant away, His Loving-Kindness – His Love – persists throughout all generations.

> ... the Soul of [Jehovah] was knit to the Soul of [mankind], and [Jehovah] loved him as His own Soul/Life ... Then [Jehovah] and [mankind] cut a Covenant, *because He loved him as His own Soul/Life*.
> Paraphrase of I Samuel 18:1, 3

The Glory of God

> Moses said, "I pray, show me Your Glory."
> Jehovah said, "I will make all My goodness pass before you, and will proclaim before you the [Covenant] Name 'Jehovah'; I will be gracious to whom I will be gracious, and will show mercy on whom I will show mercy ..."
> Jehovah descended in the cloud and stood with him there, and proclaimed the Name of Jehovah ..., "Jehovah, Jehovah, a God merciful and gracious, slow to anger, and abounding in steadfast Love [HESED] and truth, keeping steadfast Love for thousands, forgiving iniquity and transgression and sin, but will by no means clear the guilty, visiting the iniquity of the fathers upon the children and the children's children, to the third and the fourth generation."
> Exodus 33:18-19; 34:5-7

When one considers all the possible items which God could accent about His Glory – for example, omnipotence, omniscience, majesty, rule of the universe, and so forth – what is His response? *Jehovah's immediate definition of His Glory* is what His Covenant relationship embodies: His Goodness, Grace, Mercy, Steadfast Love, Faithfulness, Forgiveness and Justice.

Also note that these are *qualities*. One cannot see a 'box of mercy' or a 'bottle of grace' – a quality can only be shown in its demonstration[5]. Moses is not to see the future but only the "back" [33:23], that is, the demonstration of such things as grace and mercy from the past, which would be the 'HISstory' of the book of Genesis, which in turn forms a most fitting introduction and basic framework for the whole Bible.

What does this have to do with Covenant? Covenant is the expression of Jehovah's Glory – all these qualities are the framework as to how and why God would reach out and bind Himself to humans in such a tough and shatterproof way. And to see this Glory, Moses is protected by the "palm" – a place for cutting Covenant –, a rarely used word but the one found in Isaiah 49:16: "Behold, I have graven you on the palms of my hands" and would ultimately be where the print of the nails will be.

God's Grace

Jehovah Initiates

> If a man is to deal with God and receive anything from him, it must happen thus:
> Not that man begins and lays the first stone, but that God alone – without any entreaty or desire of man – must first come and give him a promise. This word of God is the beginning, the foundation, the rock, upon which afterward all works, words and thoughts of man must build.
> This word man must gratefully accept. He must faithfully believe the divine promise and by no means doubt that it is and comes to pass just as God promises. This trust and faith is the beginning, middle, and end of all works and righteousness.
> On the contrary God must anticipate all [of man's] works and thoughts, and make a promise clearly expressed in words, which man then takes and keeps in a good firm faith. Martin Luther[6]

There are two issues which form the foundation for the term 'Grace': The first is that God alone initiates anything which has to do with a relationship to Him. Humans do not have the capacity to outthink God; they cannot come up with an idea which would never have occurred to Jehovah, Who then would borrow from them. After God has revealed His plan, only now does mankind discover what *they* never would have imagined, and now *they* borrow concepts from that plan for their own various usages. This is why Covenant is not an adaptation of, for instance, an ancient Suzerainty Treaty, but rather it is the other way around.

> But the *free gift* is not like the offense. For if many died through one man's offense, how much more did God's Grace and the gift in the Grace of that one Man Jesus Christ abound for many.   Romans 5:15

The second essential point about Grace is that there are no strings attached. God's gifts are undeserved. Paul points out, "For there is no distinction; since all have sinned and fall short of God's Glory" [Romans 3:22-23]. We will never measure up to His standards, nor can we ever 'win' the Covenant-relationship; there is no way we can compel God to unite with us or induce Him to stick with us. In Romans 7:14-25, Paul, *as a believer*, speaks of the failings even he has when he tries to please God. If Jehovah's commitment to Covenant depended on our performance, it would be terrifying.

God's Autonomy

> Jehovah did not set His Love upon you, nor choose you, because you were more in number than any people – you were the fewest of all people! – but because Jehovah loved you, and because he will keep the *oath/seven* which he had sworn to your fathers…   Deuteronomy 7:7-8

If Jehovah is to have anything to do with us it has to be by His choice. His relationship with us is determined by *His heart*. He does not enter Covenant tentatively, but as Matthew 20:28 ("not to be served, but to serve and give His Life") and Ephesians 5:2 ("as Christ loved us and gave Himself up for us") remind us, He enters fully even at the cost of His Life, fully aware that a large proportion of "the whole world" [I John 2:2; John 3:16] would betray His Love. This is the autonomy of Jehovah in His declaration:

> I will be gracious to whom I will be gracious, and will show mercy on whom I will show mercy….   Exodus 33:18-19 (See 'Glory' above)

He *chooses* to be gracious to the whole world, providing the opportunity of Covenant to all, that is, the Covenant of oneness with Him, which is not necessarily the *special* relationship that Jehovah gives to Israel. (So, for instance, there are other faithful people outside of Abraham's family: Melchizedek, Genesis 14:18; Jethro, Exodus 18; Job.) God did and does fulfill His commitment totally – that is the center of Paul's argument in Romans 3:

> What if some did not believe? Does their unbelief nullify God's faithfulness? Never! Let God be true though every man be a liar, as it is written, "That You may be justified in Your words, and prevail when You are judged." verses 3-4

No one could claim that Jehovah has short-changed him, nor is there a question of unfairness, of moving the line of acceptance to arbitrarily exclude someone. God's offer is already accomplished – a 'done deal,' at least from His commitment. He never backs down nor backs out because of man's non-cooperation or rejection. There is no *'conditional'* to Covenant from God's perspective.

Not Unusual for a "Greater" to Approach a "Lesser"

While a Covenant is cut normally between equals, grace is not an uncommon basis for this relationship, as when prince Jonathan cuts Covenant with David – the low-class shepherd [see I Samuel 18:1-3 above]. After Covenant is cut, in terms of their personal relationship, the distinction of "greater vs. lesser" no longer applies. Indeed, Jonathan is still royalty, and David is still a vassal shepherd, but the idea of controlling because one has more power is now totally out of place. That is because the relationship is not one of power but of the heart, based not on getting but on giving the whole self without reservation, based upon the same Blood/Life flowing within both participants.

"No One Greater Than Himself"

"For when God made a promise to Abraham, since He had no one greater by whom to swear, He swore by Himself" [Hebrews 6:13]. Usually when a Covenant is cut, the participants invoke their God to be the watchdog of the relationship, to guarantee that faithfulness will be kept (in the same way that the 'state' watches over the legal protections of marriage) – but Jehovah could only invoke His own Self. He is both Participant and Watchdog, which among humans does not always work out so well. But, as will be seen, when *Jehovah* breaks Covenant, as Watchdog, He guarantees that He will pay the penalty.

B. Based on Life [נפש *(NEPHESH) Soul*]

נפש (NEPHESH) Soul, Life

> Jehovah God formed the man from the dust of the ground, and blew into his nostrils the breath of Life; and the man became a living Soul.
> Genesis 2:7

Because most people are not familiar with the original languages of the Bible, we depend heavily upon translations. Sometimes translators use different words to describe a certain word in the original language, perhaps to reflect different conditions or circumstances, or to make a sentence less awkward – or even to avoid controversy. The danger is that as we look at a translation, we may be unaware of the depth of understanding that is contained in the original word.

In order to convey what they understand certain passages to mean, translators employ a variety of words for נפש *(NEPHESH)*.[7] This key word in the foundations of Covenant is generally translated as "Soul," as well as "Life," and even as "creature." It identifies the animating power for the physical body and describes the essential makeup of a creature, particularly in how it exists in and reacts to this world. It includes the mind, the emotions, the consciousness of self as when pledging oneself by oath. It may be a euphemism for the whole person as when we might say, 'There are sixteen Souls on the bus.'

NEPHESH [Soul/Life] could be set in parallel to חי [*CHAY* - Living] [Job 9:21;33:18, 20, 22, 28], but also could be modified by *CHAY* to form "living Soul" [Genesis 1:20, 21, 24, 30; 2:7, 19; 9:10, 12; 9:15, 16; Leviticus 11:10, 46]. Although closely related, the concept of *NEPHESH* appears to contain a broader meaning than *CHAY*: *NEPHESH* means "Life" as it focuses on the essential nature of the creature, the distinctiveness of the individual, the enduring qualities marked by personality; *CHAY* is "Life" as it is daily carried on (even eternally), not so much as animating the body, but more as the *experience* of living.

The Distinctive Human

Respect for the Life / Soul

NEPHESH [Soul] is applied to both human and animal. In fact, of the twelve times where the "living Soul" combination appears in Genesis and Leviticus (above), only one [Genesis 2:7] refers to the human.

Permit a moment for a bit of moral observation regarding something which 'primitive' cultures acknowledge, but western civilization has forgotten: we share a commonality with all things living, and they deserve our respect:

> The Life/Soul of the flesh is in the Blood ... Any man of the sons of Israel, or of the strangers who dwell among you, who hunts any animal or bird that may be eaten, he shall pour out its Blood and cover it with dust.   Leviticus 17: 11, 13

As we stand contemplating the *NEPHESH* [Soul/Life] in the Blood of any creature, we glimpse an awesome mystery of God. Yes, in the course of daily living [*CHAY*] and survival we may need to take the Life [*NEPHESH*] of various creatures, but we must never do so without respect for what Jehovah has put His Hand to.

The Breath of God

Covenant is built upon the idea that there is something distinctively different in regard to the human above all other creatures on this earth. If it is not the Soul, then what is it? It is important then to pay attention to the words at the creation of the man:

> Jehovah God formed man of the dust of the ground, and blew into his nostrils the breath of Life; and man became a living Soul.
>
> Genesis 2:7 (note also Job 27:3; 33:4)

No other creature is ever described as bearing the very Breath *of God*. This suggests an intimate, personal relationship of humanity with Jehovah, a connection reflected elsewhere by "The *Spirit* (also 'Breath') of God" – in the Old Testament: רוח [*RUWACH*] (wind, breath, *spirit*); and in the New Testament: πνευμα [*PNEUMA*] (*spirit*) from πνεω [*PNEO*] (to breathe, blow, wind). It is not the Soul but this spiritual connection with God's Spirit which makes the human so unique, being an intimate connection which lies at the root of Covenant.

It is dangerous to define this distinctive part of the human as, for instance, mental prowess, the ability to think and to reason. Research in the capacities of apes in particular show that not only are they able to employ the sign language of the deaf, they have also been shown to have a sense of humor as well as the ability to initiate a question. These demonstrate more than mere mimicry. The spiritual area of the human must only be defined in regard to the special connection to God's Spirit – 'bearing His breath.' Any other basis may in the long run only create more problems than it solves.

Re-Creation

> When He said this, He breathed on them, and said to them, "Receive the Holy Spirit."
>
> John 20:22

> "The first man Adam became a living Soul." The last Adam became a Life–giving Spirit.
>
> I Corinthians 15:45

Looking at these passages, one might note that through His resurrection, Jesus echoes the creation scenario. But it is more than merely using the imagery. It is a renewal of Jehovah's intent when He first places His Breath / Spirit upon mankind; it is the restoration of the intimate and personal connection which God desires from the beginning of humanity – and even from "before the foundation of the world" [Ephesians 1:4].

Because of Jesus' in-the-flesh presence, His personal involvement to the extent of death and resurrection, and the forgiveness now made vividly real, the intimacy has become even greater in the New Testament than in the Old Testament.

The Extraordinary Power of Covenant

> Covenant is an absolute relationship that would kill its participants if it were broken.　　　　　　　　　　　　　　　　　　　Gary Piltingsrud[8]

Covenant is not merely an accessory to Life, as a ring or a medallion would decorate the body of a person. Properly speaking it is not really a commitment or an 'involvement,' although we must use those words for want of something better. It is the core Life of one person seamlessly joined to the core Life of another. It is something which cannot be broken without *Life* itself being 'broken.' It cannot be that some are 'conditional' Covenants since the relationship involves nothing less than the total person and his total Life with ramifications which reach into the future.

Since the concept is so powerful, when people want the idea of faithfulness and unbreakability, they may borrow Blood Covenant imagery, yet its forcefulness is weakened simply because they hesitate at the actual shedding of Blood and the totality it represents. So the handshake concluding the deal may evoke Covenant unbreakability, yet it cannot match the commitment and self-sacrifice which Covenant demands – *it does not have the one Blood in two persons.* It is that *unity* of Blood, not merely the Blood-letting, which makes the difference.

C. Based on Blood (Life)

The Blood = The Life [Soul]

> You shall not eat flesh with its *Life [Soul]*, that is, its *Blood*. Genesis 9:4
> The Blood is the *Life [Soul]* – you shall not eat the *Life [Soul]* with the flesh. Deuteronomy 12:23

There is a world of difference between 'The Blood *has* Life' and "The Blood *is* the Life." In the Bible, Blood and Life are identified as synonymous and, at least in concept, interchangeable – the Life is not merely *in* the Blood as if they were separate entities, the one containing the other.

> The root-idea of ... blood-friendship seems to include the belief, that the blood is the life of a living being; not merely that the blood is *essential* to life, but that, in a peculiar sense, it *is* life; that it actually vivifies by its presence; and that by its passing from one organism to another it carries and imparts life. Trumbull[9]

Wherever you read "Blood", you could insert "Life/Soul"; the reverse might sound a little awkward in some places but would not violate this understanding. Covenant is Life/Blood transfusion in its original form!

The Cutting of Covenant

The Hebrew word for Covenant [ברית *B'RITH*] means "The Cutting," because it could never be separated from Blood. Two people become "Blood-Brothers" by cutting their skin, joining the cuts (from which we get our handshake and brotherhood clasp), letting the Blood flow together, making them of 'one Blood' – one Life, one Soul.[10]

Where the 'cut' is made varies from culture to culture: most often it is some location on the *hand or arm*, however in some African cultures where the men are trained more as runners, the *leg* as a symbol of strength has been the site of choice.[11]

One Blood = One Life [Soul]

Far beyond merely some 'binding agreement,' this is a literal oneness entered into with the whole being – one's whole Life: "one Blood/Soul now flows between two persons," there is now *one Life in two bodies*:

> The inter-commingling of the blood of two organisms is, therefore ... equivalent to the inter-commingling of the lives, the personalities, the natures, thus brought together; so that there is, thereby and thenceforward, one life in the two bodies, a common life between the two friends: a thought which Aristotle recognizes in his citation of the ancient "proverb": "One soul [in two bodies]"   Trumbull[12]

It is more than friendship, and even closer than a brother (a 'milk' or 'water' relationship):

> The phrase "Blood is thicker than water" did not mean that blood-related family members were to be considered as more important than anyone else – the original meaning was, "The blood of the covenant is thicker than the water of the womb." This is reflected in "... there is a *friend* [the Covenant-related word used in II Chronicles 20:7, 'Are You not our God, ... Abraham Your friend forever?'] that sticks closer than a brother." [Proverbs 18:24].   Trumbull[13]

This is not a taking *away* of the one's Life, but the taking *in* of the other's Life, *the mingling of the Lives* – one Blood/Life – between the two persons; not only the giving of Blood, but also *the acquiring of Blood, that is, Life;* not so much a Blood-letting, as a mutual Life-Gaining.

Substitute Blood

The Red Stew

Although Blood is the most definitive indicator of Covenant-bonding, in his book Trumbull notes that substitutions are sometimes employed, such as in Malabar where a mixture of saffron and lime has been used in marriage and adoption ceremonies.[14]

A Biblical example is the well-known instance of Esau selling his birthright (with its Covenant-blessing overtones) for a *red* (אדם [*ADOM*]

– note "Adam"; from דם *DAM* "Blood") stew [Genesis 25:29-34]. Like the pact sealed by a handshake borrows the concept of unbreakability from Covenant, the oath selling the birthright (probably in front of witnesses) is sealed by this red stew (standing in for Blood) in a common meal between Jacob and Esau (which earned Esau his new nickname "Red" [*"EDOM"*]).

The Blood of the Grape

> The scepter shall not depart from Judah, nor a governor from his loins, until He to Whom it belongs comes; and to Him shall the people submit. Binding His foal to the vine and His ass's colt to the choice [red wine] vine, He washes His garments in wine and His vesture in the Blood of grapes.   Genesis 49:10-11

> Curds from the herd, and milk from the flock, with fat of lambs and rams, the breed of Bashan and goats, with the finest of the wheat – and of the Blood of the grape you drank wine.   Deuteronomy 32:14

> First we find men pledging each other in a sacred covenant, in the inter-drinking of each other's blood mingled with wine. They called their covenant-draught "assiratum," or "vinum assiratum"; "wine, Covenant-filled." By and by, apparently they came to count simple wine – "the blood of grapes" – as the representative of blood and wine, in many forms of covenanting.
>
> This mutual drinking, as a covenant-pledge, has been continued as an element in the marriage ceremony, the world over, down to the present time. ... Among the Arabs, since the days of Muhammad, wine has been generally abjured, and coffee now commonly takes its place as a drink in all ordinary conferences for covenanting. ...
>
> The Rev. Chester Holcombe, who has been a missionary in China for a dozen years or more, writes me explicitly: "I have been told that in ancient times blood was actually used instead of the wine now used as a substitute," in this wedding-cup of covenanting.   Trumbull[15]

Living Water

Remedy against the Contagion of Death:
The Red Heifer – Numbers 19

Much uncleanness in the Old Covenant is purified by a bath, a change of clothes and the change of day; however, like a deadly poison or contagious disease, mere contact with death takes a whole week – death is so destructive. *Any* contact with death or those among the 'living dead' (lepers) demands a restoration to Life. The Red Heifer's Sacrifice is given for such a reason.

Among this Sacrifice's unique features are: it is neither a *Sin Offering*, nor a *Whole Burnt Offering*, nor a *Peace/Fellowship Offering*, but "it is for purifying from sin"; the RED (that is, Blood/Life) heifer is killed OUTSIDE the camp (v 3; not at the door of *the Tent of Meeting* or by *the Altar of Sacrifice*, as is *every other sacrifice*); she is burned WITH her Blood (v 5; it is *not* poured out) along with cedar (*red*-wood), *scarlet* wool and hyssop (a combination only mentioned elsewhere for the cleansing of the leper [Numbers 14]).

The gathered-up ashes are added to *"Living Water"* [v 17] (which now becomes "the Water of Impurity" [v 9]) to be sprinkled on those whom death has touched. The mixture is sprinkled on them on the THIRD day, and on the SEVENTH[16] day – not by themselves, but only by another who is already clean – so that now they are restored to the Life of God's People (they are allowed to enter the camp) and are therefore also restored in their Covenant relationship with God.

Despite death having such power, this Sacrifice's potential is so great that apparently only six heifers are needed throughout all the generations between Moses and Jesus[17] (Jesus would be *the seventh/oath and final sacrifice!*[18]) – it is as close to an eternal sacrifice as one can get. But woe to him who does not 'need' it: "that Soul shall be cut off from among the congregation, for he has defiled *the Sanctuary* of Jehovah" [v 20].

"Living Waters"

A curious phrase – but to desert people, running water might have been considered as living and life-giving. Indeed that likely is the usage to be found in Genesis 26:19's "a well of living [*CHAY*] waters," and also in Song of Solomon 4:15. These are the only two apparently secular uses of the term in the Bible.

However in the sacrifices for the cleansing from leprosy (a living death) [Leviticus 14], "the Living Waters" is paired with "the living bird" (as opposed to the second bird, "the killed bird"), which suggests that the concept is far deeper than merely 'running water.'

The term shifts into dramatic gear in Jeremiah and Zechariah. Jehovah describes Himself as "the Fountain of Living Waters" [Jeremiah 2:13; 17:13] and in Zechariah [14:8] the end time would be characterized by "Living Waters shall go out from Jerusalem." "Living Waters" for the "Living Soul" mixed with the Sacrifice of the Red Heifer's ashes provide the antidote for death and therefore a reconnection to the Spirit of God, which in Genesis has made man "a living creature."

It would reach its climax in the New Covenant: "For I will pour Water on that which is thirsty ... I will pour My Spirit on your descendants, and My blessing on your offspring" [Isaiah 44:3], as Jesus also describes: "He who believes in Me, as the Scripture has said, out of his innermost being will flow rivers of Living Water (He spoke concerning the Spirit...)" [John 7:38-39].

"*Flowing* Water" and Unsolved Murder

Deuteronomy 21:1-9 deals with unsolved murder – innocent Blood has been shed, which therefore requires an atonement from "the city which is nearest to the slain man." Taking

> a heifer which has not been worked and which has not pulled with a yoke. The city elders shall bring the heifer down to a valley with running water, where it has not been plowed nor sown, and they shall break the heifer's neck there in the valley... All the elders ... shall

> wash their hands over the heifer ..., "Our hands have not shed this Blood, nor have our eyes seen it. Atone (KAPHAR), O Jehovah, Your People Israel, whom You have redeemed (PADAH), and do not charge innocent Blood to Your people Israel." The Blood shall be atoned for them and you shall put away innocent Blood from among you...
> Deuteronomy 21:3-9

Not the "Living Waters" as mentioned above, "flowing water" suggests the washing away of the guilt of spilled Blood. However the "atonement" comes not from the water but from the heifer's substitutionary death. Perhaps the contrast between the two might be that the "flowing water" is involved in removing – washing away – guilt, whereas the "Living Waters" – the Living Spirit, like the flow of Blood in Covenant – brings Life.

Shall I Drink the Blood of These Men with Their Lives/Souls – I Chronicles 11:15-19

David's hometown, Bethlehem, is occupied by the Philistine enemy and he wishes he could drink from its well – that is, that his home be rid of these heathens. Three daring 'sergeants' break through the lines and return with water from the town well. To David, this water symbolizes their Blood, willing to be shed for his sake, not to be drunk, but to be placed before Jehovah. Perhaps this might be accepted as within a Covenant context, since the extreme loyalty of that relationship is very evident.

The Golden Drink

> As soon as he came near the camp and saw the calf and the dancing, Moses' anger grew hot, and he threw the tables out of his hands and broke them at the foot of the mountain. He took the calf which they had made, burned it with fire, ground it to powder, spread it on the water, and then made the People of Israel drink it. Exodus 32:19-20

Powdered gold is a purgative. In suspension in water, it turns red. These two aspects speak to the restoration to Covenant with God: the sin (rebellion) must be taken away – purged – (forgiven); and the Life which has bled away must be replaced. Perhaps it is 'Living Water' in which Moses mixes the gold?

The Anointing Oil – Exodus 30:22-33

Precious and holy, this is a blend not to be copied and it cannot touch anything without that thing becoming consecrated – irrevocably set apart for exclusive use in service to God. Trumbull [for example, pp 336, 362] includes examples where the Covenanting Blood is dripped on the head; perhaps this is where the use of anointing oil comes from. Since the Blood is the Soul/Life of a person, the anointing would be a sign ('OTH?, see chapter IV below) of Jehovah's empowering Spirit for the task/role an individual is to undertake.

Consuming the Blood / Life / Soul

Respecting Life

> If anyone… eats any kind of Blood, I will set my face against that *Soul* who eats Blood, and will cut him off from his People. For the *Soul** of the flesh is in the Blood; and I have given it to you on the altar to make atonement for your *Souls**; for, as *Soul**, it is the Blood which atones for the *Soul** … Any man also of the People of Israel, or of the strangers that sojourn among them, who takes in hunting any beast or bird that may be eaten shall pour out its Blood and cover it with dust. For the *Soul** of every creature is its Blood … You shall not eat the Blood … of fowl or animal; any *Soul** who eats any Blood – that *Soul** shall be cut off from his People.
> Leviticus 17:10-11, 13-14; 7:26-27 (also Genesis 9:4) **Soul/Life*

The prohibition against consuming Blood is very strong – in fact, Jehovah is quite vehement in His condemnation – but why? Verse 13 which instructs that the Blood be poured out and covered with dust would appear to set a context of solemn respect. The prohibition is not merely for the sake of idle tradition. Blood is not merely the counterpart to a piece of meat, but represents a mystery of God's creation which we still have not figured out: the Life/Soul of a living creature.

The Vehicle of Salvation

But in verse 11 is also another reason:

> For the *Soul** of the flesh is in the Blood; and I have given it to you on the altar for making atonement for your *Souls** for, as *Soul**, it is the Blood which atones for the *Soul**.   **Soul/Life*

The prohibition is also based on how the Blood is the vehicle of atonement. But more: it is *Jehovah's gift*: "-I- have given it to you upon the altar to make atonement ..." Although the NIV makes nice reading ("given it to you to make atonement for yourselves"), there is no reflexive ("for yourselves") in the Hebrew; the sense is that *God* is the One Who places it on the altar to atone for Souls (although He uses the hands of the priest). The value then is not just that Blood contains the marvel of God's creation, nor even that it is central to atonement, but that it is God's merciful and grace-filled gift.

And this is not just for sacrificial Blood – it covers *all* Blood. As His vehicle of Atonement/Salvation, nothing is to dilute/distract/detract from the specialness of this gift and its high honor of being the vehicle of Jehovah's grace.

The Shock of Jesus' Blood

> Jesus said to them, "Truly, truly, I say to you, unless you eat the Flesh of the Son of Man and drink His Blood, you have no Life in you;"
> John 6:53

> He took the cup, gave thanks, and gave it to them, saying, "Drink from it, all of you, for this is My Blood of the new Covenant, which is poured out for many for the forgiveness of sins."   Matthew 26:27-28

After centuries of Blood being prohibited, the disciples cannot but be shocked by such pronouncements from Jesus. Yet His action is entirely consistent with the reasons why Jehovah gives the prohibition in the first place: it is the gift of salvation, the gift of atonement, not by human action, but by the LORD's grace.

And more: not just the mystery of God's gift of Life in regard to creation, *this* Blood is the mystery of God becoming part of His creation. *This* Blood is the Soul, that essence of Jehovah Himself come into the flesh. Here is the very Life of God in one sip. There is no prohibition here, but rather invitation to enter into the flow of Jehovah's Life/Blood into our lives, our veins – to enter a New Covenant.

"That You Abstain from ... Blood" [Acts 15:29]

Where is the First Church's Council Coming From?

On one hand, Jesus said, "Drink from it, all of you, for this is My Blood of the New Covenant"; yet the disciples instruct the early Church to "abstain from ... Blood" – how are we to understand this?

It is hard to imagine with how much profound respect the Blood is to be treated throughout the Old Testament: even the Blood of the animal killed in the hunt is to be covered [Leviticus 17:13]. Ezekiel 24:7-8 speaks of how Jehovah is moved to great anger at the shedding of innocent Blood and, as if that is not bad enough, that it is done openly ("on bare rock", that is, uncovered) – such additional disrespect for this precious gift increases His fury even more. After all, the Blood chiefly represents the Source of Life, God Himself: "The Blood is the Life" [Genesis 9:4; Deuteronomy 12:23]. Perhaps then the background to their prohibition is the concern that the concept of Blood might become trivialized.

A Lesson from Menstruation

When the woman is considered unclean during menstruation, it has little to do with the woman, but everything to do with the Blood, the precious River of Life ("if ... the discharge from her body is Blood" [Leviticus 15:19]). The Life which flows is now lost Life (as the danger of anemia can affirm); in fact, likewise any such issue from *a man* also makes *him* equally unclean for seven days [Leviticus 15:1-15]. For either one, on the eighth day after the flow has ceased two turtledoves are to be offered, one as a *Sin Offering*, the other as a *Whole Burnt Offering*. So also after birth:

> When the days of purification are fulfilled, ... she shall bring to the priest a lamb of the first year for a burnt offering, and a young pigeon or a turtledove for a sin offering... He shall offer it before Jehovah, and shall *atone* for her and she shall be *clean from the flow of her Blood.*
>
> Leviticus 12:6-7

Why a *Sin Offering* for something which is 'natural'? What we see now as 'natural' comes out of a world which no longer is natural the way God designed it. Lost Life is wrong, even when one does not deliberately cause it, the same as touching death (even in preparing the body of a loved one [see Leviticus 21:11]) requires the spiritual medicine through the sacrifice of Life (the Red Heifer). That we are simply participants in a broken world does not release us from being tainted by the lost Life and broken Covenant which surround us. In fact, even *the Holy of Holies* in *the Temple*, despite being where Jehovah would appear, requires yearly atonement on *the Day of Atonement* [Leviticus 16:2, 16].

Transfusions

Are the disciples intending to reject Blood transfusions when they instruct the Church to refrain "... from Blood ..."? Obviously Blood transfusions were not even imaginable back then. Since, if anything, a transfusion beautifully describes the ancient concept of Covenant with its mingled Bloods, it would be questionable that they would be concerned about this sort of use of the Blood. After all, here is the picture of strength shared, the giving of one's Life for the sake of another, the gaining of Life, and many other elements that are integral and noble within the extraordinary connection of Life found in Covenant.

In fact, if they were condemning transfusions, they would be outlawing Covenant, the very foundation of God's relationship with man, prohibiting what the Old Testament does honor (for example, the Covenant between David and Jonathan). All which the early Church seeks is to uphold respect for Blood/Life, standing against the trivializing of Blood, and *their* concern would be more in line with the above discussion in regard to menstruation. Since the Blood figures so essentially in salvation, one might assume that their concern would be against an indifference toward or even an abuse of Blood (as in pagan rites).

So Then What About Blutwurst (Blood Sausage)?

There is the danger of legalism here, of making an unbending law dictate Life. There are many times when Jesus is at odds with the Pharisees and scribes over such a method. Rightly so. In the New Testament, we are declared free from particularly the ceremonial law. Yet a law identifies a certain value: the law against murder is established because human Life is valued. Hopefully the values we arrive at go beyond the law – so in regard to "Thou shalt not kill," in his *Small Catechism*, Martin Luther explained that this commandment not only forbade hurting or harming one's neighbor, but emphasized the real spirit behind the law – St Paul's "he who loves another has fulfilled the law" [Romans 13:8,10] – by insisting on helping and befriending the neighbor (as also Jesus identified in His Parable of the Good Samaritan [Luke 10:25-37]).

Jehovah's prohibition against consuming the Blood is based on the values He identifies: it is the Life/Soul of the creature, a marvelous gift and mysterious creation of God; as well, it is the vehicle of His merciful and grace-filled atonement and therefore all Blood should be treated with even more honor.

We have been freed from the law. But what do we do with the values that underlie it? If we discard those values as well, is this sophistication, or do we merely become more crude? This is St Paul's point in his first letter to the Corinthians: "'All things are lawful for me,' but not all things are helpful... 'All things are lawful,' but not all things build up" [6:12; 10:23]. Indeed we are free. However, we may do well not to react to that freedom in a 'kneejerk' way, but rather to thoughtfully consider the values which such a law has expressed and then decide our individual course of action.

D. The Essence of Covenant

In regard to *DIATHEKE*, the New Testament word for Covenant, one may look to *The Theological Dictionary of the New Testament (TDNT)*[19], which is considered the definitive last word for every word in the Greek Bible. It strongly emphasizes the legal aspect of "Covenant" – for example, the Covenant between David and Jonathan:

> When Jonathan entered into covenant with David... "because he loved him as his own soul", he placed under legal guarantee the spontaneous impulse of this heart... This concept [*HESED*], which the OT often uses in relation to the covenant to express the faithfulness of the covenant partner, is particularly well adapted to bring out the sober legal character of the relationship established between the two concerned. *TDNT*[20]

This is not satisfying. When two North American Aboriginal natives cut Covenant, that is, form a Blood-Brother pact, is it really appropriate to say that this is done for the legal ramifications, or is it because they desire to establish a unity? It may well be that it is only a matter of viewpoint and semantics whether one uses the term 'legal' or some other way of explaining the obligation part of Covenant, yet it carries a certain dry, detached feel about it.

To illustrate the problem: suppose a North American person observes the plight of people in a famine in Africa. It touches his heart, and so he makes a substantial contribution to a help organization. It can be said that he truly cares. Another person not only makes a substantial contribution but also goes himself to the people, to look them in the face, and to do in person whatever he can do. He, too, truly cares – both truly care. Both hearts have been touched. Yet one deals 'at arm's length,' while the other becomes personally involved – you might say that his is indeed a *relationship* of deep *personal* love.

So the question which must be considered is whether God, His heart indeed touched, 'dispenses' salvation as an object 'at arm's length'; or is the goal and final product of *all* that He does – in fact, the *definition* of 'salvation' – a deeply personal relationship which literally goes on forever, not based in legal principles, but based in Love (as St John often speaks about). It is this second alternative which seems to be missing in so many discussions about Covenant. What does God really want? What is the driving force behind all which He does? When all has been said and done, just where is His heart in Covenant?

That is why God's own immediate definition of His Glory in Exodus 33:19 is such an important insight in this discussion. There is not a word about legal requirement, but rather goodness, Covenant, grace and mercy – and that is in the midst of a situation where the legal is thoroughly tromped upon (the golden calf), and Jehovah has every legal right to simply walk away. In fact, this kind of situation reflects so much of the history of the Old Testament!

Although human relationships have used the power of Covenant for personal gain, what has held God throughout the centuries? Merely legal right? Some sort of personal gain? Why does Jehovah put Himself into a relationship where He cannot back out except by death? Why does Jesus come to *share* our lives, besides just 'saving us'? When Jehovah "will wipe away every tear from their eyes" [Revelation 7:17; 21:4; Isaiah 25:8], does this not have the sense of God's personal involvement, not just His removal of the causes of crying?

There are, indeed, 'legal' aspects in every Covenant. In the Covenant between David and Jonathan, however, the legal benefit is not the essential reason – indeed, if a reason at all – for entering this relationship. It is to have a bond which would transcend all other relationships, a bond which is totally motivated by Love. There is no superior bond described anywhere else in contrast to what Covenant offers. In such a context, the legal becomes the mere servant of the Love, to indicate the depth of the commitment (as might be considered in marriage vows), but not as the binding force, which is what *Love* is to accomplish, for without such Love, the legal becomes futile.

III. Covenant Ramifications

A. *"You in Me and I in You"* [John 14:20]

What Is Mine Is Yours, for Am I Not in You?

> Of the close and binding nature of this blood-compact, ... As to its limitless force and scope, ...: One brother[-friend in blood covenant] coming to another brother's house, is in every respect regarded as free [to do as he pleases], and [is] as much at home as its owner. Nothing is withheld from him; even his friend's wife is not denied him, and a child born of such a union would be recognized by the husband as his; (for are not – as they reason – these brother-friends of one blood – of one and the same life?) [From Forbes, *A Naturalist's Wanderings in the Eastern Archipelago*, p. 452]. Trumbull[21]

Although we may object to the extent to which the oneness is taken in this case, it identifies just how powerfully the concept is understood. It is like the magician's trick where a rope would be 'cut,' then tied together, 'magic' words would be spoken, and – voila! – the rope shows no trace of being cut; no one can tell where the one cut half of the rope begins and where the other half leaves off. So also my Blood is in you, yours is in me. It is one Life – one Soul – in two bodies. There are no halves.

My Authority is in You

> Then Jonathan cut a Covenant with David, because he loved him as his own Soul. Jonathan took off his robe and gave it to David, ...
> I Samuel 18:3-4

Jonathan strips himself of his robe and gives it to David. With our variety of clothing outfits, this may seem trivial, but it is a prince's robe to be worn by a common shepherd. Here is a symbol of authority and favoritism, clearly with the idea that if you mistreat David, you answer to the royal throne, as a footnote on Esther 6:8 also points out:

royal robe the king has worn. ....Great significance was attached to the king's garments in ancient times; wearing his garments was a sign of unique favor (1Sa 18:4). To wear another's garments was to partake of his power, stature, honor or sanctity (2Ki 2:13-14; Isa 61:3, 10; Zec 3; Mk 5:27). Haman's suggestion is not only a great honor to the recipient, but it is also considerably flattering to the king: Wearing his garment was chosen instead of wealth. *Concordia Self-Study Bible*[22]

As Henry M. Stanley searches for Dr. Livingstone in Africa, he (or his proxy) cut many Covenants with various tribes. On one occasion He has to give up a precious possession, the goat whose milk he needs to soothe his ulcers. Then the wrists of Stanley's proxy (Frank Pocock)'s and of the chief are cut, joined and tied together. The chief lifts their bound wrists and declares that they are now brothers, and all are to treat Stanley as they do the chief. Later, renewing this Blood-Brotherhood, Stanley receives a scepter wrapped with brass bands. As he carries this badge of authority, throughout that area of Africa, Stanley is treated with honor and respect. The might of the chief is behind him.[23]

My Life is Your Life

with his armor, even to his sword and his bow and his belt.
I Samuel 18:4

When a Covenant is cut, different things may be accented in the oaths, specific areas of Covenant from which the participants particularly draw comfort and encouragement. The weaponry continues the message: 'YOUR enemy is now MY enemy – using my sword pledges me to fight alongside you. However, MY enemy is YOUR enemy – you hold MY sword which I can call on whenever I need help. We are so unified that one cannot be touched without the other being directly involved – my Life/Blood is yours, and your Life/Blood is mine.' The belt, symbolizing preparedness, declares readiness to give one's Life/Blood for his Covenant-partner.

It is necessary to remember, though, that no element not already covered by the total commitment of Covenant is being added – this type of ritual merely accents aspects of this relationship which may be needed at the moment. So also later when Jonathan and David cut Confirming Covenants, these do not add anything new in their relationship, but they do reassure and confirm that what their concern is, will indeed be answered.

Covenant is total, so all other rights and privileges within the scope of Covenant are always in the background. A Covenant for the sake of trade or friendship cannot escape the readiness to "lay down his Life for his friends" [John 15:13]. So, for whatever reason Abraham had cut Covenant with Mamre, Eschol, and Aner [ברית-אברם – B'RITH_ABRAM – Genesis 14:13], still these Covenant-partners risk their lives to help Abraham rescue Lot [Genesis 14:24]. The point is that one could have other agreements and treaties, but if one cuts Covenant, then that act compels the full range of commitment which Covenant demands.

Obliged

In Covenant each gives what he is and has to the other; he stands up for him; he fights for him. Without question or faltering, he *dies* for the other. <u>Anything</u> the Covenant-partner desires, without grumbling or complaint, is given without strings attached. However, the reverse is just as true – the Covenant-partner gives his own Life, withholds nothing, *not even his own son*, from his Covenant-'friend.' *The expectations toward one are EXACTLY the same expectations as toward the other:*

> What do you expect of God? His help, His presence, His Love, His individual concern for you? That He would die for you? That He should always listen to you, pay attention to you? That He would make available to you all the help and the resources that are at His disposal? If so, then that's good – you understand a lot about Covenant.
>
> But now the catch! If COVENANT, then God can have *exactly the same expectations of you* as you have of Him. He can expect YOUR help, YOUR presence, YOUR love, YOUR individual concern for Him. He can expect that YOU would die for Him, that YOU should always listen to HIM, pay attention to HIM, that YOU would make

> available to HIM all the help and the resources that are at YOUR disposal. You see, that is *COVENANT*.
>
> That is Covenant, and no, there is no half-Covenant, where you might choose the "economy" version rather than the "deluxe." No, it is an "either / or" situation: Either God's Blood flows through your veins and yours flows through His – or not.   James Lindemann[24]

That God would expect the same from me would not mean that He now would expect me to be God like He is. If I were to cut Covenant with an expert swordsman, and he expected that I now suddenly would also be an expert swordsman, he would be a fool. However, if I were the one with the gun, he might expect that I would bring that to a battle.

But a Difference in Jehovah's Involvement

> For God, having made a promise to Abraham, because He could swear by no one greater, He swore on His own Self.   Hebrews 6:13

God's involvement in Covenant has a uniqueness. Even in the New Testament's strong emphasis on the oneness with God, with being made "co-heirs with Christ," becoming part of the living Body of Christ and, of course, the Blood of the Covenant in Holy Communion – all of which profoundly speak of the unity between Jehovah and His People – a problem exists: God is still God and we will never be at *that* level, even in Covenant.

There are important reasons why Jehovah has to be more than simply 'a good ol' Buddy.' As Hebrews 6 identifies, He is the only One Who is not just participant, but also Watchman over His Covenant with humans, and in that role He stands outside of and above Covenant, even outside of and above His own participation. So when He breaks Covenant as we shall see in Zechariah, even God Himself has to pay the penalty. Jehovah is *ruled by* His own Covenant, yet as Overseer He *rules over* Covenant at the same time.

In addition, creation – and humans – also need One Who stands above the Universe, to provide and to do justice not only to those in

Covenant but to all ("He makes His sun rise on the evil and on the good, and sends rain on the just and on the unjust" [Matthew 5:45]). The Creator, although participating in His creation, must also stand outside it and therefore deserves an honor beyond that of which Covenant normally speaks. The difficulty is that Jehovah never fits neatly into any box in which our minds try to envision Him. Even in the pivotal concepts of Covenant, the box cannot help but bulge and split at the sides.

When Jehovah declares "I will establish My Covenant between Me and you ... for an everlasting Covenant, to be God to you and your descendants after you" [Genesis 17:7], He 'writes into the Covenant' His dual position as both Participant and Overseer, as Covenant-Partner and God – something of course any human-to-human Covenant could never do. Jehovah is not providing Himself a 'backdoor' by which to weasel out of Covenant obligations ('Oh, this is the area where I am God, so I do not have to stick to Covenant here'), but rather He adds an even greater layer of commitment as God into the mix, which therefore requires an additional set of responsibilities from *both* sets of participants.

Examples of this dual role as Covenant-Partner and as God would be the Tree of Knowledge with Adam and Eve, as well as the First Fruits, as in regard to Jericho. Although linked to Jehovah in the Creation Covenant, still Adam and Eve do not have any rights to the Tree of Knowledge. So also, the First Fruits of harvest and of cattle belong to the God Who provides for *all* His Creation – and since Jericho is the 'First Fruits' of the Promised Land, it is a "devoted" city [Joshua 6:17-19] that belongs to Jehovah alone. Although Covenant means common ownership, this is a level *not* shared because it involves His position as Creator and Overseer.

So when Achan takes for himself items from Jericho, Covenant *is* violated ["transgressed My Covenant" – Joshua 7:11], because he refuses to acknowledge that God is not just merely a Covenant-Partner, but also is One Who reserves His rights as the *Overseer and Creator* involved in this relationship. As these stories demonstrate, if Jehovah does not continue to occupy the second role, both Covenant and creation would descend into chaos.

Violating the Character of the Person

> The man said to Eli, "I have come from the battle; I fled from the battle today."
> He said, "What was the matter, my son?"
> The messenger answered, "Israel has fled before the Philistines, and also there was a great slaughter of the people; your two sons ... are dead, and *the Ark of God* has been captured." When he mentioned *the Ark of God*, Eli fell backward from his seat ...; his neck was broken and he died, for he was old and heavy...   I Samuel 4:16-18

What about those times when the Covenant-Partner *does not* run to the aid of Israel? Israel uses *the Ark of the Covenant* as a sort of good luck talisman, as if they could do anything they wanted and God has no choice but to follow. However, Jehovah does not allow His Person to be trivialized like that. Covenant is not an excuse by which to violate one's character and responsibilities, nor to condone unrighteousness. There is a commitment higher than to the demands of Covenant and that is to the righteousness and integrity of His own Person, not just as Covenant-Partner, but also as God.

My Covenant-Brother's Keeper

Along the same lines, although his context is a bit different, Cain's question "Am I my brother's keeper?" [Genesis 4:9] wrestles with Covenant: just how much should one care about his Covenant-partner? Does it matter if this 'brother' is in a self-destructive course of action, or would such a crisis compel intervention and discipline? After all, it is my Life/Blood in his body, as well as his Life/Blood in mine – I am affected! Would not Covenant be expected to compel corrective action?

The Covenant-People's entrance into Captivity identifies a certain maturity in the Covenant concept. Israel (both North and South kingdoms) have been in a spiritual tailspin for centuries, wanting the comfort of the Covenant-Partner, but rejecting the Overseer. Is Jehovah to respond merely in a knee-jerk (mechanical) – but *HESED*-less – gratifying of their every whim? Or would *HESED* demand that some requests be denied, or even that suffering be allowed, that is, to *not* always be 'nice' whenever the Covenant-partner calls?

He Whose *HESED* visibly struggles with His justice in regard to Sodom and Gomorrah (see "VII. Abraham Entered Covenant – D. I WILL Make Your Name Great; YOU Will be a Blessing - The Shared Nature"), is anguished of heart when He strips His partner of their Covenant Land and dignity. Yet He cannot permit their self-destructive ways to go unanswered. This is no mere dispassionate judgment – the distress pictured in Isaiah, Jeremiah and Ezekiel speak of Jehovah's distaste for the task and the yearning for a different outcome, as well as His maintaining 'a remnant' throughout all the upheaval.

B. Selflessness

Jonathan

Covenant-partners keep nothing hidden from each other – after all they are of the same Blood, and have one Life between them: David has already been anointed the next king of Israel, *two chapters* earlier [I Samuel 16:1,11-13]. In history, when a different dynasty ascends a throne, it is often at the demise of the previous regal family, so Jonathan knows that to advance David would probably spell his own doom. Jonathan acknowledges this in their first confirming Covenant (their second Covenant – see the next section "C. Subsequent Covenants"):

> *'If I am still alive*, then you will show me the steadfast Love of Jehovah, *that I may not die*; and *you shall not cut off your steadfast Love from my house forever*, not even when Jehovah cuts off every one of the enemies of David from the face of the earth.' Jonathan cut [Covenant] with the house of David ... And Jonathan made him swear *again*, because he loved him as he loved his own Soul. I Samuel 20:14-17

So when Saul later threatens David's Life:

> Saul's anger burned against Jonathan, and he said to him, "You son of a perverse, rebellious woman ... For as long as the son of Jesse lives upon the earth, neither you nor your kingdom shall be established. Now send and bring him to me, for he is a son of death."
> Then Jonathan answered Saul his father, "Why should he be put to death? What has he done?" But Saul threw his spear at him to kill him; so Jonathan knew that his father was resolved to put David to death.   I Samuel 20:30-33

Despite potentially – obviously – spelling his own doom, Jonathan still risks his Life to preserve David's – that's *Covenant!*[25] – "Greater Love has no man than this, that a man lay down his Life for his friends" [John 15:13].

Jehoshaphat

The Kingdom of Judah's King Jehoshaphat comes to visit King Ahab of the Kingdom of Israel and agrees to go to war with him [I Kings 22; II Chronicles 18]: "I am as you are; my people, your people; my horses, your horses" – is this not Covenant language? And then despite asking for the LORD's advice and receiving a very negative prophecy, they still go to war. Ahab has a brilliant idea: "I will disguise myself and go into battle, but you wear your robes."

Why does Jehoshaphat agree to Ahab's plan? Jehoshaphat would be painting a big target on his back as the only visible king on the field of battle, especially since the Arameans are apparently 'gunning for' Ahab, meanwhile Ahab would go relatively unnoticed! Why would a person put himself into such deliberate additional danger, knowing that the other is evading danger at his expense?

Is this foolishness? Or is it Covenant, in which one withholds nothing, not even his Life, for the sake of a Covenant-partner – an echo perhaps of Jonathan's willingness to die for his Covenant-partner David?

C. Subsequent Covenants

Affirmation, Assurance and Commitment
– the Confirming Covenants

A subsequent Covenant would be like a remarriage ceremony on the 40th anniversary – nothing is really changed legally, physically or relationship-wise, yet it can have many positive effects on one's relationship. As branches on a tree, every subsequent confirming Covenant often takes a specialized direction and task, yet not as if it is a separate entity but is rather firmly rooted in and affirming the Covenant below it. After all, if the Life/Blood from the first Covenant still flows in the veins and the core of one's being is joined to the core of the other's being, then what more could any subsequent Covenant provide?

Jonathan and David cut their first Covenant in I Samuel 18:1, 3. In their second Covenant [I Samuel 20:14-17], 'reopening the wound' reopens the Covenant to a specific oath to *reassure Jonathan*. However, since the whole family is already implicitly included in the first, nothing new is really added, yet it confirms that his posterity is understood as included in their Covenant. Their *third* Covenant [I Samuel 23:16-18] is *to reassure David*: during David's flight from Saul, Jonathan comes to "strengthen his hand in God." Since the original commitment is still irrevocably in effect, it also adds nothing new, but simply comforts David in that his Covenant-partner does indeed stand firmly by him.

The New Covenant Supplants Which Old Covenant?

Is it the Sinai Covenant?

> Behold, the days come, says Jehovah, when I will cut a New Covenant with Israel and Judah, not like the Covenant which I cut with their fathers when I took them by their hand to bring them out of the land of Egypt, My Covenant which they broke, though I was a Husband to them ...
>   Jeremiah 31:31-32

Before one can talk about the 'New' Covenant, it must be decided what the 'Old' Covenant is which would be supplanted. If each Covenant is a separate entity of its own, then there would be a multitude of these relationships from which to choose. Yet we constantly refer to a singular 'Old Covenant,' which makes us conclude that the many others in the history of Israel are simply additional confirming Covenants. So which one is the pivotal one?

Jeremiah here refers to the Covenant at Sinai as one which will be replaced. Indeed, that significant occasion is the first Covenant which Israel cuts as a *Nation* with God and therefore can be treated separately. In the 'New Covenant,' I Peter 2:9 affirms that those who believe in Christ will become the new "holy Nation, His own special People."

There is an Older Covenant

Yet even Sinai is 'built on the back' of an older relationship which has existed from the time of Abraham: the Circumcision Covenant. *This* bond, individual-by-individual, establishes a personal relationship with Jehovah – *every* Israelite male is placed under *this* Covenant from birth. It provides the distinctive mark which gives the Israelite his identity and separates him from the 'uncircumcised' (for example, I Samuel 14:6; 17:26); and it even provides a benchmark by which to speak about those who are unfaithful:

> Behold, the days come, says Jehovah, when I will punish all those who are 'circumcised' but are [really] uncircumcised – Egypt, Judah, Edom, the sons of Ammon, Moab, and all who dwell in the wilderness, who trim the edges; for all these nations are uncircumcised, and all the house of Israel is uncircumcised in heart.   Jeremiah 9:25-26

As will be covered later, Jehovah participated in this Covenant in a most unique way and even at Sinai there is not the degree of His personal involvement as is demonstrated in this one. For Him to become involved in any greater degree would require Him to also shed His own Blood, meaning He would have to actually become human – which happens in the New Covenant!

There is a Most Ancient Covenant

However, there is an even older Covenant, one which establishes the framework and understanding which then gives even Circumcision its context, and indeed which lays the foundation for the concept of Covenant for every culture around the world. It is the 'Creation Covenant.' In the very creation of humanity, Jehovah makes visible His heart's desire and establishes a most unique, intensely personal relationship with this small species in creation. The Bible is the story of Jehovah's action to eventually make this heart's desire a full reality forever.

Choosing the Covenant

As the description of what God most wants for His creatures, the 'Creation Covenant' provides the driving force behind *all* other Biblical Covenants (both 'Old' and 'New'), and therefore would seem not to be supplanted. On the other hand, the Circumcision Covenant has extraordinary parallels to what the 'New Covenant' offers and is the bond which provides a significant reference point in the New Testament. This is the better candidate for what will be superseded by the coming new and deeper relationship between Jehovah and His eternal People.

D. *Posterity*

Covenants – Logically – Include the Whole Family

> [Dr. J. G. Wetzstein:] "So far as may be necessary, the one must provide for the wants of the other; and the survivor has weighty obligations in behalf of the family of the one deceased." Trumbull[26]

> we do it for the purpose of assisting one another with our families, … for our wives are as one to us, and each other's children as his own, and our riches as common property Trumbull[27]

> When Grandfather died, I was feeling very sad and mentioned to one of my "uncles' [Blood-Brothers to my Grandfather] that I no longer had any grandfathers left. He was very offended, stating, 'I am also your Grandfather!' Lori Macintosh[28]

> So to say, through Abraham even Levi, who receives tithes, paid tithes while he was still in the loins of his father, when Melchizedek met him.
> Hebrews 7:9-10

> keeping steadfast Love for thousands, forgiving iniquity and transgression and sin, but will by no means clear the guilty, visiting the iniquity of the fathers upon the children and the children's children, to the third and the fourth generation.
> Exodus 34:7 (also 20:5; Numbers 14:18; Deuteronomy 5:9)

The seriousness of Covenant is reflected in how it affects even the descendants of the partners. Hebrews 7 identifies how all future generations are already present "in the loins of the father." God considers Himself still obligated to the promises to Abraham, even though over four hundred years have passed, perhaps ten generations, as Israel languishes in slavery in Egypt, when the LORD sends Moses as their deliverer. But Covenant is not merely all blessing: the curses of Covenant also descend "even to the third and fourth generation" – although God's Glory ('mercy,' 'grace' and 'forgiveness') remain available to any who turn to Him.

Sex is Not an Element

> ... the Soul of Jonathan was knit to the Soul of David, and Jonathan loved him as his own Soul... Then Jonathan and David cut Covenant, because he loved him as his own Soul. I Samuel 18:1, 3

When two men have an intense emotional bond, how should this be interpreted? A friend of this writer has a very close relationship with a couple of Native Americans, one who is a shaman. The shaman often remarks to him that they should get 'married,' however, there is no hint here of a homosexual union. What the friend finally has understood, as he began to understand more about Covenant, is that the shaman wants a Blood-Brotherhood between them. In a curious turn-around of imagery, on one hand, marriage has borrowed the concepts and power of Covenant in its rituals, and on the other hand, has lent its terminology to Covenant.

This writer recalls a sociologist who once remarked, possibly it in regard to the Roman legions, how often the men would refer to a fellow legionnaire as his 'wife' or 'husband,' thereby leading the sociologist to conclude that there was extensive homosexuality in the Roman camps. However, as the shaman's wish for Blood-Brotherhood indicates, as well as the impoverished state of the Western understanding of Covenant, such a conclusion may need to be reevaluated.

One might also consider that although in the Greek and Roman pantheons sex plays a big role in their gods' relationships with humans, intimacy with Jehovah is not described as a sexual relationship (although the metaphor of the *faithfulness* between husband and wife is often employed – which would be more in line with the shaman's concept of Covenant in terms of a 'marriage').

Here, at least between Jonathan and David, since Jehovah is very strong in forbidding homosexual relationships (Leviticus18:22; 20:13; Romans 1:26-27), this high-profile relationship does not have that element. In fact, many cultures recognize that Covenant is a relationship in which sex has no role:

> [Dr. J. G. Wetzstein:] The marriage of a man and woman between whom this covenant exists, is held to be *incest*. Trumbull[29]

> If a person is a tayo [Blood-Brother] of the husband, he must indulge in no liberties with the sisters or the daughters, because they are considered as *his own* sisters or daughters; and incest is held in abhorrence by them ... Trumbull[30]

God's idea/provision of Covenant fills an important gap in interpersonal relationships. Without it intense emotional bonds, especially between the same gender, would simply be confusing.

E. The Great Link

Because it is person-to-person at the Life(Soul)/Blood level, Covenant with its *intimate heart* investment which echoes Jehovah's heart desire, with all its other commitments, is a most powerful concept. To make a Covenant nation-wide would normally weaken its strength: it would be harder to maintain its discipline unless each person is individually bound in Covenant.

Even a nation-to-nation treaty which borrows the imagery of this relationship, perhaps even calling itself a 'Covenant,' does not have the same forcefulness. If individuals (not the leadership) within the nations refuse to honor the terms of the treaty, the 'breaking' of such a 'Covenant' would at best become an indistinct thing. Can the whole nation be held accountable for what a random individual, a 'commoner,' may do?

Yet, in Joshua 7, the whole nation *is* held accountable by Jehovah, that is, "Israel has sinned, and they have also transgressed My Covenant" [v 11], although only one man, Achan [vv 20-21], by taking for himself from Jericho what belongs to God alone, has committed blasphemy. How can the whole nation carry the guilt of what one person does?

What can guarantee that "All that the Lord said we will do" [declared at Sinai, Exodus 19:8; 24:7] is pledged by every person? And if a person only mumbles or says nothing, is he really under this Covenant? The answer is that Sinai is simply a confirmation of the relationship already established with Jehovah in the Circumcision Covenant – it does not matter whether one enthusiastically speaks out or barely mumbles under his breath – the commitment is already covered.

But the *whole nation* is guilty? The answer lies in what might be called 'the Great Link.' If my Blood flows in you, and yours in me, and if you are also in Covenant with Fred and Mary, then our Bloods flow jointly through us all. We are linked together, even when sometimes we would much rather it not be. Because of the Circumcision Covenant, all Israel is linked to Jehovah and through Him therefore with each other. Linked now by Blood and by Life [Soul] with *all* Covenant-partners there is a corporate nature and effect to broken Covenant and sin.

It answers Cain's "Am I my brother's keeper?" (Genesis 4:9) and should give second thought about an individual's responsibility toward

Covenant – AND towards all others. Indeed Covenant is not a matter of convenience, but of involvement, commitment and caring about each other.

The idea of this Great Link also therefore involves Covenants with heathen nations (forbidden – Deuteronomy 7:2) since entering into Covenant with those bound to another god means that Jehovah through these individuals would be in Covenant with that entity. This He does not accept.

F. Not to be Broken!

Covenants are Deadly

Divided We Die

> [Abram] said, "My Lord Jehovah, by what shall I know that I shall possess it?"
> [Jehovah] said to him, "Bring Me a heifer three years old, a she-goat three years old, a ram three years old, a turtledove, and a young pigeon."
> He brought Him all these, divided them in the middle, and laid each half over against the other; but he did not divide the birds in two. ... As the sun was setting, a deep sleep fell on Abram; and lo, a dread and great darkness fell upon him. ... When the sun had gone down and it was dark, behold, a smoking furnace and torch of fire passed between these pieces. On that day Jehovah cut Covenant with Abram...
> Genesis 15:8-18

I will give the men who transgressed My Covenant, who did not fulfill the words of the Covenant which they cut before Me, the calf which they cut in two and passed between its parts – the princes of Judah and of Jerusalem, the eunuchs, the priests, and all the people of the land who passed between the parts of the calf – I will give them into the hands of their enemies ... Their dead bodies shall be food for the birds of the air and the beasts of the earth.   Jeremiah 34:18-20

One practice for a Covenant ceremony is to cut at least one animal into two pieces. In a very real sense, the "broken" animal demonstrates

41

the reality of broken Covenant: there is no Life left – no Blood – just two dead pieces – just two "dead" persons.

All or Literally Nothing

Unlike light switches, Life/Blood cannot be dimmed or turned off:

> There are many forms of covenanting in Syria, but [Blood Covenant] is the extremest and most sacred of them all. As it is the intercommingling of very lives, nothing can transcend it. It forms a tie, or a union, which cannot be dissolved. In marriage, divorce is a possibility: not so in the covenant of blood. Trumbull[31]

> Yet the tie of blood-covenanting was the strongest tie known in Central Africa ... when trouble arose between Stanley and Ngalyema, the former suggested that perhaps it would be better to cancel their brotherhood. "'No, no, no,' cried Ngalyema, anxiously; 'our brotherhood cannot be broken; our blood is now one.'" Trumbull[32]

> I never heard of the blood-covenant being broken. I do not remember to have inquired particularly on this point, because the way in which the blood-covenant was spoken of, always implied that its rupture was an unheard-of thing. Trumbull, quoting Rev. R. M. Luther, former missionary to the *Karens* of Burma[33]

> ... Tolo, a chief of the Shastika Indians, on the Pacific coast, ... when he made a treaty with Col. McKee, ... was anxious for some ceremony of brotherhood that would give binding sacredness to the mutual covenant. ... he proposed the formal exchange of names. ... Thenceforward he desired to be known as "McKee." The American colonel was now "Tolo." But after a while the Indian found that ... the terms of the treaty were not adhered to by the authorities making it. Then he discarded his new name, "McKee," and refused to resume his former name, "Tolo." He would answer to neither, and to the day of his death he insisted that his name, his identity, was "lost." Trumbull[34]

Covenant is not merely an agreement or contract – it is ultimately about the circulation of Blood/Life which cannot be broken without Life being drained away, resulting in death. A *conditional*, or even a *revocable*, Covenant really makes no sense – as Siamese twins are not *conditionally* joined together neither are Covenanting-partners *conditionally* joined together – either one Blood flows between them or *they both* 'die.' Covenant is always about the flow of Life/Blood.

Cut Off

> Implied in the act of circumcision is the taking of an oath: "If I do not keep the covenant, may the destruction which is illustrated by the cutting of the foreskin, actually happen to me." This is why the LORD spoke of covenant breakers being "cut off" in Genesis 17:14. In Exodus 4:25, 12:15,30:33,38; Leviticus 7:20-25; Psalm 37; Ezekiel 14:8-17, 25:7-16. Scripture used the same verb for "cutting off" of covenant breakers as it did for the "cutting" of a covenant in Genesis 15:18.... R. Scott Clark[35]

> You shall not bow down to them, nor serve them: for I Jehovah am your God, a jealous God visiting the iniquity of the fathers upon the children unto the third and fourth generation of them that hate me
> Exodus 20:5

> [The Gibeonites] said to the king, "The man, who consumed us and plotted against us, that we should be annihilated from all the territory of Israel, let *seven* of his sons – of Saul, the chosen of Jehovah – be given to us, so that we may hang them up before Jehovah at Gibeah"... II Samuel 21:5, 6

"Breaking Covenant" is not only a religious concern, it is a distress deeply ingrained in the whole culture, even the world-wide culture. It just is not done – not on the human-to-human level, and definitely not on the human-to-divine level. This is no temporary relationship: the union of Covenant – the union of Life/Blood – cannot be trivially broken. The only way out is by death, and even then the benefits – and curses – often continue to the family, until the loss of Blood is satisfied (See *"GO'EL,"* below).

Covenants are Permanent

Jehovah is the Basis of the Permanency

Jehovah is the Originator of Covenant. The Bible is the story of His desire for such a connection to mankind, His *HESED* – His *steadfast* Love and grace are always key elements in this relationship. His Life/Blood

43

takes the central pivot in the creation of mankind (as will be discussed later). This is the foundation that St Paul identifies from which Jehovah, even with ample reason to cast Covenant aside, *still* faithfully honors the commitment of His heart – the basis of His Covenants:

> In regard to the Gospel they are enemies, for your sake; but in regard to election they are beloved for the sake of the fathers. *For the gifts and the call of God are irrevocable.* Romans 11:28-29

> What if some did not believe? Does their unbelief nullify God's faithfulness? Never! Let God be true though every man be a liar.... Romans 3:3-4

The permanency of Covenant reflects the nature of God's commitment – irrevocable.

Not Even for Deceit

The Gibeonites deceive Joshua by appearing as if they have come a great distance [Joshua 9:4-5] and Joshua never consults the Lord [9:14]. Three days after cutting Covenant, Israel discovers the truth [9:14-16] and realizes that they have cut a *forbidden* Covenant [Deuteronomy 7:1-2; 20:16-18], yet nothing can be done – *Covenant cannot be rescinded*, no matter how it is obtained.

Even a forbidden Covenant achieved by deceit stands: *Jehovah* protects it and holds its participants accountable. Centuries later, when King Saul, with 'noble' intentions, breaks Covenant by attempting an 'ethnic cleansing' of the Gibeonites, God punishes *Israel*, until David settles the Blood account [II Sam 21:1-9, see *'GO'EL'* below].

Covenant cannot be treated lightly – it is *permanent*, no matter how the partner may have abused it, been deceptive about it, or has changed in his commitment over time (as Israel does toward Jehovah). With such an irrevocable nature, consider: with whom would YOU cut Covenant? Perhaps it is for this reason that, although Covenant imagery is often borrowed, not many actually go to the depth of real Covenant.

In or Out

Since Covenant with Jehovah is entirely by grace, and God commits Himself fully and totally in Covenant, in a real way binding Himself irrevocably in this relationship, then how can Covenant be thought of as 'conditional'? As St Paul declares above, Jehovah remains faithful though every man be found false. That is, He continues to bless, He continues to guide, He continues to shape His People's destiny, He continues His discipline, He continues His grace and mercy – *He will not break Covenant throughout generations of faithfulness and generations of rebellion.* (However, the time would come when even Jehovah would finally break Covenant, yet not in rebellion and not even as a punishment to Israel, but because He would then initiate a better Covenant. Jehovah never will leave His People without Covenant.)

Should a person step out of Covenant, he steps out of its blessings, although God remains true to *His* commitment. By stepping out of Covenant, one actually attempts to *not* receive these blessings, as well as to demand the curses (actually, the logical conclusions) of being without God. Yet so often God's blessings still come ("sends rain on the just and on the unjust" [Matthew 5:45]). The moment the person 'steps back in,' Jehovah simply continues His flood of blessings upon him, however now the person willingly receives them. This is the HISstory of the Old Testament. This is the history of the Heart of God, the history of Covenant.

IV. The Covenant Mosaic

A. The Oath – To "Seven" Oneself

A Unique Number

The Hebrew number 'seven' is also a word that means "Oath" [שבע-SHABA], which is usually the word of choice for the Covenant 'oaths.'

> The importance of the number seven as representing completeness is here strongly indicated. ... The word for to swear, נשבע, literally to be *sevened*, means to have one's vow consecrated and confirmed by seven sacrifices or seven witnesses ... The number seven, says Bähr in his 'Symbolik des Alten Testament,' I., 187, 188, is the sign of the relation, union, communion between God and the world, as represented by the number three and four respectively, just as twelve is in another relation ... Its meaning, according to Bähr, among the heathen is somewhat different. There it means the harmony of the universe, and is signified by the seven stars, to which, and neither more nor less, was the power of influencing man's destiny ascribed.   *Pulpit Commentary*[36]

> Not only is the Hebrew verb "to swear" identical ... to the number seven, but also a relationship is suggested by ... Gen 21:22-34 ... Abraham seals the oath by giving ... seven ewe lambs as a testimonial witness to Abimelech, and the well is called Beer-sheba, or Well-of-the-seven/oath! Thus DBD defined *shaba'* ..., "to ... seven oneself, or bind oneself by seven things" (p. 989). Genesius cites ... evidence that in the ancient world it was not uncommon to seal an agreement by the septenary number. ...
>   In fact, we see God swearing by himself (Gen 22:16), by his holiness (Ps 89:35 [H 36]), by his right hand (Isa 62:8), and by his great name (Jer 44:26) in order that he might stress the absolute certainty and immutability of his performing that which he swore to Abraham, to Israel, and to David. See Heb 6:13-19. ...
>   An oath, *sh^ebu'a*, should be contrasted to a covenant, *b^erit*, in order to better understand both. An oath ... is a solemn verbal statement or pledge ..., while the covenant is the substance of an agreement itself. In the Hebrew idiom, one would swear (*shaba'*) an oath (*sh^ebu'a*), e.g. Gen 26:3, "I [God] will perform an oath which I swore unto

Abraham." A covenant, however, would be either established ... as in Gen 17:19, or it would be cut (karat) as in Jer 31:31, "I [God] will make (cut) a new covenant with the House of Israel." *TWOT*[37]

The 'substance' of Covenant is a remarkable *relationship* containing "oaths", which define and detail Covenant's application in this relationship. *SHABA'* is the word of choice when Jehovah describes what He swore to in Covenant with Abraham [Genesis 22:16]. Because this word has such context to it, therefore as the handshake on a deal or contract attempts to borrow the forcefulness of Covenant's commitment, so also the idea of *SHABA'* might be used outside of Covenant to describe a most solemn assurance, attempting to carry the dignity of Covenant with it.

Subliminal Messaging

A Surprising Discovery

Psychologists have discovered that the brain works faster than perhaps even it realizes. A test was once done where during a movie, a message about popcorn and soda pop was flashed for 1/3000 second every 5 seconds on the screen. Nobody noticed the additional material. Or did they? At intermission, sales of popcorn and soda pop apparently were dramatically increased during the six week period of the test.[38] It suggests that *the brain* does indeed notice!

Subliminal [sub-conscious] stimulus or messaging by even single words has been modestly effective in changing human behavior or emotions. However its reality may have been around a lot longer than we thought.

The Case Study of Jericho

Israel stands in front of Jericho, the 'door-opener' (or the 'first-fruits,' therefore wholly dedicated to God) to the *Covenant* Land. What happens here sets the tone for the conquest of that Land which had been given by Covenant Oath to Abraham. The People, with *the Ark of the Covenant/Witness* and the *seven* priests blowing the *seven* trumpets in the

48

center of the procession, are to encircle Jericho once each day for six days, however on the *seventh* day, *seven* times around [Joshua 6:3-20].

As the story is repeated aloud, at each 'seven,' the listeners *also* hear '[Covenant] Oath' – again and again would be the message in the background: '*Covenant* is at work – our Covenant-Partner is involved! He fights by our side!'

Obligation Even after Centuries

> Moses took Joseph's bones with him because Joseph had made the sons of Israel swear [*SHABA*] an oath [*SHABA*]. He had said, "God will surely visit you, and you shall carry my bones up with you from here." Exodus 13:19 (see Genesis 50:25)

In Covenant, not only do the benefits filter down to the posterity, but even the obligations. Four hundred years earlier the oath was sworn, yet Moses is compelled to fulfill its terms. Through perhaps ten generations, the commitment was handed down until it could be acted upon. So also the oath God swore to Abraham some 600 years[39] earlier [Genesis 15:13]:

> ...because of Jehovah's Love for you and because He kept the oath [*SHABA*] that He swore [*SHABA*] to your fathers, Jehovah brought you out with a mighty Hand, and redeemed you from the house of slavery, from the hand of Pharaoh king of Egypt.   Deuteronomy 7:8

God's Oath of the Seed of the Woman [Genesis 3:17], the One through Whom all nations would be blessed [Genesis 12:3], has an even greater gap of time, and yet the environment of Covenant is the same, the obligation of Covenant is the same.

Other Vows – Numbers 30

אסר אסר על נפש ['*ASAR ISSAR 'AL NEPHESH* – "to <u>bind</u> with a <u>bond</u> on his/her *Soul/Life*" – in just about every verse!] – the vows of chapter 30 are not the muttered-under-the-breath type, but rather with ceremony attached, Blood-vows perhaps with Covenant attached:

Festus, a writer of fifteen centuries or more ago, concerning Latin antiquities, is reported as saying, of this drink of the covenant of blood: "A certain kind of drink, of mingled wine and blood, was called *assiratum* by the ancients; for the ancient Latins called blood, *assir*." ...

Turning ... to the languages of the East, where the binding vow of blood-friendship was pledged in a drink of wine and blood, or of blood alone, from time immemorial, we have no difficulty in finding the meaning of "assir." *Asar* (אסר) is a common Hebrew word, signifying "to bind together" – as in a mutual covenant. *Issar* (אסר), again, is a vow of self-renunciation. Thus we have *Asar issar 'al nephesh* (אסר אסר על נפש) "To bind a self-devoting vow upon one's life" – upon one's blood; "for the blood is the life." In the Arabic, also, ... The Syriac gives *esar* ..., "a bond," or "a belt." All these, with the root idea, "to bind" – as a covenant binds. In the light of these facts, it is easy to see how the "issar" or the "assar," when it was a covenant of blood, came to be counted by the Latins the blood which was a covenant. Trumbull[40]

B. The SIGN of Covenant ('OTH – אות)

The Scar

Since Covenant is "cut," it has an essential spin-off: a 'SIGN.' As two humans cut Covenant, most often the SIGN is a scar – a continuing, indelible, and often public – reminder and guarantee of Covenant.

A woman with native-American background once described how her grandfather had three 'Blood-brothers,' and the wound from cutting the palm was picked at in order to make the scar prominent – an obvious and proud reminder of his Covenant-relationships. Such a SIGN is also a constant reminder of one's grave responsibility, and at the same time, of comfort – it is a message to any enemy that a Blood-brother has pledged to defend – and avenge – his Covenant-partner.

"To Consent, Agree"

Strong's *Exhaustive Concordance*

Strong's *Exhaustive Concordance* sees the root for 'OTH as coming from a similarly spelled "primitive root word" that means "to consent, agree." If so, this suggests a strong connection to this "SIGN" as an evidence for the ultimate of agreements.

Theological Dictionary of the Old Testament

In the *Theological Dictionary of the Old Testament*, contributor FJ Helfmeyer agrees with H Gunkel's definition of 'OTH as "an action, an occurrence, an event by which a person recognizes, learns, remembers, or perceives, the authenticity of something" [pg 170].

He continues with "The function of a sign, like its subject, shows that the main thing about it is not that it is miraculous or that it is exciting to watch, for the intention of a sign is not to terrify the onlooker, but to mediate an understanding or to motivate a kind of behavior" [pg 171].

Heltmeyer does not identify 'OTH as a specific Covenant element, yet the functions he describes (for example, signs imparting knowledge, signs of protection, signs producing faith, signs which bring to remembrance) do not exclude Covenant as, for the most part, a defining environment for 'OTH.

The *'OTH*s: More Than *Symbols* of Presence and Power

Jehovah said to Moses, "How long will this People despise Me? And how long will they not believe in Me, in spite of all the 'OTHs (SIGNs) which I have done in their midst?"   Numbers 14:11

It is true that such passages could be understood without the 'OTHs having Covenant significance. Yet when the Covenant connection is included, there is a shift of focus: Now the 'OTHs do more than show Jehovah's presence, power and authority as God, they also declare that the most intimate commitment — above all other relationships — is involved. So Jehovah's question then is not 'Why can't they see that I am God?', but rather 'Why can't they see how much I am committed to them?'

And the lack of *'OTH*s could be felt just as deeply, with the bewildered sense of 'What happened to Covenant? Do You no longer love us?'

> We do not see our *'OTH*s (SIGNs); there is no longer a prophet, and not one among us knows for how long. For how long, O God, will the enemy taunt us? Shall the enemy scorn Your Name forever? Why do You withdraw *Your Hand – Your Right Hand?* Take it from Your bosom and destroy them! Psalm 74:9-10

ZIKARON and *ANAMNESIS*

The Hebrew *ZIKARON* [Exodus 12:14; 13:9] and the Greek *ANAMNESIS* ["Do this in *remembrance* of Me" – Luke 22:19; I Corinthians 11:24,25] – "remembrance" – have a unique property:

> But what is the meaning of anamnesis, the Hebrew *zikaron* which is so difficult to translate exactly: memory, memorial, celebration, or cultic commemoration? ... [It] is the ritual recalling of a past event to restore its original virtue and, even more, the setting of those who engage in the anamnesis into the very event which the celebration commemorates. Reference may be made to the saying of Gamaliel when expounding, in the light of Exod. 13:8, the event of the Israelite Passover: "Every man in every generation must consider himself as having been personally delivered from Egypt. Every Israelite must know that he personally has been freed from slavery."
>
> Jean-Jacques Von Allmen[41]

Going beyond mere reminiscing, it speaks of where one literally relives an event, but more than that, the event comes from the past to you in the present: this is an event which *you participate in, even if you do not experience it originally yourself.* So therefore in Hebrews 7:9-10, Levi is there participating when his ancestor Abraham gives the tithe to Melchizedek. And also the *'OTH* [SIGN] of Circumcision is the witness *to* the Israelite of his *participation* in *Abraham's* Covenant.

> you shall circumcise the flesh of your foreskin, and it shall be an *'OTH* [SIGN] of the Covenant between Me and you. ... Surely the child of your household and he who is bought with your money must be

circumcised, and My Covenant shall be in your flesh for an everlasting Covenant.   Genesis 17:11, 13

Of relevant interest is that the word for the male [זכר - ZAKAR] who participated in circumcision (for example, Genesis 17:10; 34:15; Exodus 12:48) comes from the same word base from which "remembrance" [זכר - ZEKER] and "memorial" [זכרון - ZIKKARÔN] are derived. Psalm 112:6 declares "the righteous shall be for a memorial [ZEKER] forever." And in Psalm 111, remembrance, a meal, Jehovah's Covenant and His 'Grace and Mercy' (echo of His Glory) are closely connected:

> He has made a memorial [ZEKER] for His wonders; Jehovah is gracious and full of mercy. Food He has given to those who fear Him; He will remember [ZEKER] His Covenant forever.   Psalm 111:4-5

The "Mighty Hand and Outstretched Arm"

> Jehovah brought us out of Egypt with *a mighty Hand and an outstretched Arm*, with great terror and with *'OTHs* (SIGNs) and wonders.
>   Deuteronomy 26:8

> ...Thus says the Lord Jehovah: "In the day when I chose Israel and raised My Hand [in an oath]* to the descendants of the house of Jacob, and was made known to them in the land of Egypt, I raised My Hand [in an oath] to them, saying, 'I am the Jehovah your God' – in that day I raised My Hand [in an oath] to them, to bring them out of the land of Egypt into a land that I had searched out for them, 'flowing with milk and honey,' the glory of all lands."   Ezekiel 20:5-6
>   *Many translations indicate that the Hebrew "raised My Hand" should be understood in an 'oath' context.

It would seem that there is greater depth to 'mighty Hand and outstretched Arm' than is seen in terms of Jehovah's great powerfulness. Like the scars from Covenant, the Hand, the Arm and the *'OTHs* are God's reassurance to the participant, and public evidence for all others – they are His proof of His everlasting commitment to His Covenant-partner [see Psalm 136, especially vv. 10-12].

> Can a woman forget her sucking child, that she should have no compassion on the son of her womb? Even these may forget, yet I will not forget you. Behold, I have engraved you *on the palms of my Hands*; your 'walls' are ever before me.   Isaiah 49:15-16
>> ('Walls' has the same root as '-in-law,' so there may be Covenant/marriage overtones. And later in Isaiah [60:18], there is a symbolic connection of salvation to "walls": "but you shall call your walls Salvation, and your gates Praise.")

> "The Lord hath sworn by his right hand, and by the arm of his strength." It is by no means improbable, indeed, that the universal custom of lifting up the arm to God in a solemn oath was a suggestion of swearing by one's blood, by proffering it in its strength, as in the inviolable covenant of sacred friendship with God. So, again, in the striking hands as a form of sacred covenanting; the clasping of hands, in blood. Even the law courts carry the vestige of raising of the right hand by the witness when he swears to tell the truth. This act may go back to Blood-Covenant days when the palms of the hands were cut, then with the blood flowing down their upraised arms each swore allegiance to the other.   Trumbull[42]

As with 'Seven,' is there a dual thought in 'Mighty Hand and Outstretched Arm' – not just of strength, but also of Covenant relationship? This may also be part of the thought behind Psalm 74:11: "Why do You withdraw Your Hand, even Your right Hand? Take it out of Your bosom and destroy them." After all, what right does Israel have to seek God's retribution against its enemies if it were not for the Covenant relationship!

The 'Mighty Hand' of Blessing

> Then Aaron lifted up his hands toward the People and blessed them; ...   Leviticus 9:22

It is a common scene of blessing, with the hand raised and the palm toward the beneficiary. There is a curious phrase in Genesis 9:5, where shed Blood would be reckoned from "the *hand* of every animal ..., and from the *hand* of man" – "hand" here appears to be the equivalent of "soul" as a representation the whole person or animal (as, for example, in the ship's call for 'all hands on deck!'). In Covenant then, the "hand" would have more meaning than merely a convenient place to obtain Blood; it would represent the investment of all one is – one's whole soul – in this relationship. Also, the palm or the inside of the wrist would often hold the *'OTH* (SIGN) of Covenant and its commitment of one's whole being.

The raising of the hands, as Trumbull points out above in regard to the law courts, is more than a nice ritual. Such blessing is no mere well-wishing, but rather it indicates a concrete pledge in the powerful, steadfast and devoted connection of Covenant, especially since Aaron is representing Jehovah.

An interesting contrast to the raising of the hand in blessing is presented in I Samuel 15, where "Saul has set up a *hand* [often translated as 'monument'] to himself" [v 12] – the seeming arrogance of 'look at what - I- have done!' As to whether this has Covenant overtones:

> Hand is interestingly employed to mean an "ordinance" (Ezr 3:10) or a "monument" (cf. ritual stelae at Hazor) used perhaps to establish a covenant or as religious commemorations (I Sam 15:12; Isa 56:5). The Law was symbolically placed on the hand of the Israelite to remind him of its centrality in life (Deut 6:8). The instrumentality of giving ordinances and God's word was expressed with "by the hand of."
>
> *TWOT*[43]

Likely then the use of the hand in blessing is not merely a perfunctory gesture, but has Covenant significance.

"A Sign on Your Hand, Frontlets between Your Eyes" [Deuteronomy 6:8]

> HEAR, O ISRAEL, *JEHOVAH OUR GOD*, JEHOVAH IS ONE – and you shall love *Jehovah your God* with all your heart [fountain of Life/Blood], with all your Soul [Life/Blood], and with all your might [vitality of Blood = activity of Life] ... You shall repeat these words to your sons, and shall speak of them as you sit, ... walk, ... lie down, ... rise up, and shall bind them for an *'OTH* on your Hand; they shall be as frontlets between your eyes. Deuteronomy 6:4-5, 7-8; also 11:18-21

Moses commanded that his recap of Israel's history (the book of Deuteronomy) is to be bound (קשר *QASHAR*) as an *'OTH* (SIGN) on the hand. *The Theological Wordbook of the Old Testament* says that *QASHAR* is not only used to bind or tie things together, but also can be "used of a binding together of human beings" and a synonym for "to cut a Covenant." [44]

The Amulet/Phylactery

Along with Moses' command above, so also the First Fruits of man and beast are to be "as an *'OTH* (SIGN) on your hand and as frontlets between your eyes, for by strength of Hand the LORD brought us out of Egypt" [Exodus 13:16]. Similar to the scar on the palm, these things are to be a concrete reminder of Covenant:

> Hence the leathern case, or *Bayt hejab* ..., "House of the amulet," containing the record of the covenant (*'uhdah* ...), is counted a proud badge of honor by one who possesses it; and he has an added sense of security because he will not be alone when he falleth. [Eccl. 4:9,10].
>
> ... this was the custom in ancient Egypt, where the red amulet, which represented the blood of Isis, was worn by those who claimed a blood-friendship with the gods. It is a noteworthy fact, that it was in conjunction with the institution of this passover rite of the Lord's blood-friendship with Israel, as a permanent ceremonial, that the Lord declared of this rite and its token: "It shall be for a sign upon thine hand, and for frontlets between thine eyes." [See Exod. 13:11-16] And it is on the strength of this injunction, that the Jews have, to this day, been accustomed to wear upon their foreheads, and again upon their arm – as a crown and as an armlet – a small leathern case, as a sacred amulet, or as a "phylactery"; containing a record of the passover-covenant between the Lord and the seed of Abraham his friend. Not the law itself, but the substance of the covenant between the Lawgiver and his people, was the text of this amulet record. It included Exodus 13:3-10,11-16, with its reference to God's deliverance of his people from bondage, to the institution of the passover feast, and to the consecration of the redeemed first-born; also Deuteronomy 6:4-9,13-22, with its injunction to entire and unswerving fidelity, in the covenant thus memorialized. ...
>
> The two covenant tokens of blood-friendship with God – circumcision and the phylacteries – are, by the Rabbis, closely linked in

their relative importance. "Not every Israelite is a Jew ... except he has two witnesses – the sign of circumcision and phylacteries"; the sign given to Abraham, and the sign given to Moses. Trumbull[45]

On this order, the mark of the beast "on the hand or the forehead" [Revelation 13:16] would seem to have a Covenant overtone, as might the Hindu 'third eye' on the forehead, in parallel to such indicators of Covenant connection:

> To this day, as I can testify from personal observation, the Samaritans on Mount Gerizim (where alone in all the world the passover-blood is now shed...)... every child of the covenant receives also a blood-mark, on his forehead, between his eyes, in evidence of his relation to God in the covenant of blood friendship. Trumbull[46]

The Ring

> Just here it may be well to emphasize the fact, that, from time immemorial, and the world over, the armlet, the bracelet, and the ring, have been counted the symbols of a boundless bond between giver and receiver; the tokens of a mutual unending covenant. Possibly, ... this is in consequence of the primitive custom of binding, as an amulet, the enclosed record – enclosed in the "house of the amulet" – of the covenant of blood on the arm of either participant in that rite; possibly, again it is an outgrowth of the common root idea of a covenant and a bracelet, as a binding agency....
>
> The re-instatement of the prodigal son, in the parable, was by putting "a ring on his hand." And these illustrations out of ancient Egypt, Persia, and Syria, indicate a world-wide custom, so far. One's signet-ring stood for his very self, and represented, thus, his blood, as his life....
>
> The very covenant itself, or its binding force, has been sometimes thought to depend on the circlet representing it; as if the life which was pledged passed into the token of its pledging. ... On this idea it is, that many persons are unwilling to remove the wedding-ring from the finger, while the compact holds. Trumbull[47]

Superstition

> So firmly fixed was the idea of the appropriateness and the binding force of these tokens of the covenant, that their use, in one form or another, was continued by Christians, until the custom was denounced by representative theologians and by a Church Council. In the Catacombs of Rome, there have been found "small caskets of gold, or other metal, for containing a portion of the Gospels, generally part of the first chapter of John [with its covenant promises to all who believe on the true Paschal Lamb], which were worn on the neck," as in imitation of the Jewish phylacteries. These covenant tokens were condemned by Irenaeus, Augustine, Chrysostom, and by the Council of Laodicea, as a relic of heathenism.   Trumbull[48]

Wearing a Cross necklace or even 'making the "sign" of the Cross' could easily fit into this context. The validity for the Christian is that it is a reminder that in Baptism he has been 'marked' – 'scarred'? – by God so that all spiritual beings (including Satan and his devils) would know that he is in Covenant with Jehovah. It is a useful reminder of just who, and Whose, one is in this world.

However, human nature tends to turn such tools for remembrance into "good luck charms":

> Men are often tempted to rely on religious symbols and appointments, not so much to glorify God ... as to protect themselves. ... So the cross has been worn in many an evil enterprise, and carried into many battles, to defend cruel and rapacious men. So, also, men 'shout over' their Church, their English Bible, their prayer-book, or their sabbath, in a vain confidence that their relation to one of them, or to all of them, will secure Divine favour, or at all events, Divine defence, though in character and life they be no better than others who boast of none of these things. But it is all delusion ... The ark of [Covenant] could do nothing for men who by their sins had driven away the God of the ark. What a selfish man wants in religion is to have God bound to take his part and fight on his side, instead of his studying to be on God's side, the side of righteousness.   *The Pulpit Commentary*[49]

A blatant example of such an attitude is in I Samuel 4, when Israel uses *the Ark of the Covenant/Witness* as a sort of automatic guarantee of victory. That *the Ark itself*, the symbol of Jehovah's Covenant presence, would be captured [vv 17-18] is evidence that Jehovah will not be merely some talisman for mankind. In the modern age, the Cross has become either a protective charm and/or merely a decoration, no matter what the activity (therefore the terror of the vampire in fiction,[50] or the anti-God rock star who may sport a Cross even as a tattoo). Sometimes in movies a character facing danger may make the sign of the Cross on himself, seemingly more a superstitious act than a legitimate reminder of his Covenant relationship to God.

Monumental Reminders

Noah's rainbow [Genesis 9:12-13] is "the '*OTH* (SIGN) of the Covenant" [v 17], a physical reminder (even to us) that Jehovah's Covenant is real and is still valid. Other physical reminders, Covenant Monuments, often are set up at certain places as lasting — even eternal? — witnesses concerning Covenants made there:

> Thus they made a Covenant at Beersheba: then Abimelech ... and Phichol ... returned into the land of the Philistines. [Abraham] planted *a grove [tamarisk tree* (NIV)] in Beersheba, and called there on the Name of Jehovah, the everlasting God. Genesis 21:32-33

> Jacob vowed a vow, saying, "If God will be with me, and will keep me in this way that I go, and will give me bread to eat and clothing to wear, and I return in peace to my father's house, then Jehovah shall be my God, and *this stone, which I have set up for a pillar*, shall be God's house; and of all that You give me I will give the tenth to You."
> Genesis 28:20-22

> Joshua ... took a great stone, and set it up under the oak by the sanctuary of Jehovah ..., "Behold, *this stone shall be a witness against us*; for it has heard all the words of Jehovah which He has spoken to us; it shall be a witness against you, lest you lie against your God."
> Joshua 24:26-27

Not-So-Monumental Reminders

The Seven Lambs

> Abraham set *oath/seven* ewe lambs from the flock by themselves. Abimelech said to Abraham, "What are these *oath/seven* ewe lambs which you have set by themselves?"
> He said, "These *oath/seven* ewe lambs you will take from my hand, that you may be a witness for me that I dug this well."
> Therefore that place was called Beer*sheba* [*The Well of the Oath/Seven*]; because there both of them *swore an oath* [*SHABA*]. So they cut Covenant at Beer*sheba*. ...   Genesis 21:28-32

Possessing the lambs is *Abimelech*'s 'witness to Covenant' – apparently as long as these remain alive and have offspring, the Covenant is in effect.

The Scarlet Cord

After saving the two spies from capture, Rahab begs: "Now please *swear/seven* to me by Jehovah, since I have dealt kindly with you, that you also will deal kindly to my father's house and shall give to me an *'OTH* (SIGN) of faithfulness" [Joshua 2:12]. The spies agree, provided she continues to protect their lives. In the window from which they escaped the city, she is to hang a red cord as the sign of their connection in Covenant:

> A similar idea of the covenanting force of blood in the symbolism of the Old Testament and of the New, is again indicated in the fact that so many of the Christian Fathers saw a token of the blood-covenant in the scarlet cord which Joshua [sic] commanded Rahab to let down from her window as the token of the covenant whereby she was made one with the people of God.   Trumbull[51]

With this visible *'OTH*, Covenant compels Israel to preserve her and her family's lives [6:22-23] – the cord plays the same role as the ark covered with atonement ('pitch' – see later under *KAPHAR*) protects Noah and his family, or in the Passover, where the doorway of Blood protects the inhabitants from the death which is all around them.

The Robe

> Jonathan took off his robe and gave it to David, ... I Samuel 18:4

As mentioned before, this is a prince's robe to be worn by a common shepherd, the symbol of authority and favoritism, an *'OTH* to David and to others of David's connection. This may also may lend depth to the parable of the Wedding Feast [Matthew 22:11-12], where one wedding guest apparently refuses the wedding garment provided by the King (someone gathered from the highway likely does not come equipped with his own wedding garment). Although that garment would not necessarily be a Covenant *'OTH*, it evidently describes a favored status which the person rejects.

This idea would also be clearly presented by "I will greatly rejoice in Jehovah... for He has clothed me with the garments of salvation, He has put on me the robe of righteousness" [Isaiah 61:10, see Ps 132:16]; "I spread My skirt over you and covered your nakedness. Yes, I swore [*SHABA*] to you and entered into Covenant with you, and you became Mine" [Ezekiel 16:8]; "But the father said to his servants, 'Bring out the best robe and put it on [my son]'" [Luke 15:22]; and the Lamb's Bride is "granted to be arrayed in fine linen, clean and bright, for the fine linen is the righteous acts of the saints" [Revelation 19:7-8].

"The Tent of Witness" and "The Ark of Witness"

> Our fathers had *the Tent of Witness* in the wilderness, which He Who spoke to Moses commanded him to make, according to the pattern that he had seen. Acts 7:44

> I will meet you there and speak to you, above *the Atonement Cover* ("*Mercy* Seat"), from between the two cherubim which are on *the Ark of Witness*, all which I shall command for the Israelites.
> Exodus 25:22; also 30:6; Numbers 7:89

Functioning as *'OTH*s, the focal points in Jehovah's relationship with Israel, *"the Tent of Witness"* [cf. Numbers 10:11, Numbers 17:7-8, Numbers

18:2] and *"the Ark of Witness"* [particularly in Exodus, elsewhere it is called *"the Ark of the Covenant"*], are the visible witnesses of the special Covenant relationship between Jehovah and His People. But more than simply that there *is* a Covenant, they are also the reminders of *restored* Covenant, since *the Tent of Witness* has a Blood-red covering, and *the Ark of Witness* has *the Atonement* (or Ransom) *Cover* (both discussed later).

Marriage Imagery

It is no surprise that some marriage customs would use this imagery. The right arm symbolizes strength, the left arm Life. The ring on the finger/thumb on the left (Life) hand stands for the scar from the mingling of the Bloods. The joining of the right [determination, strength, volition] hands in marriage also alludes to the clasping of the hands after the palms had been cut, thus evoking the unbreakability of Covenant, *"for better and for worse, for richer and for poorer, in sickness and in health, till death do us part."*

So also the handshake, from the 'unbreakable' deal, to an expression of solidarity, to the common greeting, uses this symbolism:

> So simple a matter as the clasping of hands in token of covenant fidelity, is explicable, in its universality, only as a vestige of the primitive custom of joining pierced hands in the covenant of blood-friendship. ... But, even where hand clasping is unknown in salutation, it is recognized as a symbol of the closest friendship.　　Trumbull[52]

Negative Side to *'OTH*s

"This shall be the 'OTH to you that shall befall your two sons ..." [I Samuel 2:34] – a *negative* SIGN of Covenant, that is, that the Covenant is indeed at work, but bringing judgment not salvation. The *'OTH*s in Egypt are 'signs' that Covenant is alive and well and in full force, indicating the protection of the God Who fights for His Covenant-partner, comforting to Israel but a *negative* 'sign' for Egypt; here in Samuel it is the wrath of a Covenant perverted for selfish pleasure and gain, for all Israel to see, to realize and to take warning.

Other *'OTH*s?

Although it is a word which is associated with Covenant, perhaps not every instance of *'OTH* may specifically relate to Covenant – or do they?

> God said, "Let there be lights in the firmament of the heavens to divide between the day and the night; and let them be for *'OTH*s (SIGNs) and for seasons and for days and years." Genesis 1:14

God, just prior to His cutting of Covenant, pointed Abraham to the stars as verification of His promise [Genesis 15:5]. Elsewhere the writer has done a study on "the Ballet of the Stars," where at the birth of Jesus a remarkable series of conjunctions occur on *specific* Jewish holy days. These, in turn, describe Who Jesus is and the tasks He will fulfill as He completes the Old Covenant and initiates the New. In this way, "the heavens declare the Glory of God" [Psalm 19:1], revealing themselves to be the powerful SIGN of Covenant which the Creator had designed from the beginning.

> The People of Israel shall camp each by his own standard, with the enSIGNs (*'OTH*) of their fathers' houses; they shall camp in sight of *the Tent of Meeting* on every side. Numbers 2:2

A different word is used for "ensign" elsewhere. Recalling how Israel's Covenant at Sinai establishes them as the Nation of Jehovah, is the use of *'OTH* here, particularly in that they would be centered on *"the Tent of Meeting,"* meant to emphasize that their tribes are subservient to this national Covenant relationship with Jehovah?

> Your enemies have roared in the midst of Your Holy Place; they set up their own *'OTH*s (SIGNs) for *'OTH*s (SIGNs). Psalm 74:4

Recalling Cain's sacrifice which rebels against the sacrifice which God has demonstrated (indicated by the covering of skins, Genesis 3:21), it is no surprise to find that the rebellious would set up their own versions of *'OTH*s, perhaps as signs of Covenant with false gods or just simply for a do-it-yourself religion, perhaps also predictive of the 'mark of the Beast' in Revelation 14:9.

> Therefore Jehovah Himself will give you an *'OTH* (SIGN): Behold, a young woman shall conceive and bear a Son, and shall call His Name Immanuel.
> Isaiah 7:14

Here is the sign which identifies the culmination of the relationship in the 'Old' Covenant and the 'creation' of the 'New' Covenant.

C. The '*OTH* <u>YOU</u> Do is <u>GOD'S</u> SIGN!

In a fascinating twist, often *Jehovah's* SIGN of Covenant is not something *He* gives, but something *which mankind is to 'DO'* (for example, circumcision) – yet IN THE DOING is *GOD'S* PROOF (not *man's!*) that Jehovah and mankind are in Covenant. It is done by God's initiative and command; although human hands do it, no human has the right to claim the *'OTH* as his own accomplishment.

Even 'observing the *Sabbath*' is not merely something the faithful *do*, but, it is to be "an *'OTH* [*SIGN*] between Me and you ... that *I, Jehovah*, sanctify you" [Exodus 31:13; also Ezekiel 20:12, 20]. Occurring on the *seventh/oath* day, the *Sabbath* is *God's* evidence of Covenant *to you*, and is to be the SIGN of His Salvation [Deuteronomy 5:15], by which He brings His People rest (*Sabbath*) from their slavery. When put in these terms, precisely the same description can be applied to the New Testament practice of worship on Sunday, along with its celebration of Holy Communion, as representing the Easter Resurrection! Other such examples would be:

> [Jehovah] said, "I will be with you; and this shall be *the 'OTH* [*SIGN*] *for you* that I have sent you: when you have brought the People out of Egypt, you shall serve God upon this mountain."
> Exodus 3:12, Moses' success is to be God's *'OTH*

> They shall take some of the Blood and put it on the two doorposts and the lintel... The Blood shall be *an 'OTH* [*SIGN*] *for you*...: I will see the Blood, I will pass over you, and the plague shall not destroy you when I strike the land of Egypt.
> Exodus 12:7, 13

> Unleavened bread shall be eaten for seven days... It shall be *an 'OTH* [*SIGN*] for you *on your hand and as a remembrance* [*ZEKER*] *on your*

forehead, so that the teaching of Jehovah may be in your mouth; for with a strong *hand* Jehovah brought you out of Egypt. Exodus 13:7, 9

As one of the *'OTH*s 'which you do but is God's sign,' the *Sabbath* forms a class which includes not just the Saturday *Sabbath*, but also the *Sabbath* and *Jubilee* ("*Sabbath of Sabbaths*") *Years*. II Chronicles 36:21 declares that it will take the *seventy*-year captivity to allow the Land to finally enjoy the *Sabbath* years of rest which have been ignored throughout Israel's stay in the Promised Land.

Refusing to do the SIGN robs us. In fact, Covenant-partners endanger themselves by such negligence: had Noah not built the Ark (Genesis 6:18 – though not specified as an *'OTH* of Covenant, it can certainly fit in that class), he would have perished. Circumcision, although done by human hands, is GOD's indelible *'OTH* [Genesis 17:11] which if it is *not* done would break Covenant [Genesis 17:14]. Neglecting to circumcise his son jeopardizes Moses' Life [Exodus 4:24-26]. *God* wants this relationship! This certainly gives some weight to the New Covenant's counterparts of such things as the Sacraments and even prayer.

D. The New Name – The New Identity

> Herbert Spencer sees the correspondence of the blood-covenant and the exchange of names. He says: "By absorbing each other's blood, men are supposed to establish actual community of nature. Similarly with the ceremony of exchanging names ... This, which is a widely-diffused practice, arises from the belief that the name is vitally connected with its owner... To exchange names, therefore, is to establish some participation in one another's being." Hence, as we may suppose, came the well-nigh universal Oriental practice of inter-weaving the name of one's Deity with one's name, as a symbolic evidence of one's covenant-union with the Deity. The blood-covenant, or the blood-union, idea is at the bottom of this.
>
> Trumbull[53]

Covenant signals a radical change in Life: two persons now become one. A change in name might demonstrate this or the names might be exchanged as in the example between Tolo, chief of the Shastika Indians, and Col. McKee (along with its unfortunate conclusion, as related in a previous section).

Within this name exchange idea, Jehovah inserts the letter "*H*" ["ה"], perhaps representing His Name in the form of the breath/Spirit of God), into אברם [*'ABRAM* ("Exalted Father")], which now makes it אברהם [*'ABRAHAM* ("Father of Nations")]; likewise *SARAI* [שרי ("Princess")]'s name changes to *SARAH* [שרה ("Queen")]. Jacob, re-entering the Promised Land and returning to Covenant [Genesis 32], receives a completely new name, becoming *ISRAEL* [ישראל ("God prevails" or "Perseveres with God")].

E. The Covenant Feast

The Communal Meal

Often a meal is celebrated as part of the Covenant atmosphere. Eating together has long been recognized as a bonding together of people, just as the Covenant-vestige of shaking hands has long been recognized as a symbol of friendship. Entire households, tribes, or families may come together to share a meal or feast, further making them one, because the same food becomes part of the bodies of both sides. Even at Jacob and Laban's unique "Anti-Covenant" [below], the eating of bread appears to be part of the ceremony [Genesis 31:54].

In some instances, the elders would first feed one another, indicating the total commitment of one's physical means to sustain the other. Then, they would feed each other wine representing Blood (Life).[54] Then, the rest of the families would feed each other bread and wine. This is the ancestor to the bride and the groom feeding the cake to each other, also to the drinking of champagne (or in other instances, other liquids) with interlocked arms.

The Peace/Fellowship Offering – Exodus 29:19-26,31-34; Leviticus 3; 7:11-21, 28-36

The other sacrifices look backwards, setting right what had been broken or missing; the שֶׁלֶם [*SHELEM* – *Peace/Communion Offering*] looks forward and is more like a mini-Confirming Covenant. The root of this word, שָׁלֵם [*SHALEM*], is also the root for שָׁלוֹם [*SHALOM*. Like *HESED*, *SHALOM* is another one of those words in which there is no adequate match in English:

> **shalom.** ... the root meaning of the verb *shalem* better expresses the true concept of *shalom*. Completeness, wholeness, harmony, fulfillment, are closer to the meaning. Implicit in *shalom* is the idea of unimpaired relationships with others and fulfillment in one's undertakings....
>
> *shalom* is the result of God's activity in covenant (*berit*), and is the result of righteousness (Isa 32:17). In nearly two-thirds of its occurrences, *shalom* describes the state of fulfillment which is the result of God's presence....The peace that marks the conclusion of an agreement between ... man and God (Abraham, Gen 15:15) is couched in terms of covenant agreement....
>
> **shelem.** ... Current understanding of the meaning of *shelem* follows three main lines of thought. First, *shelem* symbolizes the gift of *shalom*... A second alternative is identified by de Vaux as "communion sacrifice," ... There is no sense of attaining a mystical union with God through these sacrifices. Rather there is a sense of joyful sharing because of God's presence....
>
> Thirdly, the fact that the *shelem* usually comes last in the lists of the offerings... argue[s] that this is a "concluding sacrifice." This derives *shelem* from the rarer Piel meaning "to complete." If this sense is correct, the NT references to Christ our Peace (e.g. Eph 2:14) become more meaningful, as he is the final sacrifice for us (cf. Heb 9:27; 10:12).   *TWOT*[55]

The name revolves around the Hebrew *shalom* and speaks not of a mere cessation of war or of a quietness of mind – actually it means "wholeness." When a jigsaw puzzle's contents are dumped out, although all the pieces are there, as long as the puzzle is not put together it is not "whole." When finally everything is as it should be and the picture can be fully seen, only then might you say that it has *shalom*.

There are many "pieces" in our lives: health; relationships with spouse, children, extended family, friends; activities and recreations; interests, attitudes, and perspectives; and many, many more. Central to this "picture," which is "the Image of God" in us, is our relationship with the Lord ... When all elements of a life are properly in their appropriate places, then we have *shalom;* but if some "pieces" are in the wrong places, some are missing, some are turned backward, some are in upside-down, and some simply do not belong, then there is no *shalom.*[56]

The other sacrifices restore the foundation of trust; this one reestablishes the mutual Covenant dedication and enjoyment of each to the other, like an *'OTH* to each other of their self-giving commitment. This Sacrifice is communion – at table with Jehovah Himself, in Covenant within His Chosen People. They 'share' the meal: God's portion by fire; the officiating priest (representing God's People) and the sacrificer by eating their portions in the presence of Jehovah. Here the sacrifice is received by the LORD, blessed by Him, and then returned to the sacrificer as something far greater.

This fellowship is echoed in the morning and evening sacrifices [Exodus 29:38-43]: "there I will meet and speak with you; there also I will meet with the Israelites ..." – as if to say, 'I am eager to meet with you *daily*, as I had with Adam and Eve before sin got in the way!' – or 'Let's do lunch (or rather, breakfast and dinner) ...'

How could one *so boldly* dine with the all-powerful Creator God of the universe? Who would be 'worthy' enough? BUT *this is done by invitation!* These sacrifices are not man's creation, but are *commanded* by Jehovah Himself! The LORD Himself opens the way by the Blood of His approved innocent victim (the *Sin Offering*; "I have given it to you upon the altar to make atonement for your Souls/Lives" [Leviticus 17:11]). Here is His Word (in Blood and flesh) that the sacrificer is fully accepted, and all which is left is the crowning fellowship with Jehovah.

Because of how Jesus redefines the *Passover Seder* meal into Holy Communion, using the *'AFIKOMAN'* (the broken, hidden middle one of three matzos) and the third cup ("the Cup of Redemption") as His own

Body and Blood, then that meal also becomes the equal to such a Covenant celebration.

F. Covenant in Odd Situations

The "Anti-Covenant"

A unique use of Covenant is found in Genesis 31:43-54 in what might be called an "Anti-Covenant." Here Laban employs the imagery of Covenant for an outcome opposite to Covenant's purpose: instead of being joined for mutual benefit and strength, he calls upon the Overseer of Covenant to enforce *separation* between Jacob and himself, to prevent Jacob from taking any more advantage of his father-in-law ["for harm" v 52], and particularly to invoke protection for his daughters (Jacob's wives). It is a creative way for Laban to have recourse should he discover that his daughters are in any way mistreated.

The "Squeeze-Play" Covenant

Sullen Cain – so quick to shed another's (Abel's) Blood – is terrified that someone (perhaps already with the idea of a *GO'EL* [see below]) will kill him [Genesis 4:9-16]. Jehovah then does a strange thing: elsewhere, the murderer forfeits his Life, but not here. The LORD gives him an *'OTH* (SIGN) and an oath ("*seven*-fold") of safe-conduct, which suggest a Covenant setting. The irony is that Cain is forced to depend on Jehovah for protection – what Cain would not do voluntarily, he now has to do involuntarily. He has rebelled against God's will, now he must find refuge in it.

G. The Live-r of Glory

The Sump of Life

The organ called the Liver may have a surprising role within the concept of the Blood.

> It is true that in many parts of the world the *liver* was made prominent as seemingly a synonym of life; but this was obviously because of the popular belief that the liver was itself a mass of coagulated blood. The idea seems to have been that, as the heart was the blood-fountain, the liver was the blood-cistern; and that, as the source of life (or of blood, which life is,) was at the heart, so the great receptacle of life, or of blood, was the liver ...
>
> Even in modern English, the word "liver" has been thought by many to represent "life" or "blood." Thus, in one of our dictionaries we are told that the word is derived from the Anglo-Saxon and the Scandinavian verb "to live," "because [the liver is] of so great importance to *life*, or animal vitality." In another, its derivation is ascribed to *lopper*, and *lapper*, "to coagulate," "from its resemblance to a mass of clotted blood."
>
> Trumbull[57]

Appearing as if the 'collection point' of Blood, the Liver represents the totality of one's Life to date: all which the person has been, all experiences and deeds, all thoughts and wisdom and strength – the Life/Soul of the person are 'contained' in the Liver.

The Glory

The only Hebrew word for Liver [כבד - *KBD*] is originally written the same as the Hebrew root word for Glory (the vowels were added later).[58] Although the two words may be unrelated, perhaps at least audibly there might be an association of concepts. The Liver, seen as the sum total of one's Life, would indeed be 'the Glory' of one's Life, representing all the person was and did.

In Exodus 33:18-19, at Moses' request to see His Glory, Jehovah would have to show His History (His Story), since indeed His Glory is His goodness, Covenant relationship, grace and mercy – it is interesting how the understanding of the 'Liver' as *the repository of Life/Blood*, would dovetail nicely with the concept of Glory in this passage, here being *the collection of God's Life*.

The Cleanser

Probably the ancient Hebrew never knew the functions that the Liver performs for the body, particularly how it is the Cleanser, taking the Blood/Life of the body, cleansing it (along with other functions), removing or neutralizing toxins (sometimes at its own self-sacrifice), and then returning the Life to the Body.

The connection between Blood and cleansing is reflected in the New Testament. If the glory of God is indeed His mercy and grace, then that which represents the totality of God's Life would find its embodiment in the Cross of Jesus, both in terms of the grace and mercy of God, as well as the cleansing of Life.

> If we walk in the light, as He is in the light, we have fellowship with one another, and the Blood of Jesus Christ His Son cleanses us from all sin. If we say we have no sin, we deceive ourselves, and the truth is not in us. If we confess our sins, He is faithful and righteous, and will forgive our sins and cleanse us from all unrighteousness.   I John 1:7-9

> ... He said to me, "These are they who have come out of the great tribulation; they have washed their robes and made them white in the Blood of the Lamb."   Revelation 7:14

> Almost everything is cleansed by Blood according to the law, and without the shedding of Blood there is no forgiveness.
>   Hebrews 9:22

The Appendage of the Liver

> You shall take all the fat that covers 'the inwards,' and the lobe of the liver, and the two kidneys with the fat that is on them, and burn them upon the altar.   Exodus 29:13[59]

"The inwards"[60] contain 'thought and attitudes'; the kidneys[61] may emphasize sensitivity and discernment; the fat seems to be the satisfactions and abundance of life, here being God's portion, perhaps as in the tithe. A surprising, notable absence is the heart, yet *the Liver* is specifically mentioned, which would be understandable if indeed the Liver is the 'sump' or summation of one's Life in the mind of the ancient, where past deeds and sins are deposited.

Many translations understand the "flap of the liver" to be only part of the liver, supposedly the *caudate lobe*. Why is the whole liver – the whole of Life – not included?

The caudate lobe is the part of the organ in direct contact with the inferior vena cava, which is the Liver's 'outlet,' returning to the Bloodstream the Life/Soul which has been processed by this organ. Perhaps sacrificing this part suggests that as the Blood/Life resumes its work, it is to be considered as sanctified? Or it reflects the concept of the tithe, or of the *Sabbath* seventh of the week, that although all of Life is in fact Jehovah's, only a portion is to be specifically dedicated to Him, yet dedicated all the same. This may be fanciful conjecture, still the question can be posed as to why it has such a prominent place in the sacrifices.

V. Restoring Lost Life/Blood

A. *No Guarantee of Faithfulness*

> If you think the New Covenant is coextensive with [that is, having the same scope as] salvation ... This is probably the most serious error in trying to understand the arguments here. Every covenant in the Bible, from Adam forward, included unbelievers. The New Covenant, in this respect, is no different. That is why Christ can promise salvation and damnation in the same breath to those in the New Covenant (1 Cor. 11, Heb. 6 and 10). Dr. C. Matthew McMahon[62]

> To be in covenant with God does not automatically imply eternal salvation – certainly not for covenant-breakers. Thus "they are not all Israel who are of Israel" (Rom. 9:6), and even in the New Covenant not all who publicly profess Jesus as "Lord" are savingly known by Him (Matt. 7:21-23). So then, the signs of circumcision and baptism definitely bring their recipients into covenant with God (and what they signify is intended as blessing), but they are not thereby personal guarantees of salvation, except for covenant-keepers. The covenant signs can also bring their recipients under God's dreadful judgment.
> Dr. Greg L. Bahnsen[63]

> For those who once were enlightened, who tasted the heavenly Gift, who became partakers in the Holy Spirit, who tasted the goodness of God's Word, of the power and of the age to come, and who then fall away, it is impossible to restore them to repentance, since they crucify again for themselves the Son of God and hold Him up to contempt.
> Hebrews 6:4-6

Covenant does not guarantee that all will be faithful. As the Old Testament vividly reveals, many who have the relationship refuse to accept it. An important note on the Hebrews passage is that it does not merely say "It is impossible to restore again ..." but rather "it is impossible to restore again *to repentance* [that is, to turn the mind around] ..." It is not that Jehovah closes the door – the Parable of the Prodigal Son demonstrates otherwise; it is that one refuses to come to *repentance* for whatever the reason he may have. But if one *does* come to repentance, how then would Covenant be restored?

B. Life/Blood is Precious

Surely, for the Blood of your Souls/Lives I will demand a reckoning; from the *hand* of every animal I will demand it, and from the *hand* of man...Whoever sheds man's Blood, by man his Blood shall be shed; for in God's image He made man. Genesis 9:5-6

Scripture clearly presents physical, human life as a specific creation of God, signified by the vital fluid in his veins, the Blood. God Himself is the Source, Originator and Terminator of that life, and no other. For this reason no man has the implicit right to take life, to shed Blood. To do so is to incur the wrath and judgment of God. In confirmation of this, Scripture reminds us that the Blood of a slain man has effects on the on-going lives of men, not because of the shed Blood-per-se does anything; but because the murderer, the destroyer was taking God's prerogatives to himself. This Biblical teaching on the shedding of Blood does not mean releasing the life-force for further activity (i.e., the Hindu doctrine of re-incarnation or like releasing a bird from a cage), rather ... the emptying of life – as emptying a bottle of precious wine into the sink – never to be recaptured again. George Kraus [64]

"For in God's image He made man" identifies the seriousness of the Life/Blood. Just as with injury and murder, which violate Jehovah's own Person through Covenant-Blood and rebel against the Giver of Life Himself, broken Covenant is to be treated with the utmost of concern. As indicated in the ceremony where once the animals were full of life but now are divided carcasses, the Life/Blood has been drained away. In fact, broken Covenant might be described as a spiritual murder and not merely a type of spiritual suicide, since the Covenant-partner is also profoundly affected (as Chief Tolo considered his identity to be 'lost').

Mention might also be made in regard to child sacrifice:

Yes, they sacrificed their sons and their daughters to demons, and shed *innocent Blood*, the Blood of their sons and daughters, whom they sacrificed to the idols of Canaan; and the land was defiled with Blood. Psalm 106:37-38

Not only is this considered murder ("innocent Blood"), but also it is regarded as the extreme violation of God's Covenant, where such is never commanded and is useless as a way to connect or re-connect with Jehovah. The one anomaly, God telling Abraham to sacrifice Isaac (Genesis 22), as the event played out is never meant to be an actual sacrifice of the child, since, despite Abraham's obedience, the LORD stops him before the sacrifice can be made. The event's purpose will be discussed later in regard to Abraham.

C. The GO'EL [גאל] – The Blood-Balancer

The Cry for Justice

"Abel's Blood for vengeance Pleaded to the skies"[65] – God is serious about His Life/Blood in humanity: even the beast which kills a man Jehovah would reckon with (stoned [Exodus 21:28,32], and since its Blood would not be properly drained, the beast could not even be eaten).

However, there is a misunderstanding in regard to what is required when Life/Blood has been spilled. This is not merely revenge (as is commonly thought in regard to "an eye for an eye" [Exodus 21:22-27; Leviticus 24:19]) – neither societal nor personal – but *accountability* for the gift of *God*'s *Life* through Covenant.

This accountability requires action since the Covenant Life/Blood has been affected, not just when there is murder or severe injury, but also when one sells himself as a slave to pay off debts, or when there is a natural death before one can produce offspring (for example, the story of Ruth). From the earthly side, there is concern because the Life/Blood of the family has been diminished, lost. It might be said that *Life* is now 'out of balance,' therefore the family would turn to the *GO'EL*, the 'Blood-balancer' – an *office* held by a kinsman whose duty it is to restore the balance to the family in whatever way is most suitable.

The Office

Another gleam of the primitive truth, that blood is life and not death, and that the transference of blood is the transference of life, is found in the various Mosaic references to the *goel*, the person authorized to obtain blood for blood as an act of justice. ... the word was ... applied to that kinsman whose duty it was to secure justice to the injured, to restore, as it were, a normal balance to the disturbed family relations. ... "that particular relative whose special duty it was to restore the violated family integrity, who had to redeem not only landed property that had been alienated from the family [Lev 25:25ff], or a member of the family that had fallen into slavery [Lev 25:47ff], but also the blood that had been taken away from the family by murder." Hence, in the event of a depletion of the family by the loss of blood – the loss of a life – the *goel* had a responsibility of securing to the family an equivalent of that loss, by other blood, or by an agreed payment for its value. His mission was not vengeance, but equity. He was not an avenger, but a redeemer, a restorer, a balancer. ...

... shows that it is not revenge, but restitution, that is sought after by the *goel*; he is not the blood-avenger, but the blood balancer.

... in some instances, all money payment for blood is refused; but the avowed motive in such a case is the holding of life as above price. ... And even where the blood of the slayer is insisted on, there are often found indications that the purpose of this choice rests on the primitive belief that the lost life is made good to the depleted family by the newly received blood. ...

In short, ... it is evident that the primal idea of the *goel*'s mission was to restore life for life; not to wreak vengeance, nor yet to mete out punishment ...   Trumbull[66]

SHALOM [שלום]

As mentioned in "IV. The Covenant Mosaic - E. The Covenant Feast - The Peace/Fellowship Offering" (above), *SHALOM* [שלום] has the focus on 'completeness' or 'wholeness,' that is, where all the pieces of life fit together properly with no holes or omissions, where everything in regard to Jehovah and to man is in its proper perspective. Although this word encompasses a far greater range of life than what the office of *GO'EL* might normally handle, still the *GO'EL* is an agent to help bring about such wholeness to life, particularly in regard to the Blood-balance of Covenant, as well as the Blood-balance of the family.

As a type of *GO'EL*, the priests in *the Temple* seek to bring wholeness to the broken Covenant of the sinner and of the People of God by the method approved by the offended party, Jehovah. The following provides two other examples of a 'wholeness' brought by a *GO'EL*: in the first, there is the brokenness of a family which has reached the end of its ancestral line and how that Blood is balanced in the birth of a child. In the second, there is a broken Covenant, and a difficult action is required to restore the brokenness to 'peace.' It is worthwhile to keep this connection between *SHALOM* and the *GO'EL* in the back of the mind whenever the word 'peace' is encountered.

The Example of Ruth

Naomi returned to Israel, bereft of husband and sons – a dead end for her husband Elimelech's family line – yet daughter-in-law Ruth faithfully stays by her side with virtual Covenant force: "your People are my People, your God my God. ... Jehovah do to me and more so, if anything but death part me from you" [Ruth 1:16-17].

When Ruth goes to glean, she 'happens' upon the field of Boaz [2:3], who 'happens' to be a *GO'EL* [v 20] in Elimelech's larger family. As 'Blood-balancer,' he is to ensure Elimelech's line would continue – not so much that he has to father the child, but that Ruth would marry within the family, so that the first male heir could be counted as Elimelech's offspring. Well informed of Naomi's plight and of Ruth's kindness to her [v 11], Boaz' initial generosity may have been because of this office.

Demonstrating strong faithfulness to Naomi, Ruth does not flirt with the young men [3:10], because in marrying someone not close enough to fulfill the brother's obligation [Deuteronomy 25:5-6], she could not raise up grandchildren to Naomi nor allow the land to remain under Elimelech's name. On the other hand, Boaz needs the permission of a *GO'EL* closer in family before he and Ruth can realize the conclusion of their attraction [Ruth 3:12-13; 4:1-12].

The result of all this faithfulness and self-discipline is a baby boy, a *GO'EL*, a "Blood-balancer" for Naomi: "Blessed be Jehovah, Who has not left you this day without a *GO'EL*. ... He has been to you a restorer of Life/Soul [=Blood]" [4:14-15]; and Ruth becomes not just David's ancestress [4:17-22], but also Jesus' [Matthew 1:5], where the promise ("a Restorer of Life/Blood") is in an even greater way fulfilled.

The Example of David

Unfortunately, the responsibilities are not always as pleasant. In II Samuel 21:1-9, even though the Gibeonites had originally acquired their Covenant by fraud, Jehovah requires an accounting for when Covenant is broken against them: "although the People of Israel had sworn [*SHABA*] to them, Saul had sought to exterminate them in his zeal..." [v 2].

Note that the restitution is not based on 'tit-for-tat' or 'eye for eye' – that *every* Gibeonite dead be compensated for. Instead, "let *seven* [*SHABA*] of his sons be given to us, so that we may hang them up before Jehovah at Gibeon on the mountain of Jehovah" [v 6]. Since *seven* is the word for Covenant oath, to bring Covenant – and Blood – back to its balance, the Gibeonites want the *oath/seven* restored. King David, as *GO'EL* for Israel, has to turn over members of his own 'family' (Israel) to the Gibeonites to redeem for broken Covenant and shed Blood [vv 6-9].

"Whoever sheds man's Blood, his Blood shall be shed by man" [Genesis 9:6] – does this not conflict with the sanctity of Life/Blood? No, because mankind is to represent the LORD ("for in God's image He made man"), and, despite the Fall, they are still His agents not only in managing the world but also in Jehovah's carrying out His overseeing of Covenant – not as individuals, but as a collective society. The policeman, soldier, judge, executioner, even a king, are not to act in their own behalf, but only as officers of the society (as the *GO'EL* is an officer of the family/society) and, above that, of God Himself Who establishes the governments (which are to reflect His Image on a larger scale).

The Biblical basis for disciplinary action is not 'rehabilitation,' nor 'deterrent,' nor 'revenge,' but a *balancing* of Blood, a *restoration* to Covenant.

Redemption for Broken Covenant

A monetary redemption for spilled Blood / broken Covenant may be arranged by the *GO'EL*. One example of such redemption is in Exodus 21:29-30, when the owner of an ox which is accustomed to gore, although warned, does not keep it penned up. If it kills someone, the owner is to die. However, "if a ransom is laid on him, then he shall give for the redemption of his Life whatever is laid upon him." In I Samuel 14:24, Jonathan unwittingly breaks a foolish oath made (before God) by his father, King Saul, and is condemned to death, yet "the people ransomed Jonathan, that he did not die" [verse 45].

Yet there is a broken Covenant which simply requires death and there is no way one can free *himself* from the penalty – it is when the Blood spilt is the Covenant Life/Blood of God first given in the Creation Covenant. Without God's Life, there is no Life:

> A brother cannot at all redeem [*PADAH* – *see next section for these words*] a man, nor give to God an atonement/ransom [*KAPHAR*] for him – for costly is the redemption [*PADAH*] of their Soul/Life which ceases forever – how can he live forever? How can he not see corruption?
> Psalm 49:7-9

A death is required, although God does have a solution for the ransom, but it will be at Jehovah's personal cost.

D. KAPHAR [כפר]
– The Ransom, the Redeeming from Sin

The *GO'EL* Established the Pattern

> Jehovah God made garments of skins for the man and for his wife, and clothed them.　　　　　　　　　　　　　　　Genesis 3:21

'Breaking Covenant' – the culture is horrified at it, demanding the direst penalties, particularly death (because the "one Soul in two bodies" has died – in a sense, been *murdered*). And with such horror on the human level, imagine what it means to break Covenant with God – this is Divine Blood! The penalty should be enormous. Since, 'well, we're only human. ...' does not even excuse broken human-to-human Covenants, how then could Jehovah's Covenant be restored? It depends on the offended Covenant-Partner. Legally He could/should demand death, but other solutions might be acceptable.

When the *GO'EL* (Jehovah) provided "coats of skins" at the cost of proxy Life to cover Adam and Eve, the pattern is established of how an Atonement (a *Ransom*) would take place. The proxy would be a victim of God's choosing, an innocent Substitute, Who would shed His Blood to restore the broken relationship with new *Life*.

> Almost everything is cleansed by Blood according to the law, and without the shedding of Blood there is no forgiveness.
> 　　　　　　　　　　　　　　　　　　　　　　　Hebrews 9:22

Since permission to eat meat came only after the flood [Genesis 9:3-4], the only source for a garment of skins prior to that event would be from the sacrifices. The skins therefore are a SIGN – but of that interesting category where although *you* may do the activity, yet such clothing is *God*'s *'OTH*, the mark and daily reminder of Jehovah's restoration of Life and of Covenant and of its cost. This provides the necessary background for the Cain and Abel story.

Atonement

Ransom

Hence another key word also comes into use: "KAPHAR," often translated as "atonement" or "forgiveness": "For the *Soul** of the flesh is in the Blood; and I have given it to you on the altar to make atonement for your *Souls**; for, as *Soul**, it is the Blood which atones for the *Soul**... For the *Soul** of every creature is its Blood in its *Soul**" [Leviticus 17:11,14; **Soul/Life*].

> The root *kapar* is used some 150 times.... There is an equivalent Arabic root meaning "cover," or "conceal." On the strength of this connection it has been supposed that the Hebrew word means "to cover over sin" and thus pacify the deity, making an atonement (so BDB).... There is, however, very little evidence for this view....
>
> Koper. Ransom. Every Israelite was to give to the service of the sanctuary the "ransom" money of half a shekel (Ex 30:12). Egypt, in God's sight, was given as a "ransom" for the restoration of Israel (Isa 43:3). This word "ransom" is parallel to the word "redeem" (*pada*, ...) in Ps 49:7. There is a warning that a man guilty of murder must be killed – no "ransom" can be given in exchange for his life (Num 35:31).
>
> From the meaning of *koper* "ransom," the meaning of *kapar* can be better understood. It means "to atone by offering a substitute." The great majority of the usages concern the priestly ritual of sprinkling of the sacrificial blood thus "making an atonement" for the worshipper.... The verb is always used in connection with the removal of sin or defilement, except for Gen 32:20; Prov 16:14; and Isa 28:18 where the related meaning of appease by a gift may be observed. It seems clear that this word aptly illustrates the theology of reconciliation in the OT. The life of the sacrificial animal specifically symbolized by its blood was required in exchange for the life of the worshipper.... It was the symbolic expression of innocent life given for guilty life. *TWOT*[67]

Pour Out the Blood Before the Altar

> ... the rest of the Blood you shall pour out at the base of the altar
> Exodus 29:12; Leviticus 4:7,18, 25, 30, 34

This instruction in regard to the Blood is not mentioned for any sacrifice other than the *Sin Offering*. It, therefore, is part of the act of ransoming – atonement. However there needs to be a distinction between the concepts of retribution and of restoration. Easily this action could be merely construed as retribution – death is required by broken Covenant, and death is poured out. But that is not the mission of the sacrifices! The intent is not destruction of Life but restoration of Covenant, to end ultimately in the *Peace/Communion Offering*.

This now falls within the concept of the *GO'EL*, whose function is to re-balance the loss of Blood. His task is to *recover* Life, to bring back what is lost, to restore Life/Blood into balance. The Blood at the altar does not just look backward to the sin but also forward to the renewed relationship.

The Day of Atonement/Redemption (Leviticus 16) – Yom Kippur (from KAPHAR)

If entering *the Holy Place* in *the Tent of Meeting* without properly honoring Jehovah is fatal (as Nadab and Abihu demonstrate – Leviticus 10:1-3), imagine entering *the Most Holy Place*, where one comes 'perilously close to God.' Yet there is one time, only once each year, on the tenth of the *seventh* month[68] when the need climaxed in such a visit: *the Day of Atonement* [Leviticus 23:27,28[69]]. Just as the priests are tainted with uncleanness by doing their God-commanded duties on the *Sabbath*, even so the holiest place on earth accumulated a taint from the sin all around it [v 16]. Along with all the camp, it would have to be atoned for/redeemed by Blood [vv 33-34].[70] As the glory in Moses' face waned without constant renewal [Exodus 34:29], so also this connection of Covenant has to be restored, revitalized, refreshed each year.

The Day of Atonement is a "*Sabbath* of *Sabbaths*" – if the *Sabbath* as "a day of rest" still allows for essential activity, this "rest of rests" allows even less: it is a day in which EVERYBODY does NOTHING, not even eat ("you shall afflict/humble your Souls" [vv 29,31 – or 'fasting'] and "do no work" [v 29; 23:32]). On this most significant day picturing Atonement

(*KAPHAR*), Israel is the portrait of utter helplessness. What clearer description could Jehovah have given of what grace is all about!

As Israel's main channel of intercession and *HESED/Love*, the High Priest's sins could restrict the flow of Covenant-Blood between Jehovah and Israel. Therefore his first sacrifice is a separate *Sin Offering* for himself *and his household*. Adding incense to coals from *the Altar of Burnt Offering*, – totally alone [v 17] – he swings a censor behind *the Most Holy Place*'s curtain to fill it with a concealing cloud [v 13 – incense often is the symbol of prayer]. Entering the smoky darkness with the sacrifice's Blood, he stands before *the Ark of Covenant*, the central point of all Jehovah's *HESED* and Covenant, and sprinkles the Blood once upon *the Atonement Cover* and then *seven* times in front of it.

By the door of *the Tent of Meeting* are two goats, both for ONE *Sin Offering*. One goat, chosen by lot, would die. Again entering *the Most Holy Place*, the Blood is sprinkled upon and in front of *the Atonement Cover*. Imagine the High Priest's relief at surviving by the intercession of prayer and the Blood of Atonement! Then mixing the Blood with his own sacrifice's, he atones the tent and the Altar of Incense, sprinkling it *seven* times.

Next is a most interesting, picturesque, and comforting sign of atonement. Part two of the ONE *Sin Offering* is the Scapegoat "Azazel" ("Very Removed")[71]. The High Priest lays his hands on this second goat and confesses Israel's sins. This goat is then led into the wilderness. What a visual reality behind the Psalmist's "As far as the east is from the west, so far has He removed our transgressions from us" [Psalm 103:12]!![72] The Atonement is done; the High Priest bathes and changes into his official vestments. After the extraordinary silence, the merry noise of the bells along his robe [Exodus 28:31-35] signals that all is well: the Atonement is accepted, their sins gone.

פדה *(PADAH) – ransom, redeem, rescue*

The semantic development of padâ is one of great significance to Christian theology. Originally, it had to do with the payment of a required sum for the transfer of ownership, a commercial term. Exodus and Le 19:20 speak of the redemption of a slave girl for the purpose of marriage. It is also used to speak of the redemption of a man's life who is under the sentence of death, as in 1Sa 14:45, when Jonathan was redeemed by the People of Israel.

The word was given special religious significance by the Exodus. When God delivered Israel from servitude to Egypt, he did so at the price of the slaughter of all the firstborn in Egypt, man and beast (Ex 4:23; 12:29). Consequently, the event was to be perpetually commemorated in Israel by the consecration of all the firstborn of man and beast to the Lord (Ex 13:12). ...

The use of *padah* and its derivatives is sometimes paralleled by other roots. Particularly it should be noted that *ga'al* [as from *go'el*] is used synonymously. Both roots have to do with redemption by the payment of ransom though it is suggested that *ga'al* basically is associated with family situations; hence, the idea of acting as kinsman. Nevertheless, the usage of both *padah* and *ga'al* in parallelisms in Hos 13:!4 and Jer 31:11, and the synonymous usage in Lev 27:27 et al. illustrate the overlapping of the two words. ...

The *kopher* sometimes parallels *padah* as in Ps 49:8 and Ex 21:30. The root *kaphar* means "... to make atonement," and the *kopher* is the ransom paid to secure favor or reconciliation.   *TWOT*[73]

The Ransom Cover

I will meet you there and speak to you, above *the Atonement Cover* ("*Mercy* Seat"), from between the two cherubim which are on *the Ark of Witness*, all which I shall command for the Israelites.   Exodus 25:22

Without its *Atonement [Ransom] Cover*, broken Covenant would compel Jehovah to move in judgment; but with *the Cover*, the door of fellowship is re-opened. Even then, the massive amount of Blood by sacrifice shed throughout the 'Old' Covenant history just is not enough to adequately atone broken Covenant – mankind could not handle the intense presence of the *Holy* God:

> Tell Aaron your brother he shall not come at all times ... before *the Atonement Cover* which is upon *the Ark*, and he shall not die; for I will appear in the cloud upon *the Atonement Cover.*   Leviticus 16:2

What a profound contrast is there in the New Testament:

> Therefore, brethren, having boldness to enter the Holiest by the Blood of Jesus, by a new and living Way which He consecrated for us, through the veil, that is, His flesh, and having a High Priest over the house of God, let us draw near with a true heart in full assurance of faith, having our hearts sprinkled from an evil conscience and our bodies washed with pure water.   Hebrews 10:19-22

The Red Tent

> You shall make a covering for *the Tent* of rams' skins dyed red [אדם "*ADAM*"], and a covering above of 'badgers' skins.
> Exodus 26:14

As with *the Atonement Cover* over *the Ark of Covenant*, over *the Tent of Witness/Meeting* is a layer of ram's skin dyed *red (Blood)*, suggesting the basis as to how Jehovah could dwell in the midst of sinful humans. Since a possible root for the Hebrew word for ram centers on 'insolence,'[74] how likely the choice it is for the *Guilt Offering* for a People who often shared that trait! The Hebrew for the supposed translation 'badger' [תחש – *TACHASH*] is unknown, but is surprisingly similar to 'serpent' [נחש – *NACHASH*] in the Genesis 3:1 account of the fall.

Ransoming a Broken *Oath/Seven*

In I Samuel 14, in regard to a battle against the Philistines, as often happened with Jehovah, the enemy destroys himself and all Israel has to do is mop up [vv 19-23]. Throwing aside consultation with the LORD [vv 18-19], perhaps attempting to force Jehovah and Israel into a quick victory, Saul rashly vows that the People would eat nothing until the day is finished – which severely weakens his own army so that they cannot fully destroy the Philistines [vv 24-32].

By evening the People, giving in to hunger, kill and eat livestock "with the Blood" [v 32]. When Saul discovers this "sin against Jehovah", he arranges so that the slaughter would be done properly with an altar built "to Jehovah" [vv 33-35]. But sin remains: an oath made before the LORD has been broken, *even though in ignorance* [vv 36-44]. When Jonathan is identified, Saul adds yet another oath, "God do so and more also" [v 44, also v 39]. When public opinion demands sparing Jonathan's Life "for he worked with God today", the broken oaths require a debt, "so the People ransomed Jonathan" [v 45].

The 'Atonement' of Salvation – Noah

Jehovah declares to Noah: "But I will establish ('confirm,' not 'cut') My Covenant with you, and you will enter the Ark ..." [Genesis 6:18]. Just like with many *'OTHs*, the Ark can be considered a SIGN, built by Noah, yet by it *God* declares *His* salvation.

In a sense, the Ark is incidental: an elaborate and well-built boat *without Covenant* would not have saved him, but with Covenant, God could have saved Noah with merely a twig. Suppose the Ark is not *perfect* and leaks profusely – no matter, because *what saves Noah is Covenant* – GOD PROMISED and Noah believes and acts accordingly (although he may have learned about "bailing out a boat"). Ultimately, the Ark is essential simply because Jehovah's command makes it necessary.

"... *pitch* it within and without with *pitch*" – Genesis 6:14 presents an thought-provoking aspect: *Only here* is the Hebrew *KAPHAR* translated as 'pitch'; *everywhere else* it is translated as 'atonement [ransom]' or something similar (every other 'pitch' is a different Hebrew word [for example, Exodus 2:3, Isaiah 34]). *KAPHAR* apparently originally does describe coal tar, and therefore that is a permissible translation, still, the *listener's* vast familiarity with the word is as 'atonement.' What then does he hear subliminally – that the Lifesaving Ark is covered with/protected by "atonement" within and without (no leaky boat any more)? *Through "atonement"* they are saved, paralleling the *Passover* [Exodus 12:7-13]!

Curiously גפר [GOPHER– "Gopher," the wood of the Ark] is an unknown word, however, note the similarity between its first letter ג (G) and the כ (K) of כפר [KOPHER "ransom" from KAPHAR – to atone], even in sound – is this perhaps a corrupted "ransom"? or a deliberate play on words? GOPHER is also the root for "brimstone" גפרית [GAPHRITH] in Genesis 19:24 and also in Psalm 11:6.

An interesting picture presents itself: the Ark is 'judgment' covered inside and out with 'atonement' – atonement faces both God and man. Also consider how *'seven'* (of each of the clean animals) figures into this account [Genesis 7:1-4].

A Sense of Futility

> For the law has a shadow of the good things to come, not the true form of them, therefore by offering the same sacrifices continually year after year it can never make perfect those who draw near. ... But in them there is a reminder of sin year after year. It is impossible for the Blood of bulls and goats to take away sins.   Hebrews 10:1-4

Josephus writes that in 70 AD 255,660 lambs are sacrificed for *Passover alone.* Numbers 28:1-29:38, Leviticus 1-6 speak of 1300 *formal* sacrifices per year X 1500 years from Moses to Jesus (not including all the other sacrifices each person may offer during the year). To truly atone for *all* broken Covenant, something much greater is required.

VI. The Old Testament: THE Foundational Covenant

A. Based on the Nature of God Himself

Grace: The First Move is Always God's

Covenant leaps out of Jehovah's Glory *as He defines it:* His Goodness, Grace, Mercy, Steadfast Love, Faithfulness, Forgiveness and Justice. His action arises from His heart, not from any anticipated benefit or need, not even from any expected response. In *EVERYTHING* God initiates the process simply because He chooses to.

B. The Creation Covenant

Part 1: MANKIND IS GOD'S AMBASSADOR

Blood(Life)-Likeness

For the Life/Soul of the flesh is in the Blood; ... the Blood is its Life/Soul.   Leviticus 17:11,14

דם	"*DAM*"	– Blood
דמי	"*ADAM*"	– the (red, Blood) man; humanity in general
אדמה	"*ADAMAH*"	– the "(red, Blood) soil"
דמה	"*DAMAH*"	– the "[Blood/Life/Soul]-*likeness* of God"

[Genesis 1:26; 5:1]

God said, "Let Us make man in Our *image*, according to Our *likeness* [*DAMAH*]: and let them rule..." So God created the man in His *image*, in the *image* of God created He him; male and female created He them.   Genesis 1:26-27

(4) It is not *[image]* which is defined and limited by *[likeness]* but the other way around. Two things are important here: (a) the similarity between *[likeness]* and the Hebrew word for blood *dam*; (b) in Mesopotamian tradition the gods in fact created man from divine blood.   TWOT[75]

Jehovah God formed the *man [ADAM]* from the dust of the *ground [ADAMAH]*, and blew into his nostrils the breath of *Life*; and the man became a living Soul. Genesis 2:7

The very center of Man's creation revolves around Blood/Life. The Hebrew cannot even say "human" *[ADAM]* without being conscious of "Blood"!

The First Covenant (The Proto-Covenant)

ברית "B'RITH" – Covenant, "The Cutting"; *associated with:*

ברה "BARAH" – to select, to choose, to eat; *but perhaps also with:*

ברא "BARA'" – to create (used for the *creation* of "*ADAM*"
[Genesis 1:27])

Does "*seven*" [Covenant "oath"] in the *seven* days of creation, have a deliberate connection to Covenant, in that the day of rest is to "rest" in the Covenant of God?

You shall keep My *Sabbath*s, for this is an *'OTH* [SIGN] between Me and you … Exodus 31:13; see Ezekiel 20:12, 20

Since the whole of the Bible revolves around Covenant, particularly between Jehovah and man; since Covenant is also a worldwide cultural pattern and therefore is very ancient; since Blood figures so prominently in the origin of humanity; therefore in the Creation account Jehovah sets *the pattern of Covenant* in creating man so that His own Life/Soul flows through him – "one Life in two persons" – perhaps echoed by "Jehovah God … blew into his nostrils the breath of *Life*" [Genesis 2:7] as man is meant to bear the Breath/Spirit of God.

The 'OTH (Sign)

THE IMAGE OF GOD

So God created man in His own *image*, in God's *image* He created him; male and female He created them. Genesis 1:27

An image is reflected only insofar as the reflecting material is able. A photograph or a mirror can give a recognizable likeness, and yet there is so much more to the original object which these images cannot show. If man is in "the Image of God," what then is he able to reflect about what God? II Corinthians 3:18 speaks of reflecting His Glory; therefore, as defined by Exodus 33:18-19; 34:5-7, it would be His Covenant relationship as well as the other qualities mentioned previously. Ephesians 4:24 chimes in with His righteousness and holiness, while I John 4:7-8 adds the New Testament counterpoint of His Love [*AGAPE*].

A Trinity!

> The God of peace Himself sanctify you wholly; and may your *spirit* and *soul* and *body* be kept sound and blameless at the coming of our LORD Jesus Christ.   I Thessalonians 5:23; See Heb 4:12; I Cor 2:14; 15:44,46

God is One God yet Three Eternal Persons, which is what the term "Trinity" encompasses. Did the first human reflect even that basic characteristic of God's nature? The Bible's answer is yes and it gives us a small window to recognize some crucial aspects about God.

This newly created human had a physical body as well as the essence which makes the difference whether that body is alive or dead – that is, the "living soul"; but especially also the "spirit," that unique connection with God which was identified earlier. These are three separate and identifiable parts to the human, and yet they work with such seamlessness that it is impossible to know where one leaves off and the other begins. To pick up a pen, the physical body does the visible action, yet it is impossible without the other parts being involved. To write great words of wisdom is the "soul" part, yet if the blood sugar level is low, they may not make much sense. Even when one prays (spiritual), generally the mind and even the body are involved.

Although this does not define how the divine Holy Trinity operates, it does give the inkling that not only is a Trinity possible, but also how it can function as a seamless unity, and possibly also how Covenant as well is meant to join two into a seamless unity.

The High Priest of Creation

> God blessed them, and God said to them, "Be fruitful and multiply, and fill the earth and subdue it; and rule over the fish of the sea and over the birds of the heavens and over all creeping beasts upon the earth."
> Genesis 1:28

Of His own design, God shares with mankind His Glory and sovereignty, His rule and government of this world-system. Adam carries the SIGN of God's Image and Likeness before all Creation, to be treated according to the honor and respect due to the Creator Himself. As the LORD's appointed ruler to creation, his management is to reflect God's management, and he is accountable to God. On the opposite side, he is high priest of creation, to bring its praise to God – as suggested in the call to creation to worship: Psalm 148; Isaiah 44:23;49:13;55:12-13.

Part 2: MARRIAGE

The Man – the Cutting[76]

"The Image of God" is the *badge*, Jehovah's SIGN, for the authority to represent God's governance over all creation, yet this task cannot to be done alone. It is not merely that the man is lonely and could not by himself multiply and fill the earth. A counterpart is required, another creation which would carry God's SIGN *to* the Man himself, just as he would bear the SIGN to her. 'Part Two' of the First Covenant is required, using a point-counterpoint of masculine and feminine traits deliberately separated and encouraged to truly represent the full range of God's rule .

> Jehovah God made a deep sleep to fall upon the man; while he slept took one of his ribs and closed up its place with flesh; Jehovah God formed the rib which had taken from the man into a woman and brought her to the man.
> Genesis 2:21-22

This also is a 'cutting' – perhaps Adam's 'strength' is not from his arm but from close to his heart (the fountain of his Life, reflecting also the center from which Jehovah operates) – ending not with two *pieces (as in broken Covenant)*, but two *persons* having one Life between them, and continued new Life (out from Blood is a child born).

> ... Because Jehovah has been witness between you and the wife of your youth... yet she is your companion and wife of your Covenant. Did He not make them one and [is there not still] a vestige of the Spirit in him? and why one? He seeks godly offspring. Therefore take heed to your spirit... Malachi 2:14-15

The Woman – Representing God to Each Other

> Then Jehovah God said, "It is not good that the man should be alone; I will make him a *helper [savior]* corresponding to him." Genesis 2:18

Helper: although the modern concept of "helper" is that of 'an expendable assistant,' the Hebrew word speaks of a person who aids someone in desperate need. A person who has fallen down a cliff needs help – not an 'expendable assistant,' but rather in essence he needs a *savior*. That is what the Hebrew word means, and, except in Isaiah and Ezekiel, it is a word everywhere else applied only to Jehovah Himself.

The 'Help of God' is the woman's *badge* for the authority to represent God: *to represent His Help/Salvation* to Creation (including to Man). Even though, sadly, in the Fall into Sin, her effort to 'help' her family instead destroys them, still her connection in regard to salvation still holds. The promise of the Savior would come not through the man, but through the woman ("*her* seed" – since throughout the Bible the child is considered the 'seed' of the man, the reformer Martin Luther maintained that this is already an indication of a virgin birth). It is only after this prophecy from God when the woman receives her name, "*EVE*" – Life!

אשה [ISHSHAH – woman; feminine of איש [ISH – man]] is the same pronunciation (although supposedly from a different root) for the *Whole Burnt Offering* (jokes aside!!). In the woman, through whom comes temptation and through whom would come the Savior, perhaps like *oath/seven*, the ear *hears* a word directly connected with broken, restored and recommitted Covenant.

Therefore mankind, both male and female, is to constantly see Jehovah's SIGN of His First Covenant *in each other*.

Common Tasks, Different Methods

Sometimes there can be confusion in regard to masculine and feminine. For instance, a traditional concept is that 'the man makes the living and the woman raises the children.' But these tasks really do not contain the range of what masculine and feminine include.

By way of metaphor, one might say that the rib and the arm both protect the vital organs in the chest, but the *methods* of carrying out this *common task* are different. The characteristics of the arm are its mobility and strength; the characteristics of the rib are its structure and flexibility. Both the rib and the arm are necessary, both are unique and are not interchangeable.

So, 'making a living' is a common task, but only partly is it to bring money into the house. How it is spent and stretched is just as necessary a method to the task as earning the money – the two form the balance, the necessary counterpoint to each other. 'Raising the children' also is a common task which requires the counterpoint of both husband and wife. While it is true that a 'one-size-fits-all' formula as to who should have which traits and methods cannot be made, it is necessary to appreciate the contribution of both and also the encouragement to further develop the traits in each other which build toward accomplishing the common tasks.

This is essential in understanding part of the dynamics of Covenant relationships. For example, that God could have the same expectations of us as we have of Him does not mean that we would do things the same way as He would. His traits and characteristics are much different from ours, His methods are different – Covenant is not based upon matching abilities. However, such tasks as to give of ourselves and all we are and have, these we actually have in common with Jehovah, which then makes Covenant a reality.

The Voluntary Servant – Blood-Likeness with God

> Be subject to one another out of reverence for Christ.   Ephesians 5:21

The concept of the shared task, but different methods, applies to St Paul's instruction in regard to the relationship between husband and wife, because his starting point is mutual subjection, mutual servanthood. Some bristle at this idea, and yet it has the best of precedents:

> If I, the LORD and the Teacher, have then washed your feet, you also ought to wash one another's feet. For I have given you an example, that as I did to you, you also should do.   John 13:14-15

> even as the Son of Man came not to be served but to serve, and to give His Life ...   Matthew 20:28

> Who is like Jehovah our God, Who dwells on high, Who humbles Himself to look after what is in the heavens and in the earth, raising the poor out of the dust; He lifts the needy out of the trash heap.
>   Psalm 113:5-7

In fact, it could be argued that when God describes Himself as One Who has fed, clothed and otherwise cared for us, such activity could describe a butler or some other servant as well. What Jesus is doing is indeed nothing novel, but rather what Jehovah has constantly been doing for His creatures – and us – all along. Having established the common task of mutual servanthood, obviously the methods would be different.

The "Pointman" (Headship)

Abbott, the historian, tells us that one characteristic of Napoleon was that he never commanded any soldier in his ranks to go where he himself was not willing to lead him. On one occasion, he ordered his army to cross a river; but seeing them hesitate to obey, the emperor spurred forward his horse crying: "Soldier, follow your general!" He was first to plunge into the river and first to reach the other side.

> Needless to say, his army to a man followed him cheering as with one voice their bold leader.
>
> Unknown

> For to this you have been called, because Christ also suffered for us, leaving us an example, that we should follow in His steps.
>
> I Peter 2:21

When St Paul describes the man as the head of the family, again human rebellion often rises to the surface, challenging why the man should have the right to boss the woman around. But if Paul is serious about mutual servanthood reflecting Jesus' care for His Bride (the Church), then the headship does not mean 'boss,' but rather echoes the call, "Come, follow Me." It is like the 'pointman' in a military patrol as it moves out to accomplish its given task: he sets the direction, speed and all the rest for the patrol who follows him – and he often is the one to first encounter the resistance of the enemy.

The Purpose

> Put on the new man, which was created according to God, in true righteousness and holiness. ... For we are members of His body, "of His flesh and of His bones." "For this reason a man shall leave his father and mother and shall cleave to his wife, and the two shall become one flesh" – the mystery of this is great, and I speak concerning Christ and the Church.
>
> Ephesians 4:24; 5:30-32

> ... man was created for a life of complete selfless love, whereby his actions would always be directed outward, toward God and neighbor, and never toward himself – whereby he would be the perfect image and likeness of God...
>
> Fr. John S. Romanides[77]

In Genesis 2:23, as Adam meets Eve, he announces, "This now is bone of my bones and flesh of my flesh" – 'everything that I am, she is' – a seamless unity. Paul identifies that this prefigures the seamless unity between Jesus and His Bride (the Church) and we begin to see the extraordinary depth to be found in God's design of husband and wife. Reaching far beyond a mere social *contract*, each marriage is to recapitulate and continue the First Covenant's unity of Jehovah's Life in and through each other, and then they are to represent His essential character (Glory) to each other and before creation.

Covenant vs Divorce

> Therefore a man leaves his father and his mother and cleaves to his wife, and they *become one flesh*. Genesis 2:24

> Therefore what God has joined together, let no man divide.
> Mark 10:9

In bold Covenant picture-language, although two, *the man and the woman* are truly ONE FLESH – ONE BLOOD – *"for better and for worse, for richer and for poorer, in sickness and in health, till death do us part."* Jehovah uses this Covenant strength to describe His relationship with His People.

> For your Maker is your Husband, Jehovah of hosts is His Name; and your Redeemer is the Holy One of Israel; He is called the God of the whole earth. Isaiah 54:5

Yet divorce enters the picture, a reality of how sin has so broken the force of Covenant – "because of the hardness of your heart" [Mark 10:4-5], and marriage ceases to demonstrate this extraordinary-of-all-relationships. In a remarkable instance, Jehovah declares that even He is divorced, from the North Kingdom of Israel:

> She saw that for all the adulteries of that faithless one, Israel, I had sent her away with a decree of divorce; yet her false sister Judah did not fear, but she too went and played the harlot. Jeremiah 3:8

The statement in Mark above recalls the lifeless carcasses divided in half, depicting broken Covenant, in Genesis 15:10, along with the carrion birds ready to pick apart the remains [verse 11]. The Hebrew word for 'divorce' comes from the same word used in 'cutting' Covenant, which is also the same word for the Covenant-breaker being 'cut off' from God's People. It is a powerful word. With humans, divorce is often the hammer by which to break the relationship, but in Jehovah's case, it is the acknowledgement of an already fractured 'Marriage' Covenant. However God's intent is to also one day call Israel again to Himself.

> For Jehovah will have mercy on Jacob, and will yet choose Israel, and set them in their own land: and the strangers shall be joined to them, and they shall cleave to the house of Jacob. Isaiah 14:1

C. Covenant (Flow of Life/Blood) is Broken

The Temptation – Genesis 3

Rebellion's Beginning

In the Temptation sequence, Satan's getting Eve to restate the command is a most important step. He is not interested in an oversight, misstep, error in judgment, ignorance, lapse in memory or the like; he wants *deliberate rebellion (that is, sin)*. Time has not changed this sequence of sin. If we ponder the times when we have 'done something wrong,' how often has the thought crossed our mind: 'This is wrong!' In fact, how often have we said, 'I know I shouldn't, but....' or 'I know I should, but ...' – is this conscience? Not necessarily! No mere 'mistake' for Satan – rather, like with Eve, he wants us determined to go ahead, even when we definitely know we should not. And broken Covenant is the result.

She must be the first so that *each person* would be a fully responsible rebel, otherwise had Adam been first, she could claim that she only followed his leadership. But since she is operating on her own, her fall is fully under her own responsibility.

Satan challenges, "You shall NOT die! For God knows ...." [Genesis 3:4-5], that is, 'your Covenant-Partner is selfish and is withholding from you – *He* is breaking Covenant!' Eve may believe she is truly being 'helper' to her husband and family in trying to 'improve' their lot, but the best of intentions is worth nothing if it is done outside the boundaries set by God.

There is the dilemma now for the man: on one hand, there is love both for the woman and for the Lord, yet on the other hand, there is brokenness and separation. The man is *not* deceived [I Timothy 2:14]; as the head, he could stop the process right here by turning to God for help. But he has no interest in doing so; yet later he is quick to blame both Jehovah and the woman for his own rebellion [Genesis 3:12]. In fact, one might well imagine him on the sidelines being cheerleader for her action.

Life is Sought Outside of Jehovah

Sadly, neither Adam nor Eve represents God any longer to each other. The woman becomes tempter, not savior, to the man. The man abandons his leadership, authority and responsibility, accepting the fruit without even a protest, eyes open without deception – he deliberately chooses rebellion. Yet when each is called to account, it is always 'somebody else's fault' – funny how things just do not change.

Like a deep sea diver with the bell helmet and the air supply pumped down from the surface, who cuts his Life-line in order to be 'free' from the restrictions of his air hose, indeed mankind is 'free' from the Life/Blood of Jehovah. Although the diver indeed may gain his freedom for about 5 minutes (from the air in his suit), from the moment the line is cut he is a dead man. In the same way, even though Adam lives 930 years, from the moment he 'cut' his Lifeline, he is a walking dead man.[78]

Without the Lifeline from Jehovah, there will be eventual physical death, but already there is spiritual (relationship-wise) death: between God and human, there is fear; between human and self, there is shame and guilt; between human and human, there is blame; between human and nature, there is irresponsibility and abuse.

Outside of God's protection and care, outside of His value of them, outside of His will, outside of being "in the likeness of God," they discover not new powers and ability, but rather how naked and vulnerable they are before all creation, and especially when facing God and His accounting.

The *GO'EL* Restores Lost Life

God's Glory: Promises! and Discipline – Genesis 3:14-19

With good cause, Jehovah could simply abandon Adam and Eve to the result from being cut off from Life/Blood, from the Source of Life. In fact, we should be surprised that He does not because we have a culture which expects Him to be fixated on sin and punishment. But instead He comes to *restore Covenant*!

The curse of the Serpent (Satan) reveals some interesting aspects of God's solution: the Serpent's food would be dust. Snakes can unhinge their jaws in order to swallow something which is 'too big for their own mouths.' Imagine the Serpent unhinging his jaw, anticipating an enormous 'prize,' and snapping closed instead upon a mouthful of dust – being defeated in what should have been his greatest 'victory.' Indeed, this would reflect the Cross, where Satan seemingly is about to achieve his greatest triumph in his rebellion (the elimination of God), yet experiences his greatest defeat in the 'Seed of the woman' (Jesus)'s death (Hebrews 2:14-15).

Neither Adam nor Eve are cursed, but instead are disciplined. Death (the ultimate weakness) will be their constant companion: for the Woman – even in the most God-reflecting moment of giving Life (birth), death and death's reminder (pain) will be present; for the man – the ground which once willingly yielded its substance, now cursed, will revolt (thorns and thistles) against the rebel, the labor will now be toil – not enjoyable work, but a struggle. "You are dust" – Satan-fodder, if you remain in rebellion.

The Pattern and Way to Restore Lost Life – Genesis 3:21

As mentioned previously, the garments of skins initiate *Jehovah's* solution to redeem mankind's sin, the shedding of innocent Blood from a victim of God's choosing to restore the lost Life. But there remains a concern: "now, lest he put forth his hand and take also of the Tree of Life, and eat, and live for ever" [Genesis 3:22] – God cares lest mankind would forever be locked into the state of broken Covenant – the best description of Hell there is.

As mankind is sent out of the Garden, a cherubim is placed to "keep" the way to the Tree of Life [Genesis 3:24]. Reasonably the guard is to prevent any entrance back into the Garden. However, the same word is used in instances as 'to preserve' and 'to maintain.'[79] Therefore the guard may be *safeguarding* the way lest it be forgotten or lost or lest mankind think itself shut out forever. This would reflect the hope of the promise of the Seed Who would redeem mankind from its sin. The thought also suggests itself that this entrance to the way to the Tree of Life would also be the place where the sacrifices were offered.[80]

D. So It Continues

Cain – Genesis 4

The Heritage of Rebellion

> In the day that God created man, in *the likeness* [DAMAH] *of God* He made him; male and female He created them;... Adam ... fathered a son in *his own likeness* [DAMAH], according to *his* image ...   Genesis 5:1, 3

The revivifying atonement of Blood is central to restoring Jehovah's Covenant – as He Himself demonstrates by the "coats of skins." This is why Abel's "firstborn of the flock" (a lamb!) sacrifice is approved. But Cain is indeed his father's son, continuing the rebellion/insolence which marked the first sin. His vegetable sacrifice is a deliberate rebellion, yet he resents its rejection and resents the contrast of how Abel's 'doing it the LORD's way' exposes his rebellion [I John 3:12].

The Voice of the Blood – the GO'EL Must Act

The "voice" of the murdered Abel's Blood cries out – for its right to live; against the injustice of murder; in horror of such casualness toward the godlike power to cease Life – this voice cannot be stilled. Abel by his lamb sacrifice had remained in Covenant, he is Blood-Brother to Jehovah – so Cain has shed *GOD's* "Blood/Life"! Again the *GO'EL* must step in to deal with lost Life – lost Blood.

Justice and Mercy for the Unjust – Genesis 4:9-16

The judgment is a sharp sentence against Cain's arrogance and defiance, and against his expectation that Jehovah should conform to Cain's desires. Where Adam and Eve were not cursed, he is. The ground that has been his delight, which had to absorb the Blood of Abel's murder, will not just resist as in Adam's discipline, it will totally mutiny against his efforts. Cain is to never feel at home anywhere [4:12], but will have the restlessness of one marked by the rest of society.

He who had no compassion, but willingly shed Blood now is afraid that he will be hunted and killed, likely by a human *GO'EL*. Jehovah's reply is to give him an *'OTH* (first use of this word) and an oath (note appearance of the concept of "*seven*") of safe-conduct. Cain, who in rebellion expected God to conform to his will, found that he is forced to do things Jehovah's way (as mentioned above in the "SQUEEZE-PLAY Covenant").

Noah: Hope Despite Judgment – Genesis 6-9

The Rebellion Deepens

According to Genesis 5, Adam dies about 130 years before Noah. Most people wish for long Life – does Adam? He is the only one who knows the before and the after of sin, and after 930 years he sees all the results of his sin: his first son is a murderer; society at large becomes worse and worse [6:5]; and then Lamech's boast [4:23-24]. One wonders what *Cain* thinks of Lamech's perversion of Jehovah's protection.

In contempt of Jehovah's Covenant-Blood, Lamech murders one who offends him. Apparently he self-righteously claims the *GO'EL*'s right to avenge, and he expects that the LORD would protect him ten times greater (more perfectly) than Cain has been protected. Likely Lamech's boast is characteristic of the degree of mankind's rebellion:

> Jehovah saw that the evil of man was great on the earth, and that every imagination of the thoughts of his heart was only evil all the day long.
> Genesis 6:5-7

The GO'EL Restores

"But I will establish ['raise up, confirm'] My Covenant with you," [6:18; 9:9,11] "the Covenant which I make ['give']" [9:12]. 'Cutting' Covenant is not used at all, but rather the word of choice is to 'raise up' the Covenant. Such a change of word suggests not the creation of a *new* Covenant, but a re-calling of the existing one, which is what this combination of words does elsewhere [Genesis 17.7, 19, 21; Leviticus 26:9; Deuteronomy 8:18].

As mentioned above, under *KAPHAR*, the Ark is built upon judgment and covered with 'atonement.' As with many *'OTH*s, Noah reveals his faith by 'doing' the SIGN of Salvation (building the Ark), yet he neither creates nor enables the salvation – the ACT of salvation depends solely upon the Covenant Promises of Jehovah: "He goes into the ark not as a mere survivor but as the bearer of God's promise for the new age" [Derek Kidner[81]].

Parallels to the Genesis 1 creation account suggest that the flood sequence is a re-calling or calling-back of the original creation[82], therefore so also a "raising up [or restoring] of the Covenant."[83] Having experienced God's salvation through 'Atonement,' Noah and his family's first act is to offer the "*Whole Burnt Offering*" [8:20] – the total-commitment sacrifice – to Jehovah in thanksgiving for His mercy.

The LORD responds with the *'OTH* [SIGN] of the rainbow.[84]

> The sign was well suited to fulfill the prime function of all covenant-signs, which is reassurance. Like the later sign of circumcision, it was the seal (Rom. 4:11) of an accomplished fact; unlike it, this could not for a moment be thought to procure it.

It has been attractively suggested that the bow would now picture to men God's battle-bow laid aside ... The obvious glory of the rainbow, however, against the gloom of the cloud, seems enough to make it a token of grace, even without the reflection that it arises from the conjunction of sun and storm, as of mercy and judgment.

The rainbow was seen as an element in God's glory by Ezekiel (1:28) and John (Rev 4:3; cf. 10:1), perhaps as a reminder of this first pledge of grace.   Derek Kidner[85]

Flesh vs. Blood

But flesh in its Soul/Life – its Blood – you shall not eat. Surely, for the Blood of your Souls/Lives I will demand a reckoning; from the *hand* of every animal I will demand it, and from the *hand* of man, from the *hand* of every man's brother I will require the Soul/Life of man.

Genesis 9:4-5

This distinction was before Israel constantly, whenever they prepared or ate a meal, or went to *the Temple* – again and again the sacredness of Blood was driven home. Today's orthodox Jew still bears witness to the seriousness with which this concept was taken. The wife bought her *Kosher Bosher* ("clean meat" bled according to Jewish law) from the *Kosher* butcher. She washed off any Blood, then applied *Kosher* salt to draw out more Blood, washing it again until there was no longer Blood to wash off. Then the meat was ready to be cooked and eaten.

Robert F. Lindemann[86]

Separating Blood from Flesh demonstrates how Life (Blood) does not mix with sin (Flesh). Flesh is the reservoir of sin's rebellion along with its death: "I know that in me (in my Flesh) nothing good dwells ..." [Romans 7:18], "the Flesh counts for nothing" [John 6:63]; but "the Blood is the LIFE." Introduced before Abraham, before the dietary commands of Moses, this concept touches the very heart of Jehovah's salvation of all mankind.

VII. Abraham Enters Covenant

A. *The Call to Covenant*

> Jehovah said to Abram, "Go from your country, your kindred and your father's house to the land I will show you. I will make from you a great nation and I will bless you; I will make your name great, and you will be a blessing. I will bless those who bless you, and whoever despises you I will curse; and all peoples of earth will be blessed through you."
> Genesis 12:1-3

The Terms
... the Land I WILL show you,
I WILL make from you a great nation and I WILL bless you
I WILL make your name great, and YOU will be a blessing.
I WILL bless those who bless you, curse those who despise you
        and all the nations of the earth will be blessed through you

Abram (Abraham) is called into an adventure of faith. Although he has nothing to offer, yet the LORD pledges to him unimaginable blessing. Throughout history, Jehovah will never back down from the promises in this call. As each believer is called to renounce the past and enter new Life, as Noah spurns the old world and in Covenant steps into the Ark, seventy-five-year-old Abram now turns his back on idol worship with its old life [Joshua 24:2-3], and steps out under God's promise, with no map, no compass, no road sign; no citizenship privileges nor protections; no extended family – he goes just with God's presence.

B. ... *the Land I WILL show you*

Learning Covenant with Jehovah – Genesis 12

One day, in Canaan, the LORD says, 'You're home!' "So he built an altar to Jehovah" [Genesis 12:7, 8; 13:18] – Abram (Abraham) owns the Land, yet will never possess it, however at every camp he builds a center of

105

worship: his immediate response is to sacrifice, to cover the new possession with Life. But a severe famine [Genesis 12:10-20] causes Abram to turn away from the promises, the call and the Land. In Egypt, claiming Sarah to be his sister (therefore marriageable, with a wealthy, childless 'brother'), he creates the very trouble he fears: Pharaoh takes her for his wife. In *HESED*, Jehovah rescues His future Covenant-partner. Significantly, only upon his return to the Land and to the first altar do we read that Abram again "called on Jehovah's Name" [Genesis 13:3-4].

Advanced Studies in Covenant – Genesis 14

Abram desperately needs help. Nephew Lot is in deep trouble, having been captured as a slave. As *GO'EL*, Abram must rescue him – but what can be done against the coalition that has just overrun the five city coalition of Sodom and Gomorrah? Mamre, Eschol, and Aner, *Covenant Blood-brothers* of Abram (*B'RITH_ABRAM* [14:13]), in Covenant obligation, step in [v 24] – but also Jehovah is part of the victory. Abram acknowledges this by giving the tithe to Melchizedek, King of Salem, priest of the Most High God,[87] as well as refusing the 'spoils' which are his by right of conquest. Not even the treasure tainted by Sodom's sin will cross Abram's hands, since it is incompatible with the LORD – after all, 'Your enemies are my enemies!' [13:13; 14:21-24].

C. I WILL Make from You a Great Nation; I WILL bless you

"And Abram Believed Jehovah" – Genesis 15:6

As Jonathan would give his armor to David, the LORD speaks Covenant directly to Abram's fears: "I am your Shield, your very great Reward" [Genesis 15:1]. Eighty-plus-year-old Abram's response is frustration: 'My chief slave will be my heir!' But no, his own son will be his heir, his descendants will be innumerable: He Who created the vast universe points to the starry sky as his SIGN. "Abram *believed*[88] Jehovah;

and it was credited to him as righteousness[89]." Despite weaknesses and fears, nagging distrust and advanced age, Abram has learned to surrender himself to the promise.

God Cuts Covenant *Almost as a Human*

But Only a Half Covenant *[Genesis 15:9-18]* – *GRACE!*

[Jehovah] said to him, "Bring Me a heifer three years old, a she-goat three years old, a ram three years old, a turtledove, and a young pigeon." He brought Him all these, divided them in the middle, and laid each half over against the other; but he did not divide the birds in two. … As the sun was setting, a deep sleep fell on Abram…
When the sun had gone down and it was dark, behold, a smoking furnace and torch of fire passed between these pieces. On that day Jehovah cut Covenant with Abram…   Genesis 15:9-18

Jehovah – not the 'big human' of mythology, but rather *the Creator Who stands apart from His creation* – comes down to *human* level, as close to becoming flesh as possible, and at this level He in Person becomes Blood-Brother to… a *human*! How astonishing this is! The only deeper act He could have done in Covenant would be to shed His own Blood – and the time will come when He does.

More so, in a normal Covenant 'cutting,' both parties must participate, but Abram does nothing to pledge or commit himself (therefore *he* cannot break Covenant … yet) – *through these pieces Jehovah alone walks* (symbolized by the smoking furnace and the torch of fire), *thereby binding Himself regardless of what Abram and his descendants might do*. Such a concrete act of *personal* involvement by Jehovah has no equivalent in the Old Testament, earning Abram the unique title, "Beloved Covenant-Friend of God" (Isaiah 41:8; II Chronicles 20:7; James 2:23). Since Jehovah alone participates in the pledge, *the foundation of 'steadfast Love' (HESED, grace) is established as the basis for God's Covenant with Abraham.*

Jehovah Under a Curse

The Lord placed himself under this curse in Genesis 15:17-21. He sealed his promise to Abraham by passing between the pieces as a sign that he would keep his promise. He received the curse upon himself in the Lord Jesus Christ who was "stricken by God, smitten by him and afflicted ... cut off from the land of the living." Galatians 3:13,14; 2 Corinthians 5:21 clearly teach that Jesus became sin and endured the curses of covenant-breaking for those who believe.   R. Scott Clark[90]

Consider the position into which Almighty God has deliberately placed Himself: irrevocably tied into this Covenant, its fate will also be His own. Like Jonathan who knows his Covenant with David will eventually spell his own doom, so also God submits Himself. He voluntarily 'paints Himself into a corner'! He will not break His commitment (Romans 3:3-4) throughout Israel's many rebellions, yet there will be a time when He ends this Covenant and submits to its curse. Jehovah, Who has poured His Life into His Covenant with mankind, will actually die.

Abram Just Has Not Got It Yet – Genesis 16

Since the promised son is not happening, Abram and Sarai 'help God out' by having a child by Sarai's servant Hagar – a legitimate practice in those days, though often with disastrous results. The result is a conflict spanning some four thousand years between Ishmael's descendants (the Arabs) and Isaac's descendants (the Jews). Yet even here Jehovah will not back away from His promises: as Abram's son, Ishmael ["God Hears"] will partake in the blessing Abram will receive ("your offspring will be as numerous as the dust/stars"), but will not be THE Son of the Promise.

NOW the Other Half – Circumcision

In Your Flesh

I will establish [again note: not 'cut'] My Covenant between Me and you and your descendants throughout their generations for an everlasting Covenant, to be God to you and to your descendants ... Every male child among you shall be circumcised... in the flesh of your foreskins, and it shall be an *'OTH* [SIGN] of the Covenant between Me and you. He that is eight days old among you shall be circumcised; every male throughout your generations ... , both he that is born in the house and he that is bought with money ..., shall be circumcised. So shall My Covenant be in your flesh *an everlasting Covenant.* Genesis 17:7-14

It might be compared to a wedding where the Bridegroom has pledged His total self, even to death, for the sake of His Bride, but she says nothing (Abram is in a trance); then 13 years later she says, "I do." *For about 13 years* Abraham simply enjoys the benefits of Covenant – Jehovah's total commitment of Himself – but now no longer merely an observer, he must *enter* the Covenant – by the Blood of Circumcision, by cutting off the 'foreskin' – merely a token action? Still, Blood flows and Covenant-Blood 'mingles.' The unmistakable *'OTH* [SIGN] is impossible to remove, evidence that "My Covenant IN YOUR FLESH is an everlasting Covenant" [Genesis 17:13].

The Pivot of Circumcision is GRACE

He received the "sign" of circumcision as a seal of the righteousness which he had by faith while he was still uncircumcised.   Romans 4:11

"Walk before Me and be perfect, without blemish" [Genesis 17:1] – by Abraham's own power? Never! Almighty Jehovah's 'Blood' *already* courses through his veins (from the first 'half' of the Covenant)! Yes, his fallen nature is still there, but God's Life/Nature is present, woven into the fabric of everything he will yet do.

This *gift of relationship* is given to the eight-day-old child, who has no knowledge, faith, or works to attract such union with God [Genesis 17:12]. Ishmael [Genesis 17:20-21], Esau [Deuteronomy 2:5-12; Hebrews 11:20], and the children of Keturah (Abraham's second wife), although not of the direct line leading to the Savior, still are encompassed under the various promises and blessings within Covenant. And the slave, who has no choice, even if he is sold to a new master, would still carry the mark of the *"everlasting Covenant"* in his flesh.

It is done by Jehovah's insistence, His initiative, His *command* – *HE* is the One Who wants this relationship with no concern whether it makes sense to mankind or not. Never in the Old Testament does God repeat *His* dramatic part in the Covenant ceremony; however each subsequent person by circumcision enters into this existing relationship, entering into and under Abraham's unique status of being 'Covenant-Friend' with Jehovah Himself. It is also important to note that Circumcision is initiated before the son of promise, Isaac, is born so that he will immediately be brought personally into Covenant with Jehovah.

Some 600 years of Circumcision[91] will pass before the Law is given to Moses (even Jesus declares that Circumcision predates Moses [John 7:22]) – *Circumcision comes not by obeying the Law, but such obedience comes after Circumcision.* And what about those descendants who never receive the Law? Clearly this relationship is "by grace through faith, not of works" [Ephesians 2:8-9].

Militant Grace in the Household of Faith

> Any uncircumcised male who is not circumcised in the flesh of his foreskin, his Soul/Life shall be cut off from his People; *My Covenant he has broken.*　　　　　　　　　　　　　　　　　　Genesis 17:14

Spiritual effects can be handed down from one generation to the next: sin is, so also is Grace. Jehovah is deeply in earnest about having this relationship with every one of His People: Circumcision involves "the place of paternity,"[92] emphasizing that Covenant is to be passed on to the following generations. The parent is held responsible – HE could bring the judgment of broken Covenant upon his child. Jehovah is so adamant about this Covenant of Grace being continued into future generations that even the chosen deliverer Moses almost dies when he ignores this parental responsibility [Exodus 4:24-26].

The Major Weakness in Jehovah's Covenant with Abraham

Because our concept of Covenant in western culture is so impoverished, we may not realize just how great an impact this relationship between God and man might have to someone experienced in Covenant practice. For instance, in Native American spirituality, although the Great Spirit (or the Creator, or the Old Man) is very much in the daily Life of His People, yet He is still separate (transcendent) from His creation. That the Great Spirit would become a literal *Blood-Brother*, mutually sharing the same Life-Blood, not just to a single noteworthy individual (a remarkable thought at that) but *to every individual* of the tribe – this is startling!

The "kicker" is that the Great Spirit is also vowing to die if and when He breaks this Covenant – which He fully intends to eventually do. That pronouncement might be bewildering to a Native American, even inconceivable that the Great Spirit could die. It is with that same amazement that we should consider this commitment by Jehovah in Covenant with Abraham.

Jehovah Himself will share *His* Blood with a human and his descendants. *God* intensely yearns for this oneness *even with the eight-day-old child* who has nothing of his own to offer – this is Jehovah's gift of grace not based upon human action but rather upon His earnest desire.

However, this awesome and mind-boggling Covenant has limped from the start – it has a major weakness: although God personally participates and fully honors His commitments and oneness, He can participate only by proxy – there is no sharing of *HIS* Blood, no 'cutting' from *HIS* side – as a Spirit, He has no Blood. The Old Testament Covenants can only yearn for a time when God will truly personally share Himself, using His own Life/Blood. Therefore all references to His Blood in the 'Old Covenant' are conceptual but not yet actual.

D. I WILL Make Your Name Great; YOU Will be a Blessing

The Shared Nature - Genesis 18

The significance of this chapter is beyond imagination, revolving not so much around the intercession of Abraham, as around the purpose why Jehovah comes. Jehovah comes looking for His 'Covenant-Friend' – Why? The answer lies in the calling promise: "*YOU will be a blessing.*"

Now fully in Covenant, Jehovah's Blood 'mingles' with Abraham's – divine Blood/Life 'flows in his veins.' Will he reflect *the Likeness and Image of God*? Can this *man* truly reflect the LORD's enormous *HESED*/Mercy? 'Your enemies are my enemies' – Sodom and Gomorrah, in rebellion toward God [Genesis 13:13], are also Abraham's enemies – a fact demonstrated by Abraham's refusal to take any of their spoil when he rescues Lot [Genesis 14:21-23]. But the nature of *HESED* is, as Jesus would later define it: "Love your enemies ..., that you may be sons of your heavenly Father" [Matthew 5:44-45]. Does Abraham truly have *Jehovah's HESED* coursing through his veins?

What greater honor can a person have, what greater blessing can a person be, than that *God* would specifically *seek out* His Covenant-partner when He 'needs' an *intercessor/mediator*! It is the very position that Jesus – and His Body, the Church – now holds.

Jehovah Finds His Intercessor

Abraham stands tall in the face of God. How awesome that a *human* wrestles with the Almighty God of the universe! But it is NOT a human wrestling with the Almighty God! It is GOD wrestling with God! What is displayed is *Jehovah's internal battle* when He must act in judgment: it is *His own HESED* in Abraham struggling with *His own justice* (which demands utter destruction against the very great rebellion of sin).

And what do we see? Look at how far backward Jehovah's justice would bend if only there were a little righteousness amid the mountains of sin! In the five cities of the territory of Sodom and Gomorrah[93] [Genesis 14:1-3], among the thousands of people, if there were only TEN righteous, *everyone* would be spared – *everyone!* Even those who really *deserve* utter destruction! If Lot and his family were counted among the righteous, then just ONE person per city (plus one from the farms) – just ONE would save a whole city whose rebellion *demanded* that God must act (as Abel's spilled Blood had cried for justice). What a powerful prophecy of the One, Who on the Cross will save the world.

A note here: some have interpreted the idea of 'righteous' as 'utterly holy,' so that no human could qualify, therefore God is 'stacking the deck' and the bargaining is really useless. However since Noah is called righteous [18:23], and Job, possibly a contemporary of Abraham, is called righteous by Jehovah Himself [Job 1:8], and even Abraham is counted righteous because of his faith [15:6], it would not seem that the standard of absolute holiness is being called for.

But in the end, how broken-hearted must have been *both* Covenant-partners when not even that paltry 'one' in each city could be found! [Genesis 19:27-28] It is understandable why Abraham had no desire to stay in that area. And there would be other intercessors yet to be sought out [for example, Moses in Exodus 32:7-14 and Numbers 14:11-21].

E. All the Nations of the Earth will be Blessed Through You

"Laughter" – The Covenant Made Visible

Is it not significant that for Abraham, the climax of Covenant should be "Laughter" – Isaac! Abraham had roared at the thought of elderly Sarah giving birth [17:17; she also laughed – 18:12-15], yet chapter 21 opens almost poetically in its thrill, joy and delight as Jehovah makes His Covenant visible in a true son and heir to Abraham "just as He said!"

Immediately, according to the LORD's command, Abraham circumcises Isaac on the eighth day, marking this new son as one who now also stands under Covenant. Abraham's utter delight gives a background to the enormous challenge to come.

A Father's Grief – Genesis 22

> An Oriental father prizes an only son's life far more than he prizes his own. ... For an Oriental to die without a son, is a terrible thought. His life is a failure. His future is blank. But with a son to take his place, an Oriental is, in a sense ready to die ... For Abraham to have surrendered his own toil-worn life, now that a son of promise was born to him, would have been a minor matter ... But for Abraham to surrender that son, and so to become again a childless, hopeless old man ... it was the giving of the one thing ... which was more precious to him than himself.
>
> Trumbull[94]

Perhaps significantly it is at Beersheba ("Well of the 'Oath/Seven'") where Jehovah commands Abraham to sacrifice Isaac. Since the Bible declares Jehovah's disgust with human sacrifice (it would have been useless as a way to appease God anyway), clearly He is not interested in a meaningless sacrifice. The issue is Covenant: will Abraham withhold *anything* from his Covenant-Partner, even his greatest treasure (his SON)? And every hope in Jehovah's Covenant is challenged: the promises hang specifically on *this* son, from whom would come the great blessings affecting the whole earth.

Although we can imagine his turmoil of heart, Abraham without apparent hesitation simply steps forward in Covenant and trusts the promise. He tells his servants *"we* will worship and then *we* will return to you" [v 5] – the plural is significant! And the response is singularly insightful to Isaac's question as to where the sacrificial lamb is: "God Himself will provide the lamb ..." [v 8].

This whole event is to make Abraham consider God's commitment to Covenant. Even if the son dies, a resurrection will be required. Jehovah must raise him up again and restore him to Abraham [Hebrews 11:17-19] since this is *specifically* THE *son of Promise*. Abraham's prophetic wisdom is fulfilled by the ram caught in the bushes – and centuries later, Jehovah will again provide His own solution, His own Lamb.

THE Father's Grief

"Your father Abraham rejoiced to see My day; he saw it and was glad" [John 8:56]. Jesus indicates that Abraham is given to understand the real nature of this event. The sacrifice Abraham does not have to make will be made by his Covenant-Partner, the Son given because of the need of His Blood-brother. The agony and grief of the Oriental father will indeed be fully felt, but by the greater Father.[95] Abraham does not just understand what God will do, he understands what Jehovah would *feel*. The Life/Blood of Jehovah runs in his veins.

And what comfort for bereaved parents! Even more than Abraham, they understand what Jehovah has felt. And God the Father fully understands their grief, having watched His own "dearly beloved" Son die – He knows the helplessness, the heartache. In Covenant, God has let us glimpse into a key element of our salvation.

F. *"Throughout Your Generations"* – Genesis 24-26

Jacob

"We have turned each to his own way" [Isaiah 53:6]

For Covenant, the LORD often does the opposite of what is usual: first, a ninety-year-old woman gives birth, and *her* child, the second born [Isaac] carries the Covenant blessing; and now, as two brothers are born, "the older [Esau] will serve the younger [Jacob]" [Genesis 25:23]. Jacob ["He Deceives/Grasps the Heel"] exploits Esau's careless attitude: for the price of a red [*EDOM* – from 'Blood'] stew, he buys Esau's birthright (the greater share in the earthly inheritance [Genesis 25:29-34], which has Covenant-blessing implications), which also earns Esau his nickname "Red" [*EDOM*].

115

Later, despite what Jehovah has prophesied, Isaac and Rebekah try to maneuver their particular favorite to get the Patriarchal Blessing (also with Covenant implications). The result is murderous anger [Esau], heartbreaking separation [Rebekah and Jacob], and a terribly disrupted family. Jacob indeed gets the promised blessing, but at unnecessary cost and without the spiritual appreciation for this gift of the LORD's Covenant.

Covenant Chases Jacob – Genesis 28

Like Abraham, Jacob has to learn about *Covenant* and its God. At Bethel, suddenly Jacob finds himself on the LORD's doorstep – the ladder to heaven. "Surely Jehovah is in this place, and I was not aware of it" [28:16]. In contrast to the family's selfish manipulations, Jacob sees angels constantly serving and carrying out *Jehovah*'s Will [28:12].

He attempts to bargain with the LORD, redefining Covenant into a conditional contract: 'IF You bring me to my uncle's house, IF You prosper me, IF You bring me back safely, THEN You will be my God, and I will give You a ten-percent commission (the tithe).' Yet *the LORD remains committed to Covenant*; in *HESED* He bestows His promises as HE wills [28:13-15]. In spite of Jacob's stubbornness, Jehovah will be with him, take care of him, and bring him back safely. The stone for Jacob's pillow now becomes a SIGN – a monument for Covenant [28:18].

Returning To Covenant – Genesis 31-32

Jacob is permitted by "the God of Bethel" to return to the Covenant Land. Jacob's Covenant-Partner HAS prospered him, not by human cunning, but by blessing [31:42]; his Covenant-Partner HAS brought him safely to his uncle's house, there to become a family [31:42], and HAS protected him from rash action by Laban [31:24]. Laban's 'Anti-Covenant' of *separation* with Jacob, "witnessed" by a pillar of stones, calls upon Jehovah to watch over them carefully while they are out of sight of each other [31:49-53].

Reentering the Covenant Land, a vision of Jehovah's "armies" doing *His* work [32:1-2] reminds Jacob that his Covenant-Partner is still busy and powerful. His Covenant-Partner HAS kept His promises, a comforting thing – but now Esau is coming with 400 men! What a struggle Jacob has! His prayer is laced with THE Covenant of Jehovah – the Covenant of Abraham – and that he is returning by Jehovah's command.

Suddenly the wrestling takes shape with a "Man," who leans over and simply throws Jacob's hip socket out of joint. Clearly the contest is by invitation, and Jacob's ability is by permission – humbling, yet reassuring!! "The Heel Catcher" hangs on – but what a difference between 'heel-catching' to deceive, and 'heel-catching' to petition! He earnestly seeks Jehovah's *"HESED* and Certainties" [v 10]. 'The Deceiver' now becomes 'Perseverer with God' (Israel), 'overcoming' and receiving the desired blessing – as Moses would on behalf of Israel later on.

Settling, But Not Settled – *Genesis 33-35*

Through Jehovah, Jacob and Esau part as brothers. Although building a "house" [33:17] and owning a piece of the Promised Land in Shechem [33:19], Jacob is not to settle in. Simeon and Levi's sordid use of the *'OTH* of Covenant, Circumcision, as an instrument of deceit and revenge [Chapter 34] curtails any such leanings, while also preventing any possibility of being absorbed by intermarriage with the Canaanites.

Commanded to return to the "Ladder" vision place (Bethel), "Israel" no longer wavers "between two opinions: If Jehovah is God, follow Him; but if Baal is God, follow him" [I Kings 18:21]. The family breaks fully with the idols they have accumulated; they "purified [themselves] and changed [their] clothes." God confirms the special name "Israel," and reaffirms the promises of Covenant first made to Abraham. "Israel" here builds an altar and raises up a stone monument/witness to this ratification of Covenant.

Joseph – Genesis 37-47

Hard Lessons

Jehovah will also need to educate and remold Jacob's favorite son, Joseph. In thoughtless naiveté or in egoism, he flaunts his privilege. He feels very secure. What a shock it must have been to be exposed to his brothers' hatred. Selling him into slavery, the brothers cover their sin by shedding an innocent victim's Blood – literally, the goat gives its Life in place of Joseph's. The ruse works, but the depth of Jacob's sorrow profoundly affects the brothers. Years later, facing possible death, they would feel their distress is the result of this episode [42:21-23].

Despite Joseph's failings, he displays a remarkable morality and echoes Jacob's tenacity, and his steadfast faith in Jehovah's Covenant sustains him when things go from bad to worse. After thirteen seemingly pointless years, many in prison[96], through 'chance' events, Jehovah brings Joseph to the position of tremendous authority and power prophesied in his dreams. Of note are the *seven/oath* years of plenty and the *seven/oath* years of famine [chapter 41] – why *seven/oath*? Are these simply a random number, or for the "knowing" listener, are they the affirmation that the Covenant, with its promises, is going forward?

"You sold me ... God sent me" [45:5]; "God intended it for good to accomplish what is now being done, the saving of many lives" [50:20]. Ultimately Joseph recognizes that his Covenant-Partner has stood with him all along, molding him, and he has 'become a blessing' even to those outside of Covenant.

On to Egypt – as Promised

Jacob and his sons have changed. The brothers offer themselves rather than let the second favorite son be imprisoned [43:13, 16-34]. Jacob's world had revolved around Joseph (supposedly 'dead') and Benjamin; and now his remaining favorite has to be risked to preserve the rest [43:14]. But Jacob's 'ace up his sleeve' is Abraham's confidence

[Genesis 22]: *Almighty God*, last mentioned at Bethel when Covenant is reaffirmed. Leaving the Covenant Land, Jacob's last stop is at Beersheba – the "Well of the Oath/Seven" – where Jehovah reaffirms His Covenant commitment [46:2-4].

Israel is now in Egypt.[97] As Jacob had to be virtually a slave in exile before he could return to the Promised Land and as Joseph had to be a slave before becoming a ruler, "Israel" has to become a slave before realizing how they are Jehovah's specially Chosen People. Only profound exposure to the LORD's Steadfast Love will shape them into a Covenant People who are to reflect His *HESED*.

VIII. Moses – Living With Covenant

A. *The Call of Moses*

As Promised, On Schedule – Exodus 1-2

Israel finds itself alongside its own servants and will learn humility and dependence on Covenant before receiving its promised status. Reflecting St Paul's "when the time had fully come, God sent..." [Galatians 4:4], reflecting the 400 years without a prophet in the intertestamental period (the span between the Old Testament and the New Testament), the LORD has apparently been quiet since Joseph, but now as the promised time [Genesis 15:13] reaches its conclusion, "remembering His Covenant" [Exodus 2:24], Jehovah's great deliverer is born humbly, under the threat of death from a jealous king.[98]

This Hebrew, specially preserved and trained as Pharaoh's 'son,' sees himself in prime position to rescue Israel. 'Helping God out', Moses' premature attempt to rescue Israel (*one* Israelite from an Egyptian taskmaster, by murdering the Egyptian) ends in him being rejected by both the oppressed and the oppressor, and, like Jacob, fleeing for his Life.

The Call of Covenant – Exodus 3-4

Chosen by God

Imagine: A rough-clad laborer with no army, no allied nations, is to wrest two million slaves from mighty Pharaoh! Without an armed revolt, they will leave "with Egypt's plunder" [3:22]. If Abraham roared at the idea of Isaac being born from someone "as good as dead," is this not also equally preposterous?

Once ready to take on Egypt one-by-one, now forty years later, Moses is reluctant. This mere man boldly and vehemently ARGUES with Jehovah! He sees only himself: "I can't!" God's answer? 'Of course, you can't! But

I can!"⁹⁹ "I AM with you" – the same word [אהיה 'HYH; a different form of יהוה YHWH [Yahweh or Jehovah] – "He is!"?] is used when God declares "I AM Who I AM!" – not a name but a verb, declaring a present-tense 'doing' God.¹⁰⁰ Pointing to the history of His Covenant, the God of History – "The God of your father, of Abraham, of Isaac, and of Jacob" – challenges Moses to test whether or not this is consistent with *ALL* which He has said and done in the past. This importance of *history* occurs again when Moses will ask to see Jehovah's Glory.

'OTHs [SIGNs]

Jehovah's second credential is *prophecy*, the concrete evidence of "I AM with you": "This shall be *the 'OTH [SIGN] for you* that I have sent you: when you have brought the People out of Egypt, you shall worship God upon this mountain" [3:12]. In faith: Noah built, Abraham traveled, Jacob entered exile, Joseph suffered – and Moses must lead. *Only in the doing* will come the *'OTH* of God's promise [3:13]. *We* want the sign *first*, but the LORD will do the opposite: *as these patriarchs obey*, they are encouraged onwards.

"I will harden Pharaoh's heart" [4:21]. Israel and its rescuer will not immediately return – *'OTHs*/wonders [4:21; see 7:3; 8:23; 10:1-2] will be done: "... I will stretch out *My Hand* and strike Egypt with all My wonders ..." [3:19-20] – His *Hand*: His almighty power to rule [for instance, Job 12:7-10; Psalms 95:4-5; 145:16] – but also His *Hand of Covenant*: "See, I have engraved you on the palms of My Hands" [Isaiah 49:16]!

Moses is given three *'OTHs* [4:1-9] meant in the first place *for Israel* [4:29-31], just as the scar in the hand confirms to the bearer that he really is in Covenant. Secondarily are the *'OTHs* also for Pharaoh [7:10-24], to declare that when he harasses the Covenant People, he battles Jehovah Himself.

The magicians duplicate the *'OTHs* [7:11-12, 22], but Jehovah's LORDship is shown as Aaron's "snake" eats up their counterfeits; they also turn water to Blood, but cannot *decrease* the suffering. Soon enough they will be outclassed [8:19] and helpless [9:11] before the Power that Moses represents.

"Israel is My firstborn son" [4:22] – *THIS* motley group of *slaves* is this supposedly powerful God's "Firstborn"?? What a giggle! What kind of honor and prestige is this? They have no might or size to make any god *want* them! And what God would let His 'favorites' be slaves? But in Covenant, Abraham's 'firstborn' *are* Jehovah's 'Firstborn' – everything which is yours is Mine, even your son is My son. If Pharaoh destroys the LORD's "Firstborn" [1:16, 22], then his own "firstborn" will be forfeit. Jehovah will act as *GO'EL* for His Covenant-partner, balancing the Blood: "Life for Life".

'Throw-away Lines'

Occasionally an incident seems merely to move the story along or to add some 'human interest' to the account. At first it might be considered a 'throw-away line' – nice to have, perhaps interesting, and even theologically useful, yet if it were not there, would it really be missed in the flow of the story? However, often there is more to it than at first meets the eye.

Exodus 4:24-26 is an example. "Jehovah met Moses and *was about to kill him*" – because Moses has not circumcised his own son. Only his wife Zipporah's spiritual insight and decisive action spares him. "Husband of Blood" [4:25-26] – Trumbull[101] points out that "Husband" is the Covenant-derived term כתן [*CHATHAN*] which speaks of Blood-marriage, or marriage with the overtones of unbreakable Blood Covenant.

That is a nice human interest story of how obviously even Jehovah's hero does not stand above Covenant: Moses has scorned placing his own "firstborn" under Covenant, but now, 'back in Covenant,' the *whole* family is included in this precious relationship to Jehovah.

But one may ask 'Why here? Why now?' – that is, how is it germane to what is happening in the larger picture, and why should it not be easily dismissed? A reason is that the relationship-setting Covenant of Circumcision, wherein *God* had bound Himself in Hesed/Love and by grace incorporated Abraham (and his family), lies at the root of what Jehovah is about to do. It sets the tone of the 'why' of the Exodus: it is not a helping of a random group of people, but rises out of the personal stake to which Jehovah has deliberately committed Himself, in these His "Firstborn," whom *He* has demanded are to be connected to Him.

Every individual is to be placed under that bond which will provide comfort, protection and participation in the "salvation" event to come – no one can be merely a "tag-along," among the Lord's People, rather he is to know that God's mighty act is specifically *for him*.

B. The Call of Israel

Israel is far more open to the LORD, and Pharaoh more cruel, than Moses expects. His shock [Exodus 5:22-23] is an experience familiar to the LORD's servants: 'I did what you wanted, and it only backfired!' Reminiscent of Abram's call [Genesis 12:1-4], Moses is sent again to Israel with Jehovah's Promise [Exodus 6:6-8].

    1) I WILL bring you out from the yoke of Egypt;
       I WILL free you
    2) I WILL redeem [גאל *GO'OL* (root word for *GO'EL*)] you
                  with an outstretched arm and mighty acts;
       I WILL take you as My own People
    3) I WILL bring you to the Land;
       I WILL give it to you as a possession.

I WILL Bring You Out From Egypt's Yoke; I WILL Free You

'OTHs (SIGNs) of Judgment

Covenant enters high gear: the first *'OTH* (SIGN) is water turned to Blood.[102] Why Blood? Being so significant to Jehovah, it is not merely for the inconvenience of it. Rather Egypt already has a 'river of Blood' from the murdered infant sons of Israel, which cries out for vengeance as Abel's Blood had, which will be answered by the final plague.

More 'OTHs – proofs that Jehovah HIMSELF is Israel's Covenant-Partner – follow, each plague challenging the Egyptian gods who 'make' Egypt powerful [Exodus 12:12; Numbers 33:4b], gods whom Israel is to leave behind.

'OTHs (SIGNs) for Repentance

> Godly sorrow brings a repentance that leads to salvation and has no regret, but worldly sorrow brings death.   II Corinthians 7:10

"I have hardened [כבד – *KABED*] his heart" [10:1]. As a noun, כבד [*KABOD*] means 'glory, honor,' specifically used for Jehovah's Glory [for example, 14:4,17]. The 'OTHs demand either repentance (submission) [9:20-21] or rejection, making either a Life which *glorifies* the LORD and reflects His grace, mercy, goodness and Covenant, or which *hardens* the heart [Isaiah 26:10] and reveals the Glory of His judgment. When Pharaoh admits "I have sinned" [9:27] and pleads "forgive my sin" [10:17], there is no surrender of will which marks true repentance. Therefore every 'OTH simply furthers his rebellion, until finally he is *forced* to acknowledge the LORD's will.[103]   However, any who will enter under the 'cover' of Covenant [12:48] will be 'saved.'

I WILL Redeem You With an Outstretched Arm and Mighty Acts;

The Passover – Exodus 12

Life For All Who Would Take It

The *GO'EL* of Israel is to redeem the Blood-balance of His People, Israel: the plagues begin and end with Blood. As defining of salvation history as the offering of Isaac is, the last plague will pour out either man's Life/Blood or a substitute's Life/Blood.   Greater than just for the immediate occasion, this *'OTH* is also an archetype which defines God's solution to the broken Foundational (Creation) Covenant.

So far an Israelite has been spared simply through his origins, but now there is neither Israelite nor Egyptian, "bond nor free" [Galatians 3:28]: if one of the 'circumcised' does not take Jehovah at his Word, he will be as any unbeliever. And the non-Israelite willing to come under Covenant [12:44, 48 – be circumcised], who follows the LORD's way, will be saved as if he is a full-Blooded Israelite.

The Passover Lamb – the Portal to Life

On the tenth day of the first month, the father, the family's High Priest, chooses a young (in its prime) male Lamb without defect (whole – holy) [12:5]. Once a Lamb is so chosen, it cannot be withdrawn, not even for a mistake or a duplication or for something which makes it no longer suitable. For four days he 'watches over' it, probably taking it to his home for safekeeping (where the children might become attached to it).

With every family performing their own sacrifice, the door lintel with its ventilation window would be ideal for lifting the lamb in order to drain its Blood onto the "threshold" (translated as "basin"). The Blood is then smeared on the doorway's two sides and top making it literally a doorway of Life. Like Noah's Ark covered with 'atonement,' inside is Life which death cannot touch, but just one step outside will bring judgment. It is the *'OTH* of Covenant [12:13], the Mark to all, even to the angel of death, that these People belong to Jehovah Himself. It will be the picture of Jesus: "I am the Door. If anyone enters by Me, he will be saved…" [John 10:9].

The Feast of Salvation

Not a bone of the lamb is to be broken [12:46; Numbers 9:12; see Psalm 34:20; John 19:36], cooked for a people ready to travel immediately. To roast it whole [12:9], Justin Martyr (c. 165) states that two wooden spits are placed at right angles to each other, stretching the Lamb out as on a Cross.

> ... *the Lord's passover* had as its second purpose a ritual demonstration that reconciled Israel [as] a community that had the privilege and obligation of living in communion with God. This bond of union was symbolized by a communal eating of the animal from which the atoning blood had been secured. Because this meal had "sacramental" significance, any remaining meat was to be burned.
>
> *Concordia Commentary*[104]

It speaks of a greater meal:

> On this mountain Jehovah of Hosts will make for all people a feast of fat things, a feast of wines on the lees, of fat things full of marrow, of well-refined wines on the lees... He will swallow up death forever; and the Lord Jehovah will wipe away tears from off all faces.   Isaiah 25:6,8

And of the greatest meal:

> Jesus took bread, blessed and broke it, and gave it to the disciples, saying, "Take, eat; this is My Body"   Matthew 26:26

In Remembrance of ...
(See *ZIKARON* and *ANAMNESIS* in IV. The Covenant Mosaic)

Even today in celebrating the *Passover*, as surely as every Israelite/Jew is 'in the loins' of his ancestor, *he is there* that fateful night, *reliving – participating in –* that great deliverance: hear, as Noah's family also did, the terrible wailing at the judgment of God; tremble, at the anguish all around as death takes its prey; marvel, to realize that God's judgment is merely a thin line, a covering of Blood – an atonement (*KAPHAR* – Noah's "pitch") – away; rejoice, to know that you have been saved, by the Lamb.

Mercy, Grace and *HESED* (Steadfast Love)

The lamb is eaten with bitter herbs (which depict slavery's harshness) and a bread not mixed with yeast (leaven[105] which sours and puffs up Jehovah's original, sweet gift; just as GRACE, Life and salvation are not to be mixed with man's self-righteousness [Ephesians 2:8-10] without it becoming 'soured' and 'full of hot air').

Israel does leave with the plunder of Egypt, not because of their great weapons of war, nor their prowess in strategy, nor their exceptionally trained army, but because of Covenant, and a Lamb and its Blood. Israel goes, being led by a visible SIGN of Jehovah's presence in the form of a pillar of smoke and fire.

The Outstretched Hand

Crossing The Red Sea: The Call to Confidence – Exodus 14

As Israel finds itself with the sea on one side, the Egyptians hard on their heels from the other, dare they trust the LORD? But Covenant means that one fights for his Blood-brother, and Jehovah will do no less:

> Do not be afraid. Take your stand and you will see the salvation Jehovah will do for you today ... Jehovah will fight for you and you will be speechless.   Exodus 14:13-14

> To Israel, ... this was salvation and redemption and the judgment of God, all in one. She could not overemphasize its importance, and therefore neither can we.   R. Alan Cole[106]

"Go forward!" – Do not stop, but march into the sea! Moses stretches out his *hand* (as Jehovah's agent, the *"Great Hand"* [14:31; 15:6, 12, 16] of Covenant?) along with the staff – which has been the *'OTH* [SIGN] of Covenant to Israel and to Pharaoh – over the sea. Jehovah separates the sea, making a dry ground over which Israel crosses. As Noah had to trust in Jehovah's plan, Israel is called on to step into the open causeway which could collapse on them.

The Covenant-Partner Fights

Egypt follows, but panics when "Jehovah looked down from the pillar" and the chariots become mired. As Moses stretches forth his hand over the sea again, the walls[107] of water collapse. The Egyptians, fleeing back toward the west run right into the water that has been "heaped" [15:8] in the west by the east wind [Exodus 14:21]. Their bodies are carried to the eastern shore, to the feet of the Israelites [14:30] – the 'signed, sealed, and delivered' proof that their "redemption" [15:13] is finalized. These Israelites will never see the Egyptians again [14:13].

When Jehovah fights, He uses the power which shaped the universe. The sea becomes a *GO'EL*: "The sea, on which Pharaoh counted for [Israel's] destruction, became first [Israel's] defense and then their avenger" (*The Pulpit Commentary*[108]). And this victory is the first instance of how the People of Covenant, the People of the Promised Messiah, will not be destroyed.

The Wilderness of "Sin"

"Then you shall know that I am Jehovah *your* God!" [Exodus 16:12] – what *HESED* and even humility Jehovah displays! Israel has seen Jehovah as a great Deliverer, but now comes the painstaking lessons about their Covenant-Partner as their Sustainer. Despite their grumbling, at Marah ["bitterness" Exodus 15:22-26], from "He Who Heals" comes a tree and a promise and the water is now Life-giving. In the Wilderness of Sin (although a very suggestive name for the English ear, it actually means "thorn, clay"), despite Israel yearning for the slavery of Egypt [16:1-3], He brings them meat and bread [16:13, 15]. Despite their suspicions that the LORD does not really care for them ("Is Jehovah among us or not?" [17:7]), the LORD provides water – this time from a rock.

The Raised Hand Conquers – *Exodus 17*

The Amalekites come to fight [Exodus 17:8-16]. As at the Red Sea, Moses' "hand" [17:11] and staff/ *'OTH* of Covenant [17:9] (possibly the background to "Jehovah-is-our-Banner" [17:15]) brings miraculous victory to these *slaves*, demonstrating again how Jehovah fights for them. In the pattern of the patriarchs, Moses immediately builds an altar in order to acknowledge the Covenant relationship which has so wonderfully saved Israel – had it not been for Jehovah, their lives would have been forfeit. It is here where Joshua [Septuagint translation: *Jesus*] makes his appearance as victor against the enemy of Jehovah's People.

I WILL Redeem You...; I WILL Take You as My Own People

Mount Sinai – Exodus 19-31

My Own People

> God said, "I will be with you. This shall be *the 'OTH [SIGN] for you* that I have sent you: when you have brought the People out of Egypt, you shall worship God upon this mountain."   Exodus 3:12

Moses dared believe such an extraordinary promise, and now he stands before the mountain – with Israel! Israel stands before the fulfillment of Exodus 6:6's second promise: "I will take you as My own People":

> If you will listen to My Voice and keep My Covenant, you shall be to Me a distinctive treasure out of all nations, for the whole earth is Mine. You shall be for Me a *Kingdom of Priests and a holy nation*....[109]
>   Exodus 19:5-6

What a task! Build a *nation* from this mass of ex-slaves – but not just any nation, a HOLY nation TREASURED by the Almighty God of the Universe; a nation where all are to be priests who can directly approach Jehovah as Covenant-Partner. This is what Jehovah yearned for and still does:

> But you are a chosen race, a royal priesthood, a holy nation, a purchased People, that you may declare the wonderful deeds of Him Who called you out of darkness into His marvelous light.   I Peter 2:9

At the Feet of Jehovah

The Hebrew word for "lightnings" [20:18] everywhere else speaks of torches or lamps, as in Abraham's Covenant [Genesis 15:17[110]]. This would be an appropriate reminder since the Sinai Covenant, as a Confirming Covenant, is renewing that most intimate relationship with all who by Circumcision are joined with Abraham to Jehovah.

Israel thought itself ready: "All which Jehovah has spoken we will do" [19:8]. However, despite preening themselves, despite their opinion of themselves, despite their special relationship with the LORD, when they witness the Majesty of God with its earth-shattering force [19:16-19; Deuteronomy 4:11-12], they decide that the cost is too high. They rebel, believing that the Covenant Jehovah, Who rescued them from Egypt in His great *HESED*, would now annihilate them. Refusing to approach the LORD "or we will die" [20:19-20], they reject His great design for them to be His Kingdom of Priests.

The Covenant Environment – Ten "Words" Or Commandments

The foundation stone of Law, the Ten Words or Commandments [Exodus 20:1-17; see Deuteronomy 5:6-21], simply identifies how Covenant affects daily Life, especially if the Creation Covenant is to be restored: they are to live out being His Life-"Image" to each other and to recognize that "Image" in others – an "Image" not to be replaced by any imitation.

Jehovah is not merely the highest but the ONLY God. His nature and His Covenant Name(s) are not incidentals to be reduced to man's imagination and abuse. His "Image" in the parents has Covenant implications ("live long in the Promised Land"). Regard for His "Image" in each other forms the background of the prohibitions against *murder* (as previously defined to Noah [Genesis 9:6]) and *adultery* (as Joseph identified as an offense against Jehovah [Genesis 39:9], a disregard of the Creation Covenant relationship). *Stealing* and *coveting* discard Jehovah's *HESED* care for His Covenanted People. *False witness* relates to the commandment guarding Jehovah's Name and His Image in one's fellow man.

Jehovah continues within the area of protecting this "Image of God", even in slaves and foreigners [Exodus 22:21; 23:9]. He will act as *GO'EL* of the weak and powerless [22:22-28]. He is to be exclusively first [23:24], with no compromise with unbelievers (lest Israel becomes ensnared and no longer serves Him with pure hearts [23:32-33]). Their Covenant-Partner will put terror in their enemies' hearts – the Covenant Angel/Messenger [23:20] is "to guard ... the way" (the same words found in Genesis 3:24): Israel's adversaries are Jehovah's adversaries.

Israel's Re-Covenant

Again Israel is enthusiastic: "All the People answered with one voice and said, 'All the words which Jehovah has said we will do.'" [Exodus 24:3; "all" is repeated 5 times in verses 3-4]. Moses erects 12 pillars (witnesses – one for each tribe) and an altar. The Blood at the *Passover* had marked their deliverance; now by one Blood – half sprinkled on the altar (and on the Book of the Covenant [Hebrews 9:19]) and the rest sprinkled upon the People – their uniqueness is marked as God's 'particular People,' their first Covenant as a Nation. It is also fifty days after *Passover*: the first *Pentecost*. In the fellowship meal (*"Peace Offering"*) of this Confirming Covenant, Jehovah again becomes visible [Exodus 24:9-11]. This is no mere entertainment, but an empowering for the leaders of Jehovah's special People.

Jehovah KNOWS Israel's fickleness and yet still desires their participation in Covenant. However, even with such mercy, Jehovah grants no favoritism when they turn their backs on Covenant: He takes the relationship very seriously. It is easy to become so focused on the man-side of Covenant with its laws and frustrations, without realizing the sheer delight God has, His earnest desire and joy at including humans into such communion with Himself. His drive toward Covenant is not based on subtle manipulation, but rather on genuine Love, hence His strongly felt disappointment when humanity just does not 'get it.'

The Tent of Meeting ("Tabernacle"/Portable Temple) – Exodus 25

The Tent of Meeting (Tabernacle; Tent of Witness) has "a cover of ram skins dyed Bloody-red ['*ADAM!*] ..." [26:14] (a picture of atonement), and a thick curtain to "separate *the Holy Place* from *the Holy of Holies*" [26:33]. Its centerpiece is *the Ark of Witness*, the SIGN (*'OTH*) of Jehovah's Covenant, the "monument" of His presence and involvement. The seat of this Covenant is *the Atonement Cover* [25:10-22] – here on the basis of atonement/ransom God will meet man.

The Lampstand holds *seven* lamps – centered on Covenant, *seven* declares its Oaths/Promises, which provide (spiritual – Revelation 4:5) light on the work of the priests. The lamps burn "clear/pure oil" [27:20-21]. On *the Table* are *the Bread of Presence (Shewbread)*, each of the twelve loaves being in a sense the embodiment of a different tribe, declaring Israel's continual presence before the LORD.

The Altar of Burnt Offering [27:1-8] dominates the outer court (the only other 'outer court' is the whole camp – the reminder to Israel that it is to be "a Nation of Priests"). One must pass through the outer court where the sacrifices are offered in order to enter *the Holy Place*, identifying that only by the Blood of a ransom can one approach Jehovah. The smoke from *The Altar of Incense* [30:1-10] represents prayer, and requires atonement [30:10] to maintain its role. The incense (prayer) has to meet Jehovah's specification [30:34-38], and has a special relationship to *the Atonement Cover*.

The Grit of Covenant

The Golden Calf – 'Have a [god] Your Way'

The 'ink' [Blood?] is hardly 'dry' on the Confirming Covenant, when Israel turns from Jehovah, despite His wonderful rescue of them from Egypt. They want a god of their own whims, a god "to go before them" whichever way *they* decide to go. With not even a protest, Aaron makes the golden calf and then announces "A festival to *Jehovah*" [Exodus 32:5]! They sacrifice *Whole Burnt* and *Peace/Fellowship Offerings* – but significantly no *Sin Offering*! – and then "sat down to eat and drink and rose up to *play* ['run wild and ... out of control' – 32:25]." Preserving an outward sham worship of Jehovah while rejecting Covenant – this goes beyond their usual petty insolence:

> ... it was precisely this identification of YHWH with Baal that was the greatest sin; even open apostasy [desertion] to Baal would have been less deadly than this 'syncretism' [mixing of religions]. R. Alan Cole[111]

The Mediator Between Jehovah and Sinful Mankind

Yet Jehovah's HESED still has its say: despite the gross unworthiness of Israel, despite His great wrath, God still holds to Covenant. As He has looked for His Covenant-Blood in Abraham [Genesis 18], God again seeks an intercessor, testing Moses' motivation and love for this "stiff-necked People" by offering to make him into a new 'Abraham' ("I will make you into a great nation" [Exodus 32:10]).

But Moses has absorbed too much HESED. With good logic little Moses faces the Judge of the Universe: neither excusing Israel, nor proclaiming their 'worthiness', but simply invoking Covenant ("*Your People*, whom *You* brought out with great power and a mighty *Hand* ... Remember *Your servants* Abraham, Isaac and Israel, *to whom You swore by Your own self?*" [32:11-14]), Moses intercedes for Israel, even mentioning how the Egyptians would delight in Israel's downfall. He proves worthy of the honor and call to be God's intercessor.

> We are not to think of Moses as altering God's purpose towards Israel by this prayer, but as carrying it out: Moses was never more like God than in such moments, for he shared God's mind and loving purpose.
> R. Alan Cole[112]

Betrayed, Yet Intercedes Again

Upon seeing what is the camp's real condition, Moses also echoes God's great anger [Exodus 32:19]. Smashing the tablets of the Law [32:19] appropriately demonstrates Israel's condition. The powdered gold calf added to water is a bitter, humbling medicine but a fascinating picture of the cleansing of Blood. Calling "whoever is for Jehovah" [32:26], Moses authorizes *GO'ELs* – his clansmen, the Levites – to slay those who *continue* to rebel against the LORD (about 0.5% of the people). By their willing obedience and by the pouring out of Blood in Jehovah's Name, the Levites are "set apart" [32:29] – anointed, consecrated to special service to the LORD.

Then Moses goes to finish the intercession: seeking *atonement* [*KAPHAR* – 32:30-33:6] and confessing Israel's sin, Moses answers 32:10 by: 'rather than me becoming a great nation, I would die for them [as atonement].' Jehovah pronounces that the rebels will be "blotted out of My book" [32:33], and the People could continue to the Promised Land, only He will not go with them. The relationship has changed despite Israel's repentance; *the Tent of Meeting* is now pitched outside the camp – Jehovah Who desires to "dwell among them" [25:8; 29:45, 46] now stands apart from them [33:7].

Working Covenant

Moses speaks with Jehovah "face-to-face, as with a friend" [33:11]. Desiring Covenant intimacy, he declares "make me *know* Your ways and let me *know* You" [33:13], and has Covenant-partner demands: "tell me Whom You will send with me" [33:12]. What calculated boldness! On *this* mountain, when Moses was first called, the great "I AM with you" was pronounced. Now he contends, 'You PLEDGED Yourself in Covenant; you MUST come when Your Covenant-partner asks!' – he knows Jehovah has voluntarily and deliberately backed Himself into the corner of Covenant and cannot deny this request. Jehovah's response is simply, "My Presence will go with you and give you rest" [33:14].

Moses presses on, satisfied with no less than His Presence: "What else will distinguish me and Your People from all others ...?" [33:16].

> Israel is always called to be distinct and different from other nations. Moses rightly sees that the chief distinctiveness of Israel lies here, in that God's presence is in her midst.   R. Alan Cole[113]

How delightedly Jehovah must have smiled at this little biped on this tiny grain of sand in the vast universe – *this* is why He had cut Covenant! The LORD is pleased with this mediator. "I *know* you *by name*" [33:17] – this meant intimacy: "I KNOW *you*" [ידע *YADA'* – to "know" by *experience*]. The name stands for a person's essential character, a symbol of his whole being, his Soul/Blood, as we saw earlier in Trumbull's account of the broken treaty between Shastika Chief Tolo and Colonel McKee.

Appropriate to a dialogue where "know" appears five times [33:12-16], Moses makes a Covenant-request: "Show me Your *GLORY*" [33:18]. This is not curiosity, Moses desires deeper intimacy with this God of all the universe. There is no hesitation. Jehovah shows him the Glory which *He* values most: "I will make My *goodness* pass before you and will proclaim My *Covenant-Name* (Jehovah); I will be *gracious* ... I will show *mercy* ..." [33:19] – My GLORY is Covenant and *HESED*.

Since this is the very core of Jehovah, Moses presses the advantage: "although it is a stiff-necked People, forgive *our* wickedness and *our* sin, and take *us* as Your inheritance" [34:9 – note the pronouns!]. What a difference from the beginning of the conversation, where God seemed so reluctant – now there is the air of enthusiasm: "Behold, I AM CUTTING a Covenant [note the present continuing sense]; I will do wonderful ... AWESOME things!" [34:10]. Rather than by the Blood of an animal, THIS renewal (confirming) Covenant will be 'cut' by the Blood of "the Amorites, the Canaanites, the Hivites, and the Jebusites" [34:11].

Still this Covenant relationship is precious, not to be mixed by Covenanting with the enemies of God [34:12-17], a warning which will go unheeded.

After spending forty days of having seen the LORD's "Glory" as no man had ever before, Moses' face literally shines from the experience absorbed into his physical being [34:29-34]. Perhaps he is closer to reflecting "the Image of God" than any human has ever been; yet it is a fading glory [II Corinthians 3:7-18]. Still, as close as Moses has been to God, when *the Tent of Meeting* is finished and Jehovah's Glory fills it [40:34-35], even he cannot enter the pure brilliance of the Presence.

The Fire of God's Presence – Leviticus 9:23-24

When *the Tent of Meeting* is completed, Jehovah declares His pleasure by consuming the *Burnt Offering* with His own fire. Fire signifies Jehovah's Covenantal presence and approval to Israel, as with the ever-present pillar of fire/smoke [Exodus 40:38]. This fire in *the Altar of Burnt Offering* [Leviticus 6:8-13], *the LORD's own fire*, is never to go out. The 'work' of the sacrifices is never 'done' – the morning will demand yet another, the evening yet one more [Numbers 28:3-4,8]. But how comforting! The fire marks God's availability: to forgive, to accept, to renew fellowship – it declares that Covenant between Jehovah and mankind is still active.

Yet the fire does go out at times – for example, for seventy years after Solomon's Temple is destroyed in the Babylonian Captivity. However it is *permanently* extinguished at the final destruction of *the Temple* in 70 AD, still not relit twenty centuries later. On the other hand, John the Baptist will point out that the One Who is coming will baptize with the Holy Spirit and *with fire* [Matthew 3:11], a new fire from the LORD's presence, not for some altar, but resting upon each believer (as the Day of Pentecost makes visible [Acts 2:1-4]).

Unclean – *The Contrast Between Death and Life*

The following chapters make Israel conscious of its identity as a consecrated Nation – a Priesthood set apart to be holy to the LORD, a People called to be separate from the world, a People focused on Life. The heart of this distinction lies in the tension between death and Life, the loss and renewal of the Blood. "Not holy" means that the Covenant is broken, Jehovah's Blood does not flow in the unholy person's veins, there is no Life. That which is dead, or dealt with dead things (vultures, etc.), or dealt with the garbage of life (pigs) stands directly opposite to such Life.

Women and Blood [Leviticus 12, 15]: since mankind sinned, childbirth and menstrual Blood are now simply lost Life: what would have been New Life now only participates in future death (as each birthing mother faces potential death, and each child will eventually die). Whenever a woman is unclean, it is *because of the Blood*, not because she is female. Why the longer time of uncleanness if the baby born is female? Because the male child assumes his own responsibility by his own Blood shed in Circumcision.

Punishment

> I am Jehovah your God... Follow My governing and keep My decrees in your daily walk of life. I am Jehovah! ... Of all the detestable things done by those who lived in the Land before you – if you likewise defile the Land, it will vomit you out as it vomited out the nations before you. Leviticus 18:3-5, 27-28

Leviticus 26 describes Covenant. Jehovah will share extraordinarily with them: abundant food, fantastic victory, complete safety; but most of all, His dwelling will be in their midst: "I will walk among you and be your God, and you will be My People" [Leviticus 26:12]. However, breaking Covenant means His absence, and they will become vulnerable – to disease, starvation, terror, defeat and exile. As the passage above reflects God's declaration to Adam [Genesis 3:17-19] and Cain [Genesis 4:11-12] of even nature abhorring the abuse of Jehovah's design, earth and heaven will resist and rebel against man [Leviticus 26:19]. If the People still do not catch on, it will get worse: "then I will walk contrary to you in fury" [v 28]. The result will be horrible.

Yet whenever there is repentance, Jehovah will eagerly resurrect Covenant: "then I will remember My Covenant with Jacob ... with Isaac ... with Abraham, and I will remember the Land" [Leviticus 26:42]. And in spite of all which will happen, "I will not reject them, nor will I hate them, to consume them, *to break My Covenant with them*" [v 44].

Acceptance at Last

The LORD brings Covenant into visible reality for Israel, agreeing to live at the hub of their Life together. Like a shell around *the Tent of Meeting* [Numbers 1:48-53], the tribe of Levi, already "set apart" by Blood and by the ransom for Israel's firstborn [Numbers 3:40-51], is guardian of the holy things [Numbers 8]; the rest of the People then camp three tribes to each corner of the compass, forming a Cross with *the Temple of God* at its center [Numbers 2].

Further acceptance comes in *the Aaronic Blessing* [Numbers 6:22-27]: "So shall you put My Name on Israel, and I will bless them." In three short sentences is wrapped up the nature of Jehovah (His "goodness") and His Covenant: He will sustain and protect; He will demonstrate HESED; He will bring His Rest ("peace") – and He will delight in His People. In return, as each of the twelve tribes brings their gifts at the consecrating of *the Tent of Meeting* [Numbers 7], for the moment Israel is willing to be His People.

Give It to You as a Possession

The Land

A year of preparation has passed (for example, building *the Tent of Meeting*), but ahead lies *the Covenant Land*. David Plotz makes an interesting observation about the Land:

> According to the Lord, the *land* is alive – the land itself can be purified or defiled, the land can rise against the people... Until this passage, I never fully understood that when God makes His covenant with Israel, He is actually making a three-legged deal: He makes a covenant with His people, *for His land*. Maybe that's why so much of Genesis is about real estate. Maybe that's why, for many faithful Jews, being Jewish in America, Canada, or France is not being wholly Jewish at all: they are cut off from the land that is our covenant with God. We're

not His Chosen People anywhere. We're His Chosen People on His Holy Land. And that's why the land must be pure.   David Plotz[114]

Struggling with Covenant

The Ark of the Covenant leads the People [Numbers 10:33] as a shepherd, along with the pillar of Cloud which goes before them – these must be quite impressive of Jehovah's leadership but they also make the coming rebellions stand in contrast even more. Sure enough, Israel has another cloud, but this one follows them and is a black one – complaint: If they are so special and Jehovah so gracious, then why are they not going first-class, why are God and Moses ignoring or withholding what is 'owed' them (shades of Adam and Eve!)? First comes the sigh [Numbers 11:1], then the infectious discontent of the "rabble" [v 4], then outright rebellion: "Israel *turned* and *wept*" [v 4]. Like wildfire, dissatisfaction sweeps the WHOLE camp.

In the oneness of Covenant, God's anger burns and Moses sees evil [v 10]. But can a human handle God's wrath? 'Burned-out' Moses explodes in bitterness, overstates his case [vv 11-15] and later snaps, "Where am I to find all this meat?" [vv 21-22]. The LORD allows him to blow off steam and, recognizing Moses' underlying emotional fatigue, makes seventy elders share the spiritual responsibility.

Then declaring Jehovah's Covenant-Hand is not crippled [11:23], the People get their meat, with a 'kicker': they will detest what is so yearned for. Quails come in unbelievable numbers, but without properly curing their kills, many get sick; the greedier ones bring judgment upon themselves, hence "The Graves of Greed" [v 34].

Even Miriam and Aaron rebel, challenging Moses' right to speak for Jehovah – as if Moses had taken the privilege upon himself. However Moses is a unique and privileged prophet: more than a spokesman, he is an embodiment of Covenant – a SIGN of the Covenant between Jehovah and Israel. As long as Moses leads Israel, they KNOW they are in Covenant. In the *HESED* of Jehovah, humble Moses prays for his enemies.

At the Covenant Land threshold, they pause to send spies to explore it [Deuteronomy 1:19-25]. Rather than directing them 'to inspect the Land as a new acquisition' as Jehovah had told Abram, Moses may have incited rebellion by instructing: "See ... whether the people are weak or strong, few or many. ... What kind of towns ... are they unwalled or fortified?" [Numbers 13:18-19] – unnecessary questions, since their Covenant-Partner will fight for them.

So, focused on the inhabitants, most of the returning spies are vehement: "we were in our own eyes as grasshoppers ..." [13:33] and Israel resorts to their favorite pastime: 'grumble and weep' [14:1-2]. On the other side Joshua and Caleb, Moses and Aaron, powerfully hold Covenant before Israel, declaring Jehovah as the deciding factor for victory.

But, in trying to elect a new leader [Numbers 14:4] and attempting to stone Moses [14:10], Israel makes God *very* angry. Echoing Mt Sinai [Exodus 32:7-14], Jehovah speaks of destroying Israel, again offering to Moses to be a new 'Abraham.' Moses' reply is still Covenant-based and filled with HESED, and he fights 'dirty,' using Jehovah's own declaration of His Glory [Exodus 33:19; 34:5-7] against Him, and then points out how His honor would not be glorified among the nations, especially Egypt. Again, Moses wins – or rather, Jehovah's HESED in Moses wins.

Pardoned, yet the consequences remain: this People are turned back from "the land which I lifted up My Hand to cause you to live in it" [Numbers 14:30]. That privilege will be for a generation spiritually prepared to conquer through Covenant. Because of the sins of the fathers, the children will have to wait [14:33-34].

But does Jehovah really mean it? What if they repent *hard enough* and *really* demonstrate their willingness to now follow Him, especially since they are now *so sincere* and *as long as He goes their way*? So they attempt to take the Covenant Land by themselves – without Moses, or *the Ark of the Covenant*, or the pillar of cloud and fire – without Jehovah. And they are decimated.

Even Moses Trips

A water shortage raises Israel's famous grumble, 'You brought us here to die! Why did we ever leave Egypt?' [Numbers 20:4-5] Perhaps Jehovah wanted to tie this occasion together with the evidences of Covenant: as Aaron had held out his staff and the plagues came, as Moses had lifted his hand and the Red Sea parted – with this SIGN in hand, Moses is to merely *speak* to the rock – Jehovah's *Word* is to be effective.

Already 'burnt out' [Numbers 11:11-15], Moses again feels that Israel's rebellion is HIS problem alone. It is a small but significant slip of the tongue, "Shall <u>we</u> bring forth water to you ..." [v 10]. And then in great personal anger and frustration, he hits the rock twice. He has acted as if there were no Covenant-Partner, making himself the source of the Life-giving water. He has not honored – 'sanctified' – Jehovah.

> But the biblical viewpoint would refer to the holiness of God not only to the mystery of his power, but also to his character as totally good and entirely without evil. Holy objects therefore ... are not merely dedicated, but dedicated to what is good and kept from what is evil. ... "Man was made in the image of God and capable of reflecting the Divine likeness. And as God reveals himself as ethically holy, he calls men to a holiness resembling his own" (ISBE, "Holiness").
>
> *TWOT*[115]

"Whoever keeps the whole law, yet stumbles at just one point is guilty of breaking it all" [James 2:10]. Not even 'the Lawgiver' is exempt! The great mediator by which the Law came [Exodus 20], through whom Jehovah had shown Himself powerful with "a mighty Hand" [Exodus 3-14], who talked with Jehovah "face to face" [Exodus 33:11] and had seen His Glory [Exodus 34:5-7] – it takes only one sin to keep even him out of the Covenant Land, even though it is seemingly *minor* compared to Israel's grand rebellions![116]

However, his punishment is also an act of *HESED*: Moses is not rejected, instead God understands him. Worn out by Israel, to now lead them into the Covenant Land with its new demands – this and Numbers 11 demonstrate that it would be too hard on this Covenant-partner.

Despite Moses' terrible disappointment, Israel experiences a dramatic lesson, and the LORD demonstrates His *HESED* – His loving care – to both.

"As Moses Lifted Up the Serpent" – *Numbers 21*

Israel is beginning to change: they do not gripe when confronted by Canaanites who are raiding them! Instead they come with a vow to Jehovah, and in battle against these enemies, their Covenant-Partner fights alongside them. But complainers are not far away: they are impatient with the tedium of wandering. The result: "fiery" serpents whose bites cause death. Israel's 'fox-hole' religion surfaces quickly, as they run to Moses in repentance.

Since the solution is so simple, "When anyone is bitten, when he sees [the Seraph which Moses made], he shall live", perhaps the plague is not just punishment but also a filtering of Israel. Up until now, the plagues and their resolutions are general. But with this 'salvation,' only those who take Jehovah at His Word survive. Those who do not, who will not, who think it too easy, who do not want to bother, who add on more requirements, etc., are unmistakably weeded out – not by Jehovah's fault, but by their own refusal.

It IS easy! All it requires is faith in God's promise to simply LOOK at the model of the serpent which Moses put on the pole. He does not have to identify its shape, nor count its scales, or even see it clearly – from the distance he may only see the glint in the sun, but that is all he needs. As the snakes are subsequently cleared from the camp, imagine the boldness: 'go ahead and bite me! All I have to do is look up and the bite becomes meaningless.' What a picture of God's salvation, which Jesus would later draw upon [John 3:14-15]![117]

C. A New Attitude Surfaces

The old generation of gripers is passing away. At the Well of Beer, they SING[118] [Numbers 21:16-18] – quite a contrast to the complaining only a chapter before! Then with Sihon's defeat [21:21-31], Israel begins to taste the fulfillment of promise, of Covenant. For once they are becoming settled [v 25]. What a difference in the spies who go to Jaazer, whose report leads Israel to take the area! With Jehovah's personal Word of Covenant-victory ("I have given him into your hand" v 34), Israel stands against Og of Bashan and wins, and "possessed his land".

Balaam Meets Israel's Covenant

"The LORD Your God Turned Curse into Blessing" [Deuteronomy 23:5]

From the aspect of Covenant, this delightful yet serious interlude, filled with its own humor, sets the tone for the conquests – Covenant is at work for Israel: 1. The "Fear" precedes them as prophesied in Exodus 15:15-16; 23:27-28 and Deuteronomy 2:25; 2. *Jehovah* interferes with any attempts to curse Israel; 3. Instead, only blessing is to be their lot; 4. His Covenant plan will continue.

Afraid of Israel, King Balak sends for Balaam to curse them, but Jehovah steps in to forbid the prophet [Numbers 22:12]. The second time, although Balaam is allowed to go, Jehovah is angry [22:22 – "stationed himself in the way, as an enemy against him"], perhaps because Balaam thinks that Jehovah has been 'bought out.' "I have come out as an enemy because your way is contrary to Me" [v 32] – making yourself enemy to Jehovah's Covenant-partner makes you Jehovah's enemy. Balaam is warned to speak Jehovah's Word, or else.

Despite many altars and sacrifices on "the High Places of Baal" [22:41], Balak, who only sees a wizard for hire, is angry because his employee does not perform as contracted. His problem is that he never sees that God is *the Initiator* not *the Servant* of prophecy; the prophet speaks Jehovah's Word, he does not command Jehovah.

The first prophecy [23:7-10] is Jehovah's deliberate affirmation to the nations of His Covenant with Israel. Israel will stand, never swallowed up by the nations (v 9 – not even after four millennia – not in the Babylonian Captivity, nor the fall of Jerusalem in 70 AD, nor in Nazi Europe). Indeed Covenant is being fulfilled: "Who can count the dust of Jacob?" [v 10; see Genesis 13:16].[119] On top of that, the end (of the People?) will be enviably blessed! [v 10]

The irony of the second prophecy [23:18-24] is that Balak wants the King of Israel[120] [v 21] to curse His own People. But Jehovah will not back down from nor reconsider His Covenant with Abraham [vv 19-20]. "He has seen no iniquity in Jacob" [v 21] – *THIS People*?? But in Covenant-*HESED*, forgiveness is to be found, "and I remember their sin no more" [Jeremiah 31:34; Isaiah 43:25]! In that same Covenant, there is protection [v 22] and a formidable Foe [v 24] – NOT by magically controlling the gods, but by Covenant with Jehovah ("see what God has done" – v 23).

The third prophecy [24:3-9] intensifies the picture: Israel will be blessed like an Eden [vv 5-6]. His waters will overflow, his King exalted [v 7]. "God ... shall eat up the nations His enemies, and shall gnaw their bones, and pierce them with His arrows" [v 8] – *Jehovah will fight for Israel* [end of verse 9]. Like the hole in a dike now releasing torrents, prophecy runs on [vv 17-24]. Now the message includes the sphere of the Covenant-Partner Jehovah and His ultimate victories: "a Star" and "a Scepter shall arise" [v 17], "One out of Jacob shall have dominion" [v 19].

Subterfuge, the Blood-Debt and the GO'EL

Balaam proposes to Midian a far more successful plan than cursing [Numbers 31:16]: the victory would not come by the ability of fighting-men, but by the weakness of desire. Israel's persistent problem throughout its history is in trying to mix religions, committing "whoredom" – not just with the Moab and Midian women, but also with their idols, thereby breaking the Creation, the Circumcision, and the Mosaic Covenants.

The discipline is severe: the chiefs/ringleaders, who encourage this "fornication", are executed and their bodies hung from poles. An example of the boldness of these "chiefs" is Zimri who, despite the camp being in penitential mourning, openly 'entertains' one of the Midianites in his tent [Numbers 25:6]. As a type of *GO'EL*, Phinehas (Aaron's grandson) executes both of them on the spot [vv 7-8] and "the plague of death was stopped."

Until now, Israel's rebellion has been of its own doing, but here, it is at Midian's deliberate enticement, and 24,000 of Israel die – Jehovah's own Covenant-Blood has been shed, a Blood-debt which requires 'balancing.' As the *GO'EL* responsible to balance lost Blood to 'the family,' Moses is to avenge this loss by striking Midian [25:16-18]. Finally six chapters later the LORD insists that he perform this duty before he dies [31:2].

With a thousand soldiers from each tribe [Numbers 31:4-5]; with Phinehas, the new Covenant representative [v 6] and with the holy vessels of Jehovah (their Covenant Warrior-King) at their head, Israel goes to war, thoroughly routing the Midianites, and losing not a man [v 49]. But like inept Keystone Cops, they bumble their mission: although executing the mastermind of the plot (Balaam) [v 8], they preserve those who caused the Blood-debt: the Midianite women [v 9]! In anger [vv 14-17], Moses insists that they complete the Blood-debt, and so prevent any new Midian-inspired problem.

This event exhibits the use of *The Water of Impurity (the Red Heifer)*, since even soldiers in battle become unclean from their association with death [v 19]. Everything they picked up as booty has to be cleansed, by washing or by fire before it can enter the camp. Since all Israel suffered the Blood-debt, they will share half-and-half with the soldiers in the plunder. All, in turn, will share a portion with the priests and Levites.

The Covenant of Peace

Paralleling the Levite consecration of Exodus 32:28-29, for his zealous honoring of Jehovah, the 'atoning' Blood-shed at the execution of Zimri and the Midianite woman affirms the "everlasting priesthood" [Numbers 25:13] to Phinehas's family.

This signals a change. In the past, the head of the family held the domain of the priesthood; for example, at the original *Passover* he performed the sacrifice which signaled salvation for his family. Although he remains the priest of his family, now in the larger community, with a more centralized worship center (and after Israel's apparent rejection of "a nation of priests"), as well as for the sake of order and accountability, the pattern of responsibility has shifted. Only a few – here, a certain family – will be allowed to exercise the priesthood on behalf of the People – a not unusual idea in a larger worship context:

> For thus it is written in I Pet. 2: "You are a chosen race, a royal priesthood, and a priestly royalty." Therefore we are all priests, as many of us as are Christians. But the priests, as we call them, are ministers chosen from among us. All that they do is done in our name; the priesthood is nothing but a ministry.   Martin Luther[121]

> For every high priest chosen from men is appointed on behalf of men for the things in regard to God, so that He should offer gifts and sacrifices for sins.   Hebrews 5:1

The authorization occurs through a "Covenant of Peace [*SHALOM*]" [v 12] reminiscent perhaps of the *Peace Offering*, a type of Communion sacrifice. This is a curious title. Does it suggest a different *kind* of "wholeness" and integrity? Or is it simply emphasizing a quality within the normal Covenant environment (as the subsequent Covenants of Jonathan and David emphasized Covenant aspects in reassurance to each other) as an empowerment for the role of *community* priest which Phinehas and his descendants now have?

Final Preparations

Passing on the Leadership

Moses' death is near and he inquires who the next leader of the People will be [27:12-23]. His aide, Joshua, whose spiritual allegiance is proven ("in whom is the Spirit" – v 18), is officially designated: publicly "lay your hand on him" [v 18-19] (Covenant symbolism?) – the authority [v 20], the responsibility, and the guilt (like the High Priest's) will fall to this new leader. "You shall put *some* of your honor on him" [v 20] – without the same deep Covenant-relationship as Moses had, Joshua will receive instructions through the High Priest [v 21].

Dividing the Covenant Land

The tribes of Reuben, Gad and Manasseh upon finding themselves already in very fertile land suitable for livestock, desire to settle on the "wrong" side of the river [32:1-5]. Moses is concerned: will they take their ease while the rest of the People labor to clear the Covenant Land, even discouraging the rest as when the 10 spies had brought back a 'discouraging word'? No, they assure him, as part of the Covenant People they will see that the Covenant Land is settled as Jehovah had promised. So Moses consents, warning that Jehovah does not take His Covenant lightly and if they sabotage it, "be sure your sin will find you out!" [32:23]

What a spiritual and psychological boost to have the Covenant Land already divided up before they ever step foot on it! [chapter 34] Now each individual will be fighting not for an idealistic concept, but for his very own home! Covenant is taking concrete reality!!

Looking Behind Before Looking Ahead

For Israel on the threshold of THE Covenant Land, with all the mystery of the unknown future, Numbers 33 is essential in what it emphasizes: 'look at what Jehovah of Covenant accomplished every step of the way, to bring us here at this point of time!' Israel is right in the middle of the march of Covenant to its completion – of which the Covenant Land is an essential step. 'Now get out there and clean out that Land!' – "drive out the inhabitants ... destroy their graven images ... demolish their high places! Possess the Land and dwell in it (it's yours, I gave it to you!)!" [vv 52-53]

D. Deuteronomy
– Moses' Last Will and Testament

The Prologue

Moses is about to die, but what can he bequeath to all Israel? Only what he aimed for all along: that they be in Covenant as he knew Covenant. As he was shown the 'goodness' of the LORD in a vision, so he shows them the goodness of Jehovah within their history – the concrete basis of Covenant. But part of the legacy is also that they BE *Jehovah's* People before and to the world. Therefore He begins, not with the *Passover*/Exodus as the grand display of Jehovah's Love (which future prophets use as THE central reference point), but rather when they left Mount Sinai, where they had cut Covenant with Jehovah – Moses is emphasizing *THEIR* Covenant relationship.

However, significantly, this *Last Will and Testament* is based on the Abrahamic Covenant. They are at the doorstep of the first Covenant Promise: the Land "sworn [*SHABA*] to your fathers, to Abraham, to Isaac, and to Jacob" [1:8]; and in recounting Jethro's advice [1:9-17; see Exodus 18:21-27], he emphasizes the fulfillment of Covenant Promise Two: "I will make from you a great nation" [Genesis 12:1-4]. Throughout Deuteronomy, the phrase *"Jehovah your God"* shows up an extraordinary number of times, pounding home that everything in this Book is linked to "your" Covenant.

Yet once before the People had stood at the threshold of the Covenant Land [1:18-33]. They had turned away in fear and distrust of their Covenant-Partner's power, ability, and commitment, so the LORD slammed the door to the Land [1:34-36] (even on Moses' shirttail – v 37) and gave this Promise to the next generation [vv 38-40]. Their vain attempt to obtain the Covenant Land was without the Covenant-Partner, "for I am *not* in your midst" [1:42].[122] Then when they wept, not in repentance but because they did not get what they wanted, Jehovah would not hear – the Covenant phone-line was 'out of order.'

However, "If we are unfaithful, He remains faithful, since He is not able to deny Himself" [II Timothy 2:13] – in Covenant, Jehovah is still their God, and the Promises will be accomplished [2:7]. Now that the new generation is ready ("all the men of war had finished dying" – v 16), Jehovah turns their faces again to the Covenant Land.

When Sihon stood in the way [2:24-37], Jehovah and Israel as Covenant-Partners executed judgment on him [vv 24, 30-31]. The bonafide giant [3:11], Og, "*Jehovah our God* also gave ... into our hands" [v 3]. Israel tasted victory ("not a city too high for us; *Jehovah our God* delivered all before us" – 2:36) and settled in ("begin to possess, in order to possess" – v 31): three Israelite tribes now have their land – the People are already a fourth of the way home! "Your eyes have seen all which *Jehovah your God* has done ... so Jehovah shall do to all the kingdoms ... do not fear them; for *Jehovah your God* – He shall fight for you!" [3:21-22].

Jehovah our God is Israel's ever-present defense ("by trials, 'OTHs, wonders, war – by a mighty Hand and an outstretched Arm" [4:34]), their strength lies in wisdom, understanding, "righteous statutes and governing" [vv 6-8]. "Guard yourself, guard closely your Soul/Life [= Blood] lest you _forget_" [4:9, 15] your first-hand experience with *Jehovah your God* and His majestic imparting of His Law [vv 11-13, 15], lest you instead fall into false god worship [vv 16-19].

"Guard yourselves lest you _forget_ Covenant with *Jehovah your God* ... *Jehovah your God* is a consuming fire, a jealous God" [4:23-24]. "When [you] ... have done evil in the sight of *Jehovah your God*, ... I call the heavens and the earth to witness against you ... you shall soon utterly perish from off the Land ... Jehovah shall scatter you ..." [vv 25-28]. "But when you seek *Jehovah your God* ... with your whole heart and all your Soul/Life ... then you shall return ...; for *Jehovah your God* is a merciful God; He will not forsake you off, nor destroy you, nor _forget_ the Covenant of your fathers which He swore [SHABA] to them" [vv 29-31]. The greater Covenant underlying all of this is the Covenant with Abraham, the Circumcision Covenant [Genesis 12:1-4; 15:12-21; 17:1-14].

The Sinai Covenant

"*Jehovah our God* cut Covenant with us at [Sinai], ... not [merely] with our fathers ... but with *us* ... face-to-face" [5:2-4] – the Circumcision Covenant and this Confirming Covenant are essential – they involve 'OUR' Blood. "*Jehovah our God* revealed to us His Glory and His greatness, His voice we heard ... we have seen that God speaks with man and he lives" [v 24]. BUT they then say, 'He's *too* close, this is *too much* Covenant, *too much* oneness, give us distance, or else we will die!' [vv 25-27]. Covenant creates such a tension that Israel is uncomfortable – they want distance.

Underlying the Covenant relationship is "I am *Jehovah your God* ..." [5:6]: *your* God, Who comes in *HESED*, not in the sense of 'if you obey, then I'll free you from Egypt,' but rather "We were slaves to Pharaoh in Egypt, and Jehovah brought us out with a mighty Hand. Jehovah gave 'OTHs and great wonders and calamities ... before our eyes; ... in order to bring us in, to give us the Land which He had sworn to our fathers ... " [6:21-25]. This sense of Covenant echoes in the *Sabbath*, remembering "*Jehovah your God* brought you from there by a mighty Hand and an outstretched Arm ..." [5:15].

"HEAR, O ISRAEL, *JEHOVAH OUR GOD*, JEHOVAH IS ONE" – the only One, "there is no other, there is no God except Me" [Isaiah 45:5].[123] Israel, separate and distinct among ALL nations, is to have no Covenant, intermarriage, or sympathy for other religions – "For you are a holy People to *Jehovah your God*. *Jehovah your God* has chosen you to be a treasured People to Him," not because of numbers, but because of Love/*HESED* and Covenant [7:6-8]. "Know therefore that *Jehovah your God* – He is *The God*, the faithful God, keeping Covenant and steadfast Love [*HESED*] to all who love Him ... to a thousand generations, and repaying those who hate Him, to their face, to destroy them ..." [7:9-11].

In turn, "*Jehovah your God* shall keep Covenant and steadfast Love [HESED] with you which He swore [SHABA] to your fathers, and will love you, bless you, and multiply you. ..." [7:12-13].

When you have doubts, "remember [ZECHER] that which *Jehovah your God* has done to Pharaoh ... which your eyes have seen, the 'OTHs, the wonders, the mighty Hand, the outstretched Arm with which *Jehovah your God* has brought you out. ... You shall not tremble before them, for *Jehovah your God* is among you, a mighty and terrible God" [7:18-21].

Jehovah your God humbled you these forty years, "to test you, to know what is in your heart" [8:2]. You endured puzzlements [v 3], blessings [v 4], and discipline [v 5], and you remained true! – Now watch out lest in future success and contentment you think, "My power and the might of MY Hand have brought me this" [v 17]; and you forget *Jehovah your God*, Who upheld you, Who "gives you power ... that He may establish His Covenant which He swore [SHABA] to your fathers" [v 18]. Breaking Covenant will make you as defenseless against Jehovah's wrath as anyone else outside Covenant.

"So, Israel, what has *Jehovah your God* asked of you [in return for such HESED/Love], but to fear [solemn respect] *Jehovah your God*, walk in all His ways, love Him, and serve *Jehovah your God* with all your heart and Soul/Life" – this is *Jehovah your God*, the God of the UNIVERSE, Who could have chosen anyone He wanted! [10:12-14; also 11:1-9; 18-22]. So live the Covenant *inside*: not just on the outside [v 16], as the center of everything you do [v 20], because Jehovah IS a God of HESED/steadfast Love (look at how He fulfills Covenant!) [vv 21-22]. This is "a Land which *Jehovah your God* cares for, the eyes of *Jehovah your God* are constantly upon it" [vv 8-12] and He will bless it for your sake [vv 13-15]. However, woe to you if you lose sight of Him and turn to other gods [vv 16-17]!

"I set before you a blessing and a curse: a blessing if you obey *Jehovah your God's* commands ... and a curse if you will not obey ..." [11:26-28]. This Covenant is not remote, to be chased down, earned, or sought from a distance – "The Word is very near to you, in your mouth and in your heart, that you may do it" [30:14]. It is not complicated or philosophical; it is simply Life or death, blessing or curse. It is not whether you will stumble, but whether you will turn away from Covenant. The angels of heaven and the physical universe – two witnesses – will testify to your choice. Choose! Choose Life and blessing, choose to love Him, choose to listen and to cleave to Him, choose the Jehovah of the Covenant with your fathers, with Abraham, with Isaac, and with Jacob! [vv 15-20].

Outside of Covenant, the curses will come [vv 20-23]: futility, frustration, disease, pestilence, emptiness, loss, madness, slavery; "and you shall be an astonishment, a proverb, and a sneer among all people" [28:37]. "Then shall all these curses come upon you, they shall pursue you and overtake you until you are destroyed[124] ... They shall be on you for an 'OTH and for a wonder on your seed forever" [vv 45-47]. Other nations will stand bewildered at what went so wrong. The reason? "Because they have forsaken Covenant with Jehovah, the God of their fathers" – what is inconceivable in human Covenants has been done in Covenant with Jehovah [29:24-28].

So do not toy with false-god worship [16:18-22], nor tolerate its practice [17:2-7]; do not play at wondering how the former occupants honored their gods [12:29-32]; do not split gifts of worship with spiritual junk-food sellers (fortune-tellers or occultists, like spiritists and witches [18:9-13]). ANYONE – prophet, family member, or townsman – encouraging you in these things (you'll know the counterfeits by their lies), not only are you *not* to be afraid of them, but they are to die without mercy [13:1-11; 18:20-22].

As the Circumcision Covenant stands above Moses' Covenant, therefore *Jehovah our God* will never forget His Promise. Like the Father running to His returning prodigal son, when you turn back to Covenant, He will already be at your side! [30:1-3] No matter where you are – even in the farthest heavens, He will gather you back to the Covenant Land, and will bless you [vv 5-6].[125] There will be a better circumcision: a whole new heart; and the curses will be upon your enemies instead. You will be given a most reliable Source for information: "a Prophet[126] from among you ... One like me; to Him you shall listen" [18:15, 18].

So obey *Jehovah your God*'s will: worship Him where HE puts His Name, not according to YOUR ideas but according to HIS way – only then will you really "rejoice before Jehovah" [12:4-14]. And *Jehovah your God* will proudly display you before all nations as His very own People [12:18-19; 28:1, 9-10]. Every part of your Life from field to home will be blessed [vv 2-6, 11-12]; in war and in abundance, the presence of your Covenant-Partner will be evident [vv 7-8].

As you offer your First Fruits in *the Temple*, you shall confess: 'I declare today to *Jehovah our God*; I, whose history is that of homelessness and suffering; I, plucked from Egypt "by a mighty Hand and an outstretched Arm, with great terror, with '*OTH*s (SIGNs) and miracles"; I, given this good Land: I owe everything to *Jehovah my God* and His Covenant! Here, LORD, I give you the First Fruits – what You wanted, yet so little next to what You give!' [26:1-10] "and you shall rejoice in all the good things which *Jehovah your God* has given to you" [v 11].

A Unique People!

You are a chosen People in Covenant with *Jehovah your God*, His Personal Treasure, consecrated and set apart from the world and its death [14:3-20]. In this uniqueness (separateness), your garment fringes mark you as distinct [v 12] with a hope others do not have. So you treat your body differently (it belongs to your Covenant-Partner – 14:1-2), and since *Jehovah your God* gives you this Covenant Land freely, you help your (Covenant-)brother in need. "Your heart shall not be grieved when you give to him, for because of this *Jehovah your God* will bless you" [15:10-18].

Lest innocent Blood be shed, the "Cities of Refuge" will protect the accidental killer [19:1-13]. In the case of unknown Blood-guilt, the nearest town must release the guilt by breaking a heifer's neck next to an "everflowing stream", washing their hands of the death, claiming no knowledge of the crime, washing off the guilt of the town into the stream which carries away it and the "Life/Blood" (heifer's and "murdered individual's") – "and the Blood shall be forgiven them" [21:1-9].

You will do justice to your brother who dies childless by raising up children to his family, or else be disgraced among Israel [25:5-10]. Your righteousness according to the Creation Covenant is to be evident in regard to marriage [22:17-18; 20-30; 24:1-4] and to the uniqueness (separateness) of the sexes [v 5].

Does real power lie in a numerous, well-equipped army? *"Jehovah your God* is with you!" [20:2]. His presence, symbolized by the priest, reminds you of the past and of Covenant: "for Jehovah your God goes before you, to fight for you ..., to save you." When you do go to war for the LORD, you will be especially clean, because *"Jehovah your God* walks in the middle of your camp, to deliver you and to give up your enemies before you" [23:14].

Although preserving the Ammonite and the Moabite, you will not support them because of their treachery [23:3-6]. Still, remember that it is here where *"Jehovah your God* turned [Balaam's] curse into a blessing to you, because *Jehovah your God* loved you" [v 5]. In the *HESED* of Jehovah, you shall not despise your brother the Edomite, not even your enemy the Egyptian (in whose "house" you had lived for four hundred years [v 7-8]).

Moses' Song

Jehovah your God will fight and your enemies will not stand a chance [31:1-5]. So, in Covenant, you have every reason for strength and courage, for *Jehovah your God* is going with you, "He shall not fail you nor forsake you!" [vv 6-8]. Still, Israel will fall so far from Covenant that "I shall forsake them and hide My Face from them" [vv 16-18].

So they must be given a song, like the tune you cannot forget, to haunt them as a witness against them. A second witness will be the account of Jehovah's goodness – His *TORAH*, His commandments, His blessings and curses – which lie at the heart of His Covenant, placed into *the Ark of the Covenant* [vv 24-27]. The two witnesses of the heavens and the earth will hear their vow of Covenant, so that Israel's rebellion can claim neither ignorance nor misrepresentation [31:28-30].

Jehovah our God, The Rock, will be the constant throughout Israel's faith and rebellion. Despite Jehovah's wonderful blessings, watch how they will reject Him! He leads them, supports them, and abundantly feeds them [32:6-14]; but the self-satisfied "Righteous One" ("Jeshurun") will abandon God, the Rock of his salvation, Who has created this People. Preoccupied with demons – non-gods – they will forget their Rock [vv 15-18].

As if spitting with distaste, Jehovah declares He will hide His Face from His sons and daughters. If they follow non-gods, then they will be a non-people! [v 21]. In an anger reaching the depths of Hell, He will sap every strength of theirs, scattering them, but not so that an enemy can claim responsibility for their misfortune. The only explanation for such ease in conquering them is that their "Rock had sold them ... Jehovah had given them up" [v 30]. As the *GO'EL* of Blood-Covenant, Jehovah will administer His vengeance [v 35].

Yet His *HESED* will win out: Jehovah will have compassion on a Nation which is nothing, on a People who are stripped of all their false supports [32:36-38]. Now they will finally know that there is absolutely no other god of any kind but their Jehovah [v 39]. Now as *GO'EL* of the Covenant, He will take vengeance on the enemies of Israel, and their judgment will be greater than any visited upon His People.

Moses' Farewell And Patriarchal Blessing
[Chapter 33]

Jehovah of Israel's Covenant, Who loves "all the saints in Your Hand" [33:3], will bless the tribes – particularly *Judah*, who will be prominent in Israel, experiencing Jehovah's victory; and *Levi*, so faithful during Israel's faithlessness, who will declare Jehovah's judgments, teach Israel, and intercede for them ("burn incense"). There is none like the God of Jeshurun, your eternal Refuge; Who is not bound to this earth, Whose Arms of Covenant are under you, Who fights your enemy before you.

Israel will need no other protector, and will experience blessings which shower from heaven. "Who is like you? A People saved by Jehovah, the Shield of your help ... the Sword of your majesty!" [v 29]

The Death of Moses

Moses' yearning has surfaced in 3:23-27, "Lord (*ADONAI*) Jehovah, You have *begun* to show Your servant Your greatness, and Your mighty Hand! ... could I please go over and see this wonderful Land?" But one 'little' sin keeps him out – "Jehovah was angry with me because of *your* words, ... that I might not go into the good Land ... (I must die here); ... but you shall pass over and shall possess this good Land" [4: 21-22].

According to Jehovah's word, Moses ascends Mount Pisgah to die. Perhaps as 'part 2' of his vision of the "Glory of Jehovah" [Exodus 33:19-23], he sees *the Covenant Land of Israel*, not just as a yet-unsettled Land of Promise. After struggling so hard for forty years on behalf of this People, perhaps Moses is shown what is to come – the continued History of the Goodness of Jehovah and of His Salvation. It certainly would be appropriate. There on the mountain Moses dies and is buried as Jehovah chooses.

But what Moses' death implies! – a frightening thought to anyone earning their way into the "Covenant Land"! He had the best chance of achieving the Promise: honored as chosen by Jehovah Himself; he had seen God's Glory; they had talked "face-to-face as with a friend." His faith weathered Israel's idolatries and rebellions, and he even won arguments with Jehovah! He knew intimately and followed the Law like no other man and was the High Priest Aaron's High Priest. "Never since has a prophet like Moses arisen in Israel" [34:10]. Yet one little sin stops him *dead* at the door of the Promise. All that the Law can do is view the Promise from a distance.

It requires a Joshua (the Greek Septuagint translation: Ἰησους – Jesus!) – to "cause them to inherit the Land" [3:28].

IX. Time with Jehovah – Israel's Worship

A. The Priests

The Priests – Exodus 28

Meant to be a "Nation of Priests," Israel now instead has an official priesthood: representatives and spokesmen for when they gather as one. As Adam mediated between God and creation, Aaron and his sons bear responsibility for the spiritual state of Israel, raising the worshippers before the LORD and then conveying His response (forgiveness, communion, etc.). "You shall serve as a service of gift" [Numbers 18:7] – serve BY grace, FOR grace: similar to if not actual *GO'EL*s, the Priests restore the Blood-balance within Covenant, through the method which the Offended Party allows in the place of the offender's own Life. Especially with the *Sin Offering*, they demonstrate Jehovah's grace: no one could offer his own sacrifice – one's standing before the LORD is not due to his own effort.

The two altars represent these priestly duties: *the Altar of Incense* (intercedes for the People), and *the Altar of Burnt Offering* (brings Jehovah's *HESED* to this treasured Nation, including *teaching* Israel the *TORAH* (often translated as "the Law") so that they might know the need and benefit of the sacrifices [Deuteronomy 33:10]).

Beyond an honor, it is a burden. On the High Priest's shoulders [28:12] and over his heart [28:29] are the names of the tribes, so that all he does is constantly in their name. His robe [28:31-35] has bells "so that he will not die" – so that when he enters *the Most Holy Place*, literally risking his Life, the People would listen and pray for him. Over his forehead is "Holy to Jehovah" [28:36], and he will "bear the iniquity of the sacred things" [28:38][127]; "You ... shall bear the sanctuary's iniquity; and you ... shall bear your priesthood's iniquity ..." [Numbers 18:1,3,5]. In the sacrifices and in interceding, the LORD would call the priests to account.

But Israel also has responsibility toward the priests. By Numbers 18, challenges to the priesthood had brought death and plague upon Israel, so that it became obvious that "bearing the iniquity" of the priestly office was no trivial matter. Of all the tribes, the priests and Levites would be 'homeless,' having no tribal land possession: "I am your portion and your inheritance" [Numbers 18:20]. In response, Israel is to support them through their offerings and the "ransom" of the firstborns. This would be a "Covenant of Salt"[128] [Numbers 18:19] to the priests and Levites.

Aaron the High Priest

How could Jehovah use Aaron, so prominent in the "Golden Calf" and the later Numbers 12 rebellions, as the special link between Himself and man, the link of intercession/forgiveness?? The wonder is that a SINNER, obviously not because he is 'good enough,' is chosen by Jehovah to serve Him. In *HESED*, the LORD makes him worthy: as Jehovah's hands, Moses washes Aaron and his sons [Exodus 29:4],[129] and then dresses them in the marks of their office [vv 5-6]. The special Anointing oil is poured only on the High Priest Aaron's head – an equipping by the Holy Spirit for his special service – and then the sacrifices are performed as required.

B. The Sacrifices

All Life Is Mine!

Leviticus 17 revolves around v 11: "The Blood is the Soul/Life, is the Atonement." Verse 3 seems to indicate that every animal slaughtered, even for meat, must be acknowledged before Jehovah at *the Tent of Meeting* – the shedding of Life/Blood is not trivial, no matter its source, and specifically is not to be eaten. The drained Blood is to be sprinkled upon *the Altar of Sacrifice* – evidence of respect not to the animal, but to the Source of all Life on earth. Perhaps this reaches back to pre-Noah days, when every animal which was killed WAS a sacrifice! Still, if not done in rebellion, the penalty for eating Blood is a relatively minor uncleanness: "wash your clothes and take a bath" [v 15].

This practice discourages isolated sacrifices [v 5] and since *all* animals are brought in, no false god worship would go unnoticed [v 7]. The only exception is the animal killed in the hunt, whose Blood is poured on the ground and then covered.

The Main Sacrifices – The Cost of Restored Communion

One might call the sacrifices *'OTHs*, because although done by human hands, they are Jehovah's gift, *His* work: "For the Soul/Life of the flesh is in the Blood; and *I have given it for you* upon the altar to make atonement for your Souls" [Leviticus 17:11] – SIGNS that Covenant is alive and active. Since the whole nation was originally supposed to be priests, the ordination sacrifices should have been all Israel's ordination, God's desire which is carried over into the New Covenant [1 Peter 2:5] in regard to all believers in Jesus. Therefore the ordination sacrifices are here highlighted:

The Sin Offering –*Exodus 29:10-14 (See Leviticus 4; 6:24-7:7)*

"The Soul/Life which sins, it shall die" [Ezekiel 18:20][130] – broken ('torn apart') Covenant means Life is forfeit, therefore the *Sin Offering* is to redeem (atone, ransom) this lost Life/Blood and pronounce forgiveness to the one who shattered the unity of Covenant. Such redemption comes only through the Life of a blemish-free, approved substitute in its prime. The sacrificer lays his hands upon it, identifying it with himself ('This is me!'), and, confessing his sins, makes it his Sin-Bearer. Its sin-tainted Life/Blood is *not* a gift to Jehovah, but rather as lost Life, it is poured out at the base of *the Altar of Burnt Offering* (which drained into a waste area).

"Burn the ... flesh, its skin and its dung outside the camp; it is a *sin offering*." Flesh is the lodging place of sin and represents sin's clinging nature. Unclean and rejected by God, unusable for any worthwhile purpose, even food, it is not to remain before the LORD, but burned in the

161

garbage dump. Only "all the fat around the inner parts, the fatty covering of the liver, and both kidneys[131] with the fat on them"[132] are burned on *the Altar of Burnt Offering*.

The Whole Burnt Offering – *Exodus 29:15-18 (See Leviticus 1; 6:8-13; 7:8)*

But forgiveness IS NOT enough! God declared "You are *holy*, for I Jehovah your God am holy" [Leviticus 19:2]; "You are to be *perfect*, as your Father in the heavens is perfect." [Matthew 5:48]. Although forgiveness does wipe away the Life/Blood-debt of rebellion, the sacrificer's Life now has many 'empty spaces' where holiness[133] should have been (actually the whole Life!) – *which is not perfect*! Again an innocent victim's Life/Blood is required to fill those gaps. Not only is Life required to *redeem* lost Life, but more Life is required to *replace* what should have been.

The עלה [`OLAH – *Whole Burnt Offering*[134]]'s root means "to ascend, to go up." Perhaps this refers to the sacrifice's smoke ascending to heaven, or to the *sacrificer* who is raised in status as if he had never broken Covenant – 'righteous' – and therein celebrates a joyful recommitment to Jehovah.

As a *cleansed* sinner, the sacrificer takes an animal according to Jehovah's specifications, and identifies himself with it by laying hands on its head. This Life/Blood is not poured out, but offered upon the Altar. Representing the *new* Life, it is given to the LORD – man's 'return pump' of Life has begun to function again. The body is cut up; the "inner parts and the legs" are washed (the inner Life and daily walk are 'Baptized'); then ALL of it is burned upon *the Altar* – offering the whole/holy Life and body of the cleansed sinner, of all he is and has. The smell of burning meat and fat is a pleasing aroma[135], because its center is obedience – the obedience of a Life following the LORD's command and will.

Unlike the *ordination Whole Burnt Offering* where Moses performs this sacrifice as an act of God's grace, in the *normal Whole Burnt Offering* the sacrificer apparently does the killing and much of the preparing of the body himself [the Leviticus passages]. Still the effects of this offering are by grace, since the benefits come not because of the perfectly prepared sacrifice, but because of the innocent Life/Blood of the victim which is shed on the sacrificer's behalf – an *'OTH* done by the individual, yet is Jehovah's gift of Life to him. Likely this offering is in St Paul's mind when he wrote: "I urge you therefore, brethren, by the mercies of God, to present your bodies as a living sacrifice, holy and well-pleasing to God, which is your reasonable service" [Romans 12:1].

The Peace/Fellowship Offering

This fellowship/communion meal is discussed in "IV. The Covenant Mosaic, E. The Covenant Feast."

Special Differences for the Priest - *Exodus 29:19-37*

Different from the ordinary *Peace/Communion Offering*, the *Ordination Sacrifice* has some extra features: some Blood is applied to the tip of Aaron's and his sons' right ears, right thumbs, and right great toes. As the victim encompasses two directions (God and man), so also the new priest encompasses two directions: his *ear* is turned toward Jehovah, to speak God's Word to the People; but he also is to listen to Israel and bring their prayers before Jehovah Himself by interceding for them.

So also his *hand* is turned two ways, serving both God and man. But he is not to be careless: his hand of ability, power, authority and COVENANT is holy, having grave responsibility to not be linked with anything less than holy. His *foot* signifies the 'walk' of the priest, how he travels Life's pathways: his conduct, manner, attitudes, speech, preoccupations, etc. are all to reflect his responsibility toward Jehovah and toward his spiritual charge.

After the rest of the Blood is sprinkled upon the Altar, *some of that Blood is mixed with anointing oil [v 21] and sprinkled upon the sacrificer.*[136] Oil is often the symbol of the empowering of the Holy Spirit.

The *Ordination Sacrifice* has another difference: normally the officiating priest receives the right thigh [vv 27-28], but here it is Jehovah's [v 25] – in other words, the ordination is done by the Hand of the LORD, through grace and steadfast Love/*HESED*. The breast, normally for the priests in general [Leviticus 7:30-34], is Moses' share [29:26]; and the rest of the ram is for the newly ordained [vv 31-34].

Still Needs Atonement

Not always are all three types of sacrifices offered each time the sacrificer comes before the LORD. One may merely express his commitment and devotion in the *Whole Burnt Offering*, or his joy in the *Peace/Fellowship Offering*. Yet despite the idealistic picture of how the *Sin Offering* redeems the sinner from broken Covenant's death, and the *Whole Burnt Offering* restores him to righteousness, the truth is that the rebellion of sin is still present. Even *the Peace/Communion Offering* must also speak of "atonement/redemption" [v. 33]. The problem is that the Sacrifices' working material (the animal victim) just does not measure up to the need. Something more powerful and longer lasting is required if one is to end up in eternal Covenant-communion with Jehovah.

Other Sacrifices

Numbers 19 – The Water of Impurity (The Red Heifer)

Discussed previously under "II. The Basics of Covenant, C. Based on Blood (Life) – Substitute Blood – Living Water"

Leviticus 2 – The Grain Offering (Also 6:14-23)

It was the only bloodless offering, but it was to accompany the burnt offering (see Nu 28:3-6), sin offering (see Nu 6:14-15) and fellowship offering (see 9:4; Nu 6:17). ... The cooked product was similar to pie crust. The worshiper was not to eat any of the grain offering, and the priests were not to eat any of their own grain offerings, which were to be totally burned (6:22-23). The Hebrew word for grain offering can mean "present" or "gift" and is often used in that way (see Ge 43:11). The sacred gifts expressed devotion to God (see v. 2).

Self-Study Bible[137]

Leviticus 5:14-6:7 – The Trespass/Guilt Offering (Also 7:1-6; Numbers 5:5-10)

This is a modified *Sin Offering* including restitution (in those cases where that is possible).

How much Life/Blood it takes, not just to forgive, but to finally experience restored Covenant! The immensity is multiplied by the thought that **each** sin/rebellion *requires* this sequence of sacrifice. Yet animal Life/Blood is no substitute for *God's* Life/Blood in the human – they can only allude to what is necessary. A permanent solution can only be established by the Blood from the Source of Life, Jehovah Himself.

C. The Festivals

The Three Important Festivals

Establishing the festivals of *Unleavened Bread* (and *Passover*),[138] of *Harvest* (*Pentecost, the Feast of the First Fruits*), and of *Ingathering* (*the Feast of Booths, the Fruit Harvest Festival*), ALL the men of Israel are to appear before "Lord (*ADONAI*) Jehovah"[139] at least these times each year [Exodus 23:17; 34:23]. Not just national and agricultural occasions, they center in His salvation in Covenant, reaching back to Eden and forward to Jesus' work and Resurrection (*Passover/Unleavened Bread*), to the *First Fruits* and the beginning of God's new *nation* (*Pentecost* - Acts 2), and to *the Last Day* (*the Harvest Festival*[140]).

In describing these festivals, a crucial comment is made in regard to worship: "No one comes before Me empty-handed" [Exodus 23:15; 34:20][141] and "Bring the best of the First Fruits ..." [23:19]. The worship experience is never for the worshiper to ask 'What do I get out of it?',

'Does it please me?', but 'What does Jehovah *deserve* from me, according to His Covenant and *HESED* shown to me?'

The Feasts

Redeeming the Time (Daily, Weekly [Sabbath], Monthly [New Moon])

Life is now tainted by sin's rebellion – Adam and Eve would certainly understand that: daily life will no longer be the same. How then can one even hope to have a 'good' day, in terms of his relationship to Jehovah?

St Paul writes what sounds like an odd idea: "Redeeming the time" [Ephesians 5:16; Colossians 4:5], yet this is exactly what Israel is instructed to do: every morning (beginning of the workday) and every evening (beginning of the next day), no matter if a festival or other occasion, a lamb is sacrificed [Numbers 28:1-8] – each 'day' begins with a consciousness of Jehovah's redemption. The *Sabbath* begins with *two* additional lambs [vv9-10], and the new month adds two bulls, a ram, *seven* lambs and a goat *Sin Offering*. For God's People, all of their time is to be centered in the LORD's Covenant.

The Sabbath, the Sabbath Year and the Year of Jubilee

The *Sabbath Day* is for man *and beast* to "refresh" them – Jehovah, as Creator and Sustainer, commands "the Image of God" to reflect His care of His creatures[142] (mankind itself is also one). Not just a tradition or commandment, *seven* relates the *Sabbath* to Covenant – it is an *'OTH* [Exodus 31:13] of Jehovah's Covenant relationship, of *His* sanctifying His People and especially of His Salvation [Deuteronomy 5:15]. Breaking *Sabbath* carries the equivalent force as breaking Covenant [Numbers 15:32-36].

The *Sabbath Year* (every *seventh* year) is for *the land* to rest – to lie uncultivated. In the previous six years, the necessary food or money for the year would have to be stored up: "I have commanded My blessing on you in the sixth year ..." [Leviticus 25:21]. Whatever grew in the seventh year is not to be harvested, but is available to everyone and anyone, rich and poor alike, even to the wild animals [Exodus 23:10-11]. In the reason given for the Babylonian exile from the Promised Land, seventy (*seven/oath*) times *completion*) years would tie into Covenant:

> [The king of the Chaldeans] took into exile ... to fulfill the word of Jehovah by the mouth of Jeremiah, until the land had enjoyed its *Sabbath*s. During all the days of desolation it kept *Sabbath*, until seventy years were fulfilled.   II Chronicles 36:20-21

Since apparently the *Sabbath Years* were never kept, the *Jubilee Year* with its greater economic demands would be even the more resisted (some criticize its potential economic chaos). In this *Sabbath* of *Sabbath Years* (the fiftieth year), almost all land returns to its original owner/family, every Hebrew slave becomes free – and, most of all, everyone depends on Jehovah to care for them – which might not be so bad if it did not follow on the heels of a *Sabbath Year*. *The Year of Jubilee* makes it two years in a row of depending on Israel's Covenant-Partner to supply their needs for survival.

The principle behind the *Jubilee Years* is in Leviticus 25:23 and 55: "because the land is Mine and you are aliens and My tenants. ... for the sons of Israel are My servants – My servants whom I brought out of Egypt. I am Jehovah your God." Beginning on *the Day of Atonement/ Redemption,* here is the reality of Atonement made visible, a truly new beginning for everyone and everyone is to act in anticipation of this Atonement. So when the land is sold or an Israelite sells himself into slavery, it is to be with the awareness that *the Jubilee Year* will return them, therefore their price would be adjusted accordingly [vv 14-17] – because Jehovah is the true owner of the People and of the Covenant Land and HE is greater than any human deals.

The Passover (Feast of the Unleavened Bread) – *Also Leviticus 23:3-8*

The *Passover* was discussed previously in the section concerning the Exodus from Egypt.

Numbers 9:1-14 provides for a mandatory second *Passover* celebration, assuming there is good reason for missing the normal date (for example, for some uncleanness), because *Passover* is not optional: he who refuses to celebrate the *Passover* "shall be cut off from his People ... he shall bear his sin" [v 13]. Deuteronomy 16:1-8 restates the *Passover* regulations in light of settling in the Covenant Land.

The Festival of First Fruits

As the first male opening the womb is Jehovah's, as the Tithe is Jehovah's, so also when the grain harvest begins, the first of the harvest belongs to the Giver of all good gifts [Leviticus 23:9-14]. Numbers 28:26-31 specifies that two bulls, a ram, *seven* lambs, and a goat are to be sacrificed.

> In regard to the festival year, there is a bit of a puzzle in that, although "*the Festival of the First Fruits*" is indeed linked to the *Pentecost* celebration in Numbers 28:26, in Leviticus 23:11 there is also apparently a "first" of the First Fruits ceremonies – "*the Feast of the Unleavened Bread*" – which begins on *the day after Passover (the Passover* is referred to as "the *Sabbath*"). The Israelite is allowed to now eat from the grain as it is harvested [v 14]. When Jesus dies in 33 AD, the next day is a double *Sabbath* – both *Passover and* Saturday (the normal *Sabbath*) – and He rises on *this day following "the Sabbath."*
>
> The Feast of the Unleavened Bread marks the transition from the barley harvest to the wheat harvest, and equally so, the Resurrection marks the transition to the new harvest of the New Covenant. As the Israelite now eats the "untainted" (unleavened) first bread from the new crop, it is also the day when the risen Jesus is known to the Emmaus disciples in the "Breaking of Bread" [Luke 23:30-31, 35], the name the early disciples give to Holy Communion [Acts 2:42, 46; 20:7; I Corinthians 10:16]. As Jesus' People now follow His instructions, "Take and eat, this is My Body given for you" every Sunday following, they sample the First Fruits of the Resurrection, which gives the frame of reference to Paul's words:

> But Christ has now been raised from the dead, He has become the First Fruits of those who have fallen asleep.... But each in his own order: the First Fruit Christ, then those who are Christ's at His coming.
> I Corinthians 15:20, 23
>
> James Lindemann[143]

The Festival of Weeks (Harvest – Pentecost)

Seven full weeks, starting the count *on the day after Passover*, is Israel's 'Thanksgiving Day' [Leviticus 23:15-22].[144] The bounty of the land is shared with the priest, and the command to have *HESED* on the poor and the alien is repeated. "You shall rejoice before *Jehovah your God* ... and you shall remember that you were a slave in Egypt ..." [Deuteronomy 16:11-12].

This also celebrates when Israel stood at the foot of Mount Sinai and became the Nation of Israel – a parallel to the beginning of New Testament Church at the feast of *Pentecost* [Acts 2].

The Festival of Trumpets (Rosh Hashanah)[145]

The first day of the *seventh* ('oath' and *Sabbath*!) month (a half year opposite to *Passover*) is for having a "blast" – of trumpets – to celebrate the joy of a new agricultural year [Leviticus 23:23-25]. Since the lunar year is shorter than the solar year and a thirteenth month is occasionally added to realign the seasons, this feast also lets everyone know that *the Day of Atonement* is near. Numbers 29:1-6 commands a bull, a ram, *seven* lambs, and a goat be sacrificed.

The Day of Atonement/Redemption (Leviticus 16) – Yom Kippur[146]

This is discussed previously on "V. Restoring Lost Life/Blood, D. *KAPHAR* – Atonement – The Day of Atonement/ Redemption." After the great ceremony depicting the removal of sin, there is still *the Burnt Offerings*, re-dedicating the Priest and the People, and cremating *the Sin Offerings* outside the camp. Ritually all is well between God and His People

– yet THAT day *still requires* an additional *Whole Burnt Offering*; and a bull, a ram, *seven* lambs and a goat are also sacrificed [Numbers 29:7-11], as well as the usual *daily* sacrifices – 16 in all.

The Festival of Tabernacles (Booths; Ingathering)[147]

Five days later (half year from *Passover*) comes *the Feast of Tabernacles*, a joyous time with the LORD that lasts a week – a rejoicing beyond all other feasts [Leviticus 23:40; 29:12-38; Deuteronomy 12:12,18]: "for *Jehovah your God* shall bless you in all your increase, and in every work of your hands; and you shall truly rejoice" [Deuteronomy 16:13-15].

The sacrificial requirements are enormous: the first day, a goat *Sin Offering*, thirteen bulls, two rams, and *fourteen*[148] lambs are sacrificed. It is the same each day (less one bull from the day before), until the eighth day, when one bull, one ram and *seven* lambs are offered – all in addition to the usual daily sacrifices. This volume declares an increased communion between Jehovah and mankind, as it celebrates Israel's freedom (from Egypt), living in "booths/tabernacles" (tents) at the foot of Jehovah's mountain, experiencing His care for them.

In the background is this festival's dependence on *the Day of Atonement*'s necessary sacrifices for forgiveness and renewed Life and how, although it rejoices in the blessings of Jehovah, still it limps – every day yet another *Sin Offering* (the goat) must be sacrificed – *the Day of Atonement*, recent as it is, just is not enough!

X. Different Circumstances, Same Covenant

A. Settling the Land

Joshua – The Six Hundred Year Dream Becomes Real

Preparations

Imagine the thrill: despite the loss of Moses, the camp's excitement must have been electric – this is the chosen generation, the time is now, and the Covenant Land promised to Abraham is about to be their new home. Those on 'the wrong side of the river' reflect the rest of the nation's enthusiasm, 'Tell us what to do, where to go; we fully accept your authority. Any rebel will be put to death, so be strong and confident!' [1:16-18]. With Israel's face turned toward the Covenant Land, two men are sent to spy out Jericho.

Joshua gets his final pep-talk from Israel's Covenant-Partner:

> I will not fail you nor forsake you. Be strong and courageous, for you shall cause this People to inherit the Land which I swore [*SHABA*] to their fathers to give them. Only be strong and very courageous to heed all the teachings [*TORAH*] which Moses charged you ... Have I not commanded you? Be strong and courageous; do not be afraid nor discouraged; for *Jehovah your God* is with you in all the places where you go.   1:5-9

"I Claim This Land in the Name of ..."

With supreme confidence, in contrast to the first twelve spies [Numbers 13], the two spies come back: "Truly Jehovah has given all the land into our hands! All the inhabitants of the land have melted before us!" [Joshua 2:24]. Now comes the long awaited thrill: *the Ark* is on the move! The time has come! The symbol of Jehovah's presence moves out ahead of the People [3:4] – Jehovah will be 'point man'[149]: He will meet first any problems they encounter.

The first problem is the flooding Jordan River [3:15], but as "the feet of the priests bearing *the Ark of Jehovah*, Lord (*ADONAI*) of all the earth, rest in the waters of the Jordan, its waters shall be cut off...By this you shall surely know that the living God is among you!" [3:13, 15-17,10]. Twelve stones, one for each tribe, from where one cannot go (mid-river), will be "the *'OTH* (SIGN) among you" [4:5-6]. Facing a Covenant Land yet to be conquered, here is a reminder of Jehovah's great power and resourcefulness, as well as a clear warning that Jehovah will not be thwarted [4:24; 5:1].

The first generation (now dead), although themselves circumcised, ignored circumcising their sons, so Israel has to now return to Covenant [5:2-9]. Imagine: how ridiculous to cross *into* enemy territory *and then deliberately, immediately incapacitate every male, especially of fighting age!!*[150] Yet the pattern reflects the Circumcision Covenant with Abraham: the Patriarch is already surrounded by Covenant before he and his whole household are circumcised (and incapacitated). So also Israel, surrounded by Covenant, re-enters into this personal bond with Jehovah.

Then they have a *holiday*, celebrating the *Passover* with the seven-day *Feast of Unleavened Bread.* What guts! or faith (you pick); and how demoralizing for the enemy – the ultimate 'psyching out'![151] Jericho, who is very aware of Israel [2:9], must have been driven crazy at Israel's utterly casual concern for the business of war. Yet what better way to face the conquest of the Covenant Land than by focusing on Jehovah's commitment and power as the *Passover* recalls their release from Egypt.

What a time of dramatic change for Israel: now they are in the Covenant Land, the manna ceases [5:12], and no longer is there the pillar of cloud and fire [Exodus 40:38; Nehemiah 9:19-22]. Yet Jehovah has not deserted them: as their Covenant-Partner He stands near Jericho with His sword drawn [5:13-15]. The Captain of Jehovah's Army (Jehovah Himself?) will fight for Covenant-partner Abraham's children.

Jericho

What is so significant about Jericho? Here is a walled city, meant to be impenetrable. It is 'the door-opener' to the Promised Land. Will they fail, will they become exhausted and become discouraged, or will they conquer? What happens here will set the tone for the conquest of the Land given by Covenant. Does this bond have any real value in a situation like this?

Jericho is also the First Fruits of this Covenant Land, and therefore belongs [is "dedicated"[152]] to only Jehovah: "You shall certainly keep away from the 'dedicated' thing, lest you make yourself 'dedicated' by taking from that which is 'dedicated' and make the whole camp of Israel 'dedicated' and bring trouble to it" [6:18].

There are no siege works, just a silent army merely marching around the city once each day for six days [Joshua 6:3,6-11] – a most unique offensive tactic! Imagine Jericho's utter bewilderment – and fear! With *the Ark of the Covenant* leading the procession and '*seven/oath*' constantly ringing in the background: *seven/oath* days, on the *seventh/oath* day after *seven/oath* rounds, the *seven/oath* priests blew their *seven/oath* trumpets, the People roar and Jericho's walls mean nothing. Jehovah fights in a most marvelous way: Abraham's Covenant-Partner's 'oaths' are coming true, God's People are easily victorious.

Joint Accountability

When Achan takes items for himself, he commits *blasphemy*[153], taking what belongs to God alone; and like pulling a blanket over them, his theft pulls Jericho's 'dedicated' status over Israel. The tables are reversed: as Israel had been Jehovah's instrument of judgment, now the heathen town of Ai is God's instrument against Israel – without Covenant, Israel is as vulnerable to God's judgments as any heathen nation is [7:11-12].

Why such harshness? Because the interconnectedness of Covenant-partners answers Cain's question "Am I my brother's keeper?" The principle of Ezekiel 33:8 is not some 'future' responsibility: "When I say to the wicked, 'O wicked one, you will surely die,' and you do not speak to dissuade him from his ways, that wicked one will die for his sin, but I will hold you accountable for his Blood." Therefore when a soldier enters the town in only his battle-dress, but leaves pregnant (with the robe rolled up under his tunic and panting from the weight of the gold and silver) – surely others notice, yet say nothing.

Once the sin is removed, Ai is easy pickings for Israel. The Captain of Jehovah's Army gives the command [8:18], and since apparently only the inhabitants are now 'dedicated' [8:26] for the *GO'EL*'s Blood-balancing for Israel's loss of Life, its spoil is available for Israel [8:2,27].

Deceived

The Gibeonites use a different tactic: instead of *fighting*, they *deceive*, appearing as if they had come a great distance [9:4-5]. Neglecting to consult with Jehovah, Joshua cuts a forbidden [Deuteronomy 7:1-2; 20:16-18] Covenant, but Covenant nonetheless, which cannot be rescinded. When Gibeon is attacked [10:5], Israel has to fight – but *their* Covenant-Partner is also at hand [v 8]: "Jehovah devastated them before Israel and ... showered great hailstones out of the heavens" [vv 10-11]. To finish the work, through his Covenant-Partner ("for Jehovah listened to the voice of a man; for Jehovah fought for Israel"), Joshua commands and the sun and the moon slow down for an extra day's worth [vv 13-14].

The Israelite captains set their feet upon the necks of the kings, "for so shall Jehovah do to all your enemies ..." [10:25] – which the following conquest demonstrates [10:29-43; 11:16-18]. But it is not easy! As Pharaoh had rejected the *'OTH*s of the Plagues, so also all Canaan rejects what Israel's phenomenal victories declare. Instead they try to overpower Israel (and Jehovah) [11:19-20]. Chapter 11 describes quite a coalition set up against Israel [vv 1-5], but as the LORD promises, this vast multitude lies vanquished the following day [vv 6-14].

Settling Down in the Land

"Joshua controlled the whole Land" [11:23] – yet all the inhabitants are not removed at once "lest the Land become desolate" [Exodus 23:29-30]. Still, what a thrill as each tribe actually *receives* its allotment. What had been dreamed about, promised and fought for, now is reality. But they are not done: interspersed are battles being fought and territories not yet conquered. However, for the first time in the whole history of Israel, from Abraham down, the Covenant Land is actually *theirs*.

In a pointed aside, Caleb surfaces as an eighty-five-year-old man [14:10-11], still as nimble and ready for battle as when he spied the Covenant Land as a forty-year-old. Remember those giants the first spies had bemoaned [Numbers 13:32-33]? THAT'S the Land he wants! [Joshua 14:6-12]. And a walled city of giants just cannot handle this 'elderly' warrior [15:13-15] – not when Jehovah is Caleb's Covenant-Partner!

Israel becomes complacent – Judah [15:63], Joseph [16:10], and Manasseh [17:11-13] cannot clear their territory "because the *Canaanite* wished to live in this land" [v 12]! Joshua has to almost boot the remaining *seven(!)* tribes into taking their areas [18:2-7]. Finally all is finished [19:51]. The trans-Jordan tribes are released [22:1-9] and are misunderstood when they build a magnificent altar at the Jordan: is this a rebellion against Jehovah [vv 16-20]? No, this is 'not for sacrifice, but a witness of our being in Covenant – a witness to not neglect our obligations and for the rest of Israel to not exclude us' [vv 27-28].

The Solemn Re-Commitment of Covenant

At Shechem – where Abraham is first told that this was his Covenant Land [Genesis 12:6-7], where Jacob makes the LORD exclusively his God [Genesis 35:2-4], where Joseph's bones are buried [Joshua 24:32], lying between the Mount of Curses (Ebal, with its stones with the law written on them [Deuteronomy 27:1-8]) and the Mount of Blessings (Gerizim) – here Israel is to renew Covenant, which forms a parenthesis around the Covenant Land's conquest [Joshua 8:30-35; 24:1-28].

As Moses spoke parting words, so Joshua wants last words with the People he led during its most wonderful time. Echoing Moses' Last Will and Testament (Deuteronomy), he speaks of all Jehovah has done and still does for them [Joshua 23:3-5, 9-10, 14]: from Abraham, Isaac, Jacob and Esau, to the great salvation from Egypt, to the Covenant Land; from the battles won on Jordan's far side, to city after city which were conquered on this side; an inheritance where Israel has not built, planted, or earned – this is how Jehovah has shown Himself in Covenant.

Joshua throws down the challenge: 'follow Jehovah or follow the 'gods' which give you nothing; but as for me and my house, we will serve Jehovah' [24:14-15]. If they turn away, the nations will be the death of them [vv 12-13]; Jehovah will not back away from His curses [vv 19-20].

The response is full of the heady enthusiasm of the People's recent conquest of the Covenant Land: 'Far be it from us to forsake Jehovah to serve other gods; for Jehovah our God – He brought us out of Egypt and has done these great *'OTH*s, He preserved us in all the way and among all the people through whom we have passed, and Jehovah cast out all the inhabitants before us – we will serve Jehovah, for He is our God' [24:16-18].

Joshua's flat-out contradiction is 'reverse psychology': 'You cannot serve Jehovah! He's too holy and jealous – He will not play games when you forsake Him, but will come down hard on you. Choose another, more easy-going god; Jehovah is too dangerous!' [24:19-20]. Israel insists, "No, we will serve Jehovah!" [v 21]. He replies, 'Then blame no one but yourselves – you will be your own accuser when you fail! If this is your choice, then you had better follow through on it: remove your false gods and center your heart on Jehovah, Israel's God!' [vv 22-24].

"Joshua cut Covenant with the People and set on them a statute and judgment"[154] [24:25] and a stone will be the second witness (the People themselves are the first) of this occasion [24:26-27]. So closes another extraordinary period of time within Israel's history, a time when a far-off promise made to a lone man over six hundred years earlier becomes a reality.

Judges – Accountability for Spiritual Ownership of the Covenant Land

Progress and Regress

Judges describes how the clearing of the Covenant Land continues. At Jehovah's direction [1:2], Judah and Simeon combine strengths to clean up both of their allotments, this time capturing Jerusalem and other places, yet still not doing too much in the valleys "for they had chariots of iron" [1:19]. Even then the Jebusites in Jerusalem are not "dispossessed." In fact, Israel has made many Covenants with a number of the inhabitants, merely making them tributaries rather than dispossessing them.

Time passes and a new generation arises who fall into the predicted trap: "The sons of Israel did evil ... and served the Baalim, and forsook Jehovah, their fathers' God ..." [2:11-13]. They intermarry with the inhabitants [3:6], deliberately rebelling against Jehovah's command [Exodus 34:15-16; Deuteronomy 7:3]. In response, "Jehovah's anger burned against Israel, He gave them into the hand of plunderers, ... He sold them into the hand of their enemies" – Jehovah's Hand of Covenant is against them as He had sworn [2:14-15].

He has not abandoned them, sending 'judges' who rescue them; but before long the cycle would begin again. Finally, Jehovah announces that He deliberately will leave the Canaanites in the Covenant Land longer, in order to make Israel wrestle with its infidelity to Covenant [2:20-22; chapter 3]. Still, when Israel cries out to Jehovah, He raises up 'saviors': Othniel [3:9], Ehud [v 15] and Shamgar [v 31] and Deborah.

"Has not Jehovah gone out before you? ... Jehovah destroyed Sisera ..." [4:14-15], Deborah together with Barak defeats Sisera with his "900 chariots of iron", while Sisera is given the ultimate disgrace for a warrior, to be killed by a 'housewife' Jael [v 21; see 9:54].

Gideon

Again Israel refuses to obey, so Jehovah "gave them away", this time to Midian, an old enemy [6:1], who saps their strength by constant raids and demands. Israel cries out for a deliverer but gets a prophet instead (at first), who calls them back to Covenant (to true repentance) [vv 7-10].

Then as Abraham and Moses were called, so is Gideon: "Jehovah is with you, mighty warrior!" [6:12]. Is this some bad joke – 'Right, and where is Jehovah now? ... and who am I to do this?' Jehovah insists, "I am with you!" [v 16]. "Then do for me an *'OTH* (SIGN)" [6:17] is Gideon's reply. When his courtesy meal is consumed *by fire* and the stranger disappears [v 20-21], he realizes this is Jehovah's messenger and fears for his Life[155], but is reassured, "Peace to you" [v 23].

His first step is not heroism on the battlefield, but confrontation of sin. By Jehovah's command, 'bold' Gideon by night destroys the Baal worship items and erects an altar *solely* to Jehovah [6:25-27], which enrages his fellow Israelites. However his father stands square against them: "Will you plead for Baal? Will you save him? He who pleads for him shall be put to death; if he is a god, let him contend for himself!" [v 31]

The call to repentance works. Transformed from cowering Israelites who worship idols [6:2-6], Gideon's fellow tribesmen follow Jehovah and Gideon against a foe who has beaten them all along [v 34]. Yet *Gideon* could not believe the LORD would actually use *HIM*, and so comes the 'fleece test,' in which Jehovah accommodates him [vv 36-40].

"Lest Israel glorify itself against Me, saying, 'My own hand has saved me'", of the 32,000 which answer the call [7:4], 99.1 out of every 100 soldiers are sent home, leaving only 300 against 135,000 [7:12; 8:10]. Faced with his handful against so many, Gideon's apprehension is anticipated; Jehovah invites His "mighty warrior" to visit the enemy camp and listen. To Gideon's credit, he and his page go alone and come back with an earful: "This is nothing but the sword of Gideon ... a man of Israel; God has given Midian and all the army into his hand" [v 14].

Near midnight, suddenly the Midianite camp is surrounded by torches, trumpets and shouting; in terror and in disorientation, Israel's Covenant-Partner "set every man's sword against his companion" [7:20, 22]. After capturing the two Midian kings, Gideon, although unwillingly, assumes the role of *GO'EL* in balancing the Blood-debt of his 'family' by executing the kings [8:18-21].

Such success makes Israel hunger for a king more tangible than Jehovah, and Gideon is their best candidate. But for him the position is already filled: "Jehovah shall rule over you" [8:22-23]. Later, by intrigue and murder, his son Abimelech ("Father of a King") is made king over Shechem to disastrous results for both [9:7-56]. Of the spoils of war, Gideon keeps only the (nose)-rings for himself, out of which he makes a golden ephod – a future stumbling block to him and his family, as well as for Israel [8:27].

Jephthah and Samson

Again Israel falls spiritually, adding gods from the surrounding nations, and again Jehovah "sold them." Again they come to the LORD with the repentance of convenience, but this time He is not buying: 'Go and cry to the gods you have chosen – It's their job to save you in the time of distress' [10:14]. In response the People clean up their act and Jehovah becomes sympathetic toward them [v 16].

His chosen deliverer, Jephthah, is an outcast, a prostitute's son rejected by his kin, the leader of pirates/hoodlums [11:1-3]. But when battle looms, suddenly everyone appreciates the man they know he is, and later agree he should remain their leader [v 10]. Despite not being allowed to participate in the major festivals [Deuteronomy 23:2], Jephthah has a remarkably focused faith on Jehovah alone [v 11], which is strengthened [v 29].

Unfortunately, he attempts to persuade Jehovah by means of a vow[156] [11:30-31, 34-39] – but the LORD does not need to be *convinced* to save His

People. Who knows what he expected would "come out the doors of my house to meet me when I return" [v 31]. Sadly, it is his only child, his daughter.[157]

Soon enough Israel is again running down 'the road to trouble.' Anticipating Israel's future freedom from the Philistines, through an "Angel"[158], Jehovah promises Manoah and his wife a boy, a special deliverer who will be a Nazarite[159] for his whole Life, even from the womb [chapter 13].

A 'fun-loving' playboy, Samson's great strength does not reduce his great weaknesses: women and vanity. Despite the command not to intermarry [Exodus 34:15-16], Samson insists to his father: 'Get this Philistine woman for me, for she is pleasing *in my own eyes*' [14:3]. Still, Jehovah can use even man's rebellion to accomplish His purposes and allows this opportunity to set the stage for a weakening of the Philistines.

Samson's vanity in his strength is the basis of his riddle [14:14], which initiates a chain of death and destruction. Brave Judah is willing to sacrifice Jehovah's deliverer for the sake of peace, but neither Jehovah nor Samson are finished yet, providing yet another rout of the Philistines [15:14-19]. His continued fascination with forbidden (Philistine) women seems contrived to toy with his enemies [16:1-3]; however, Delilah plays the better game.

"Sporting" with her, he reveals that if his *seven/oath* locks of hair[160] [16:13] were shaved off, it would break the Nazarite vow (and Covenant); the pipeline to Jehovah would be cut and he would lose his strength [vv 17-19]. Now *he* becomes the "sport" of the Philistines [16:23-25], but without the distractions he could pray: "O Lord Jehovah, remember me, I pray, and strengthen me, I pray, this time only, O God, let me be avenged" [16:28] – I shall be *GO'EL* for my two eyes. With the death of the Philistine elite, Samson creates more havoc than in all the rest of his Life.

"What Has Light To Do With Darkness?" [II Corinthians 7:14-16]

"I have wholly consecrated my silver *to Jehovah* for my son to make a carved image, a molded idol" [17:3]. The terrible sin Israel committed with the Golden Calf is to be repeated: this is not just an idol, but an idol named Jehovah! It is alongside a houseful of *"TERAPHIM"* (household gods), an ephod, and a consecrated "son" (a Levite) as priest [vv 5,10-13]. "Now I know that Jehovah will do me good ..." [v 13] – won't Jehovah be so thrilled with me!

Some Danites want a new place to settle and their spies recognize the priest. After settling in, the Danites steal the gods, the ephod, and the priest [18:17-20] and become comfortable with their acquired idol worship [vv 30-31].

In Gibeah another situation ends in a civil war. In the wilderness' merciless conditions, hospitality is more than friendliness and the lack of hospitality could end up as manslaughter. So when an Israelite couple stop overnight in this Israelite town and a scene reminiscent of Sodom and Gomorrah [Genesis 19:1-11] occurs (rowdies wanted to "know" the travelers), this event is viewed with horror. It is inexcusable and calls for drastic action. The man will be *GO'EL* for his family, but Israel will also be *GO'EL* in regard to its own and Jehovah's honor [20:6,8-11].

Refusing to give up those responsible, the tribe of Benjamin implicitly condones their activity [20:12-13]. But Israel is following Jehovah, and in the third battle, with a better strategy, "Jehovah struck Benjamin before Israel" [20:35]. Benjamin is left with only 600 men, all without family or homes [v 47]. Since Israel has vowed that no daughter of theirs would marry a Benjaminite, if Jehovah's law of no intermarriage with the nations is obeyed, this tribe would become extinct and Israel would no longer be Israel [21:1-4].

However, since Israel has been *GO'EL* for its and Jehovah's honor, whoever had rejected this responsibility is to die [v 5]. It is discovered that Jabesh-Gilead could not have been bothered with such gross sin in the midst of Israel. From the destruction of that city, 400 virgin women are found for the Benjaminites [21:8-13]. The remaining 200 would be *seized* from the girls at Shiloh, so that it is not a 'giving' of their daughters to Benjamin.

B. A King! A King!

Samuel – I Samuel

A Nazarite for Life

Hannah, childless and distraught, "vowed a vow" for a son, "I will give him to Jehovah all his Life, and no razor shall go upon his head" [I,1:11]. High Priest Eli blesses her [v 17] and so does Jehovah: Samuel is born. Hannah brings the young boy to *the Lord's House* as promised [vv 20-28], and then erupts into praise of the LORD for lifting up the empty, the despised, and the helpless [2:1-10]. "The child served Jehovah before Eli" [I,2:11] and "grew up with Jehovah" [v 21] gaining "stature and favor both with Jehovah and with men" [v 26].

Eli

By contrast, Eli's sons abuse the priesthood, "despised Jehovah's offering" [I,2:12-17] and "lay with the women who served at *the Tent of Meeting's* door" [v 22]. Despite warning them that a priest deliberately sinning has no mediator [vv 23-25], Eli keeps them in office and is himself warned of Jehovah's wrath [vv 27-36]: "why do you kick at My sacrifice ... and honor your sons above Me?" [vv 29-30]. Broken Covenant will 'break' his family, the *'OTH* [SIGN] being that the two sons will die on the same day [v 34]. Then Jehovah will "raise up a faithful priest, who shall do all which is in My Heart and in My Soul/Life", and "walk before My anointed forever" [I,2:35].

Samuel, Meet Jehovah

One night Jehovah calls young Samuel, who answers as Eli instructed, "Speak, O Jehovah; Your servant hears" [I,3:9-10]. Thus begins an era in which "the Word of Jehovah" is as significant a part of Israel's Life as it had been with Moses, and Jehovah "let none of [Samuel's] words fall to the ground [unfulfilled]" [v 19]. This first message is distasteful, pried from young Samuel only by Eli's curse "God do so to you – and more – if you hide anything" [I,3:17]. The time of warning is over; Eli's judgment, based on "the iniquity of which he was aware" [v 13], will have no mercy, not "by sacrifice nor by offering forever" [v 14]. Eli does not resist Jehovah's judgment, but quietly accepts it [v 18].

"Ichabod"

As if it were a 'good luck charm' to compel the presence of "Jehovah of hosts, dwelling between the cherubim", *the Ark of Covenant* is brought into battle with Eli's two sons as its guardian/bearers [I,4:3-4]. But Jehovah will not be manipulated. The battle is lost and the sons killed as promised [v 11; see 2:24]. What kills Eli, though, is that *the Ark* is captured [vv 17-18]. The birth of Ichabod ("Where is the Glory?") pictures the reality: Covenant is in shambles, therefore Jehovah's goodness, HESED, and compassion – *the Glory* – "had gone into captivity from Israel" [vv 19-22].

But *Jehovah* is not defeated! That the 'god' Dagon has not bested Jehovah is clear when the idol is found in the position of submission to *the Ark* [I,5:3]. The next day, the same thing occurs, however now its head and *"palms of the hands"* lay separate [v 4]. But rather than acknowledge the message [6:6], the Philistines remove the object [5:10-12] that brings them such discomfort [vv 6, 9] and upsets their religion [v 7].

How they send it back proves that Jehovah's 'Hand' has humiliated their 'god' [I,6:2, 9, 12]. The unguided, never-yoke-broken, recently-calved cows go directly to the Levite town of Beit Shemesh, who delightedly respond with *Whole Burnt Offerings* and sacrifices [vv 14-15]. But there is no room for indifference around Jehovah – "Who can stand before Jehovah, this holy God?" – as curiosity kills *seventy* who look inside *the Ark* [v 19-21].

Israel repents as Samuel calls them back to Jehovah [I,7:1-6], which upsets the Philistines. Firmly resolved but war-shy Israel nervously gathers at Mizpah [vv 6-8] and pours out water (see II,14:14 ; perhaps as a stand-in for Blood, or for 'Living Water'?). Samuel offers a *"whole"* Whole Burnt Offering[161] possibly emphasizing *complete* surrender to their Covenant-Partner, and the LORD so terrifies the Philistines that Israel simply mows them down [vv 10-11]. The Philistines fade into the background, because "Jehovah's Hand was against the Philistines all Samuel's days" [v 13]. The memorial-stone for the victory is aptly named "Ebenezer ['Stone of the Help'] ... So far has Jehovah helped us" [v 12], a contrast to the Ebenezer of chapter 4:1.

Saul – I Samuel

"A King! A King!"

Wisely, Israel does not want Samuel's sons to lead them, since the sons have gone the same way as Eli's [I,8:1-3]. But, rather than asking for Jehovah's opinion, they want 'what everybody else has' [vv 5, 20] – a KING, who would "go out before us and fight our battles" [v 20]. Jehovah reminds the upset Samuel that He their Covenant-Partner is the One rejected – which is quite in character for Israel [vv 6-9].

Do they know what they ask for? The king, unlike the humble prophet/judge, will care more for his own pomp and majesty, adding taxation, conscription, and forced labor, mostly for his and his courtiers' enjoyment and comfort [vv 10-18]. And even if the king were as righteous and just as Samuel, what guarantees that his sons would be the same? Israel will be stuck with them. But the People are determined to have their king [I,8:19].

Saul - What Could Have Been

From once decimated Benjamin comes Saul [I,9:21]. Searching for donkeys [vv 3-5], he returns anointed as king.[162] Jehovah, although rejected, maintains *HESED*/Covenant care for His People [v 16; 10:7]: the use of holy oil [10:1] declares this as no mere political office but that accountability and protection go right to Jehovah of Covenant. Three 'OTHs (SIGNs – I,10:7, 9) confirm Samuel's action, but most of all, Saul has a "new heart" [v 9] and becomes a "new man" under the Holy Spirit's power [v 6].

Although rejected as King and Savior, Jehovah proves His involvement through a lottery indicating Saul as king [I,10:17-24], deliberately squelching party politics (no campaign ads!!). The People reply by acclamation. Samuel defines the kingdom's justice/rule (Israel's 'constitution') and sets it before the LORD [v 25]. Some still rebel: "How can this one save us!?" [v 27]. The answer lies not in Saul but in Jehovah Who "delivered Israel" [I,11:13].

Jabesh-Gilead, rebellious in Judges 21, is willing to compromise itself by cutting a treaty-'Covenant' with an old oppressor, the Ammonites [see Judges 11]. But this 'Covenant' would be cut by destroying the right eye of every man in the city – a move designed to specifically disgrace Israel, not to accomplish the equality of Blood-Covenant.

When Jehovah utterly defeats Ammon, Saul's kingship is affirmed by anointing, by lot, and by victory. Some wish to drive the point home by annihilating all rebellious Israelites, however King Saul intervenes – Jehovah's victory over His enemies will not be marred by an inquisition [I,11:12-13]. Samuel's response is to allow everyone a second chance at Gilgal "to renew the kingdom there" [vv 14-15].

"He Must Increase, I Must Decrease" *[John 3:30]* – *I Samuel*

In a modesty matching John the Baptist's [John 3:27-30], Samuel hands over the limelight to Saul [I,12:1-2]. But before stepping back, he challenges interpretations of his ministry. Has he been greedy or improper? Israel affirms his honesty and truthfulness, which Samuel translates into an oath before Jehovah [v 5].

Therefore without selfish motive, Samuel identifies again Israel's spirit of rejection which saturated their desire for a king [I,12:6-12]. Their Covenant-Partner has always wonderfully protected and delivered them, but they reject this relationship, desiring instead the lesser connection to a human king. Well, they have their king – now what? Their individual and communal obligations of Covenant have not changed a bit, and, for the sake of discipline, Jehovah displays His dissatisfaction over Israel's undiminished leanings toward rebellion [vv 13-17].

Like the teenage beer party that is great fun until someone is killed in a drunken accident, Israel's lark after a king is sobered by the LORD's anger at their rebellion [I,12:18-19]. Yet in *HESED* and Covenant, He ("His great Name" – v 22) will not abandon *His* People, and the Covenant-Blood flowing within compels Samuel never to cease praying for this People [vv 20-23]. Yet, Israel plays close to the edge of destruction [vv 24-25].

"What Have You Done?" – *I Samuel 13:11*

Facing an impressive Philistine horde and an Israelite army melting away in fear, Saul decides to offer sacrifices himself rather than wait for slowpoke Samuel [I,13:8-10]. His defense is "I forced myself" [v 12] – with no hint of repentance for his disregard of Jehovah's prophet. Unimpressed, Samuel declares that the kingdom will go to "a man according to [Jehovah's] own Heart" [I,13:14].

Meanwhile Saul's son, Jonathan, and his armor-bearer attack the Michmash outpost [I,13:15-16, 19-23] – but what are two against so many? However Jonathan understands Covenant: "we will cross over to these *uncircumcised*; perhaps Jehovah will work for us, for it is not difficult for Jehovah to save by many or by a few" [14:6]. He then seeks an *'OTH* to show that the mighty Covenant-Warrior, Jehovah, has "given them into our hands" [v 10] – which is provided [v 12]. Indeed, the two of them are responsible for twenty dead.

But the Covenant-Partner is not finished: "The earth trembled, for it is a shaking of God" [I,14:15]. From then on, the battle is, as often with Jehovah, one where the enemy destroys himself and all Israel has to do is mop up [vv 19-23]. Throwing aside consultation with the LORD [vv 18-19], perhaps attempting to force Jehovah and Israel into a quick victory, Saul rashly has the People vow to eat nothing until the day is finished – which severely weakens his own army so that they cannot fully destroy the Philistines [vv 24-32].

By evening the People give in to hunger and kill and eat livestock "with the Blood" [I,14:32]. When Saul discovers this "sin against Jehovah", he arranges so that the slaughter will be done properly with an altar built "to Jehovah" [v 33-35]. But sin remains: an oath made before the LORD has been broken, *even though in ignorance* [vv 36-44]. When Jonathan is identified, Saul adds yet another oath, "God do so and more also" [v 44, also v 39]. When public opinion demands sparing Jonathan's Life "for he worked with God today", the broken oaths require a debt, "so the People ransomed (*PADAH*) Jonathan" [v 45].

The Test of Amelek – I Samuel

"You shall strike Amelek and devote utterly everything of his" [I,15:3] – but "Saul and the People had pity on Agag, and on the best of the flock, the oxen, ... and the lambs, and all which is good" [v 9]. The sin of Achan is repeated and condemned: "I have repented[163] that I caused Saul to reign as king" [v 11]. By preserving Amelek, Saul destroys his second chance: despite his 'good intentions' of saving these things 'for sacrifice,' he has placed his ideas above Jehovah's command.

"You rejected ... He rejected ..." [I,15:23, 26]: rebellion, witchcraft, "iniquity" ("nothingness": God's idea of idol-worship), "idolatry" ("*TERAPHIM*": 'good-luck charm' gods) are all ways to seek something – anything – other than the LORD. Although acknowledging his disobedience, Saul blames it on the People [v 24], thus indicating his own poor leadership. The torn prophet's robe signifies that Jehovah[164] has passed Saul by and that this judgment is final [vv 27-29]. Saul seems resigned as Samuel completes the work this king should have done [I,15:30-33].

Since the relationship of prophet and king is now ended, although it anguishes Samuel, Jehovah reveals that His plan, His Covenant will still move forward with a new king.

David – I & II Samuel

The LORD's Anointed

As when one gets nervous when a police car enters a highway, so why has Samuel come to Bethlehem [I,16:4]? No worries; he is just 'making rounds and offering a sacrifice there', however also covertly anointing the next king [vv 5,1]. Passing by the rest of Jesse's sons, David is brought in from the flock and is chosen and anointed.

However, Saul also knows that his days are numbered, his dynasty will end. Every day this weighs on him, increasing his suspicion, increasing his despondency, increasing his resistance to Jehovah's will, chased by a conscience that neither asks for nor has forgiveness.[165] 'By coincidence' David is picked to use his music to soothe Saul's troubled mind, thereby giving this future king an introduction to court life [I,16:14-23].

Goliath

Saul himself a physical 'giant,' especially backed by Covenant, could easily make mincemeat of Goliath, whose armor, though impressive and intimidating [I,17:4-7], is nothing against Jehovah. But Covenant no longer backs Saul, and this battle might just be the prophesied end to his reign. Since Israel does not know about this, all they see is his fear and therefore assume that Goliath is indeed an impossible foe [vv 11,24].

Bearing an ancient version of the 'care package' for his brothers[166], David comes and with the sharpness of innocent youth cuts right to the issue: if Covenant exists, then Goliath is nothing. By defying Israel, this "uncircumcised"/non-Covenant person defies GOD [I,17:26]. Rebuked for such 'impertinence', David replies, "Was it not a word?" [v 29] – a truism, perhaps a 'Word' from Jehovah, from one anointed (seemingly as a prophet?) and possibly tutored by Samuel.

David volunteers, "I'll fight this Philistine" [I,17:32]. How can David do such a thing, with neither training nor size to go toe-to-toe in armed combat [vv 33,38-39]? But David has faced frightening foes before, and "Jehovah, Who delivered me from the hand of the lion and the hand of the bear, shall deliver me from the hand of this Philistine" [v 37].

Goliath is astounded at this audacity, but David replies, "I come to you in the Name of Jehovah of hosts, the God of Israel's armies ... All this company will know that not by sword nor spear does Jehovah save, for to Jehovah belongs the battle, and He has given you into our hand" [I,17:45,47]. With one stone, one shot, despite such marvelous armor, the mighty Goliath is felled. Thus begins David's rise to fame as "a man of war", and initiates his fleeing for his Life, due to Saul's jealousy [I,18:5-11].

Jonathan

"Jonathan loved him as his own Soul/Life" and they cut Covenant [I,18:1,3; 20:17]. This son of King Saul presents a most interesting character, one which powerfully prefigures Jesus, the Son of *the* King, "full of grace and truth" (John 1:14). This Covenant is very one-sided: Jonathan gives everything: his clothing, armor, etc. – signs of royal approval; he stands against the wrath of his father, risking his Life in defense of David [I,20:30-31]; and then he gives his Life, permitting David to become king. Never once does he express jealousy, but is always willing to protect and advance his Covenant-partner [v 14-15,31; 23:16-18]. In return, all David can give is Covenant-friendship. Only long after Jonathan is gone can David return the kindnesses which had been given to him.

"On the Lam"

Saul's jealousy even kills priests who have unwittingly helped David escape [I, 21:1-9; 22:9-23]. David flees to Gath (Philistines!!), but finds no refuge there. When Keilah, an Israelite town, is threatened, despite his few numbers, he defends them, for *his* Refuge promised, "I will give the Philistines into your hand." Although he is their savior, the town would betray him, so David runs on, until Jehovah diverts Saul's attention [I,23:7-15,19-29].

Imagine his men's frustration when David has Saul right in hand yet will not kill "Jehovah's anointed" – not once, but twice! [I,24; 26]. But the LORD's Covenant is not based on convenience, nor to take matters into one's own hands, despite what opportunity shows up: "Jehovah forbid that I should do such a thing to my master, Jehovah's anointed, or stretch out my hand against him; for he is Jehovah's anointed" [I,24:6]; "Who can stretch out his hand against Jehovah's anointed and be guiltless? ... As Jehovah lives, Jehovah will strike him; or his day to die shall come; or he will go into battle and perish" [I,26:9-10].

The End of Saul – I & II Samuel

As he gets farther from the LORD, the more desperate Saul becomes, even to where he consults the occult for help – an outright breaking of Covenant. Yet, to reassure the woman's safety he swears [*SHABA*] "by Jehovah, 'As surely as Jehovah lives, no harm shall befall you'" [I,28:10]. Something is different about *this* séance when Samuel appears which causes the medium to recognize Saul [I,28:12] – perhaps the séance REALLY works for the first time because *God* steps in. It ends in a curse: Saul and his sons "will be with me [Samuel]. The LORD will also hand over the Israelite army to the Philistines" [v 19]. The next day, so it happens [I, 31; I Chronicles 10].

An Amalekite opportunist thinks he will be rewarded, not only by bringing Saul's crown and armband, but also by supposedly being the one who removes David's antagonist [II,1:1-16]. He has not counted on

David's spirituality nor Jehovah's morality. The 'gods' of the heathen support the winner, whoever he may be, but not so with Jehovah. Despite Saul's rebellion, reminiscent of the Image-of-God-authority invested in Adam still present after the first sin, "Jehovah's anointed" still carries the weight of God's authority and protection behind it – it is not to be discarded at one's whim and convenience.

David mourns the loss of "Jehovah's anointed" and of his Covenant-brother, Jonathan.

Winning the Kingdom

David is anointed again as Judah's king [II,2:4] but Israel is yet to be won at the cost of civil war [II,2:12-3:1], complete with a defector (Abner – II,3:6), treachery (Joab, perhaps thinking himself as a *GO'EL*, kills Abner in Blood revenge – II,3:18-30)[167], and a coup [II,4:5-8]. David's answer to the participants of the coup is the answer of a true *GO'EL* of the nation: "when wicked men have slain a righteous person in his own house on his bed, should I not therefore also require his Blood at your hand, and consume you from the earth?" [II,4:11]

Rather than gloating over his enemies, his reaction at the deaths of Saul and Jonathan, the execution of Saul's "killer", his reaction to the deaths of Abner and Ishbosheth (Israel's 'king'), and the execution of the coup participants indicate David's humility and bring healing to Israel. They are now ready to accept him as king over all the Covenant Land [II,5:1-5; I Chronicles 11:1-3], so the elders and David cut Covenant with each other.

If this is truly Covenant, then it brings an interesting dimension to kingship, since he does not see himself as the People's superior, lording it over them, but rather standing at an eye-to-eye level with them, in keeping with the shepherd image [II, 5:2] in Deuteronomy 17:20.

Jerusalem is finally captured and made Israel's capital, while David "went on and became great, and Jehovah, the God of hosts, was with him" [II,5:10; I Chronicles 11:4-9] – as demonstrated by the double defeat of the

Philistines: the first being where "Jehovah had broken through on my enemies" [v 20; I Chronicles 14:8-12], the second being when the ambush waited for "the sound of marching/stepping in the tops of the weeping trees ... for God shall go out before you to strike the Philistine army' " [vv 23-24; I Chronicles 14:14-15].

A Home and a House

The celebration of bringing *the Ark of Covenant* to its permanent home (Jerusalem) is marred by the death of Uzzah, who touches *the Ark* to steady it. But Jehovah has not withdrawn His Covenant *HESED*, as the blessing on Obed-edom demonstrates [II,6:11; I Chronicles 13:13-14]. As *the Ark* is brought into the city according to Jehovah's commanded procedure [I Chronicles 15:1-15], it is a time for praise [I Chronicles 16:1-36; see Psalms 105,106] and for *Whole Burnt Offerings* and *Peace Offerings* [vv 13,17-18] – since Jehovah renews His relationship to the nation, it is fitting to dedicate oneself and experience communion/peace with Him.[168]

However, Jehovah's *Ark* does not even have a "house" like David has [II,7:2; see I Chronicles 17]; yet that does not bother Israel's Covenant-Partner, Who "walked up and down among all Israel" [v 7]. Instead, having taken David from the shepherd's homelessness, He will now build *him* a "house" (a dynasty with a High Point, the Messiah) [vv 8, 11-13, 16]. His offspring will build Jehovah's house, one to whom "I will be His Father, and he shall be My son" [v 14]. "David came in and sat before Jehovah" [v 18] – what a Covenant-comfortableness with the universe's Creator! His psalm is of overwhelmed gratitude echoing with Covenant themes [vv 18-29].

The following chapters describe how Covenant reaches a sort of climax, as "Jehovah gave David victory wherever he went" [II,8:6, 14] – even over the much-feared chariots, victory over treachery and malice [II,8:3-13; II,10; I Chronicles 18:3-13; 19], and victory through others' appreciation [II,8:9-10; I Chronicles 18:9-10]. In response, David dedicates the spoils of war to the LORD, to be used for the building of *the Temple* he would never see.

Covenant Obligations

In a lull after settling the country and fighting foes, David still has Covenant commitments both with Jehovah and with Jonathan [See I,20:14-16,42]. A search for Saul's household "that I may show him *HESED* because of Jonathan ... that I may show the *HESED* of God to him" [II, 9:1, 3], turns up a living son to Jonathan, Mephibosheth, whom David treats as his own, so that he "ate continually at the king's table" [vv 11,13]. This is dangerous because David exposes himself to potential treachery by allowing a former dynasty access to the throne – but of such are Covenant's risks! Indeed, Mephibosheth *is* involved in a conspiracy, yet David will only exile him, not have him executed – of such is Covenant's commitment!

Great Faith Falters, "But There is Forgiveness with Thee" *[Psalm 130:4]*

Not even God's beloved saints are free of the need of a Savior. David, whom in war "Jehovah preserved wherever [he] went" [I Chronicles 18:6, 13], in the season "when kings went to war" [II, 11:1; I Chronicles 20:1], stays home. He is distracted, perhaps more by his success and power than by the pretty woman, and he sinks into a most sordid sin: adultery with Bathsheba ("Daughter of the *Oath/Seven*") and the murder of her husband, "a mighty one" – one of David's faithful elite [II,23:39; I Chronicles 11:41].

Most of all, he also has broken Covenant with Jehovah and the People. The once strengthening closeness of his Covenant-Partner is gone; yet how could David show any remorse without revealing to the kingdom what he has done? While he lives empty of God, in the quagmire of sin and guilt, the child is born [II, 11:27].

Jehovah does not give up on David: as He came to restore communion with Adam and Eve, so He sends Nathan to restore David to

Covenant. In response to Nathan's parable, David declares, "the man who has done this is a 'son of death'" [II,12:5]. Imagine his surprise to hear Nathan's reply, "YOU are that man!" [v 7]. David responds, probably with relief, by confessing, "I have sinned against Jehovah" [II,12:13].

His Covenant-Partner would not have withheld blessings, so how utterly unnecessary all this has been! [II, 2:8]. Therefore, as Adam and Eve's sin still continues in its effects, so also David's sin dogs his family: immorality (Amnon's rape of Tamar – II,13:), rebellion (Absalom – II,15-18), death, and dishonor would mark David's family – he really will be "a son of death" – worthy of death, the penalty for adultery [Leviticus 20:10].

"Jehovah has put away your sin" [II, 12:13] – an immediate demonstration of Jehovah's *HESED*/mercy. Yet now "the enemies of Jehovah" [v 14] have opportunity to ridicule God based on the hypocrisy of His People. As *GO'EL*, Jehovah will balance the loss of Blood, but rather than David, the child will die, despite David's prayer [v 18]. In humility, David acknowledges the supremacy of the Lord's ways. In forgiveness, a new son is born, whom Jehovah loves: Solomon ("peaceful" – peace with Jehovah?), or Jedidiah ("beloved of Jehovah") [vv 24-25].

David's Psalm in II Samuel 22 has undertones of the Noahic flood as he recounts his Covenant-Partner's saving ability, although it may also refer to something more recent. See how Jehovah bends the universe's powers for His Covenant-partners' sake! His final words in chapter 23 heavily emphasize Covenant in which nothing is or will be withheld from one who remains in Covenant (even if the road is at times a bit rocky).

The *GO'EL* concept also has a big part in Absalom's restoration [II Samuel 14] after murdering Amnon for the rape of his sister Tamar [12:23-38]. To get Absalom reinstated, Joab has a woman tell the story of her two 'sons,' one who killed the other in manslaughter. Now Blood-balancing is demanded, which would destroy this 'widowed mother's' only heir. As king, David forbids the *GO'EL*-of-Blood from taking any more action [II Samuel 14:11]. Verse 14 emphasizes the inability to recover lost Life, but also the Lord's Blood-balancing through mercy and redemption. The woman then says in effect, 'If Jehovah shows mercy, and you would show mercy to me, why not to your own family?' Trapped in this logic, David allows Absalom to come home, but only under a sort of house arrest. Since Absalom is not repentant, David's forgiveness actually sets the stage for Absalom's later rebellion.

The Census and the LORD's House – II Samuel

God allows [II,24:1] and Satan incites [I Chronicles 21:1] David to number his fighting men. Since no threat compels this, it is more like a miser counting his money – he is treasuring and glorifying the wrong thing. He is so determined that not even his military advisors can dissuade him [II,24:3]. Yet David's conscience pulls the reins in on him, and he confesses before the LORD [v 10]. Given the choice, David prefers to be punished directly from the Hand of his LORD, which means three days of plague (echoes of Israel's 40 years of wandering).

But *Jehovah*'s heart is torn and when the three days are ended, He cries out "Enough!" [II,24:16; I Chronicles 21:15].[169] The angel stops at the threshing floor of Araunah, where David is commanded to build an altar [II,24: 18-19]. Although the land is freely offered to him, David defines an essential point about sacrifice: "I will not offer to Jehovah what is yours, nor offer a *Burnt Offering* which costs nothing" [I Chronicles 21:24]. The heart of the LORD is expressed when He Himself sends fire from heaven to light the sacrifice which ends the episode [v 26].

This now sanctified place is where Solomon's Temple will be built [I Chronicles 22:1]. Because of Blood shed in the wars and in adultery, David has dealt too much with death for him to build the house for "Jehovah the God", a house signifying the restoration of Life [v 8]. Like Moses at least seeing the Covenant Land from afar, so David could at least begin the preparations and planning for the great Temple [v 5;28:11-19].

Now, all which is left is that Solomon should "be strong and courageous, and act; do not fear nor be afraid, for Jehovah God, my God, is with you; He will not fail you nor forsake you until you have finished all the work of service for the house of God" [I,28:20]. Turning to Israel, they respond with joy, "because with a whole[170] heart they offered willingly to Jehovah" [I,29:9].

Solomon

The LORD's Anointed – *I Kings*

David's son Adonijah moves to usurp the throne, but the prophet Nathan and Bathsheba collaborate to warn David, who responds by having Solomon anointed as king [I,1:1-53]. Then David gives his parting advice to his son, encouraging him to stay true to Covenant [2:2-3], so that the promises in Covenant will continue, especially in that a son of David should always occupy the throne of Israel [v 4].

The Course is Set, With Wisdom and Knowledge from Jehovah

Jehovah asks His Covenant-partner what he would like as a coronation present. Solomon already displays great wisdom by asking for "a hearing[171] heart" [I,3:9] and for "wisdom and knowledge" [I Chronicles 1:10] to equip him for his task. The LORD responds by giving him an extraordinary wisdom (yet this renowned wise man would also prove to be one of the most foolish), along with what he had not asked for. The uncommon wisdom is acutely demonstrated in the famous story of the two mothers and their babies [I Kings 3:16-28] and in the visit of the Queen of Sheba [*Oath/Seven* – I,10:1-13; II Chronicles 9:1-12].

The Temple At Last! – *I Kings*

In his fourth year Solomon begins *the Temple* of which David had dreamed – a house befitting the eternal Covenant-Partner [I,5-7; II Chronicles 2-4]. He locates *the Temple* on Mount Moriah [II Chronicles 3:1], where perhaps "in the Land of Moriah" Abraham went to sacrifice Isaac [Genesis 22:2]. During the building program, Jehovah reaffirms His

Covenant-presence, reminding Solomon and Israel to remain faithful [I,6:11-13].

The Temple dedication [I,8:2] occurs during the month of *the Festival of Trumpets, the Day of Atonement* and *the Festival of Tabernacles*. Since the People are dismissed on the 23rd of the month, if the dedication and *the Festival of Tabernacles* each have their own seven-day celebration, then the dedication begins on *the Day of Atonement* and ends with the Sacred Assembly at the end of *the Festival of Tabernacles* [II Chronicles 7:8-10]. Having the dedication connected with these two feasts is suggestive, especially in the sense that now *the Ark of Covenant* with its *Atonement Cover* has a permanent home, all Israel is finally 'home' as well.

In response to the *Whole Burnt Offerings* (the 'wholly giving of self') and the *Peace/Fellowship Offerings* (communion with Jehovah Who dwells among us) [I,8:62-64], the LORD displays the cloud of Glory [vv 10-11] reminiscent of the Exodus [Exodus 18:21-22; 19:18; 40:34], to which another reference is made in regard to the tablets of the *TORAH* "when Jehovah cut Covenant with Israel" [v 9].

Throughout the construction and now in the dedication, Solomon refers to "the Name" of the LORD [for example, I, 8:16, 17, 18, 29, 43, ...], the special Covenant Name identified at Moses' call.[172] His plea [vv 33-40, 46-50; II Chronicles 6:24-31, 36-39] is that "God be true though every man be a liar" [Romans 3:4], because THIS God "keeps Covenant and *HESED*/steadfast Love" [v 23; II Chronicles 6:14]; "He will not forsake us nor leave us" [v 57]. 'LORD, also listen to all who come because they have heard of "Your great Name, Your strong Hand and Your outstretched Arm"' [v 42]. Fire comes down and consumes the sacrifices [I Chronicles 7:1-3], just like when *the Tent of Meeting* had been dedicated [Leviticus 9:24].

Again Jehovah appears to Solomon to declare that *the Temple* is accepted, "My eyes and My heart shall be there forever" [I,9:3] and "If My People, who have taken My Name upon themselves, are humbled and pray, who seek My face and turn back from evil ways, I shall hear from

Heaven, I will forgive their sin and heal their land" [II Chronicles 7:14]. However, should Israel ignore and disgrace Covenant then the curses will come: "this House which I have sanctified for My Name I shall cast away from before My face" [II Chronicles 7:20]; "Israel shall be a proverb and a sneer among all peoples ... everyone passing by [this House] shall be astonished ... 'Why has Jehovah done this to this land and to this house?'" [vv 7-8].

The Foolishness of the Wise – I Kings

Despite his great wisdom through which he could see the truths of human nature, how curiously blind Solomon is spiritually. In the culture of that day, mimicking Covenant's *'OTH* as when Abraham gave Abimelech *seven/oath* sheep as the 'monument' of their Covenant, often treaties between nations are sealed by one king giving a daughter to the other in marriage, implying that as long as the marriage lasts, the treaty lives also. But marriages to 'heathens' are expressly forbidden [Exodus 34:14-16] since they will "turn his heart aside," and these many wives [Deuteronomy 17:17] do exactly that [I,11:3-8]: Solomon even builds temples for and sacrifices to his wives' gods. Covenant is so soon broken.

Jehovah essentially states, 'I even warned him in person, twice!' But Solomon's conscience is nothing like David's. Therefore the Kingdom will be split as were Solomon's spiritual loyalties [I, 11:9-13]: ten tribes will follow Jeroboam [vv 26-43]. Possibly Ecclesiastes is written in his last days, where Solomon's spiritual wisdom finally catches up with him and he realizes the emptiness of anything other than having the LORD's approval.

The Split Kingdom

Rebellion (that is, 'Transgression') and "the Sin of Jeroboam" – I Kings

Solomon's rebellion against God's law has taken its toll: the seeds for revolt are sown, perhaps because of his emphasis on wealth, and/or perhaps because many resisted the compelled support for heathen worship systems. Indeed there is the feeling of being overburdened [I,12:4; II Chronicles 10:4], perhaps by the taxes and the conscription (the 'draft') necessary for erecting Solomon's various buildings and heathen temples. Son Rehoboam's lack of wisdom creates the fulfillment of God's promise to split the kingdom [I,12:15-16; II Chronicles 10:15]. Only Jehovah's intervention prevents a civil war [v 24; II Chronicles 11:1-4].

The ten tribes ("Israel")'s King Jeroboam begins "Jeroboam's Sin" which dogs the heels of every subsequent 'northern' king: to prevent Israel from worshipping at Jerusalem (the only place where the LORD "placed His Name," where Covenant could be renewed) which risks the possibility of all Israel being reunited, a heathen religion is created [I,12:26-30] with its own priests and calendar parodying God's feasts [vv 31-33; 13:33]. Meanwhile, the Levites and all who remain true to Jehovah migrate to Judah [II Chronicles 11:13-14, 16-17; 15:8-9].

A prophet declares that judgment is Jehovah's answer.[173] As Jeroboam points, commanding to seize the prophet, his hand withers, restored only by the prophet's prayer [I,13:1-7]. However, when the prophet himself disobeys the LORD's command, he also is judged [vv 8-32]. Jeroboam rejects all these warnings.

At the death of Jeroboam's son, God still counts Himself as tied to Israel in Covenant: "My People Israel" [I,14:8] and pronounces an extreme punishment upon every male, man and child of Jeroboam's family [vv 10-14]. Israel too will be judged because of their endorsement of Jeroboam's new religion, as well as augmenting it with the old Canaanite Asherah (nature idols, such as Ashtoreth, goddess of nature and reproduction) religion.

Meanwhile, the Fall of the South – *I Kings*

Rehoboam "reigned ... in Jerusalem, the city where Jehovah put His Name" [I,14:21-22] – HERE is the site GOD chose for His legitimate religion, yet Jehovah is not convenient to their desires [vv 23-24]. Judah's fall is either as rapid or faster than the northern kingdom's fall away from

Covenant – II Chronicles 11:17 emphasizes that the piety lasts only three years, and then the sin becomes so great that already by the fifth year Egypt overruns the southern kingdom (Judah and Jerusalem) [v 25-26; II Chronicles 12:1-9]. Rehoboam does repent but is left with a paltry substitute for the wealth and glory which once was the kingdom's [vv 27-28; II Chronicles 12:5-8].

His son, Abijam/Abijah carries on his father's foolishness ("his heart was not whole with Jehovah his God" – I,15:3), yet "for David's sake [Covenant!] Jehovah his God gave him a lamp in Jerusalem" [v 4]. Still the LORD will 'serve a purpose': Abijam/Abijah is quick to refer to Him in the appeal to the northern tribes to reunite and "not fight with Jehovah, the God of your fathers" [II Chronicles 13:4-12], and the LORD does not abandon them when "they depended on Jehovah" [v 18].

Yet the Spiritual Southern Cross Does Shine Through – I Kings

However, there are also courageous, faithful kings. The third king, Asa, "did what was right in Jehovah's eyes" [I,15:11] and whose "heart was whole with Jehovah all his days" [v 14]. When threatened by Ethiopia's overpowering force, Asa confidently turns to his Covenant-Partner: "There is none beside You to help between the great and him who has no strength" [II Chronicles 14:11].

After the victory, Jehovah admonishes faithfulness: "be strong and do not let your hands weaken, for there is a reward for your work" [II Chronicles 15:7] – which encourages Asa to redouble his efforts to be rid of the idols, etc. which the People have grown to accept. Of the plunder, they sacrifice *seven/oath* hundred oxen and *seven/oath* thousand sheep, and enter into Covenant "with all their heart and with all their Soul" [vv 12,15]. Asa even kicks out his own mother from the royal court [v 13; II Chronicles 14:2-4, 15:16-17] because of her idol worship. Yet "the 'high places' are not removed" [v 14] – a constant failing of many kings.

To break the northern king, Baasha,'s blockade [I,15:17-22; II Chronicles 16:1-6], Asa forgets Jehovah's personal stake in Covenant [II Chronicles 16:7-10]. Instead he looks to a human solution, a Covenant with Ben-Hadad of Syria: "[Remember] the Covenant between my father and your father! I send to you gold and silver – now break your Covenant with [the northern king]" [I,15:19; II Chronicles 16:3]. If "Covenants" between nations do not have the same depth and Blood-totality as the personal relationship has, does it mean that political expediency and money trump the horror of breaking Covenant? Or is it that the "older" of the two Covenants should have priority? Either way, Asa opens his kingdom to continual harassment by other nations. Despite his intention to be godly, Asa's pride makes him do very unfortunate things [II Chronicles 16:10].

If You Thought the South was a Problem, Just Try the North!

Jerusalem is Jehovah's favorite because there He has "placed His Name," yet both north and south are under the Covenant which reaches all the way back to Abraham. Therefore even in the north, the LORD is deeply concerned with its steep drift into idolatry. And although God could use a non-believer as His *GO'EL* [I,15:25-34] accomplishing His judgment against the house and sin of Jeroboam, yet Baasha himself falls under the same condemnation at the hand of Zimri and *his* short-lived reign [I,16:11-20].

The following dynasties are a hodge-podge of intrigues and coups, yet each one is rarely an improvement over the last. Repeatedly comes the refrain "the sin which he did, to cause Israel to sin," until the climax in faithlessness is reached when Ahab ascends the throne: "Ahab… did what was evil in Jehovah's eyes above all who were before him. It came to pass, as if it were merely a trifle that he walked in the sins of Jeroboam …, that he took a wife, Jezebel … of the Sidonians, and went and served Baal, and bowed himself to it" [I,16:30-31], and then goes on to child sacrifices [v 34].

Elijah – I Kings

Elijah is the North's primary prophet, raised up to counter Ahab's great evil. Immediately as the attention turns to him, the scene is one of judgment, a drought, and he is sent to the brook Kerith (from *KARATH* – as in 'cutting' a Covenant) to be supernaturally kept alive until the brook dries up [I,17:1-7]. Then he is sent to Zeraphath ('refinery') in the very heart of the Baal worship country from which Jezebel came, to a widow whom Jehovah has "commanded to feed him" [v 9]. Both she and Elijah are bewildered that her only son dies [vv 17-24] – are they not doing what the Lord commands? However, like the raising of Lazarus, Jehovah chooses the route of death in order to reveal something greater: now in no uncertain terms the widow understands just Who the God is that she is dealing with.

Why Do You Go On Limping?

After three years, Elijah confronts Ahab [I,18:17-18]. Gathering "Israel" (the North) at Mount Carmel, Elijah stages a challenge: "How long will you limp between two opinions? If Jehovah is God then follow Him, otherwise go chase after Baal!" [v 21]. Then to prove his point, he challenges the 450 prophets of Baal with the 400 prophets of the Asherah to prepare a sacrifice on their altar, but they cannot light the fire – only their god is to do that.

Sarcastically he taunts these prophets, 'perhaps your god is busy talking, or in the washroom, or on a trip, or even sleeping – yell louder!!' The prophets, seeking to attract Baal's attention and indicating their genuine earnestness, slash their bodies "until Blood flowed" [v 28]. But "there was no sound, no answer, *no one who cared*" [v 29].

Elijah takes twelve stones – one each for ALL of Israel's tribes (not just the northern ten), makes an altar "in Jehovah's Name" [vv 31-32], then drenches it three times [vv 33-35]. It just takes a simple prayer and fire descends on the altar which literally consumes everything, even the water. Israel's response is to proclaim from their knees, "Jehovah, He is THE

God!" [v39]. The false prophets are seized and executed at the river Kishon (whose root word means "snare, lure") and now finally the rains come.

I'm So Alone!

Queen Jezebel is not impressed. She threatens Elijah with the same thing which happened to her favorite prophets and he goes into a tailspin. Hiding out on a mountain, Jehovah asks why he is there and Elijah pours out his story: Israel has thoroughly disregarded Covenant and he is ineffective against it all – "I, I alone, am left" [I,19:10; see contrast in I,18:22]. Having the prophet stand out on the mountain, "Jehovah passed by" [I,19:11], yet He whose Glory is not based in power and majesty, but in kindness, goodness, mercy and Covenant, "was not found in" the ensuing windstorm, earthquake, and fire, but rather in the whisper.

There is work yet to be done – Covenant is still operating – there are still *seven/oath thousand*[174] totally faithful in Israel still to be ministered to, and Elijah is to prepare the way for three who will deliver Jehovah's judgment against the rebellious North: Hazael, an enemy of Israel [II,8:7-15]; Jehu, who will act as *GO'EL* and houseclean Israel (although not enough); and Elisha, who will take the mantel of Elijah.

Elisha is hard at work, plowing with the twelfth of twelve yoke of oxen (symbolic of Israel?) – yet, as the disciples would for Jesus, he leaves all for the LORD's work. Elijah on the other hand is not now retired – he still has five chapters and a few more kings to go. Rather it is like what one pastor told his intern, "Because you are here, it does not mean I will do less work, but rather now more work will get done."

King Ahab of the North

Ahab presents himself as very foolish. At times he seems to actually seek the LORD's will, and then will turn around and deliberately rebel; Jehovah on the other hand shows Himself extraordinarily merciful (*HESED!*) to one who so often spiritually endangers Israel of the North.

Ben-Hadad comes to abuse Ahab; yet despite facing an enormous army Ahab willingly follows a prophet's commands [I,20:13-21]. It is a call to repentance, "See, I give it into your hand today, and you will know that I am Jehovah" – the Covenant-Partner will exert His will. Round two, however, is fought to demonstrate that the Covenant-Partner of Israel is not some piddling little god, but rather the Creator of all things: "Because the Syrians have said, 'Jehovah is God of the hills and not God of the valleys'; therefore I deliver all this great multitude into your hand, and you will know that I am Jehovah!" [I,20:28]. Reminiscent of Jericho, a six days prelude leads to open battle on the *seventh/oath* day [v 29].

But then Ahab just cannot get it right. Instead of destroying the enemy of Israel, he *Covenants* with them [I,20:34]. The reaction of Jehovah is extreme. The penalty for the prophet's disobedience [vv 35-36] is severe because Jehovah demonstrates that His commands cannot be taken lightly. For this same reason, Ahab will experience the result of thinking that God can be so flippantly compromised.

Naboth's Vineyard

A little boy in a man's body is a sad and dangerous thing. King Ahab pulls a temper tantrum because he does not get what he wants [I,21:1-5]. At stake here is not just family heritage, but also this is the Covenant Land GOD gave to *each* family, never to be sold (remember "the Year of Jubilee"? [Leviticus 25:23; Numbers 36:7]). Ahab's argument is not just with Naboth, it is with Jehovah Himself.

Jezebel's solution is easy: accuse Naboth of blasphemy and treason [I,21:8], and the result is obvious [vv 13,14]. Now nothing stands in Ahab's way – except Elijah, who delivers a very unpleasant condemnation and prophecy [vv 21-24]. Ahab really does repent [I,21:27], and Jehovah demonstrates His nature by delaying the doom. One would think that the LORD would be so tired of Ahab's rebellions and sin that any gesture of repentance would make no difference. But being true to His Glory, Jehovah responds with *HESED* even to Ahab.

Ahab's Death – *I Kings*

The South's King Jehoshaphat comes to visit and is willing to go to war with Ahab [I,22:2-4; II Chronicles 18:1-3]. But Jehoshaphat wants to make sure the LORD agrees with them – which He does not, as the prophet Micaiah foretells [v 17; II Chronicles 18:16]. Still, Jehoshaphat agrees to be dressed out in his kingly garments, while Ahab makes himself look like a common soldier. Is putting himself in danger simply foolishness on Jehoshaphat's part or is he bound by a Covenant relationship? Yet despite Ahab's various ways of trying to thwart God, "a man drew his bow by chance...." [v 34; II Chronicles 18:33]. All which Jehovah has prophesied comes true.

Jehoshaphat of the South – *II Chronicles*

Asa's son, Jehoshaphat ("whom Jehovah judges), Jehovah approves of, "for he walked in David's earlier ways" and "Jehovah established the kingdom in his hand" [17:3,5]. In his third year he sets the nation to learn God's Word [vv 7-9], to which the Covenant-Partner responds with peace from the surrounding nations [vv 10-11]. Although not pleased at Jehoshaphat's assisting Ahab [19:2], the Covenant-Partner does not visit judgment against the king.

Meanwhile Jehoshaphat continues to be Jehovah's ambassador "from Beersheba to the hill country of Ephraim, and brought them back to Jehovah, the God of their fathers" [19:4]. Reflecting his Covenant-Partner's Life/Blood flowing through him, he instructs the judges to "judge not for man but for Jehovah" [vv 6-7], and to the leaders "so shall you do in the fear of Jehovah, faithfully and with a holy heart" to judge, in *GO'EL* language: "between Blood and Blood, between governance [*TORAH*] and commandment, statues and judgments" [vv 9-10].

But a faithful and earnest heart toward the LORD does not insulate him from the world's challenges: Syria attacks with a mighty multitude. Jehoshaphat's immediate response is to consult Judah's Covenant-Partner [20:3-4]. His prayer is wise, starting with praise – which not only glorifies

God but also re-orients the pray-ers' thinking and attitude [vv 6-9]. Then laying the problem before Jehovah, his claim is based on Covenant: "they repay us by coming to drive us out of Your possession, which You have caused us to possess" [v 11].

Little can match the majesty of Jehovah's answer: "You shall not fear nor be afraid before this great multitude, for the battle is not yours, but God's. Tomorrow, go down against them; ... You shall not fight in this: station yourselves; *stand and see* the salvation of Jehovah with you... do not be afraid nor fear..." [20:15-17]. Jehoshaphat responds with absolute confidence, encouraging the People to believe, even commissioning *singers* to precede the army.

"When they began to sing and praise," the Covenant-Partner "set ambushes" against Syria [20:22]. The enemy camp becomes a brawl in which each kills the other. Israel only has to gather up the spoils – apparently not a bad haul. Not only does Jehovah "cause Israel to rejoice over their enemies" [v 27], but also "the fear of God was upon all the nations of the land when they heard that Jehovah [the Covenant-Partner] had fought against the enemies of Israel" [v 29].

The Short Life of Ahaziah (North) – *II Kings*

Ahab's son Ahaziah follows his father and "provoked Jehovah the God of Israel" [I Kings 22:53]. Not long after ascending the throne he descends through a lattice from an upper room. Probably internally injured, he sends to Baalzebub ("husband of the fly") for word whether he would recover [II,1:2], but Jehovah replies through Elijah, "Is there not a God in Israel that you must ask of Baalzebub, god of Ekron?" [v 3]. Displeased with the message, Ahaziah sends the army after Elijah. After the first two detachments go out in a *blaze* of glory, Elijah is told to go with the very respectful third detachment [vv 9-15]. The message has not changed, and Ahaziah dies.

'Brother' Jehoram becomes king. He is a little better, having gotten rid of the Baal worship-objects. However "he clung to Jeroboam's sin, by which he made Israel to sin" [3:2-3] – in other words, he maintains a separate worship from what, where and how God had commanded.

Elijah, NOW It is Time to Go Home – *II Kings*

With almost a liturgical lilt, at places (Bethel, Jericho, and the Jordan) key to Covenant reaching all the way back to Abraham, there is point-counterpoint between Elijah and Elisha: "Stay here…" "As Jehovah lives, I will not leave you", with the refrain of the "sons of the prophets" in the background [2:1-7]. In an act that evokes Covenant memories of Israel leaving Egypt and then of entering the Covenant Land, Elijah and Elisha cross the Jordan into the wilderness.

"That I may have a double portion of your spirit" [II,2:9] – Elisha claims the firstborn's right of inheritance, not of earthly goods, but of the spiritual, in order to carry on the work of his "father"/mentor. It is not something bequeathed through a will – only Jehovah can give it, an element within Covenant. If Elisha witnesses Elijah's parting, then the LORD would so equip the successor with what he desires [v 10].

"My father, my father, the chariot of Israel and its horsemen!" [II,2:12] – a chariot and horses of fire separate the two and Elisha does watch Elijah disappear upward in a tornado(?). "Where is Jehovah, Elijah's God?" [v 14] – with Elijah's mantle, which has been left behind, crying out in grief, Elisha strikes the waters of the Jordan and again the river parts to allow him to cross. Jehovah has kept His Covenant.

Elisha

Elisha is Established as Prophet of Jehovah – *II Kings*

Through Elisha, Jehovah performs a series of miracles, establishing this prophet as indeed His spokesman: The first comes immediately [II, 2:19-22]: to heal "evil" water, which he does by using salt – the symbol of preservation and permanence. The second is the awesome warning that the office of prophet is not to be trivialized: forty-two children – a gang –

decide to make fun of this man of God and are 'consumed' in their ridicule [vv 23-25].

The next two miracles depict Elisha as *GO'EL*: in the miracle of the endless oil [II,4:1-7], fellow Israelites, of the "sons of the prophets", are redeemed from threatened slavery; in the next, the Bloodline of the Shunamite family is preserved twice, not only in the miraculous birth of a son (as per Abraham and Sarah) [vv 8-17], but also in a resurrection [vv 18-37]. More miracles follow: a terrible-tasting stew is transformed by adding flour [vv 38-41]; and "the People" are fed with only twelve loaves of bread, yet still have leftovers [vv 42-44].

After Such Righteousness, Such Treachery – II Chronicles

In the South, Jehoshaphat's son, Jehoram, may follow his father, but not in his footsteps. As soon as he is powerful enough, he murders all his brothers, as well as "leaders in Israel" [21:4]. His wife is "Ahab's daughter" and he follows Ahab's godlessness [v 6; II Kings 8:17-18].

God declares Himself as *GO'EL* for His People and for Jehoram's brothers' innocent Blood. Jehoram and his house are terribly punished [21:12-20] and he is given the unique honor (?) of the epitaph: "he departed to no one's regret" [v 20]. Still, "Jehovah would not destroy David's house, for the sake of the Covenant He cut with David..." [v 7; II Kings 8:19: "... since He promised him to give him a lamp to his seed for ever"].

Jehoram's oldest surviving son, Ahaziah, whose mother is Ahab's daughter, listens to the same counselors as his father, and so the spiritual climate of Judah does not change [22:1-5; II Kings 8:25-27].

Naaman Learns of Jehovah's Grace – II Kings

Naaman, a well-respected general "because by him Jehovah gave great victory to Aram," is also a leper [II,5:1]. In a celestial irony, Jehovah shows that mercy responds not to pride, power or money, not even to exclude an enemy of Israel, but springs entirely from grace. What is required of this leper is simple and without circus: a baptism, powerless by itself ('this little dinky river' [v 12]), but connected to God's promise will effect a miraculous cure.

It is too easy for Naaman. Let him prove his worth and he will be satisfied, or make God's requirements fit his sensibilities and he will be willing [vv 11-13], but to do something so ... so ordinary? Still is it really so much to ask? Naaman relents and experiences Jehovah's mercy – he has met the true God [vv 14-15].

Elisha refuses payment [II,5:15-16], the message being that God's grace is *grace* – fully and totally from out of *Jehovah*'s will and heart, definitely not by man's hand, not even by token payment. Gehazi, Elisha's servant, feels that just a *little* payment cannot hurt, but he receives more than he bargains for, receiving Naaman's leprosy as well [vv 20-27]. Jehovah does not fool around when it comes to describing His grace and mercy.

The Covenant-Partner's Sense of Humor – and Mercy – II Kings

The king of Aram wants to ambush the Israelite king, who always seems to know and is prepared [II,6:1ff]. Is there a traitor? No, Elisha is "telling the king of Israel the words which you speak in your bedroom" [v 12]. Elisha's servant is appalled – the Aram army surrounds the house to capture one man – until through Elisha's prayer he sees the Covenant-Partner's army [II,6:15-17]. Struck with "blindness" (perhaps unable to recognize their surroundings), the Aram army is led deep into enemy territory (to the capital of the North Kingdom, Damascus) and is given their "sight" back. The Israelite king is eager to demolish the Aram army, but Elisha maintains that they are to be fed and sent back to the Aram king [II,6:21-23], who leaves Israel alone after that.

Ben-Hadad's Invasion of the North – II Kings

Syria decides to conquer Israel, and in the midst of the siege, even bird droppings command a price as food [II,6:25]. When Israel's king discovers how people are reduced to cannibalism, he, in keeping with human nature, blames God (and his prophet, Elisha) for these results of Israel's rebellions [vv 25-31]. Although wearing sackcloth [v 30], the king impatiently demands and attempts to force Elisha's cooperation [vv 32-33].

Yet the astounding mercy of Israel's Covenant-Partner has a solution: by the same time the next day, food will be so plentiful that it will be sold extraordinarily cheaply [II,7:1]. "Impossible!" is the king's captain's retort, to which Elisha replies that he will see it but never get close to God's miracle [vv 2]. Using four unwanted castoffs (lepers), God reveals His 'impossible' solution: Syria thinks they hear a great army marching toward them and have fled, dropping everything on their way. Indeed, the resulting booty is as if the 'windows of heaven had opened,' and judgment also descends upon the unbelieving captain [vv 16-20].

A Pause for the HESED of Jehovah – II Kings

Within this time period, Elisha has told the woman whose son he has returned to Life to go into some other land because of the "famine" that is coming [II,8:1] – possibly Ben-Hadad's siege is part of that. At the end of the *seven/oath* years, she just 'happens' to appear before the Israelite king as he is reviewing Elisha's great deeds. Rather than having to convince the king to return her land, he is well prepared to do that, as well as to give her the benefit of everything the land produced while she was away [vv 3-6].

Hazael and Jehu – Jehovah's Word to Elijah Took Shape – II Kings

Hazael is sent to Elisha to find out whether Ben-Hadad will survive a particular illness [II,8:7-9]. Elisha's reply is that the illness will not threaten his life, but he will die anyway. Staring intently at Hazael until he is embarrassed, Elisha weeps at all the destructive and cruel things Hazael will do to Israel because he will be the next Syrian king [vv 11-13]. Upon Hazael's return, the prophecy begins [vv 14-15].

In the North, Elisha sends a "son of the prophets" to anoint Jehu as Israel's king and Jehovah's *GO'EL* against Ahab and Jezebel's house due to the slain prophets' Blood [II,9:1-10]. Acclaimed by fellow commanders, Jehu rises up against Joram/Jehoram (of the North) at Jezreel [vv 11-16]. Joram meets this commander at Naboth's vineyard, there to "balance the Blood" of Naboth's family as God had promised Ahab [vv 11-26]. Jehu is *GO'EL* also against the murderer, King Johoram (of the South), executing his son Ahaziah, visitor and close relative to Joram [II,9: 27-28; II Chronicles 22:5-9], and then later also executing the North's "royal princes" [10:13-14].

The aged Jezebel apparently thinks she might be temptress to Jehu, although also mockingly calling him a "Zimri." His response is simple: "throw her out of the window" [II,9:30-33]. After casually having lunch, Jehu and friends go back to bury Jezebel only to find that the dogs also had had lunch (on her) – as the LORD had promised [vv 34-37].

Jehu invites all the North's city councils to either fight for Ahab's house, or join him (which they wisely do) [II,10:1-5]. As a *GO'EL* for Israel ("Now know that nothing of Jehovah's Word shall fall to the ground, which Jehovah spoke against the house of Ahab" [v 10]; "Come... see my zeal for Jehovah" [v 16]), he demands the death of Ahab's descendants [vv 6-8], friends, and priests [v 11]. When "brothers" of the now deceased Ahaziah, king of Judah, come to "greet the king [Ahab] and queen [Jezebel]'s sons" [v12-14], they also suffer the same fate.

Claiming to outdo Ahab in devotion to Baal, he proposes the grandest sacrifice ever (along with a party/orgy?) [II,10:18-21][175] and gathers out of Israel even the casual Baal worshipper. After making sure that no Jehovah-follower is accidentally mixed in [v 23], when the sacrifices begin, the largest sacrifice is that of the execution of the Baal-worshippers and the destruction of their idols and temple (making it into an outhouse!) [vv 24-28]. As prophesied to Elijah, Jehu is Jehovah's *GO'EL* for Israel, reminiscent of the wilderness purges.

Yet despite his apparent high regard for Jehovah and His will, Jehu still "did not turn from Jeroboam's sin" [v 31] – he just could not allow Israel

211

to worship Jehovah the way He commanded. So the LORD continues to whittle away at the North Kingdom's territory.

Joash /Jehoash – II Kings

Athaliah, mother of the late southern king Ahaziah, decides that being queen is too nice to share, so she destroys every heir to the throne [II,11:1-3; II Chronicles 22:11]. However, Ahaziah's sister, Jehosheba ("Jehovah's *Oath/Seven*"), wife of priest Jehoiada, steals Ahaziah's baby son Joash from the gallows, protecting him in "the house of Jehovah" for *seven* years [vv 2-3; II Chronicles 22:11-12].

Jehoida spends the next six years gaining alliances with the army captains, until in the *seventh* year they "cut Covenant and took an *oath/seven* with them in Jehovah's house" [II,11:4; II Chronicles 23:1]. These captains go out and gather the Levites and the chieftains of the families from the land, who also "cut Covenant in God's house" [II Chronicles 23:2]. On the appointed day, all boldly step out to proclaim Joash as king [II,11:5-12; II Chronicles 23:4-11]. Athaliah is not pleased, but that does not last long [II,11:13-16; II Chronicles 23:12-15].[176]

With enthusiasm Jehoida "himself and all the People and the king" cut Covenant with the LORD "that they should be Jehovah's People". After ridding the city of its Baal worship, they return "to Jehovah's house to offer *Burnt Offerings* to Jehovah ..., with rejoicing and with singing, according to the order of David" [II,11:17; II Chronicles 23:16]. Years later, after straightening out the collection of tax for temple repairs, along with instituting a proper accounting structure for the money, Joash brings *the Temple* back to worshipful condition [II, 12:4-16; II Chronicles 24:4-14].

But this piety does not outlive Jehoida. Despite warnings from Jehovah's prophets, the king's slide into rebellion after Jehoida's death is rapid, even to where Zechariah, Jehoida's son, at the king's command, is stoned to death in *the Temple* court for warning Judah how God is turning his back on them [II Chronicles 24:15-22].

Even with Syria's much smaller army [II Chronicles 24:23-24], the LORD executes judgment against Joash. To appease Syria's Hazael, Joash plunders *the Temple* and sends it all to him [II Kings 12:17-18]. Acting as *GO'ELs* "because of the Blood of Jehoida the priest's sons" but without such authority, Joash's servants assassinate him (he is not buried with the kings [II Chronicles 24:25-27]). In turn his son, Amaziah, has to be *GO'EL* against the assassins, but respects the law by not executing their whole families [II,14:5-6; II Chronicles 25:3-5].

Amaziah's Rule – II Chronicles

Amaziah is an acceptable king [II, 25:2; II Kings 14:3-4], but those "high places" still have to go. Also looking to human solutions, he hires Israelite (North) mercenaries, only to be told by a prophet that the Covenant-Partner (Who was not consulted first) does not allow that, since: "Jehovah has power to help or to cause to stumble" [v 8]. Now that the damage is done, the angry released mercenaries raid some Southern towns.

Amaziah discovers that indeed God can do powerful things for His Covenant-partner, yet he carts home the Edomite gods whom Jehovah has defeated, to worship! [II,25:14]. And, like his father, he refuses to listen to the prophet sent to warn him [vv 15-16]. He then refuses to listen to any argument (because "it was from God") opposed to going to war against the North and it fails terribly [vv17-24].

"From the time that Amaziah had turned aside from following Jehovah, they plotted against him ... and killed him" [II,25:27] – there seem to be those within Judah who feel strongly about Jehovah being Judah's only God, and they continue to be *GO'EL* on His behalf.

Meanwhile in the North – II Kings

Jehoahaz, Jehoash, and Jeroboam II continue the sins of Jeroboam's namesake, that of diverting worship from Jehovah. Still, Jehovah's *HESED* does not desert this segment of His Covenant People. At first, Jehoahaz is put into the hands of Hazael of Syria [II,13:3], but when he "sought the face of Jehovah, Jehovah listened to him ... and gave a deliverer/savior to Israel" [vv 4-5]. Yet despite no real spiritual change in the country [v 6], still "Jehovah saw the affliction of Israel, very bitter; and none was bound nor was free, there was no helper to Israel. Jehovah had not said that He would blot out Israel's name from under heaven, but saved them by the hand of Jeroboam the son of Joash" [II,14:26-27].

The Death of Elisha – II Kings

Elisha is about to die and Jehoash is devastated, repeating Elisha's words when Elijah was taken [II,13:14]. Shooting a symbolic arrow, Elisha declares, "The arrow of Jehovah's deliverance, and the arrow of deliverance from Syria" [v 17]. But the symbolic striking of the ground is too few to destroy Syria [v 18-19]. Jehoash will indeed smite Ben-Hadad of Syria three times, but it will not be enough to completely stop Syria.

So Elisha dies. In a side event, a dead man is hurriedly thrown into Elisha's tomb when a raiding party happens by, and as the body touches Elisha's bones, the man revives [II,13:20-21].

The Final Spiral

Back to the South – II Chronicles

Uzziah is a good king, a spiritual king, who falls into the trap of pride. He has "set himself to seek God" [II,26:5, II Kings 15:3-5], he loves the Land [v 10]; Jehovah helps him [v 7], he is "wonderfully helped" [v 15]. But he grows proud, demanding the right to do a priest's privilege [II,26:16-21]. While a heathen society has no problem with this, Jehovah separates the functions of king and priest to balance each other. Uzziah is willing to stand against the priest Azariah and eighty warrior-priests until the LORD steps in by touching the king with leprosy, a leprosy which remains for the rest of his Life.

His son, Jotham, follows in his footsteps, except for the foolish pride [II, 27:2; II Kings 15:3-4]; however, the People are not quite sure that the

LORD is the only One to worship. Still, "Jotham became mighty because he ordered his ways before Jehovah" [v 6].

Unfortunately his single-mindedness does not survive. His son, Ahaz, "walked in the ways of Israel (the North)'s kings", taking up even Baal worship and the practices of the nations once driven out of the Covenant Land [II, 28:2-4]. In punishment, Judah is harassed by many, particularly by the North's King Pekah.[177] Ahaz looks to Assyria for help only to be victimized by them [II, 28:16-20; II Kings 16:7]. So he worships the Syrian gods "because they were helping Syria" [vv 23-24; II Kings 16:10-18]. At death he is buried, but not with the kings of Judah [v 27].

The North's Final Descent – II Kings

In fairly quick succession, Northern kings rise and fall [II,15:2-30] with the refrain that each does evil in the sight of the LORD, particularly in continuing the "sin of Jeroboam." Hoshea is a little better than the rest, but tries to rebel against Shalmaneser of Assyria who now 'owns' the North. In a real way, the North ceases to exist as God's People as Assyria takes many captives and resettles the Covenant Land with 'heathens' [II,17:24-25; 18:9-10].

II Kings 17 is a eulogy for the North, outlining what led to its death. Despite how Jehovah had done remarkable acts to bring Israel from Egypt to the Covenant Land, both North (Israel) and South (Judah) stand condemned. They fear other gods, secretly disobey Jehovah, refuse to reject the practices of the nations which God has driven out, and "made for themselves, of the lowest of them, priests …" His prophets are not heeded; they "hardened their necks", rejecting His Covenant [v 15], and sold themselves to do evil [vv 13-20]. As if simply astounded at such things, the chapter repeats how Israel still does not learn, trying to continue its playing of both sides of the fence, continuing the brokenness of Covenant [vv 29-40].

Because they do not listen to Jehovah their God, transgressing His Covenant, ignoring Moses [II,18:12], "So Jehovah showed Himself very angry and removed them from His presence" – and although only Judah is left, it is not because they are so obedient [II,17:18-20]. So Jehovah casts off the seed of Israel, afflicting them and giving them into the hand of plunderers.

Hezekiah Clings to Jehovah – II Chronicles

Southern king Hezekiah "clung to Jehovah and did not turn aside" [II Kings 18:3], and "did what was good, and right and true before Jehovah his God" [II, 31:20-21]. Deeply troubled by "the sin of our fathers" and how Israel has become "a trembling, an horror and an hissing", Hezekiah opens his career by reopening *the Temple* so that he might cut Covenant again with Jehovah, God of Israel [II,29:3-10].

Wiithin two weeks *the Temple* is ready[178] and so there is a worship of rededication and repentance in which the Blood of *seven* bulls, *seven* rams, *seven* lambs, and *seven* goat-lambs are sprinkled upon the altar "for a *Sin Offering* for the kingdom, for the sanctuary, and for Judah ... to make atonement (*KAPHAR*) for all Israel" [II, 29:20-24]. The People's response overwhelms the priests, so the Levites have to assist them [vv 25-35]. Finally reaching a breather, everybody is astounded at how suddenly this all happened [v 36].

Since this does not happen in time to prepare for the *Passover*, Hezekiah opts to celebrate it in the second month, and invites what is left of the North: Come, "return to Jehovah, the God of Abraham, Isaac, and Israel ... for Jehovah your God is gracious and merciful and will not turn His face from you if you turn back to Him" [II, 30:1-9]. The messengers mostly encounter mockery, but still many come, and from the South (Judah), "God's HAND was to give to them one heart to do the commandment ..." [v 10-12].

Jerusalem is purified from idol worship[179] and the *Passover* is a great celebration, even for those from the North who do not have time to become ritually clean – but through Hezekiah's prayer "Jehovah ... healed the People" [II, 30:13-20]. Unwilling to break the mood, the celebration lasts an extra week, and when the priests "rose and blessed the People, their voice was heard and their prayer came to His holy dwelling-place, to Heaven" [vv 21-27].

With renewed conviction, God's People clean up the Covenant Land, even in the North. The various idol worship centers – even the "high places" which had constantly spiritually dogged the heels of Israel – are broken down, even the serpent which Moses had raised in the wilderness, which had become a god to Israel, is destroyed [II,31:1; II Kings 18:4].

Then the People started giving to the LORD, "heaps upon heaps," so much so that extra room had to be made in *the Temple* to hold it all [II,31:2-12]. Finally after *seven* months ("Day of Atonement" month) it is all finished.

Sennacherib Meets Israel's Covenant-Partner – II Chronicles

Hezekiah "rebelled against the king of Assyria," so Sennacherib comes to master Judah and apparently Hezekiah at first humbly offers tribute [II Kings 18:7,13-16]. But Sennacherib wants more – he is going to conquer Jerusalem. Hezekiah prepares his land and his People for war: "Be strong and courageous, do not be afraid nor cast down before the king of Assyria ... for with us is more than with him. With him is an arm of flesh, but with us is Jehovah our God to help us, and to fight our battles" [II, 32:7-8].

Sennacherib taunts Jerusalem and mocks Jehovah's ability to save it [II, 32:9-19; II Kings 18:17-37]; when Hezekiah turns to Jehovah, through the prophet Isaiah he is reassured that Sennacherib will be neutralized [II Kings 19:1-7]. Sennacherib's messenger returns to find his master suddenly fighting on a second front. Yet Sennacherib does not give up and taunts Jerusalem and mocks Jehovah yet again [II Kings 19:10-13].

Turning again to the Covenant-Partner of Israel, Hezekiah is informed by Isaiah that the LORD mocks Sennacherib:

> I did it; from days of old I planned it. Now I brought it to pass that you should make desolate ruin-heaps of fortified cities ... But your sitting down, and your going out, and your coming in – I've known it

all – even your rage against Me and your arrogance... therefore I will put My hook in your nose and a bridle in your mouth and I will turn you back by the way you came... II Kings 19:25-28

Meanwhile there is hope for Israel: "those who are left shall again take root downward and bear fruit upward ... the zeal of Jehovah of Hosts shall do this ... For I will defend this city, to save it, for My own sake, and for My servant David's sake" [II Kings 19:30-31,34]. That night "the angel of Jehovah went out and struck 185,000 in the Assyrian camp; and they rose up in the morning and behold all of them were dead bodies" [v 35]. "So Jehovah saved Hezekiah and ... Jerusalem... and he guided them on every side. Many brought gifts to Jehovah to Jerusalem and precious gifts to Hezekiah king of Judah, and he was exalted in the sight of all nations" [II, 32:22-23].

Hezekiah's Illness – Physical and Spiritual – II Kings

Isaiah is sent to tell Hezekiah that his illness will lead to death and therefore to prepare for it. Hezekiah cries out and weeps before the LORD. Before Isaiah is even out of the courtyard, Jehovah turns him around with good news for the king: in three days he will be healthy, he will live yet fifteen more years, and will be free of Assyria [II, 20:1-6].[180] As reassurance, God allows a marvelous sign to Hezekiah, where the shadow on the sundial goes back ten steps [vv 8-11; II Chronicles 32:24].

But then Hezekiah foolishly ("his heart was lifted up, ... God left him to himself, to test him and to know all which was in his heart" [II Chronicles 32:25,31]) shows a potential conqueror, Babylon, the wealth of his kingdom, which Isaiah condemns because Babylon will indeed cart it all off one day [II, 20:12-19]. II Kings 20:19 describes Hezekiah as unconcerned about such a prophecy as long as it does not occur in his own lifetime – there is no intercession made – although II Chronicles 32:26 indicates that "Hezekiah was humbled for the pride of his heart, ... so that the wrath of Jehovah did not come upon them in the days of Hezekiah."

Manasseh – II Chronicles

What is troublesome about Manasseh is that he is born after Hezekiah's illness, within those fifteen years of grace. One would think that Hezekiah would have devoted special time with the boy to instill a high regard for the LORD and His extraordinary mercy. Yet Manasseh is only twelve upon accession to the throne [II,33:1; II Kings 21:1], so who knows. Whatever did happen between this new king and his father, Manasseh sets out to undo all the reforms his father had accomplished [vv 2-10; II Kings 21 2-9].

Finally Jehovah pronounces judgment: "I am bringing evil upon Jerusalem and Judah, so that whoever hears of it, his two ears will tingle. ... I abandon the remnant of My inheritance, and give them into their enemies' hand" [II Kings 21:10-16]. Manasseh is led off to Babylon in chains, there to finally 'discover' "Jehovah his God ... Jehovah of his fathers" [II,33:11-12]. Allowed to return to Jerusalem, "Manasseh knew that Jehovah, He is God" [v 13]. He rebuilds Judah's defenses and removes the altars which he had built – is it so long ago? – to false idols. However, "the People still sacrificed in the high places, only to Jehovah their God" – better, but still not God's will! [vv 14-17]

Son Amon has not learned his father's lesson and so he rebuilds all which his father has torn down [II, 21-23; II Kings 21:19-22]. His end is by assassination [vv 24-25; II Kings 21:23-24].

Josiah – II Chronicles

Eight year-old Josiah does "what was right in Jehovah's eyes, and walked the ways of his father David, and did not turn to the left nor to the right" [II, 34:2; II Kings 22:2]. "There was no king like him, who turned to Jehovah with all his heart, and with all his Soul/Life, and with all his might" [II Kings 23:25]. At sixteen "he began to seek the God of his father David", at twenty he begins to cleanse the Covenant Land (even in the North) of idol worship, and at twenty-six he begins the cleansing and rebuilding of *the Temple* [II, 34:3-13; II Kings 22:3-7; 23:4-20,24].

Long buried, the Book of the Law is finally discovered and read before the king, who is overcome with humility at the judgment which Israel/Judah deserve [II, 34:18-21; II Kings 22:8-13]. Turning to Huldah the prophetess, he is told, "Behold I will bring evil on this place ... and My wrath shall be poured out on this place, and it shall not be quenched ... [but to Josiah:] because your heart was without defenses and you were humbled ... your eyes will not look upon all the evil I shall bring upon this place" [vv 23-28; II Kings 22:15-20].

Josiah's response is to call God's People together and re-affirm Covenant – "the Book of the Covenant" is read to all, and then Covenant is cut "before Jehovah, to walk after Jehovah, to keep His commands, testimonies and statues with all the heart, and with all the Soul/Life" [II, 34:29-33; II Kings 23:1-3]. The next step is the *Passover*. Josiah himself provides lambs for the People and the oxen for the *Whole Burnt* and the *Peace Offerings*, "and there had not been a *Passover* kept like it in Israel from the days of Samuel the prophet" [II, 35:1-19; II Kings 23:21-23].

Still the axe hangs over Judah's head: "Jehovah did not turn away from the fury of His great anger" [II Kings 23:26-28]. As Balaam learned that God could even speak through the mouth of a jackass, so God could use the mouth of the heathen king of Egypt. But Josiah will not listen and therefore dies in battle [II, 35:20-24; II Kings 23:29-30]. Among his mourners is the prophet Jeremiah [II,35:25].

The Final Slide into Captivity – *II Kings*

Of the final kings, the resounding bell is that they do evil in the sight of the LORD. Josiah's first son, Jehoahaz is quickly taken to Egypt, there to die. His brother, Eliakim/Jehoiakim lasts longer but is no spiritual improvement and is in turn taken to Babylon in chains because of his rebellion against Nebuchadnezzar [II,23:31-24:7; II Chronicles 36:1-8]. More and more, Judah is overrun and decimated by its enemies.

Jehoiachin has a brief reign, in which Babylon plunders *the Temple* and Jerusalem; Mattaniah/Zedekiah refuses to be humble before Jeremiah and rebels against Nebuchadnezzar (despite his vow before Jehovah of allegiance to the Babylonian king) [II, 24:8-20; II Chronicles 36:9-13].

Jehovah has not abandoned His People yet – "Jehovah, the God of their fathers, sent to them by the hand of His messengers rising early and sending, for He had pity on His People and on His dwelling-place; but they mocked the messengers of God, and despised His words, and scoffed at His prophets...until there was no healing" [II Chronicles 36:15-16].

The siege against rebellious Zedekiah is terrible, and his punishment by Babylon is heartrending, as the last thing he sees before his eyes are destroyed are the deaths of his sons [II,25:1-7]. Jerusalem is left a smoking carcass, – its walls in ruins, its People carted off to Babylon – and *the Temple* is demolished [vv 8-21; II Chronicles 36:17-20]. The determination of Israel to rebel continues even after this devastation as Nebuchadnezzar's appointee governor is assassinated, which further scatters the People as many run away to Egypt [II,25:22-26].

Epitaph of the South

"He took into exile in Babylon those who had escaped from the sword, which became servants to him ... to fulfill the word of Jehovah in the mouth of Jeremiah, until the land had enjoyed its *Sabbath*s. During all the days of desolation it kept *Sabbath*, until seventy years were fulfilled" [II Chronicles 36:20-21]. It is interesting how obedience to the LORD is tied into stewardship of His gifts, here the proper use of the Covenant Land.

Yet in spite of all the agony and grief which Israel has given Jehovah, neither II Kings nor II Chronicles end with destruction and punishment as the final thought. Instead the last note is hope, that the LORD has not abandoned His People. II Kings 25:27-30 records how King Jehoiachin is raised up and honored by the Babylonian king, while II Chronicles 36:22-23 points to Cyrus' proclamation: "Jehovah, the God of the heavens, ... has appointed me to build Him a house at Jerusalem, which is in Judah. Whoever is among you of all His People, may Jehovah his God be with him. Let him go up."

C. Exile and the Return

Ezra

The Covenant-Partner Makes His Move

If He Whose "*HESED* ... is from everlasting to everlasting" [Psalm 103:17], Whose Love (in Abraham) struggles with His justice in regard to Sodom and Gomorrah (who were His enemies), then in the Babylonian Captivity, how His heart must break to do such a thing to this People He has determined to Love.

Yet for Jehovah, Covenant is unbreakable – He will not abandon His People. Babylon is defeated by a very special nation called the Persians. Although never in Covenant terms, a deep friendship is established between Persia and Israel which will endure through the centuries, even to the coming of the Magi (one of the six ruling castes of Persia) to honor the birth of Jesus.[181]

King Cyrus of Persia declares he has responsibility laid upon him by Jehovah to have Israel rebuild their temple and nation. This sounds almost too good to be true. In fact, it would seem as if it is contrived by the Hebrew writers, except – how else does one explain the migration back to Israel and the sanction to rebuild their religion and identity? And this takes place in the *first year* of Cyrus' reign!

"The People Gathered As One Man to Jerusalem"

Israel comes, thousands of some clans, just the "sons of" in other clans; priests, singers, tradesmen, forty-two thousand of them. They come with the vessels from Solomon's temple, returned to them by Cyrus' treasurer. Determined to no longer play games with God, it is Jehovah and Him alone they will worship. The urgency is to give their worship a home, but even before that, they will worship. In spite of their fear of local reaction, they will worship. Only after this do they begin raising up the place where Jehovah's Name will once again dwell. A prominent figure in this restoration is Jeshua (Joshua, Jesus – "Yahweh saves" – [3:2, 9; 4:3]).

Israel's refusal to truly repent had brought the Exile upon themselves. But now, offering new hope and new Life, how significant that the first festivals they celebrate are *the Day of Atonement* and (although not mentioned) the following *Feast of Tabernacles* [3:4]. *The Day of Atonement* is a wonderfully strong image of forgiveness and reinstatement with Jehovah, while *the Feast of Tabernacles* celebrates how God had brought Israel to this Covenant Land once before. Although only a remnant of Israel now, the symbolism is profound.

Rejoicing with a Broken Heart

It has been like holding one's breath for seventy years, how they have waited for this moment. The young see the foundation being laid as the proof that no longer are they the disenfranchised of the nations, and raise their voices in unbridled thanksgiving. But the older ones know what they have lost. How they must have feelings akin to Adam and Eve's, who even when times were good, would still have known what Life was like before and how they were responsible for the loss. Like a dam bursting its gates, they grieve – grieve for the loss of their treasured Temple, grieve for the loss of family and friends, grieve over the lost childhoods of their offspring, grieve that once what was so magnificent will never be again.

If You Cannot Beat 'Em, Distract 'Em! – Ezra 4:1-24

The old temptation is Satan's first line of defense. What had brought Israel to its downfall was not just that they ignored God, but had included false gods as partners to Jehovah. The present heathen inhabitants' intention to help in the rebuilding may not have been malicious, yet subtly it would leave a sense of obligation and mutual cooperation – which could tempt the returnees to again include false gods in their worship. The reply of the heads of the families is wise; it is, in essence, 'No, this is our job to do – we need to do it this way' [3:3].

But how often the 'well-meaning' of people, once they feel rejected, turns to offense and anger! The 'helpfulness' is simply a thin veneer over self-pride, which when denied immediately transforms into a vitriolic nastiness. The wisdom of the chiefs is vindicated: the heathen inhabitants had wanted ownership in *the Temple*, so that they could use it as they felt pleased to do, rather than to obey Jehovah.

At this time, only *the Temple* is being rebuilt, not the city walls. The concern is not what happens to the city; instead the point is that Israel is reconnecting with its Covenant-Partner. Still the soft underbelly is that Jerusalem's history has been long on rebellion and past insurrections come back to haunt these Jews. The work is forcibly stopped.

In the second year of Darius' reign, the prophets Haggai and Zechariah, along with Zerubbabel and Jeshua, finally take heart again and restart the rebuilding. The governor Tattenai requires proof authorizing them to do this work, but is willing to let them continue until something definite comes from Darius ("God's eye was upon the elders of the Jews, and they were not stopped" [v 5]). His letter to Darius is neither inflammatory nor worried, as he recounts the Jews' defense. Their plea is to a decree which Cyrus had made; he simply asks for verification.

The story proves true, even to the dimensions which the new temple is to take. Darius goes on to instruct Tattenai not only to not interfere but also to provide expense money, sacrifices and whatever else is needed so that they might pray to "the God of heaven" on behalf of the king. And then Darius adds teeth with a rather effective punishment for anyone messing with "this edict." As well, God is called upon to also protect this temple. Without further problem *the Temple* is finished.

The New Beginning – Ezra 6:16-22

The dedication is extravagant, yet only a token compared to the dedication of Solomon's temple [I Kings 8:62-66; II Chronicles 7:1-10]. When they had first re-entered Jerusalem, they celebrated *the Day of Atonement* and *the Festival of Tabernacles*; now they celebrate the other half year's great festival, *the Passover* and *the Feast of the Unleavened Bread.* The irony is that the joy of this *Passover* is not from the release from a heathen king's tyranny, but from a king's help and encouragement to rebuild their faith and nation.

Ezra Leaves Babylon

It is now when Ezra first arrives on the scene, some 80 years after the first group had returned to the Covenant Land. The journey takes four months, possibly because he gathers a new group of re-settlers with him [7:28; 8:1-20], although it seems that many are also simply migrating back because of King Artaxerxes' open door to the return. On Artaxerxes' part, he generously provides for the re-establishment of the worship of Jehovah, "to honor Jehovah's house in Jerusalem" [7:27].

Ezra sees his mission particularly in leading the resurrected nation back into the *TORAH* of Moses, "which Jehovah, the God of Israel, had given" [7:6]; "for Ezra had devoted himself to the study and observance of Jehovah's *TORAH* and to teaching its decrees and laws in Israel" [v 10]. Artaxerxes himself acknowledges the importance of this as he gives charge to Ezra [v 25-26]. In all this, Ezra recognizes "God's good Hand" [v 9], "Jehovah my God's Hand was upon me, I was made strong" [v 28] – would there be the *added* sense of Covenant in regard to the Hand?

TORAH

In regard to "the *TORAH*" or "the Law":

> The word tôrâ means basically 'teaching' whether it is the wise man instructing his son or God instructing Israel. The wise give insight into all aspects of life so that the young may know how to conduct themselves and to live a long blessed life. {Pr 3:1f} So too God, motivated by love, reveals to man basic insight into how to live with each other and how to approach God....
> ...In addition, the book of Deut itself shows that the law has a broad meaning to encompass history, regulations and their interpretation, and exhortations. It is not merely the listing of casuistic

statements as is the case in Hammurabi's code. Later the word was extended to include the first five books of the Bible in all their variety.

Covenant precedes law; and the law was given only to the nation which had entered into covenant with God [although in the sense of moral principle, law is as old as human sin and God's governance, Ge 3:7 Ge 9:6 Ge 26:5. -R.L.H.]. The law specifically is the stipulations of the covenant. But in the broad sense of law, namely God's teaching, covenant plays the central part. Law and covenant may parallel one another, {e.g. Ps 78:10} Since they are so closely tied together, to break one is to break both. Their interconnection is further witnessed to in that the tables of the testimony were placed in the ark of the covenant and a copy of the book of the law placed beside it as a perpetual witness to the covenant between God and his People. {Ex 40:20 De 31:26}

The law, as well as the covenant, brings with it blessings or curses. He who follows its precepts will be blessed (De 29:9 [H 8]), but whoever breaks them will be cursed (De 29:20-21 [H 19-20]). Following the law is the source of life; it makes life a joy and lengthens its days. {De 6:1-2} On the other hand, as the standard it tests Israel to determine whether they follow God completely or not. {De 8:2 Jud 3:4}
TWOT[182]

As indicated, *TORAH*, although commonly thought of as "the rules and regulations," actually contains a wealth of material greater than that. More specifically, since *TORAH* commonly refers to the "Books of Moses" (Genesis through to Deuteronomy), as we have seen, this is the story of Jehovah's Glory [*KABOD*] as defined by Him: His goodness, kindness, mercy, Covenant relationship, forgiveness and justice. It describes the struggle of *HESED* with judgment, and the first glimpses of God's eternal solution to the problem of mankind's sin. It wrestles with the reality of Jehovah's Life/Blood flowing in the veins of mankind, from God's satisfaction with an intercessor to His anger at flippancy toward this most intimate of relationships. Within this is the proper treatment of a Covenant-partner, whether in regard to the LORD, as Donor or Recipient, or to a fellow human, also as recipient or donor.

"So We Fasted and Petitioned Our God"

The dilemma is familiar: we represent an all-powerful God – but who should we turn to for help? What kind of statement does this make before the world? For the People returning to Jerusalem, safety is a real concern as they travel the robber-infested wilderness routes. Yet Ezra feels awkward asking for the king's protection, so the most sensible thing is to fast and humble themselves, and ask *the King* – Jehovah [8:21,23].

Believing he has the LORD's blessing, he entrusts for the journey the twelve heads of the priests with the gold and silver for *the Temple*, impressing on them the holiness of this task. His confidence in the LORD is not dishonored: "The Hand of our God was on us, and He delivered us from the hand of the enemy" [v 31]. Now comes a poignant statement: "The sons of the exiled, who had come out of the captivity, offered *Burnt Offerings* to the God of Israel" [v 35].

"I Sat Horrified" [9:4]

Imagine the scene: Those who return, who have been humbled by Jehovah through the captivity, who are investing their lives in rebuilding the center of their faith – are sabotaging what they have so long wished for and for which they have risked so much. Through intermarriage with the heathens occupying the Covenant Land, they are committing the same sin which is responsible for the captivity, the sin of Solomon: syncretism – allowing other gods to share in the devotion which belongs to Jehovah alone. God forbids such intermarriage.

Ezra is absolutely appalled. History threatens to repeat itself, but this time would God's wrath have any limits – especially after the LORD showed such mercy in bringing them back to this Covenant Land?! It is a most *deadly* game to play. What should he do? By the time of the evening sacrifice, he knows where he has to start: confession. The People are one, and he is their leader – this is no Pharisee; the guilt falls on his shoulders as well. Soon he is joined by many who share his despair at this sin.

Finally Shechaniah proposes that they renew Covenant by cutting Covenant again [10:3], and be determined to remove this rebellion against Jehovah's will. He assures Ezra that he has the full backing and support of the People there. The leading priests, Levites, and all Israel take an *oath/seven* to do what is proposed [v 5].

All the Remnant are commanded to come to a convocation upon penalty of forfeiture of place and property should they refuse. The difficulty (beside the pouring rain) is that the separation from the heathen wives should be done in an orderly fashion. It is agreed that the elders and judges of each town be empowered to locally oversee this task. Over a hundred men are found to be guilty of this kind of rebellion, who "gave their hands in pledge" – using the symbolic strength of Covenant – and presented a ram as a *Guilt Offering* [v 19].

Nehemiah

The Heart Breaks

Meanwhile, back at the palace (Artaxerxes', some twelve years later), Nehemiah's heart is torn by news of the Remnant's difficulties and vulnerability to attack, since the city's walls and gates are still in ruins. Characteristic of the Remnant, Nehemiah cries out in fasting and repentance to Jehovah, "the great and awesome God Who *keeps (SHAMAR*, as in "*keep* the Garden" [Genesis 2:15], and other passages) Covenant and *HESED* to those loving Him and *keeping (SHAMAR)* His commands" [Nehemiah 1:5]. Again it is not '*their* sin' but "*we* have sinned...both I and my father's house" [v 6], and like Moses in the wilderness before him, he pleads '*You* said: "but if You will turn to Me...I will gather them'" [v 9].

Ready to risk his Life for his People, Nehemiah comes without his courtly smiles before the king. Normally one's little Life is unimportant before the king, but this king is genuinely concerned about his cupbearer (a most trusted and important position). Nehemiah's request is daring – yet it is readily accepted. The king has no reservations in providing for this cupbearer's needs, even to sending an armed escort with him, "according to the good Hand of my God on me" [v 8].

"They Made Their Hands Strong for Good" [2:18]

Of course it is not without opposition, but to oppose Nehemiah is to risk rebellion against the king. Still Nehemiah is careful not to let his task be known as he goes by night to survey the damaged walls. Once finished, though, he approaches his fellow Jews and tells them not only about how "the Hand of my God was upon me," but also about the king's support. The response is enthusiastic work from the Jews.

At first there is scorn from the heathen officials. The Remnant responds with prayer, then more work. Then there are vague, half-veiled threats. Again the Remnant prays, and then posts a guard. Nehemiah reminds the People that they have their Covenant-Partner to fight at their side. The resistance does nothing overt, but the Remnant cannot relax their vigilance – "did their work with one hand and held a weapon in the other" [v 17].

Selfishness

Ezra had been alarmed at the spiritual Russian roulette of inter-marrying with the heathen, now Nehemiah is horrified at how the Israelite is willing to subject his own brother into financial enslavement. For seventy years the Remnant had longed to be free from foreign slavery, and now their fellows – God's People – are plotting to put them back into literal slavery – forcing them to sell themselves and their children to pay off debts in the middle of a famine. They are violating Moses' prohibition against usury [for example, Leviticus 25:36], as well as violating common decency within brotherhood, allowing the heathen the opportunity to ridicule further these 'God-fearing' People!

Those responsible have no defense. Instead they agree to restore to their brothers what has been taken. To compel their word, Nehemiah calls for the priests and under their authority makes those responsible swear an *oath*/*seven* to do as promised. Further, should anyone break this oath, "he shall be shaken out and emptied" [5:13] – reminiscent of the torn carcasses of broken Covenant. The People praise the LORD and the oath is kept.

Meanwhile, Nehemiah shows that he practices what he preaches. For his twelve years as governor in Judah, "out of reverence for God," he refuses to tax the People beyond the subsistence level of the government. And especially at this time, most of the income goes to feed the People working with him, as he works among the People on the wall. He prefers Jehovah's approval over amassing a fortune [v 19, 14-15].

"But I Prayed, 'Now Strengthen My Hands'" [6:9]

The human enemies try many ruses to dishearten and frighten the Remnant. They attempt to draw Nehemiah out to 'a conference' (possibly to kill, or detain, or embarrass him), but he refuses, 'What I am doing is more important than what you propose!' [6:3]. Then to the invented plot to make Nehemiah king, he answers, "it is from *your* heart you contrive them" [v 8]. They want to "weaken our hands, [so I prayed] 'Make my hands strong!'" [v 9].

If they could not get him to come out, then maybe they could make him so fearful he would hide inside. Shemaiah, seemingly paranoid about assassins, begs Nehemiah to seek asylum in *the Temple*. But the man who works side-by-side with his People will not run away and hide and will not allow himself to be discredited.

The wall is finally finished – in only 52 days! How awkward for the enemies because it seems very plain that Jehovah is behind this work to restore "the place where I shall set My Name." The wall has been rebuilt, security has been restored, but watchfulness is still required. Spies and treachery are close at hand, especially since one enemy, Tobiah, well connected by marriage to those close to the action, constantly needles Nehemiah.

"Do Not be Sorry, for the Joy of Jehovah is Your Stronghold!" [8:10]

For seventy years there was a spiritual wilderness for the Remnant – they have been without Temple; many without teachers; and many without Scripture (the *TORAH*). Imagine the intense excitement as they stand before their new temple as the scrolls of the Torah are opened, and Nehemiah and the Levites help them to understand what is read to them. As at the dedication of *the Temple*, what a mixture of emotions! Do you weep at the sense of loss which the sins of their People had created, or do you laugh with delight at the privilege of being at the wonderful start of a restored relationship with Jehovah?

The Levites give them direction: This is a holy day! The knowledge and understanding of God's will has returned to the midst of His People! So go "eat the fat, drink the sweet, share.... and make *great* rejoicing" because "the joy of Jehovah is your stronghold" [vv 9-12]. Indeed, it is a day the LORD has made happen.

So, rather than be discouraged, the People gather to find out more, and discover that in this very month is an important festival, the Festival of Booths. How extraordinarily appropriate for a People just coming in out of wandering in the spiritual wilderness of the captivity! Such celebration as theirs is something not seen since the days of Israel's first entering the Covenant Land under Joshua.

"Leaning on the Everlasting Arms" – 9:1-73

Re-established with Jehovah, the Remnant pauses to think through what this relationship has meant and should mean to them. So they separate themselves from the heathen inhabitants, and in fasting and prayer, under the leadership of the Levites, they review the incredible *HESED* of God.

Despite the Covenant God cut with them [v 8], despite receiving "the Land You had raised Your Hand to give them" [v 15], their fathers rebelled; they refused to remember and did not obey. Yet, echoing

Jehovah's own description of His Glory, they now confess, "But You are a God ready to pardon, gracious and merciful, slow to anger and of great *HESED*, and did not forsake them" [v 17]. Again and again, when they had cried out to Him, the LORD had answered and sent messiahs (saviors) [v 27] to bring them back to the *TORAH* [v 29], but they still acted proudly and sinned.

Still "God – the Great, the Mighty, the Fearful One, Who keeps Covenant and *HESED*" [v 32] never forsook His People. Since He has now brought them back, they ask that although they deserved all which their fathers had brought upon themselves, would Jehovah now take note of their condition and of their renewed submission to His will as they cut a Covenant with Him [v 38]?

Recommitment and Repopulating the "Holy City" – *10:1 - 12:26*

"Entering into a curse and an *oath/seven*" [10:28-29], rather than simply the father as spokesman for the family, each man, woman, son, and daughter recommit themselves to God's Law. They will not compromise their faith by marrying the heathen; they will faithfully observe the *Sabbath* and the *Sabbath Year*; God's House will be financially taken care of; the First Fruits, firstborn, and tithes will be given to the LORD as commanded – "We will not forsake the house of our God" [10:39].

Jerusalem, here first called "the Holy City" [11:1], now has its temple and its wall. But where are the People? Chosen by lot, every tenth family is to move into the city from the outlying areas and the seed for a new Jerusalem is established.

Dedication Celebration – *12:26-47*

The People spiritually and physically are in place, *the Temple* is rebuilt, the wall is rebuilt. Now is the time to thank God and dedicate particularly the wall. The celebrants and mass choir are divided into two groups, each on opposite walls, then together in *the Temple*. One can only wonder about the musical possibilities for that day – choir counterpointing choir, echoing each other, drawing to a unified crescendo; the congregation in the city being drawn into song, "so that the joy of Jerusalem is heard even afar off" [v 43]. *The Temple* is not as magnificent as Solomon's, but after all the People have been through, perhaps the joy is even greater.

The Temple storerooms are prepared, allotments for the singers and the gatekeepers are set, the priests and the Levites are provided for – Jerusalem is open for worship!

How Hard It Is to Put the LORD First – 13:1-47

With such a precious treasure restored, certain officials still do not grasp that they can lose it all again. The priest Eliashib sets aside Temple storerooms as private storage for the heathen Tobiah (who had attempted to sabotage the building of the wall). So also have the Levites and the singers been neglected in regard to their stipends. When Nehemiah returns to Jerusalem, he 'reorganizes' just a bit, and sets honest men in charge.

Nehemiah reminds the leaders that their doublemindedness is part of the reason for the destruction of Jerusalem – was once not enough? The *Sabbath* also is not being observed as a day of rest and focus on Jehovah. Israelite and heathen alike enter Jerusalem to trade on the holy day. When the merchants who are locked out on the *Sabbath* simply camp by the wall, he informs them that the next time he will "send a Hand against them" [v 21].

Again, the problem of intermarriage with the heathen surfaces, especially where the children have no interest in things 'Jewish' [v 24]. Nehemiah's displeasure – striking some and pulling out their hair [v 25] – is quite evident. Yet his concern is valid: that is what Solomon had done, which started Israel's disintegration and brought God's judgment [vv 26-27]. Finding the problem even within the priesthood, action really needs to be taken.

Likely there are some, perhaps many, who disapprove of such stringent commitment to God's Law. Nehemiah turns to Jehovah and basically says, 'LORD, You judge!'

Esther

The story is most unique in the Bible in that it never mentions God directly, yet the Covenant relationship to Jehovah flows throughout it. The Covenant-Partner moves subtly and deftly in such instances as when King Ahasuerus (Xerxes) could not sleep, so he has recent history read to him. There he finds he has not honored Mordecai for the service he had rendered, and so on the very morning Haman would have Mordecai hanged, Haman has to parade through the city proclaiming the merits of Mordecai. The wisdom of Esther and her preservation also is significantly guided by the LORD.

Of interest is Mordecai's warning, "If you are completely silent at this time, relief and deliverance will arise for the Jews from another place, but you and your father's house shall be destroyed. Who knows if for such a time as this you have come to the kingdom" [4:14]. Apparently it is at the *Passover* when Haman hatches his own 'ultimate solution to the problem of the Jews' (Hitler was not the first, but ended up with a similar fate).

The result of the victory of their Covenant-Partner is "a time of happiness and joy, gladness and honor... feasting and celebrating" [8:16-17], "as the time in which the Jews rested[183] from those who hate them, the month which is turned for them from anguish to joy, from mourning to optimism, ...days of feasting and joy, of sending presents, and giving gifts to the poor" [9:22].

XI. Poetry

A. *Job*

What was That All About??

Covenant is not an obvious theme in Job; however, since the Covenant-name "Jehovah" is used, it can be assumed that such a relationship between God and Job forms the background to the story. This adds an extra dimension to the account, especially in Job's bewilderment at what is happening to him. After all, if he is in the kind of depth relationship in which there is complete openness, then why is God not telling him what is going on? What Job does not comprehend is the deafening silence from God.

It is not the loss of his family, nor the loss of his wealth, nor the bitterness of his wife, nor the agony of the body, nor the empty comfort of his 'friends' – what distresses Job the most is that God makes no effort to enlighten him. Although he frequently asks 'why?', God never answers his plea.

Yet Job never lets go of the relationship and therein lies his success. In spite of the silence from God, Job fully expects that the relationship is not broken. In fact, his statement:

> For I know that my *GO'EL* [Redeemer] lives, and in the end He shall stand above the dust; and after [this] my skin is destroyed, yet in my flesh I shall see none other than God (Whom I shall see for myself and my eyes shall behold). How my heart yearns within me! 19:25-27

demonstrates profound confidence not only of standing in the presence of God in the resurrection but also that the balancing of lost Blood will indeed take place on his behalf [*GO'EL*]. But in his frustration and suffering, He wishes that God would just end his Life here so that this final destiny can be established.

Still, it is difficult. What wears away at him is that his Covenant-Partner seemingly does not care about him — and that's not Covenant! God apparently does whatever He intends, whatever the cost might be, and there is no changing Him. Job does not begrudge Jehovah His reasons; it is just that without knowing what is going on, Job feels robbed of all purpose for his own Life, robbed of his reason for living. Why should he continue day after day — not that he would commit suicide, but is there really any point to 'getting up in the morning'?

A Gritty Look at Covenant Yet Covenant None the Less

So far in the Bible, it has been necessary to identify Covenant's extraordinary relationship with God and what that means to humanity. That Jehovah would Himself enter into such a personal and close relationship with humans is beyond imagination. How important it is to focus on this extraordinary privilege and the awesomeness of God's commitment in this relationship: His eagerness, His close participation in the lives of the People to whom He has chosen to be bound, His *HESED* which will not give up, yet also His justice which will not be neglected.

The book of Job reminds us that Jehovah is both Participant and also Overseer of Covenant; yes, there is a remarkable equality between the two Covenant-partners, yet He still is also God, the human is not. The LORD does bring mankind up into such a close relationship, yet He is also the One "upholding the universe by His Word of power" [Hebrews 1:3]. Therefore there are many things in the Kingship of God which man cannot be privy to, which he cannot even begin to comprehend.

Even when Jehovah finally does speak directly to Job, Job is never given the answer why all this has happened. The real issue in regards to unfortunate events is not a matter of explanation but of trust. After all, is not trust the greater element in any Covenant, even over openness? If I go into battle, I need to *depend* on my Covenant-partner, that even if I do not fully understand what he is doing, I still can count on the fact he will be there by my side. Openness is not enough.

The whole story (which we are allowed to see) indicates Jehovah's message as: 'I am God, I have power far beyond yours, and I have concerns which are far beyond yours. However, no matter what the apparent circumstances may be, you are not forgotten or thrown aside. I will be there.' Jehovah is involved from beginning to end – in fact, the story even happens at His instigation. Covenant does not insulate the human from God doing things which stretch one's faith.

Covenant with an unseen and only occasionally communicative God is difficult. We tend to think that Abraham had regular conversations with God, but consider that in the thirty years between God's call and the birth of Isaac only a few episodes of dialogue with Jehovah are recorded. How much of God's silence to Job did Abraham himself experience? We do know that his bewilderment once reached the point where Abraham took matters into his own hands and Ishmael was born.

So, even though the idea of Covenant with God should be a most exhilarating concept, a concept loaded with extraordinary privilege, still the reminder of Job is that God is greater than Covenant and operates *also* beyond this relationship. However, conversely, this activity does not in any way reduce the intimate bond which Covenant declares.

"Jehovah Turned Job's Captivity, when He Prayed for His Friends" [42:10]

Modern translations, in attempting to make the text more readable, may change a word for something which flows more smoothly. However, there are times when it might be better that the word in its stark awkwardness be left untouched. Other versions use "fortunes" instead of "captivity" – which may not violate the sense of the passage, but can still miss an important point.

There are many words which we might have used in this sentence, if we were writing the original story. 'Fortunes' would indeed be one, 'afflictions' might be another, or 'distress' or a number of other such words – all of which are in the Hebrew language. But the chosen word is "captivity." That causes a bit of puzzlement. 'Affliction' we can understand, but "captivity" – that he is locked up, bound up? Just what can it mean?

Perhaps it is the illness which imprisons him, but more likely it is spiritual in nature. Reading the section describing the 'comfort' of Job's 'friends,' it is not hard to imagine that by the end of the section, Job is ready to cross off his friends' names in his little black address book. Things get kind of nasty by the time all are finished talking. Job is accused of some pretty bad sins, and the friends are described as useless and empty – a perfect recipe for the breaking of friendship.

But Jesus and St Paul both describe the nature of God as loving His enemies [Matthew 5:44-45; Romans 5:10]. Indeed we see that nature vividly displayed in God and Abraham's dialogue over Sodom and Gomorrah. So the problem facing Job now becomes a Covenant issue. Quite possibly the captivity which is referred to is a dark cloud of anger in Job's heart. At this point, God's LifeBlood's flow in Job's veins has been dramatically diminished – the flow has been clamped down – chained down, if you will.

Again, Jehovah looks for His intercessor. The 'release from captivity' is when Job *prayed for his tormentors*. This prayer has a dramatic ability to refocus the pray-er's attitude and heart: rather than 'eating his heart out' – in seeking revenge, or even in desiring that they would suffer corresponding disasters so that they would understand his distress (to which they probably would never connect) – instead he practices *HESED* and intercession, and leaves the rest in the LORD's hands. With this, Jehovah's LifeBlood is released and He can be again the special Partner which Covenant describes.

B. The Psalms

(The passages in this section are not an exhaustive listing but a representative sample.)

Why? How Long?

Although basically not adding much new in terms of defining Covenant, the Psalms do indeed follow Job. In many ways, both record the difficulty of translating Covenant into daily Life. Both struggle with the times of silence and the feeling of being abandoned by the Covenant-Partner during the times of waiting, during the times when it seems as though evil is triumphing, during the times when one seems to be inundated and overwhelmed by catastrophe: "Why, O Jehovah, do you stand far off? Will you hide in times of trouble?" [Psalm 10:1]; "Jehovah, how long will You look on? Rescue my Soul/Life from their devastation..." [Psalm 35:17]; "O God, You have cast us off; You have broken us; You were angry – take us back again!" [Psalm 60:1]; and even "They have conspired with one heart together and cut a Covenant against You" [Psalm 83:5].

> O God of vengeance, Jehovah God of vengeance, shine forth! Lift Yourself up, O Judge of the earth; give just repayment to the proud. ... O Jehovah, until when shall the wicked triumph ... They kill the widow and the alien, they murder the orphan, yet they say, "Jehovah will not see, the God of Jacob will not catch on."   Psalm 94:1-3, 6-7

It is the struggle of maintaining faith. It seems like attempting to step forward while the flood waters are tearing at your legs to pull them out from under you. Yet time and again, despite the bleakness of the picture, the Psalmist does make that step forward in hope: "Jehovah, You have heard the desire of the humble; You will establish their heart; Your ear will hear" [Psalm 10:17]; "I will thank You in the great assembly; among a mighty people I will praise You" [Psalm 35:18].

But Jehovah is a Fortress to me, and my God the Rock of my refuge. He turns back on themselves their own iniquity, and in their own

wickedness He shall cut them off; Jehovah our God shall cut them off.
Psalm 94:22-23

Psalm 44 presents a perplexing scenario: the description in verses 9-14 reflect the judgment of God in Deuteronomy 28 should faithless Israel break Covenant; and yet "All this has come upon us; but we have not forgotten You, nor have we dealt falsely with Your Covenant. Our heart has not turned back, nor have our steps swerved from Your way" [vv 17-18]. This cannot be the cry of Israel in captivity, since the captivity is the result of Israel's faithlessness. However, St Paul refers to this passage in Romans 8:36, where he sees it describing himself and his co-workers in Christ, who experience all sorts of persecution *because* they are doing God's will, and he sees it as a necessary element in the Gospel's invasion of Satan's territory.

Broken Covenant

Psalm 78 summarizes the history of Israel from the Exodus through to David, accenting the broken Covenant [vv 10, 37]; how they "did not remember His Hand" [v 42] and ignored His *'OTH* (signs) in Egypt [v 43]; how He got so angry during the time of the Judges that He "delivered 'His strength' into captivity, and 'His glory' into the enemy's hand" [v 61]. In fact, Psalm 95's version actually ends on the note of judgment.

Yes, we know the history of broken Covenant, but the Psalms also wrestle with the *experience* of such results:

> For Your arrows pierce me, and Your Hand presses down on me. There is no soundness in my flesh because of Your anger, nor wholeness [*SHALOM*] in my bones because of my sin. For my iniquities have gone over my head; as a heavy burden they are too heavy for me. My wounds stink and fester because of my foolishness. I am twisted, I am doubled over; I see gloom all the day long, for my confidence has been fully burned, and there is no wholesomeness in my flesh. I am numb and severely broken; I howl because of the turmoil of my heart.　　　　　　　　　　　　　　　Psalm 38:2-8

> For my days are dispersed like smoke, and my bones are scorched like a hearth. My heart is beaten down and withered like grass, so that I

> forget to eat my bread. Because of the sound of my groaning my body sticks to my skin. ... I lie awake, and am like a bird alone on the housetop ... For I have eaten ashes like bread, and mingled my drink with weeping, because of Your anger and wrath; for You have plucked me up and flung me away. Psalm 102:3-10

Yet the counterpoint of broken Covenant is Jehovah's mercy: "they were not faithful in His Covenant, but being merciful, He atoned (*KAPHAR*) [their] iniquity" [Psalm 78:37-38], as well as His reassurance: "I will not violate My Covenant, nor alter what goes out of My lips" [Psalm 89:34]. Again the history and the theology we already know, but the psalmists sing of the yearning for forgiveness and the exhilaration of re-instatement:

> Hide Your face from my sins, and blot out all my iniquities. Create in me a clean heart, O God, and renew an established spirit within me. Cast me not from Your presence, and take not Your Holy Spirit from me. Restore to me the joy of Your salvation, and uphold me by Your grace-given Spirit. Psalm 51:9-12

> Bless Jehovah, O my Soul; do not ignore all His benefits; Who forgives all your iniquities, Who heals all your diseases, Who redeems [*GO'EL*] your Life from destruction, Who crowns you with steadfast Love [*HESED*] and tender mercies, Who satisfies your mouth with good things, so that your youth is renewed like the eagle's.
> Psalm 103:2-5

Helper

> The salvation of the righteous is from Jehovah – their Refuge in the time of trouble. Jehovah helps them and delivers them; He will deliver them from the wicked, and will save them, because they flee for refuge in Him. Psalm 37:39-40

As noted when we first met the word group for "Helper" in Genesis 2 at the creation of Eve, this is more than merely assistance, but rather has the sense of 'rescue' and 'saving,' a most common theme in the Psalms. The difficulty here might be in the assumption that Jehovah should help because, after all, He is God and should 'owe' it to His creatures to be available to them. However, the reason why *we* could call on Him to help is because He has bound Himself in Covenant and therefore has pledged Himself to be 'on call' for His Covenant-partner.

> In Your righteousness deliver me and rescue me; bend Your ear to me, and save me! Be to me an unconquerable Refuge which I may continually enter – a Stronghold and a Fortress where Your command is to save me ... O my God, deliver me from the hand of the wicked, from the palm of the unjust and ruthless man. Psalm 71:2-4

> Freely I will sacrifice to You; I will praise Your Name, O Jehovah, for it is good, for He has snatched me out of all trouble and my eye has looked down upon my enemies. Psalm 54:6-7

> In distress I called on Jehovah; He answered me in the boundlessness of Jehovah. Jehovah is for me – I will not fear. What can man do to me? Jehovah is for me as One Who helps me; therefore I shall look down on those who hate me. ... You deliberately pushed to make me fall, but Jehovah helped me. My Strength and Song is Jehovah, and He is Salvation to me. Psalm 118:5-7, 13-14

And again, it is not merely the theology of needing God's help, but also the experience of it – from in the midst of the need:

> My God, my God, why have You forsaken me and are far from my deliverance, far from the words of my cry? My God, I call by day but you do not answer, and in the night, I am not silent. ... I am a worm and not a man, a reproach of mankind, and despised by the people. ... I am poured out like water, and all my bones are spread apart; my heart is like wax – it is melted in the midst of my bowels; my strength is dried up like a potsherd and my tongue clings to my jaws.
>   Psalm 22:1-2, 6, 14-15

to the delight of receiving that help:

> When Jehovah turned back the captivity of Jacob, we were like those who dream. Then was our mouth full of laughter and our tongue full of singing; ... Jehovah has done great things for us and we are thrilled.
>   Psalm 126:1-3

GO'EL

> Let the speech of my mouth and the meditation of my heart be pleasing to You, O Jehovah, my Rock and my *GO'EL*. Psalm 19:14

The idea of "Helper" can go so far as to call on Him to be *GO'EL*, to bring Life and His People back into balance:

> In pride the wicked pursues the poor – let them be taken by the plots which they have contrived. ... Arise, Jehovah God! Lift up Your Hand! Do not forget the dejected. ... But You have seen, for You take note of trouble and provocation, to repay it by Your Hand. The unfortunate one commits himself to You; You are the Helper of the orphan. ... Jehovah, You have heard the longing of the dejected; You will establish their heart; Your ear will hear, to bring justice to the orphan and the crushed, that the men of the world may oppress them no longer. Psalm 10:2, 12, 14, 17-18

> For He will deliver the needy who cries, the poor also, and the one who has no helper. He will have compassion on the poor and needy, and will save the Souls/Lives of the needy. He will redeem/avenge [*GO'EL*] their Soul/Life from deceit and injustice; and precious shall be their Blood in His sight. Psalm 72:12-14

> You have with Your arm redeemed/avenged [*GO'EL*] Your People ... Psalm 77:15

> A Father to orphans and a Judge for widows is God in His holy dwelling. God sets the lonely into homes; He sets the captive into prosperity; but the rebellious dwell in a dry land. Psalm 68:5-6

And perhaps with Covenant emphasis:

> O my God, deliver me from the hand of the wicked, from the palm of the unjust and cruel. For You are my hope, O Jehovah GOD; You are my Trust from my youth. Psalm 71:4-5

Yearning for the Covenant-Partner

> O God, You are my God; earnestly I seek You; my Soul thirsts for You; my flesh longs for You as in a dry and exhausted land without water. In the Holy Place I have perceived You and looked upon Your

power and Your Glory. Because Your *HESED* is better than Life, my lips shall praise You. Psalm 63:1-3

Exuberance of Covenant

I was glad when they said to me, "Let us go into the house of Jehovah." Psalm 122:1

O Jehovah, our Lord, how majestic is Your Name in all the earth, Who has set Your Glory above the heavens! ... When I see Your heavens, the work of Your fingers, the moon and the stars which You have established, what is man that You remember him, and the son of man that You visit him? Psalm 8:1, 3-4

I will bless Jehovah at all times; His praise shall always be in my mouth. My Soul/Life shall boast in Jehovah; the humble shall hear of it and be glad. Magnify Jehovah with me, and let us exalt His Name together! Psalm 34:1-3

It is good to give thanks to Jehovah, and to sing praises to Your Name, O Most High; to make known Your *HESED* in the morning, and Your faithfulness every night, on an instrument of ten strings, on the lute, and on the harp, with harmonious sound. Psalm 92:1-3

Oh come, let us sing joyfully to Jehovah! Let us shout in triumph to the Rock of our salvation. Let us come before His presence with thanksgiving; let us shout in triumph to Him with psalms, for Jehovah is the great God, and the great King above all gods. Psalm 95:1-3

An unmistakable emphasis in the Psalms is the reoccurring keynote of joy, joy in Jehovah's deliverance, joy in His creation, joy in being His Covenant-connected People.

Psalm 119

Psalm 119 is a book of Psalms all on its own, having chapters begun in the consecutive order of the Hebrew alphabet. A great emphasis in the book is on 'the *TORAH*,' which can make the Psalm seem to be merely an extensive demand for obedience, but actually it attempts to set the environment of what the connection of Covenant involves. Knowing, understanding, and following what Covenant requires are important: the 'teachings' are a guide to the righteous, especially for the young. But also "I will see wonderful things from Your *TORAH*" [v 19]: we have a defense from the reproach and scorn of others [vv 22-23], as well as clarity and confidence about our Covenant-relationship ("make your Word sure to Your servant" [v 38]).

Above all, there is a solid basis for hope: "Remember the Word to Your servant, on which You have made me hope. This is my comfort in my affliction, for Your Word has given me life" [vv 49-50]. It can be known what pleases our Covenant-Partner and He can be depended upon for what He has promised ["I looked for Your favor with all my heart, favor me according to Your Word" v 58]. And we have confidence in the things He will do for us: "I know, O Jehovah, that Your judgments are right, and in faithfulness You afflicted me. Please let Your *HESED* be for my comfort, by Your Word to Your servant" [vv 75-76].

In seeing the wonderful things in the *TORAH*, we discover "Your fidelity is to every generation" [v 90] – from Adam and Eve, to Abraham, even to rebellious Israel in the Wilderness – therefore "I will never forget Your precepts, for by them You gave me Life" [v 93]. "By Your precepts I know; so then I hate every false way" [v 104]; "I hate doubting thoughts, but I love Your *TORAH*" [v 113]; "let me not be ashamed of my hope!" [v 116]; "Your testimonies are wonderful, therefore my Soul keeps [guards, preserves, watches over] them" [v 129].

Meanwhile, we *have needed* Your help: "I cry out with my whole heart; O Jehovah, answer me and I will keep Your statutes" [v 145]; "Hear my voice by Your mercy, O Jehovah; give me Life by Your judgment!" [v 149]; "Plead my cause and redeem [*GO'EL*] me; give me Life according to Your Word ... according to Your judgments ... according to Your *HESED*" [vv 154, 156, 159].

Let my cry come before You, O Jehovah; give me wisdom according to Your Word.

Let my prayer come before You; deliver me according to Your Word.
My lips shall utter praise when You have taught me Your statutes.
My tongue shall respond to Your Word, for all Your commandments are righteousness.
Let Your Hand help me for I have chosen Your precepts.
I long for Your salvation, O Jehovah, and Your *TORAH* is my delight.

vv 169-174

A Final Important Thought

My God, My God, why have You forsaken Me? Why are You so far from helping Me, and from the words of My groaning?   Psalm 22:1

As Jesus reminds us as He hangs on the Cross, the grand fulfillment of the Covenant significance in the Psalms will focus on the Individual Who IS the *reality of Covenant* between Jehovah and mankind, of God in human form, of one yet at the same time two. Therefore each Psalm describes Jesus in a far more perfect way than they also describe us.

C. Proverbs

Distancing From Covenant

Proverbs follows very much along the same lines as Psalm 119, where it emphasizes knowledge, understanding, and wisdom in regard to the right way, God's way, as opposed to the fool's way. It and even the Psalms seem to represent a shift in thought in regard to Covenant: perhaps as society becomes more 'sophisticated,' that is, more focused on a larger community than on simple family structures, Covenant becomes more of a static institution than a vibrant process.

Rather than on the relationship in action (such as how Mamre, Eschol and Aner are there when Abraham needs them, or the relationship between David and Jonathan, or Moses arguing with Jehovah in defense of Israel), the emphasis here appears to center on the 'duty' and the mental aspects (that is, the right thinking, the right understanding, the right wisdom, the right actions). This is not to say that these do not belong to Covenant, however perhaps the dynamic aspect has been lost. An example of the difference would be how one may speak of marriage in terms of its energy and personal involvement, as represented by the Song of Solomon, as opposed to speaking of it in terms of the mechanics, a listing of marriage do's and don'ts.

Indeed both sides have their place, yet perhaps this shift of perspective reflects the earlier stages of what we have today, where we know *about* Covenant, but we no longer really know *Covenant*. Even though we have vestiges of Covenant in our society, we have been so far removed from the concept that we have to have special studies or read special books to find out what it is all about. We know its mechanics, we just do not really know its relationship as an everyday, common slice of Life.

Striking Hands

"One suffers evil when he is surety for a stranger; but one hating strikers [of Palms] is safe" [11:15]; "A man lacking heart strikes the Palm; he pledges in the presence of his friends" [17:18]; "Do not be one of those who strike the Palm, who are sureties for loans" [22:26] – these proverbs are strongly against the practice of "striking the Palm," which may have Covenant connection:

> There seems, indeed, to be a gleam of this thought in Job 17:31:
> "Give now a pledge, be surety for me with thyself;
> Who is there that will strike hands with me?"
> The Hebrew word *taq'a* (תקע) here translated "strike," has also the meaning "to pierce" (Judg. 4:21) and "to blow through," or "to drive through" (Num. 10:3); and Job's question might be freely rendered: Who is there that will pierce [or that will clasp pierced] hands with me, in blood friendship? Thus, suretyship grew out of blood-covenanting.
> Trumbull[184]

Perhaps this is a practice adopted from Covenant which either parallels or is the parent to the practice of 'shaking hands on a deal' by which the participants consider the deal unbreakable. It also is suggestive of the modern "high five" which shows solidarity between people who have a common interest.

Friend

> My son, if you are surety for your friend, you struck your Palm for a stranger! You are snared with the words of your mouth, captured by the words of your mouth. Do this then, my son, when you come into the Palm of your friend, go humble yourself and demand [release] to your friend. 6:1-3

Although the imagery of Covenant may be used, the relationship is not there. "Friend" as used here is not the same word as the one describing the unique Covenant sense of "friend" which is used when Abraham is called the "Friend of God" [II Chronicles 20:7; Isaiah 41:8], which also is used in 18:24: "A man of friends [the word used in 6:1-3] may be shattered, but there is a [Covenant-]friend who sticks closer than a brother."

Had the Covenant-Friend word been used in 6:1-3, then there would have been a tension which would instruct the wise to refuse helping out the Covenant-partner, as opposed to the withholding of nothing which the Covenant-partner requests (for example, Mamre, Eschol, and Aner risking their lives in Abraham's need [Genesis 14]). Even though one may, by the use of its imagery, act as if Covenant were at work, Solomon declares that such financial dealings only make strangers out of friendly people. After all, such relationships just do not have the backing, the depth and the trust which Covenant provides.

The Seven Pillars

> Wisdom has built her house, she has hewn out her *seven/oath* pillars;...
> Come, eat of my bread and drink of the wine I have mixed. 9:1,5

Chapter nine opens with what might indicate that Wisdom is grounded in Covenant, speaking of *seven/oath* pillars, where the word for pillars first shows up in the "pillar of cloud ... pillar of fire," the 'OTH (Sign) of the Covenant–Partner Who leads the Israelites through the wilderness. If so, then the meal which Wisdom proposes may be more than just a simple metaphor, but may also allude to the Covenantal meal, as well as the *Peace Offering*. This would not be inappropriate in its allusion to a connection, a oneness of Wisdom with the Source of Covenant.

No Irresponsibility

> [Although] Hand be joined to Hand, the evil one shall not be acquitted, but the seed of the righteous escapes. 11:21

> An abomination to Jehovah is everyone proud in heart: although Hand be joined to Hand, he will not be acquitted. By mercy and truth iniquity is atoned, and in the fear of Jehovah men turn from evil.
> 16:5-6

Although there may be different possible understandings here, a Covenantal perspective could make sense. As discussed previously, Covenant ("Hand be joined to Hand") is not a permission for irresponsibility, it is not a protection for evil, it is not an attempt to make responsibility hang in limbo as one blames the other for evil. Perhaps "proud in heart" might be the picture of one who thinks he is above everyone else, even above the law, and therefore does not have to pay attention to the effects on others. Yet if that one comes to his senses and turns from his evil, then Covenant now has value, there is hope, there is mercy and atonement/ransom [*KAPHAR*].

D. Ecclesiastes

Ecclesiastes does not seem to have anything to contribute to the understanding and development of the concept of Covenant, other than despite the frustration, inequities and injustices of Life, God will step forward and resolve all things according to what is righteous and good.

E. Song of Solomon

The Song of Solomon is a beautiful description of the vibrancy of Love. Although it does not define any new elements nor does it use the key symbolisms within Covenant, it does identify the intensity of the heart which is found therein, with its emotions, yearnings, and delight, here particularly in the Marriage side of this bond. Since the relationship between Jehovah and His People, both in the Old Testament and in the New, is often described as a Bridegroom and His Bride, this book reminds us that Covenant is no mere formal relationship but has its roots in the *total* person.

XII. The Prophets

A. Isaiah

In Search of a *GO'EL* and Intercessor

If the *GO'EL* is the Blood-balancer whose task is to pay attention to the orphan and the fatherless, to the mistreated and the poor, as well as to the 'bigger' items such as the end of a family line (the book of Ruth) and murder, then in numerous places Isaiah is in search of a *GO'EL*:

> So when you spread out your Palms, I will hide My eyes from you; also when you multiply prayers, I will not hear – your hands are full of Blood! Wash yourselves; purify yourselves; remove your evil deeds from before My eyes. Stop doing evil, learn to do good; seek justice, rebuke the oppressor; defend the orphan, plead for the widow.
> 1:15-17

If Jehovah's Life/Blood is flowing in their veins, then the picture would be as Abraham who intercedes on behalf of Sodom and Gomorrah, or as Moses who uses God's own definition of His Glory [*KABOD*] against Him in defense of Israel. But rather what is here is *not* His Life/Blood:

> ... He looked for justice, but behold, Bloodshed; for righteousness, but behold, a cry of distress. ... Woe to those who draw depravity with cords of falsehood, and sin as if with a cart rope;... Woe to those who call evil good, and good evil; who put darkness for light, and light for darkness; who put bitter for sweet, and sweet for bitter! Woe to those who are wise in their own eyes, and cunning in their own sight! Woe to men 'mighty' at drinking wine, woe to men 'bold' in mixing liquor, who justify the wicked for a bribe, and turns the righteous man aside from righteousness!
> 5:7, 18, 20-23

> For your Palms are defiled with Blood, and your fingers with iniquity; your lips have spoken deceit, your tongue has muttered iniquity. No one calls for righteousness, nor does any one judge in honesty. They trust in confusion and speak emptiness; they conceive perverseness and bring forth wickedness. ... Their feet run to evil, and they hurry to

shed innocent Blood; their thoughts are thoughts of iniquity; desolation and destruction are in their paths. The way of peace they do not know, and there is no justice in their ways; they have made themselves crooked paths; whoever walks that way shall not know peace.   59:3-4, 7-8

There is no one seeking justice, defending those who are helpless and in need, and there is no intercessor for those who stand under judgment:

> I looked closely, but there was nobody; among them there was no counselor, who when asked, could answer a word. ... Why, when I came, was there no man; and when I called, was there none to answer? ... He saw that there was no man, and He was amazed that there was no intercessor ... I looked, but there was no one to help, and I was astonished that there was no one to uphold.   41:28; 50:2; 59:16; 63:5

> But this is a People preyed upon and plundered; all are snared in holes and hidden in prison houses; they are for plunder, and no one delivers; for spoil, and no one says, "Bring back!" Who among you will give ear – who will heed and listen in the time to come? Who gave Jacob for spoil, and Israel to the robbers? Was it not Jehovah, He against Whom we have sinned? For they would not walk in His ways nor listen to His *TORAH*. Therefore He poured on him the fury of His anger and the fierceness of war; it has blazed on every side of him, yet he did not know; and it burned him, yet he did not take it to heart.
>   42:22-25

Where is the *GO'EL?* Where is the intercessor? Where is the Abraham or the Moses to plead for those who have made themselves the enemies of God?

That Which is No God

Not only is there no concern for those in need, but Israel turns to something which is total foolishness: idols. Think of the silliness: a man cuts down a tree, chops it up, uses some for mere firewood to cook over, then carves a piece of it into an idol and falls down before it as if it were a supreme god [44:14-19]. It is on the same order as the "lucky" rabbit's foot which sure was not very lucky for the rabbit.

> So also is their land full of idols; they worship the work of their own hands, that which their own fingers have made. People bow down, and each man humbles himself – do not forgive them. 2:8-9

The same kind of delusion has made the People look anywhere else than to Jehovah:

> When they say to you, "Enquire of those who are mediums and spiritists, who whisper and mutter," should not a People consult their God, rather than for the living to seek the dead? 8:19

> You are exhausted by the multitude of your counsels; let now the astrologers, the stargazers, and the new moon fortuneteller stand up and save you from what shall come upon you. 47:13

The delusion will go even farther:

> Because you have said, "We have cut a Covenant with death, and with Sheol we have made an agreement. When the overwhelming scourge passes through, it will not come to us, for we have made a lie our refuge, and we have hidden in deception." 28:15

Ultimately, as the final chapter of II Chronicles [36:20-21] identifies, even the land itself suffers because Israel has discarded their precious relationship with Jehovah:

> Even the Land is defiled under its inhabitants, because they have passed over the *TORAH*, slid by the statutes, and broke the everlasting Covenant. Therefore a curse has devoured the Land, and those who dwell in it are accountable. Therefore those who dwell in the Land are burned, and few men remain. 24:5-6

The Filthy Rags

> But we are all like an unclean thing, and all our righteousnesses are like filthy rags; we all fade as a leaf, and our iniquities, like the wind, have taken us away. 64:6

An interpretation for "filthy rags" is that these were menstrual rags, stained with Blood. Why this image? Because here is lost Life, a badge of the Life lost under the broken Creation Covenant. Rather than something to be paraded before the LORD and the world, this supposed 'righteousness' simply exposes the insensitive perversion of dignity and piety.

The Hand and the Arm of Jehovah

"I will turn My Hand against you, and thoroughly purge away your dross..." [1:25] begins the warning that the Hand of Jehovah will bring not rescue this time, but the curses of broken Covenant.

> Therefore the anger of Jehovah is kindled against His People; He has stretched out His Hand against them and struck them, and the hills trembled. Their carcasses were like filth in the midst of the streets. For all this His anger is not turned back, but His Hand is stretched out still. 5:25

"His anger is not turned away, but His Hand is stretched out still" is repeated in chapters 9 (vv 12, 17, 21) and 10 (v 4), in a section which describes the terrible results of the curses of Covenant, of what happens when the Life/Blood of Covenant has been drained from the Land. This is the LORD's deliberate action, not merely happenstance:

> Behold, Jehovah's Hand is not shortened, that it cannot save; nor His ear heavy[185], that it cannot hear. But your iniquities wedge between you and your God; and your sins have hidden His face from you, so that He does not hear. For your Palms are defiled with Blood, and your fingers with iniquity; your lips have spoken deceit, your tongue has muttered iniquity. 59:1-3

"That He may do His work, His abnormal business, and bring to pass His bond service, His foreign task" [28:21] – as we see in the wrestling of Abraham (Jehovah's *HESED*) with Jehovah (His justice) [Genesis 18], as we see in the Lord's self-description of His *KABOD* (glory) as "goodness, Covenant, grace, and mercy" [Exodus 18:19], such punishment is not His delight – it is foreign to His heart. Yet Justice against such abuse of Covenant will not be ignored by a righteous God.

However Covenant will not be abandoned either! Chapter 14 indicates a turn in the relationship as the Hand of Covenant now describes the defense of Israel and that "His Hand is stretched out" [vv 26, 27; also 23:11; 31:3)] bringing terrible punishment on the nations which have abused His People. Like an '*OTH* (SIGN), "The descent of His Arm" [30:30] will be terrifying for the nations, but comforting for His People: "My Arms will judge the peoples ... and on My Arm they will trust" [51:5].

> Fear not, for I am with you; do not anxiously look about you, for I am your God. I will strengthen you; yes, I will help you; yes, I will uphold you with My righteous Right Hand. ... For I, Jehovah your God, will strengthen your right hand, saying to you, 'Fear not, I will help you.'
> 41:10, 13

And within Covenant, His People will occupy a most honored position among all nations;

> For Zion's sake I will not be silent, and for Jerusalem's sake I will not rest, until her righteousness goes forth as brilliance, and her salvation as a burning torch. The nations shall see your righteousness, and all kings your glory. You shall be called by a new name, which the mouth of Jehovah will name. You shall be a crown of beauty in the Hand of Jehovah, and a royal diadem in the Palm of your God. 62:1-3

However, that Arm "made bare ... in the eyes of all the nations", where "all the ends of the earth shall see the salvation of our God" [52:10] begins a fascinating section, because 'the Arm of Jehovah" [53:1] comes within a description of One absolutely destitute and destroyed, not powerful; the Cesspool of "*our* transgressions, ... *our* iniquities; the chastisement for our peace" [53:5], not a gloriously superior Master.

Jehovah, Our *GO'EL*

> He saw that there is no man, and was stunned that there was no intercessor; so His own Arm rescued for Him; and His own righteousness undergirded Him. For He put on righteousness as a breastplate, and a helmet of salvation on His head; He put on the garments of vengeance for clothing, and wrapped Himself with zeal as

a cloak. According to their works, so He will repay: fury to His adversaries, recompense to His enemies... 59:16-18

For the day of vengeance is in My heart, and the year of My Redeemed [from *GO'EL*] has come. I looked, but no one was helping, and I was stunned that no one was bearing the weight; therefore My own Arm rescued for Me; and My own fury undergirded Me. I have trodden down the peoples in My fury, made them drunk in My fury, and poured their [Blood] on the earth. 63:4-6

No one else is to be found, therefore Jehovah Himself steps in to be *GO'EL*. "Jehovah stands up to contend, and stands to struggle with the People" [3:13] – in the following verses He takes the leaders to task for "plundering" and "crushing My People"; and in 25:4 He is declared as the protector of the helpless: "For You have been a Refuge to the poor, a Stronghold to the needy in his distress, a Shelter from the storm, a Shade from the heat."

Yet Covenant does not mean that He will support His Covenant-partner no matter what. Those who break Covenant will be confronted with their rebellion, and if they do not repent, then the judgment of broken Covenant must be visited upon them – those "with outstretched necks and wanton eyes, walking and mincing as they go" [3:16] will become "desolate" [v 26].

> Enter into the rock, and hide in the dust, from the terror of Jehovah and the splendor of His majesty ... They shall go into the caves in the rocks, and into the holes in the dust, from the terror of Jehovah and the splendor of His majesty, when He arises to make the Land tremble ... To go into the clefts of the rocks, and into the crags of the rugged rocks, from the dread of Jehovah and the splendor of His majesty, when He arises to shake the Land mightily. 2:10, 19, 21

Still, if the scene with Abraham in regard to Sodom and Gomorrah is indeed the picture of the struggle within God between *HESED* and judgment, then the situation with Israel and Judah would have to be very bad for such judgment to be visited upon them. "The splendor of His Majesty" – although God primarily describes His 'Glory' in terms of goodness, grace and mercy, in the following chapter 34 of Exodus, He also reminds us that His Glory includes justice, "who will by no means clear the guilty" [v 7] – those who will not repent. Yet despite all this, when there is repentance, His grace and mercy remain close at hand, "forgiving iniquity and transgression and sin" [also v 7].

> Therefore Jehovah waits to be gracious to you and will rise up to have mercy on you. For a God of justice is Jehovah; blessed are all those who wait for Him. For the People in Zion shall live in Jerusalem; you shall surely not weep. Certainly He will be gracious to you at the sound of your cry; when He hears it, He will answer you.   30:18-19

It is especially in the last third of Isaiah that there is a dramatic shift, where "Jehovah, our *GO'EL*" becomes a resounding 'bell of hope':

> "Remember [*ZEKER*] these, O Jacob, and Israel, for you are My servant; I have formed you, you are servant to Me, O Israel, you will not be forgotten by Me! I have blotted out, like a thick cloud, your rebellion, and like a cloud, your sins. Return to Me, for I have redeemed [*GO'EL*] you."
> Sing, O heavens, for Jehovah has done it! Shout, you lower parts of the earth; break forth into singing, you mountains, O forest ...! For Jehovah has redeemed [*GO'EL*] Jacob, and glorified Himself in Israel. Thus says Jehovah, your *GO'EL*, He who formed you from the womb: "I am Jehovah" ...   44:21-24

> "For your husband is your Maker, Jehovah of hosts is His Name; and your *GO'EL* is the Holy One of Israel; He is called the God of the whole earth. For Jehovah has called you like a woman abandoned and hurt in spirit, like a wife from youth when you were despised," says your God. "For a mere moment I left you, but with great compassion I will gather you. With a little wrath I hid My face from you for a moment; but with everlasting *HESED* I will have mercy on you," says Jehovah, your *GO'EL*.   54:5-8

The Redeemed

"But the Redeemed [*GO'EL*] shall walk there, and the Ransomed [*PADAH*] of the LORD shall return" [35:9-10; see also 51:11] – as One Who brings the Blood back into balance, the *GO'EL* ransoms His People. And since "You have sold yourselves for nothing, you shall be redeemed

[*GO'EL*] without money" [52:3]; on one level, the ransom that is paid will be the Blood of the very oppressors themselves:

> I will feed those who oppress you with their own flesh, and they shall be drunk with their own Blood as with sweet wine. All flesh shall know that I, Jehovah, am your Savior, and your *GO'EL*, the Mighty One of Jacob.   49:26

> But now, thus says Jehovah, Who created you, O Jacob, and He Who formed you, O Israel: "Fear not, for I have redeemed [*GO'EL*] you; I have called you by your name; You are Mine. ... For I am Jehovah your God, the Holy One of Israel, your Savior; I gave Egypt as your atonement [*KAPHAR*], Ethiopia and Seba in your place; you who have been precious in My sight, who have been glorified [*KABOD*], and whom I have loved; therefore I will give men in your stead, and people for your Life. ... Everyone who is called by My Name, whom I have created for My Glory [*KABOD*]; I have formed him, yes, I have made him." ... Thus says Jehovah, your *GO'EL*, the Holy One of Israel...   43:1-4, 7, 14

But there is a larger ransom to be paid, not to outsiders in regard to a transitory slavery, but rather a spiritual Blood-balancing in regard to sin, a ransom paid for all by One from 'among us':

> He is despised and rejected by men, a Man of agony and One Who knows calamity; One from Whom we averted our faces; He was despised, and we did not regard Him. Surely He has borne our calamities and carried our agonies; yet we appraised Him as punished, struck by God, and oppressed. But He was wounded for our rebellion, He was crushed for our iniquities; the chastisement for our peace [*SHALOM*] was upon Him, and by His stripes we are healed.
> All we like sheep have gone astray; each of us has turned to his own path; yet Jehovah has laid on Him the iniquity of us all. He was oppressed and He was afflicted, yet He did not open His mouth; like a lamb led to the slaughter, and a sheep before its shearers is silent, so He did not open His mouth.
> He was taken from oppression and from judgment, and who will ponder His generation? For He was cut off from the land of the living; for the rebellion of My People He was punished. ...
> It pleased Jehovah to crush Him; He has put Him to grief. When You make His Life/Soul an offering for sin, He shall see His seed, He shall prolong His days, and the delight of Jehovah shall prosper in His Hand. He shall see the travail of His Soul, and be satisfied. By His

knowledge My righteous Servant shall make many righteous, for He shall bear their iniquities. Therefore I will allot to Him a portion with the great, and He shall divide the spoil with the strong, because He poured out His Life/Soul to death, and He was numbered with the rebellious; He bore the sin of many, and made intercession for the rebels. 53:3-12

"My righteous Servant" faces an impossible task: Psalm 49:7-8 speaks of the inability to give to God a ransom for oneself (Revised Standard Version) nor one's brother (King James Version). *KAPHAR*, as in *the Day of Atonement*, has the sense of redemption, and the imagery of the whole sacrificial system is based on a substitutionary victim ransoming the People – which is no permanent solution since the sacrifices needed to be constantly repeated. So how can this "Servant" have the ability to redeem an innumerable amount of people, the "us all" in the passage?

In Genesis 14:24, Mamre, Eschol, and Aner put their lives on the line for Covenant-partner Abraham – would the LORD do any less for His People, especially since Covenant is His own design? In Genesis 15:17, the imagery is that Jehovah participates, He Himself and not by proxy, in the Covenant with Abraham. Now "we" are in need, "our" lives are threatened, what then should "we," as Abraham's offspring[186], expect from "our" Covenant-Partner?

> Therefore the Lord Himself will give you a *'OTH* [sign]: Behold, the virgin shall conceive and bear a Son, and shall call His Name "Immanuel" ["God with us"]. 7:14

Although the Hebrew uses simply a "young woman" in this verse, in the Jewish translation into Greek called the "Septuagint," made two hundred years *before* Jesus is born, of all the Greek words which might be used, it is startling that the rabbis choose the specific word, "virgin." Obviously God Himself steps into human history in a most unique way:

> For a Child is born to us, a Son is given to us; the government will be upon His shoulder; and His Name will be called Wonderful, Counselor, Mighty God, Everlasting Father, Prince of Peace [*SHALOM*]. Of the increase of His government and of peace [*SHALOM*] there will be no end, upon David's throne and over his kingdom, to establish it and

uphold it with judgment and righteousness from now up until forever. The zeal of Jehovah of hosts will do this.   9:6-7

That this Child will be called "Mighty God, Everlasting Father" may raise no eyebrows in most ancient civilizations, since their kings are often considered at least demigods. But not so in Israel! Through the mouth of a prophet, especially with a God Who declares "For My own sake, for My own sake, I will do it... My Glory [*KABOD*] I will not give to another" [Isaiah 48:11] – if Jehovah Himself steps in, then here will be that ability to deal with the sin of "us all." Indeed this Child will need to be THE "Mighty God."

You are a Covenant

> Behold! My Servant whom I uphold, My Elect One in Whom My Life/Soul delights! I have put My Spirit upon Him; He will bring forth justice to the nations... Thus says God Jehovah,... Who gives breath [Life[187]] to the people on [the land], and spirit to those who walk on it: "I, Jehovah, have called You in righteousness, and will hold Your hand; I will preserve You and *give You as a Covenant to people*, as a Light to nations, to open blind eyes, to bring out prisoners from the prison – those who sit in the darkness of confinement. I am Jehovah, that is My Name; and My Glory [*KABOD*] I will not give to another, nor My praise to carved images.   42:1, 5-8

> Thus says Jehovah, the *GO'EL* of Israel, His Holy One, to the Despised of Life/Soul, to the Loathed of nations, to the Servant of rulers: "Kings shall see and rise, princes also shall worship, because of Jehovah Who is faithful, the Holy One of Israel, Who chose You. ... In an acceptable time I have heard You, and in the day of salvation I have helped You; I will preserve You and *give You as a Covenant to people*, to restore the earth, to cause them to inherit the desolate inheritance; that You may say to the prisoners, 'Go forth'; to those who are in darkness, 'Reveal yourselves.'...   49:7-9

What is notable here is that "My Servant..., My Elect One in Whom My Soul [Life, hence Blood] delights" [42:1] will *not* be *like* a sign or representation or initiator of Covenant, but rather would *be* the Covenant. Truly in the ancient world, when a treaty between countries is made, often the daughter of one king would be given to the other king in marriage, and that daughter somewhat embodied the treaty – as long as the marriage lasted, the treaty lasted. But despite how a treaty may borrow from this relationship, it is not a true Covenant. This here is not a picture of two countries in agreement, but rather of *Life* from the Creator Himself that would bring Light, sight and freedom; this "Servant" is to be that very flow of Life which Covenant has always described.

But by definition, Covenant means two persons becoming one – so how can any *single* person *be* Covenant? That is like saying a person *is* marriage. That doesn't make sense and therefore is this prophecy to be symbolic only? Or does He Who designed Covenant have something greater in mind, something reflected in "Immanuel," where God in this Elect One would be *the reality of two in one*, the reality of Covenant 'in the flesh'? And God has to be personally involved since His Glory will not be attributed to any other than Himself. The difference here is expressed primarily in regard to His Spirit's presence forever with those who by entering into *this* Covenant become one with this "Servant."

> "The *GO'EL* will come to Zion, and to those who turn from rebellion in Jacob," says Jehovah. "As for Me, this is My Covenant with them ... My Spirit Who is upon you and My words which I have put in your mouth, shall not depart from your mouth, nor from the mouth of your descendants, nor from the mouth of your descendants' descendants," says Jehovah, "from this time and forevermore." 59:20-21

Yet this is not only to the Chosen People – it is also "Behold, I will lift My Hand to the nations, and set up My standard for the peoples..." [49:22]; "Also the sons of the foreigner who join themselves to Jehovah, to serve Him, and to love the Name of Jehovah" [56:6-7] – for all this is to be "an everlasting Covenant" [55:3-4; 61:8], "'My steadfast love [*HESED*] shall not depart from you, nor shall the Covenant of My peace [*SHALOM*] be removed,' says Jehovah, Who has mercy on you." [54:10].

> Surely You are our Father, though Abraham was ignorant of us, and Israel would not acknowledge us; You, O Jehovah, are our Father; Our *GO'EL* – from everlasting is Your Name. 63:16

B. Jeremiah

No Intercession

Jehovah has been driven so deeply into disgust toward the deliberate rebellion of His People, that there is nothing which He will allow which can ransom Israel and Judah from the judgment which broken Covenant demands – whereas Isaiah is in search for an intercessor, here there will be none:

> But you, do not pray for this People, nor lift up a cry or prayer for them, nor intercede to Me; for I will not hear you.
> 7:16; also 11:14; 14:11

> "Do not enter the house of mourning, nor go to lament or bemoan them; for I have taken away My peace [*SHALOM*] from this People," says Jehovah, "even *HESED* and compassion." 16:5

> ... Even if Moses and Samuel stood before Me, My Soul/Life would not turn toward this People. Take them away from My face, and let them go out ... For who will pity you, O Jerusalem? ... You have forsaken Me, ... you have gone backwards, therefore I will stretch out My Hand against you and destroy you; I am weary of relenting!
> 15:1, 5-6

In fact, although the prophet had indeed once interceded for them, he finally shares in Jehovah's anger:

> Shall evil be repaid for good? They have dug a pit for my Life/Soul! Remember how I stood before You to speak good for them, to turn away Your wrath from them! Therefore deliver their sons to the famine, ... Let their men be the slain of death, their young men killed by the sword in battle ... Jehovah, You know all their counsel against me, to kill me. Do not atone [*KAPHAR*] their iniquity, nor blot out their sin from Your sight; but let them stagger before You: deal with them in the time of Your anger.
> 18:20-21, 23

False Religion

Ultimately, the pivotal issue comes back to "Because they have forsaken the Covenant of Jehovah their God, and worshiped other gods and served them" [22:9]. The derision which God has for idols in Isaiah is echoed here:

> ... who say to a tree, 'You are my father,' and to a stone, 'You gave me birth.' For they have turned their back to Me and not their face; yet in the time of their trouble they will say, 'Rise up and save us.' But where are your gods which you have made for yourselves? Let them arise, if they can save you in the time of your trouble – for as the number of your cities are so are your gods, O Judah. 2:27-28

> For the customs of the peoples are empty; for one cuts a tree from the forest, the work of the workman's hands, with the ax. They deck it out with silver and gold; they fasten it with nails and hammers so that it will not wobble. Like a decorated fencepost, they cannot speak; they must be carried, because they cannot walk. Do not be afraid of them, for they can on their own do neither evil, nor good ... a piece of lumber is a doctrine of emptiness ... Everyone is stupid in his knowledge; every metalsmith is shamed by the idol, since his molded image is deception – there is no breath/spirit in them. They are emptiness, a work of delusions; in the time of their reckoning they shall perish. 10:3-5, 8, 14-5

They became a 'water'-less – a 'Living Water'-less – wasteland, forsaking "Me, the Fountain of *Living Waters*." Instead they have "hewn themselves cisterns – broken cisterns which can hold no water" [2:13; see 17:13], having a 'Life' based on the emptiness of false gods, a false religion supported by prophets who lie:

> The prophets prophesy lies in My Name. I did not send them, I did not command them, I did not speak to them; a false vision, a worthless divination, and the deceit of their heart they prophesy to you. 14:14

> "I have heard what the prophets said who prophesy lies in My Name, saying, 'I have dreamed, I have dreamed!' ... They scheme to make My People forget My Name by their dreams which each man tells his neighbor, as their fathers have forgotten My Name for Baal! The prophet who has a dream, let him tell his dream; but he who has My Word with him, let him speak My Word faithfully. What is the straw to the grain?" says Jehovah. 23:25-28

But what literally disgusts God is the sacrificing of children – "the Blood of the innocents (... which I did not command or speak, nor did it come into My mind)" [19:4-5], "nor did it come into My heart" [7:31].

Consider how, when Jehovah commands Abraham to enter into Covenant by Circumcision, He specifically includes the eight-day-old child [Genesis 17:12]; and even Moses is about to be killed for apparently not bringing his son into Covenant [Exodus 4:24-26] – it is no wonder then that child sacrifice would never come into God's heart, because His heart yearned for the Covenant relationship, not for a different kind of cattle for sacrifice. So strong is His rejection of such sacrifices, that He turns it around: rather than a sacrifice being thought of as food for the gods [Psalm 50:12-13], they would be forced to eat their own children in the coming terrible siege [prophesy: 19:9, Leviticus 26:29; Deuteronomy 28:53; fulfillment: II Kings 6:29].

The Reoccurring Note of Justice

Although the foolishness of idol worship is particularly galling to the LORD, how often a major pivot for the judgment facing Judah is justice – that if the king will not 'balance the Blood,' then Jehovah will step in and do major spiritual correction.

> ... Hear the Word of Jehovah, O king of Judah, ... "Do justice and righteousness, and deliver the robbery victim out of the oppressor's hand. Do not maltreat nor do violence to the stranger, the orphan, or the widow, nor shed innocent blood in this place. For if you resolutely do this word, then kings who sit on David's throne shall enter the gates of this house, riding in chariots and on horses, he and his servants and his people. But if you will not heed these words, I swear [*SHABA*] on Myself," says Jehovah, "that this house shall become a desolation. ... Woe to him who builds his house without righteousness and his upper rooms without justice, who uses his neighbor's service without pay and gives him nothing for his work. ... Did not your father eat and drink, and do justice and righteousness? Then it was well with him. He judged the cause of the poor and needy; then it was well. Was that not to know Me?" says Jehovah. "Yet your eyes and heart desire nothing but your greed, to shed innocent Blood, to oppress and to extort."   22:2-5, 13, 15-17

The Loyalty That Should Have Been There

Chapter 35 recounts the example of the Rechabites' faithfulness in obeying the instruction of their father Jonadab to not drink wine. It is a vivid contrast to how Israel could have been faithful but simply refused:

> I also sent you all My servants the prophets, rising up early and sending them,... But you have not inclined your ear, nor heeded Me. The sons of Jonadab, son of Rechab, followed their father's command, with which he charged them, but this People does not obey Me. Therefore thus says Jehovah God of hosts, the God of Israel: "Behold, I bring on Judah and on all the inhabitants of Jerusalem all the calamity which I have pronounced against them; because I spoke to them but they did not listen, and I called to them but they did not answer." 35:15-17

Jehovah vs. Jehovah

But this coming judgment is no dispassionate reaction by the LORD. In Genesis 18:23-32, Abraham and Jehovah struggle with each other over the judgment of Sodom and Gomorrah, or rather, the *HESED* of God in Abraham struggles with the justice of God, to where justice eventually concedes that, in addition to Lot and his family, only one additional righteous person per city would be enough to save the territory. This same struggle is evident in Jeremiah, where again only one righteous person could save the whole city:

> Run to and fro through the streets of Jerusalem; see now and know; and seek in her open places if you can find a man – anyone who does justice, who seeks truth – and I will pardon her. 5:1

Even as judgment is knocking at the door, the LORD is still considering "if that nation against whom I have spoken turns from its evil, I will reverse the distress which I intended to do to it" [18:8], "that everyone may turn from his evil way, then I will forgive their iniquity and their sin" [36:3; also 26:3].

Go and proclaim these words toward the north, and say: 'Return, backsliding Israel,' says Jehovah; 'I will not cause My anger to fall on you. For I am merciful,' says Jehovah; 'I will not keep anger forever. Only recognize your iniquity, that you have rebelled against Jehovah your God, and have scattered your ways to strangers under every green tree, and you have not obeyed My voice,' says Jehovah. 'Turn back, O backsliding children,' says Jehovah; 'for I am married to you. I will take you, one from a city and two from a family, and I will bring you to Zion.' 3:12-14

"And You Would Not!" [Matthew 23:37; Luke 13:34]

God has such a dream for Israel – "that they may become My People, for renown, for praise, and for Glory; but they would not hear" [13:11]; He has tried again and again to prevent the culmination of judgment, "rising up early and speaking, but you did not hear, and I called you, but you did not answer" [7:13 (v 25; 25:3-4; 26:5; 29:19; 32:33; 35:1; 44:4)].

> Now therefore, speak to the men of Judah and to the inhabitants of Jerusalem, saying, "Thus says Jehovah: 'Behold, I am fashioning a calamity and devising a plan against you. Turn now each one from his evil way, and make your ways and your doings good.'"
> But they say, "It is hopeless! So we will walk according to our own thoughts, and each will obey the stubbornness of his evil heart."
> 18:11-12

He has given them 'the benefit of the doubt' and has tried to shake them loose from their rebellion, but still they would not turn back to the true bond of Covenant:

> ... You struck them, but they feel no pain; You debilitated them, but they refuse correction. They have made their faces harder than rock; they have refused to return.
> Therefore I said, 'Surely they are poor, they are foolish; for they do not know the way of Jehovah, the judgment of their God. I myself will go to the great men and speak to them ...' But these have altogether smashed the yoke and torn off the bonds.
> Therefore a lion from the forest shall slay them, a wolf of the deserts shall destroy them; a leopard will stalk their cities. Everyone

who goes out from them shall be torn in pieces, because their rebellions are many; their backslidings have increased.

How shall I pardon you for this? Your sons have forsaken Me and have sworn by non-gods ... Shall I not reckon with them for these things? ... On such a nation like this shall My Soul/Life not take vengeance? 5:3-9

The height of their rebellion is to break even the Covenant they had made with each other which is cut within their Covenant with the LORD:

Thus says Jehovah, the God of Israel: "I cut Covenant with your fathers in the day when I brought them out of the land of Egypt, out of the house of bondage, saying, 'At the end of seven years every man set free his Hebrew brother, who has been sold to him; when he has served you six years, you shall set him completely free from you.' But your fathers did not heed Me nor inclined their ear.

"You were now turned and had done what was right in My sight — proclaiming liberty every man to his neighbor; you even cut Covenant before Me in the house which is called by My Name. But you turned again and disgraced My Name, and every one caused his male and female slaves ... to return and brought them into subjection ..."

Therefore thus says Jehovah: "You have not heeded Me in proclaiming liberty ... Behold, I proclaim a liberty to you, ... — to the sword, to pestilence, and to famine! And I will remove you to terror within all the kingdoms of the earth. I will give the men who have transgressed My Covenant, who have not performed the words of the Covenant which they made before Me, when they cut the calf in two and passed between its parts ... I will give them into the hand of their enemies and into the hand of those who seek their Life..." 34:13-20

When even the animals, "the stork in the heavens ... the turtledove, the swift, and the swallow" [8:7] are aware of "their time," "no man repented of his wickedness, saying, 'What have I done?' ... My People do not know the judgment of Jehovah" [8:6-7].

For you were deceitful in your hearts when you sent me to Jehovah your God, saying, 'Pray for us to Jehovah our God, and tell us all which Jehovah our God shall say and we will do it.' I have this day told it to you, but you have not heeded the voice of Jehovah your God, in all which was sent you. Now therefore, fully know that you shall die by the sword, by famine, and by pestilence in the place where you desire to go to dwell. 42:20-22

So Judgment will Descend

From the beginning of the book, "...They have turned their back and not their face to Me" [2:27-28] is answered in 18:17, "I will show them [My] back and not the face in the day of their calamity." The "outstretched Hand and strong Arm" – instruments of Covenant which hold warning to those who would threaten Israel – now will turn against Covenant-breaker Israel in "anger and fury and great wrath" [21:5]. "Because they have defiled ... My inheritance with the carcasses of their detestable and disgusting things" – heaped garbage in Jehovah's living room, so to speak – "I will repay their iniquity and their sin double" [16:18].

> ... therefore behold, I, even I, will utterly forget you and cast out from before My face you and the city which I gave you and your fathers. I will lay an everlasting disgrace upon you, and a perpetual shame, which will not be forgotten. 23:39-40

> You have done more wickedly than your fathers, for behold, no one listens to Me – each one follows the twists of his own evil heart. Therefore I will cast you out of this Land into a land which neither you nor your fathers know; and there you shall serve other gods day and night, where I will not give you favor. 16:12-13

> I will give them as an object of horror and evil to all the kingdoms of the earth, to be a disgrace and a proverb, a sneer and a curse, in all places where I shall drive them. I will send the sword, the famine, and the pestilence among them, till they are consumed from the Land which I gave to them and to their fathers. 24:9-10

The judgment will follow even those who think they can escape by running away to Egypt:

> "... all the remnant of Judah, who went to the land of Egypt to dwell there, shall know whose words will stand, Mine or theirs. And this shall be a SIGN ['OTH] to you," says Jehovah, "that I will punish you in this place, that you may know that My words will surely stand against you for affliction." 44:28-29

Yet the Grief of God

In wrath against the rebellion and broken Covenant Jehovah has to act, yet heaven echoes with a sob:

> I have forsaken My house, I have left My heritage; I have given the dearly beloved of My Life/Soul into the hand of her enemies.   12:7

> Therefore you shall say this word to them: "Let My eyes run down with tears night and day, and do not let them cease; for, with a great shattering, the virgin daughter of My People has been crushed with a terrible blow."   14:17

> Is Ephraim My dear son? Is he a pleasant child? For as often as I spoke against him, I earnestly remember [ZEKER] him still; therefore My inward parts cry aloud for him; I will surely have compassion on him, says Jehovah.   31:20

> He strung His bow like an enemy; He reared up His Right Hand like an adversary, He killed all who were pleasing to the eye in the tent of the daughter of Zion; He has poured out His fury like fire.
> Lamentations 2:4

And Jeremiah is also overcome:

> My heart within me is broken because of the prophets; all my bones shake. I am like a drunken man, and like a man overcome by wine, because of Jehovah, and because of His holy words.   23:9

Holding Fast to Hope

Jehovah has been spit on, slapped down, scorned, given mocking worship and outright rejection, yet despite His justifiable wrath this punishment is not what really lies deep in His heart. Even already "from afar" He anticipates when He will gather to Himself "*all* the families of Israel, and they shall be My People..., I have loved you with an everlasting Love; therefore with *HESED* I have drawn you" [31:1-3].

> For I will set My eyes on them for good, and I will bring them back to this Land; I will build them and not tear them down, I will plant them and not uproot them. I will give them a heart to know Me, that I am

Jehovah; and they shall be My People, and I will be God to them, for they will return to Me with their whole heart. 24:6-7

"For I know the plans which I envision for you," says Jehovah, "plans of peace and not of evil, to give you a future and a hope. Then you will call upon Me and come and pray to Me, and I will listen to you. You will seek Me and find Me; when you search for Me with all your heart, I will be found by you," says Jehovah. "I will turn away your captivity, I will gather you from all nations and from all the places where I have driven you ..." 29:11-14

There will be repentance even from "Ephraim" (Israel): "You have chastised me, ... turn me back, and I will be turned... Surely, after my turning, I repented; ... I was ashamed and humiliated..." [31:18-19]. Amazingly, the door still is not shut against this rebellious People: "For Israel is not forsaken, nor Judah, ... though their land was filled with sin against the Holy One of Israel" [51:5], and Covenant can still be relied on:

Do not abhor us, for Your Name's sake; do not disgrace the throne of Your Glory. Remember [ZEKER], and do not break Your Covenant with us. 14:21

Despite what appears to be the worst of disasters, Jehovah's Covenant-Partner is to thrive even in exile, and is to pray for the well-being of the place wherever they find themselves:

Build houses and dwell in them; plant gardens and eat their fruit. Take wives and beget sons and daughters; and take wives for your sons and give your daughters to husbands, so that they may bear sons and daughters and multiply there, and not diminish. Seek the peace [SHALOM] of the city where I have sent you into exile, and pray to Jehovah for it; for in its peace [SHALOM] you will have peace [SHALOM]. 29:5-7

There will be a 'salvation' which will replace the great rescue of Israel from Egypt: the benchmark of God's mercy will become "As Jehovah lives, Who brought back the children of Israel from the land of the north and from all the lands to which He had expelled them" [16:14-15].

> Thanksgiving shall go forth from them, the voice of those who are merry; I will multiply them, and they shall not be a few; I will also glorify [*KABOD*] them, and they shall not be insignificant. His sons shall be as before, and his congregation shall be established before Me. I will punish all of his oppressors. ... "You shall be My People, and I will be your God."
> 30:19-20, 22

In the midst of shattered Covenant after generations of rejection, God will still demonstrate His righteousness by *His* faithfulness to His Covenant, particularly to David:

> Thus says Jehovah: "If you can break My Covenant with the day and My Covenant with the night, so that there would not be day and night in their time, then My Covenant may also be broken with David My servant, so that he shall not have a son to reign on his throne, and with the Levites and the priests, My ministers."
> 33:20

And along with that declaration of faithfulness comes a powerful example of hope even when it seems all, even their Land, is lost. Jeremiah is instructed to buy a field in chapter 32, "For thus says Jehovah of hosts, the God of Israel: 'Houses and fields and vineyards shall be bought again in this land'" [v 15]. Yet Jeremiah cannot divorce himself from the extreme confluence of emotions: on one hand is the evidence of Jehovah's commitment to Israel throughout the past:

> You brought Your People Israel out of the land of Egypt with SIGNs [*'OTH*], with wonders, with a strong Hand, with an outstretched Arm, and with great terror; You have given them this Land, of which You swore to their fathers to give them – a land flowing with milk and honey.
> 32:21-22

yet in front of him is the horror-filled present which has to be journeyed through before the hope will materialize: "Look, the siege mounds! They have come to the city to seize it ... You said to me, O Lord GOD, 'Buy for yourself the field for silver, and call witnesses'! – yet the city is given into the hand of the Chaldeans" [v 24-25].

Still in the midst of the bleakness of the moment, "Behold, the days are coming,... when I will perform that good thing which I have promised" and "the voice of joy and the voice of gladness, the voice of the bridegroom and the voice of the bride" will be heard again in the land, to "Praise Jehovah of hosts, for Jehovah is good, for His mercy endures forever" [33:14, 11]. The "Branch of righteousness ... shall execute judgment and righteousness in the earth" [v 15] and:

> Behold, I will bring it health and healing; I will heal them and reveal to them the abundance of peace [*SHALOM*] and truth. ... I will cleanse them from all their iniquity in which they have sinned against Me, and I will pardon all their iniquities in which they sinned and in which they rebelled against Me. Then it shall be to Me a name of joy, a praise, and an honor before all nations of the earth, who shall hear all the good which I do to them; they shall be awed and tremble for all the goodness and all the peace [*SHALOM*] that I make for it.   33:6-9

Yet God will not be blind to continued disobedience:

> "It shall be, if they will learn carefully the ways of My People, to swear [*SHABA*] by My Name, 'As Jehovah lives,' as they taught My People to swear [*SHABA*] by Baal, then they shall be built up in the midst of My People. But if they do not obey, I will certainly tear out that nation and destroy it," says Jehovah.   12:16-17

The *GO'EL* to 'Balance the Blood'

Wrath will be directed toward all who cause suffering to this Covenant-partner still treasured in God's heart:

> "It shall be, when seventy years are fulfilled, that for their iniquity I will punish the king of Babylon, his nation, and the land of the Chaldeans, – I will make it a perpetual desolation. So I will bring on that land all My words which I have declared against it ... Many nations and great kings shall be served by them also; and I will repay them according to their deeds and according to the works of their own hands."
>
> Thus says Jehovah God of Israel to me: "Take this wine cup of wrath from My Hand, and cause all the nations, to whom I send you, to drink it. And they will drink and stagger and go mad because of the sword that I will send among them." ...
>
> "For behold, though I begin to bring calamity on the city which is called by My Name, should you go utterly guiltless? You shall not be

guiltless, for I will call for a sword on all the inhabitants of the earth," says Jehovah of hosts. ... "Jehovah will roar from on high, and utter His voice from His holy dwelling; He will roar mightily over His sheepfold. With a shout, like those who tread grapes, He responds against all the inhabitants of the earth. A tumult will go to the ends of the earth, for Jehovah has a quarrel with the nations; He will bring suit against all flesh. The wicked He will put to the sword, ... Behold, evil shall go forth from nation to nation, and a great tempest shall be stirred up from the ends of the earth."   25:12-16, 29-32

Therefore all those who devour you shall be devoured; and all your foes, all of them, shall go into captivity; those who plunder you will be for plunder, and all who prey upon you I will give for prey.   30:16

In 23:19-20 and in 30:23-24, the "violent whirlwind" of God's judgment, which "will dance on the head of the wicked; the anger of Jehovah will not turn back until He has executed and carried out the intents of His heart" ends with the statement: "In the latter days you will understand it with wisdom." Simply put: 'when it all shakes out' – when those in power come to realize that their power is not self-attained but only loaned to them and when the false prophets discover their sources are counterfeit, then all will discover the (unpleasant, for many) reality that Jehovah is the only real God.

Perhaps we are surprised that Babylon is to now experience the LORD's wrath precisely for being the instrument of God's judgment. The condemnation, however, apparently stems from Babylon's arrogance. As a point of comparison, some 'primitive' cultures have a small ritual of apology and thanks to the spirit of the deer or animal they have killed in the hunt, humbly recognizing that this is a sad necessity to maintain their tribe's existence. But not so Babylon – they had exulted in the destruction and murder they had wreaked on Israel, therefore:

"Because you had glee, because you gloated, you destroyers of My heritage, because you are fat like a heifer in new grass, and you bellow like bulls" ... Because of Jehovah's wrath it will not be inhabited, but will be desolate – all of it. Everyone who goes by Babylon shall be stunned and hiss at all her plagues. ... for it is the vengeance of Jehovah. Take vengeance on her! As she has done, do to her! ... Repay her according to her work; according to all she has done, do to her; for against Jehovah she has been haughty, against the Holy One of Israel.

Thus says Jehovah of hosts: "The children of Israel, as also the children of Judah, were oppressed; all who captured them have held them fast; they refused to let them go. Their Redeemer [GO'EL] is strong; Jehovah of hosts is His Name. He will earnestly prosecute their case, that He may give the Land rest, and trembling to the residents of Babylon."

"The cruelty done to my flesh be upon Babylon," the inhabitant of Zion will say; "and my Blood upon the inhabitants of Chaldea!" ... Therefore thus says Jehovah: "Behold, I will defend your case and take vengeance for you. ... As Babylon caused the slain of Israel to fall, so at Babylon the slain of all the earth shall fall."

50:11,13,15, 29, 33-34; 51:35-36, 49

Yet even this is not merely punishment without a goal:

> O Jehovah, my Strength and my Fortress, my Refuge in the day of distress, to You the nations shall come from the ends of the earth and say, "Surely our fathers have inherited lies, emptiness and that which has no value." ... Therefore behold, this time I will make them know: I will make them know *My Hand* and My might; and they shall know that *My Name is Jehovah*. 16:19, 21

"For Jehovah has redeemed [*PADAH*] Jacob, and ransomed [*GO'EL*] him from the hand of one stronger than he" [31:11] – the ultimate purpose of watching this play out is to give hope in the midst of a rough road:

> O Jacob My servant, do not dread, nor be terrified, O Israel, for I am with you; for I will make a full end of all the nations to where I have driven you, but of you I will not make a full end ...
> 46:27 (also 30:10-11)

And an Even Greater Hope

> "In those days and at that time," says Jehovah, "The iniquity of Israel may be sought, but it does not exist; and the sins of Judah, but they shall not be found; for I will forgive those whom I preserve." 50:20

In regard to the "whirlwind" passages above, from our vantage point in the New Testament's "latter days," we who have seen the Cross, the suffering, the abandonment and the death of Jesus, realize even more profoundly how that "violent whirlwind" descended upon the One Who is described earlier in chapter 23:

> ... I will establish to David a Righteous Branch; a King shall reign and act wisely, and do justice and righteousness in the earth. In His days Judah will be saved, and Israel will dwell safely; this is His Name by which He will be called: JEHOVAH OUR RIGHTEOUSNESS.
>
> 23:5-6

And there will be a new Covenant, "an everlasting Covenant which will not be forgotten" [50:4-5], "an everlasting Covenant with them, where I will not turn away from doing good to them" [32:40]:

> Behold, the days are coming, says Jehovah, when I will cut a new Covenant with the house of Israel and with the house of Judah not like the Covenant I cut with their fathers in the day that I took them by the hand to bring them out of the land of Egypt, My Covenant which they broke, though I was a Husband to them, says Jehovah. But this is the Covenant which I will cut with the house of Israel after those days, says Jehovah: I will put My *TORAH* in their inward parts, and write it on their hearts; I will be their God, and they shall be My People. No more shall they teach each man his neighbor, and each man his brother, saying, 'Know Jehovah,' for they all shall know Me, from the least to the greatest of them, says Jehovah. For I will forgive their iniquity, and will remember their sin no more. 31:31-34

Lamentations

This short book is a vivid first-hand struggle with the judgment of God. As often happens with a person who is grounded upon the LORD, even when overcome with the sense of loss and despair, hope still weaves itself throughout the background and keeps surfacing. In spite of the sense of abandonment, this person of faith just cannot let go of hope or of dependence on the *HESED* of Jehovah. 'This *will* end and our God *will* restore us' – because of His relationship with us, His promises, and especially His Covenant (although not explicitly stated as such).

This I restore to my heart, therefore I have hope. Through Jehovah's *HESED* we are not consumed, because His compassions fail not.

They are new every morning; great is Your faithfulness. "Jehovah is my portion," says my Soul/Life, "therefore I hope in Him!" 3:21-24

Chapter 3 starts in a very personal way, as if the speaker is both observer and victim of the LORD's devastation, the counterpoint to Isaiah's "Man of Sorrows" as a firsthand account:

> I am the man who has seen affliction by the rod of His wrath. He led me and made me walk in darkness and not in light. Surely He has turned His Hand against me all day long. 3:1-3

It is indeed Covenant: 'your destruction is mine, I cannot separate myself from it.' And since Isaiah's Anointed One *is* the New Covenant, the guilt, the condemnation, the destruction, will all be His; His will be not *a* suffering, but *all* suffering. He will be no mere detached Observer, but Participant; not just Redeemer, but also the Redeemed:

> You came near on the day I called on You, and said, "Do not fear!" O Lord, You have pleaded the case for my Soul/Life; You have redeemed [*GO'EL*] my Life. 3:57-58

C. *Ezekiel*

"Behold, It Has Come... The End Has Come... Behold, It Has Come" [7:5-6]

> I came to the captives at Tel Aviv ... I sat where they sat, and remained there being appalled among them *seven/oath* days. 3:15

Can one possibly fathom the anguish of Soul which is reflected in the cry of 7:5-6! For 430 days, a day for each year of Israel's rebellion, and a number reflecting Israel's stay and subsequent slavery in Egypt [Exodus 12:40-41], Ezekiel has borne the iniquity of God's People [Ezekiel 4:3-8]. In the death of his wife, he depicts the stupefied grief of loss in 24:16-24, demonstrating how the People will, without being allowed a whimper, watch the desecration and destruction of the jewel of their identity: *the*

Temple. It will be a time of "sighs/groans too deep for words" [Romans 8:26].

"The Land is Filled With Crimes of Blood" [7:23]

> Son of man, will you judge, will you judge the bloody city? Yes, show her all her abominations!
> Then shall you say, 'Thus says the Lord Jehovah: "The city sheds Blood in her midst, that her time may come; and she makes idols within herself to defile herself. ... Behold, the princes of Israel: each one has used his power to shed Blood in you. In you they have disdained father and mother; in your midst they have oppressed the stranger; in you they have abused the orphan and the widow. You have despised My holy things and profaned My *Sabbath*s. In you men of slander have caused Blood to be shed; in you are those who have eaten [sacrifices] on the high places; in your midst they have devised schemes. In you the nakedness of the father has been uncovered; in you they have humiliated a woman who is set apart during her uncleanness. One has committed abomination with his neighbor's wife; another lewdly has defiled his daughter–in–law; and in you another has violated his sister, his father's daughter. In you they have taken bribes to shed Blood; you have taken interest and excess; you have profited from your neighbor by extortion – and Me you have forgotten," says the Lord Jehovah. "Behold, I have struck My Palm at the dishonest profit which you have made, and at the Bloodshed which has been in your midst.   22:2-3, 6-13

The curious phrase, "I have struck My Palm," seems to carry the idea of 'slapping the table' or 'pounding the fist into the other hand' in anger. Although not every instance where "Palm" appears necessarily indicates Covenant connection, could this have been the Covenantal version of 'rending the clothes in grief' [for example, II Samuel 3:31 and II Chronicles 34:27]? It certainly is in reaction to the abuse of position and power of those in authority: "Enough, O princes of Israel! Turn away violence and oppression, do justice and righteousness, and stop extorting My People" [45:9].

There is no refuge from the onslaught of lies, especially from the politicians, who are "like wolves tearing prey, to shed Blood, to destroy Souls/Lives, and to get dishonest gain" [22:27]. Those in spiritual leadership "... have spoken emptiness and prophesied lies ... who envision emptiness and who divine lies; ... they have caused My People to stray, saying, 'Peace!' and there is no peace" [13:8-10] and the women "who sew amulets on their sleeves... Will you hunt the Souls/Lives of My People, and give life to the Souls which come to you?" [v 18] – they "put to death Souls who should not die, and keep alive Souls who should not live, by your lying to My People who listen to lies" [v 19]. They, "with lies, have saddened the heart of the righteous, whom I have not made sad; and have strengthened the hands of the wicked, so that he should not turn from his wicked way to keep him alive" [v 22].

Not even the priests are a protection from the disintegration of the Covenant People:

> Her priests have violated My *TORAH* and defiled My holy things: they have not divided the holy from the common; they have acknowledged no difference between the unclean and the clean; they have hidden their eyes from My *Sabbath*s, so that I am dishonored among them.
> 22:26

> Woe to Israel's shepherds who feed themselves! Should not the shepherds feed the flocks? You eat the fat and clothe yourselves with the wool; you slaughter the fat ones, but you do not feed the flock. You have not strengthened the weak, you have not healed the sick, you have not bound up the broken, you have not brought back what was driven away, you have not sought the lost; but with force and cruelty you have ruled them.
> 34:2-4

The People are callously left as victims: "Because My Sheep became prey – My Sheep became food for all the beasts of the field from having no shepherds; My shepherds did not search for My Sheep, but the shepherds fed themselves and did not feed My Sheep ... Behold, I am against the shepherds, and I will require My Sheep at their hand ..." [34:8-10].

In strong language, God will assert His Lordship: "Behold I Myself will search for My Sheep and seek them out" [34:11], "I will tear off your veils ... you shall no longer envision emptiness nor practice divination; I will deliver My People out of your hand, and *you shall know that I am Jehovah!*" [13:21, 23].

"Sacrificed Their Sons Whom They Bore To Me"
[23:37]

> You have taken your sons and your daughters, whom you have borne to Me, these you sacrificed to (your false gods) for food. Is your prostitution such a small thing, that you have slaughtered My sons and delivered these to them by causing these to pass through the fire?
> 16:20-21

Since in Covenant what is mine is yours, then Israel's children do not belong to Israel: since the male child is circumcised on the eighth day, the child is now 'one' with Jehovah Himself; besides, the first-born male "is Mine" [Exodus 13:2; 22:39; 34:19-20]; and the daughter also is to be *sheltered* under Covenant. Not only is Israel not free to use their children as they please, but then to use what is *Jehovah's* in order to worship an idol, to shed *His* children's innocent Blood, is the epitome of their blatant utter disregard of their Covenant relationship with Jehovah.

> For they have committed adultery, and Blood is on their hands. With their idols they have committed adultery, and even their sons whom they bore to Me they caused to pass through the fire, to devour them. Even this they have done to Me: they have defiled My sanctuary in that day and polluted My *Sabbath*s, for when they had slaughtered their children for their idols, on that day they came into My sanctuary to pollute it; and indeed thus they have done in the midst of My house.
> 23:37-39

Not only is such shedding of Blood already an act of rebellion, but it is treated with pride without a hint of humility: "For her Blood is in her midst; she set it on a high rock; she did not pour it on the land to cover it with dust" [24:7]. Therefore in response God will turn it into an unmistakable billboard: "That it may raise up fury and take vengeance, I have set her Blood on a high rock, that it may not be covered" [v 8].

Indeed, it is a pattern that what God has given to His People is used to worship their idols: "My gold and My silver, which I had given you ... My oil and My incense before them. Also My food which I gave you ... you set it before them as sweet incense..." [16:17-21]. But the irony is that as they scurry around to worship their false gods, the ultimate conclusion of their actions will be the desolation of their families:

> I have defiled them by their own gifts, that by making to pass through the fire [sacrifice] all their firstborn, I might make them desolate and that they might know that I am Jehovah. 20:26

Whereas the sacrificed children were to be "food" for the gods, the desolation would be even more pronounced:

> Therefore fathers shall eat their sons in your midst, and sons shall eat their fathers ... because My sanctuary you have defiled with all your idolatries and with all your disgusting things, therefore I also will withdraw; My eye will not spare, nor will I have any pity ... So shall My anger be spent, and I will cause My fury to rest upon them, and I will be consoled; ... Then your altars shall be desolate, your incense cups shall be broken, and I will throw your slain before your idols. I will lay the corpses of the children of Israel before their idols, and I will scatter your bones around your altars. 5:10-11, 13; 6:4-5

"His Idols in His Heart" [14:4]

Is it in anger or is it in amazement that the all-knowing Jehovah watches an absurd attitude (which unfortunately is still quite modern) play out: "Son of man, have you seen what the elders of the house of Israel do in the dark, every man in the room of his idols? For they say, 'Jehovah does not see us, Jehovah has abandoned the land'" [8:12]. The condemnation of "the idols in the heart" while one still attempts to maintain a holy façade, gives us pause even two and a half millennia later:

> ... "Everyone of the house of Israel who sets up his idols in his heart, and puts the stumblingblock of his iniquity before his face, and then comes to the prophet – I Jehovah will answer him, according to the multitude of his idols, that I may catch the house of Israel by their heart, all who are estranged from Me by their idols. ... I will set My face against that man and make him as a sign ['OTH] and a proverb, and I will cut him off from the midst of My People. Then you shall know that I am Jehovah ... that the house of Israel may no longer stray from Me, nor be defiled again by all their transgressions, but that they are to be My People and I am to be their God," says the Lord Jehovah.

"Therefore say to the house of Israel, 'Thus says the Lord Jehovah: "Turn, and be turned from your idols, and turn your faces away from all your abominations." ' " 14: 4-5, 8, 11, 6

Here is the struggle of Covenant in terms of real Life – the flow of the joint Blood, the flow of the mutual Life, which is to be both visible and also to run to the deep and hidden recesses of all which a person is, has run headlong into the secret pet sins, the way of Life which will destroy not only the individuals but the nation. The heart of Jehovah still yearns that Israel turn away from this uninhibited rush to ruin but instead of Israel saying to God, "You have cast all my sins behind Your back" [Isaiah 38:17], God declares "Because you have forgotten Me and cast Me behind your back, therefore you shall bear the penalty of your lewdness and your prostitution" [Ezekiel 23:35]. Their persistency compels unrelenting progress toward the frightening judgment, "I am against you":

> Therefore thus says the Lord Jehovah: 'Behold I am against you – even I! – and will execute judgments in your midst in the sight of the nations. I will do in you what I have not done, and the like of which I will not do again, because of all your abominations.' 5:8-9

> Behold, I am against you and will draw My sword out of its sheath and cut off from you both righteous and wicked …. My sword shall be drawn from its sheath against all flesh from the Negev to the north, and all flesh will know that I, Jehovah, have drawn My sword out of its sheath; it shall not return anymore. 21:3-5[188]

The Watchman: "Why Should You Die?"

The job of the watchman is essential: people's lives depend on his warning. If he is negligent, then he is the same as a murderer; but if he is faithful then for anyone who does not heed the warning, "his Blood shall be on his own head" [33:2-6]. Ezekiel is a spiritual watchman, to warn the wicked from his way, to warn the righteous from turning from God's way. Anyone who heeds the warnings "will surely live"; anyone who ignores the warning "shall die in his sin," but because the "watchman" (Ezekiel) has fulfilled his responsibility, he will not be accountable [3:16-21; 33:7].

The judgment is coming, the warning is sounded, and the plea is to "turn and live!" The presence of the captivity confirms how the sins of the fathers can indeed have ramifications for their descendents, "upon the children and the children's children" [Exodus 34:7], but the watchman calls each individual to decide his own personal fate. He who conforms to God's way will 'weather the storm' of captivity, but he who rebels will die – not just as an earthly result, but also as the parallel of the spiritual state:

> "Behold, all Souls* are Mine; the Soul* of the father, also the Soul* of the son, is Mine; the Soul* who sins shall die. But a man who is righteous and does what is just and right; ... who has walked in My statutes and kept My judgments to deal faithfully – He is righteous; truly He shall live!" says the Lord Jehovah. ... "The Soul* who sins shall die. A son shall not bear the iniquity of the father, nor a father bear the iniquity of the son. The righteousness of the righteous shall be upon him, and the wickedness of the wicked shall be upon him." ...
> "Do I desire at all the death of the wicked?" says the Lord Jehovah, "Is it not that he should turn from his ways and live? ... Turn, and be made to turn from all your rebellions, so that iniquity will not be your stumbling-block. Cast away from you all the rebellions which you have rebelled, and make yourselves a new heart and a new spirit, for why will you die, O house of Israel? For I have no pleasure in the death of one who dies," says the Lord Jehovah, "so turn and live!"
>   18:4-5, 9, 20, 23, 30-32 (also 33:10-11, 18-20) [*NEPHESH (Life)]

Sadly, Ezekiel's task will be one of frustration: "But the house of Israel is not willing to listen to you, for they are not willing to listen to Me; for all the house of Israel, they are strong of head and hard of heart" [3:7]. "Lo, you are to them as one who has a beautiful voice singing a love song and playing an instrument well; for they hear your words, but they do not do them. When this comes to pass – as it surely will – then they will know that a prophet has been in their midst" [33:32].

> Therefore, son of man, [pack your bags] for captivity, and go into captivity by day in their sight. You shall be exiled from your place into another place in their sight. Perhaps they will realize, though they are a rebellious house.   12: 3

No Longer Could Any Human "Stand in the Gap"

> "Even were these three in their midst: Noah, Daniel and Job; they would deliver [only] their own Souls/Lives by their righteousness, … neither sons nor daughters would they deliver; only themselves would they deliver, and the land would be desolate.
>
> "Or if I bring a sword on that land … and I cut off from it man and beast, even if these three men were in its midst, as I live,… they would not deliver sons nor daughters, but they would deliver only themselves.
>
> "Or if I send a plague into that land and pour out My fury on it in Blood, to cut off from it man and beast, even though Noah, Daniel, and Job were in its midst, as I live," says the Lord Jehovah, "neither son nor daughter would they deliver; they by their righteousness would deliver [only] their own Souls/Lives."   14:14, 16-20

Noah, righteous in the midst of a world gone depraved; Job, of whom God Himself proclaimed, "there is none like him in the earth, a perfect and upright man, who fears God and turns away from evil" [Job 1:8]; and even Daniel, "greatly beloved" [Daniel 10:11,19], who willingly takes upon himself to confess "my sin and the sin of my People Israel, and presenting my supplication … for the holy mountain [Jerusalem] of my God" [Daniel 9:20] – yet not even they are of powerful enough stature to counter Israel's overflowing cup of repugnant spiritual treachery. Indeed there is no human that can fend off the judgment against the nation:

> "So I sought a man among them who would make a wall, and stand in the breach before Me for the sake of the Land, that I should not destroy it; but I found no one. Therefore I have poured out on them My rage; with the fire of My wrath I consumed them; on their own heads I have put their ways," says the Lord Jehovah.   22:30-31

> My eye shall not spare nor will I have pity upon you; but I will put your ways upon you, and your abominations shall be in your midst; and you shall know that I am Jehovah! … My eye will not spare, nor will I have pity; according to your ways I will give to you, … And you shall know that I am Jehovah Who strikes. … though they cry in My ears with a loud voice, I will not hear them. …
>
> The iniquity of Israel's and Judah's houses is exceedingly great, the Land is filled with Blood, the city is full of perversity; for they say, "Jehovah has forsaken the Land, and Jehovah does not see!" But I –

My eye does not spare, and I will not have pity, but on their own head I will put their deeds. 7:4, 9; 8:18; 9:9-10

Discarded Love and Covenant

Chapter 16 presents Jehovah's compassionate affection for Israel, using the metaphor of one who has actively nurtured his beloved as she grew and matured, until the time when they are joined in Covenant:

> "Not an eye had pity on you, ... when I saw you trampled in your Blood, I said to you in your Blood, 'Live!' ...; and you grew, and matured ...
>
> "I passed by you and looked on you, behold, your time was the time of love; I spread My skirt over you and covered your nakedness. I swore [SHABA] to you and entered into Covenant with you," says the Lord Jehovah, "and you became Mine. I washed you in water; I washed away your Blood from you, and anointed you with oil. I clothed you with embroidered cloth ... with fine linen and covered you with silk. I adorned you with ornaments, and put bracelets on your hands, and a chain on your neck." 16:5-11

Yet His Beloved used the very beauty He had given her to sell herself:

> But you trusted in your beauty, played the harlot ... Such things have come and should not be! You have also taken things of beauty, My gold and My silver, which I had given you, and made for yourself male images and played the prostitute with them. You took your embroidered clothes and covered them, and you put My oil and My incense before them. Also My food which I gave you ... you put it before them as sweet incense 16:15-19

However, she had not *sold* herself, nor does she even prostitute herself for free: "How feeble is your heart! ... You are an adulterous wife, who takes strangers instead of her husband. To all prostitutes they make a payment, but you make payments to all your lovers..." [16:30, 32-34]. Perhaps it is startling for some to see the depth of feeling on Jehovah's part: "I was broken/crushed by their adulterous heart which has turned from Me, and by their eyes which wantonly look to their idols" [6:9].

In chapter 20, God traces His steadfast commitment to Israel, from when He chose Israel and "raised My Hand to the descendants of the house of Jacob" in His Covenant oath to Abraham; and then followed through on His Covenant in the Exodus, "I made Myself known to them in the land of Egypt, I raised My Hand to them, saying, 'I am Jehovah your God'"; then fulfilled one of His promises, "to bring ... into a Land that I had searched out for them, 'flowing with milk and honey,' the glory of all lands" [verses 5-6].

With such a dramatic demonstration of His commitment 'under their belt,' it would seem a simple step to "throw away the abominations...., and do not defile yourselves with the idols of Egypt" which has been shown to be nothing. Yet upon entering the very Land of Promise, "they saw all the high hills and all the thick trees, there they offered their sacrifices and provoked with their offerings... nor did they forsake the idols of Egypt" [20:28, 8]. Their blatant disregard for Covenant is then echoed in their Covenant with Babylon, a Covenant made in the Name of Jehovah [II Chronicles 36:13]:

> "Say now to the rebellious house: 'Do you not know what these things say? Behold, the king of Babylon ... took [Judah's] king's offspring, cut Covenant with him, and made him enter into an oath ['ALAH] ... that the kingdom might be humbled and not lift itself up, to keep his Covenant that it might stand. But [Judah's king] rebelled ... Will he prosper? Will he who does these things escape? Shall he break Covenant and be delivered?'"
> "As I live," says the Lord Jehovah, "surely in the place of the king who made him king, whose oath ['ALAH] he despised and whose Covenant he broke – in the midst of Babylon he shall die. ... He despised the oath ['ALAH] by breaking Covenant; behold, he gave his Hand and [still] has done all these things, he shall not escape."
> Thus says the Lord Jehovah: "As I live, surely My oath ['ALAH] which he despised, and My Covenant which he broke, on his own head I put it ... for the treason he committed against Me."   17:12-20

And Israel's disregard of Covenant causes this special and unique ("we are distinct, I and Your People, from all other people" [Exodus 33:16]) relationship between Jehovah and His People to be violated: "When you brought in the sons of foreigners, uncircumcised in heart and uncircumcised in flesh, to be in My sanctuary to defile it – My house – ... they broke My Covenant because of all your abominations. You have not kept charge of My holy things, but you set them to keep charge of My sanctuary for themselves" [44:7-8]. "For thus says the Lord Jehovah: 'I will deal with you as you have done, who despised the oath ['*ALAH*] by breaking Covenant'" [16:59].

The special word for remembrance, ZEKER, which should bring a person back to Covenant fidelity, is used instead against those who think that merely the existence of a Covenant ("who have *sworn/seven oaths/seven*"), broken or not, should insulate them; they will discover that the King of Babylon "will bring their iniquity to remembrance [ZEKER], ... in that your transgressions are uncovered, so that your sins are seen in all your doings – because you have been remembered [ZEKER], you shall be taken by *the Palm*. ... I will pour out My rage on you; I will blow against you with the fire of My wrath...; Your Blood shall be in the midst of the Land. You shall not be remembered [ZEKER], for I Jehovah have spoken" [21:23-24, 31-32[189]].

Equally so those who in insolent pride refer to the Covenant promises, "Abraham was only one, and he possessed the Land; but we are many; the Land has been given to us as an inheritance" (perhaps the ancient version of 'possession is nine-tenths of the law'), yet "You eat with Blood, you lift up your eyes toward your idols, and you shed Blood.... You rely on your sword, you commit abominations, and a man defiles his neighbor's wife. Should you then possess the Land? ... Then they shall know that I am Jehovah, when I have made the Land a devastation and a desolation because of all their abominations which they have done" [33:24-26, 29].

Yet Covenant will not die! "But I will remember [ZEKER] My Covenant... and I will raise up an everlasting Covenant with you. Then you will remember [ZEKER] your ways and be ashamed.... I will raise up My Covenant with you, and you shall know that I am Jehovah, that you may remember [ZEKER] and be ashamed..., when I atone [KAPHAR] for you for all you have done" [16:60-63].

> I will cut with them a Covenant of peace [SHALOM], and it shall be an everlasting Covenant with them; I will establish them and multiply them, and I will put My sanctuary in their midst forevermore. ... and I will be their God, and they shall be My People. The nations shall know that I, Jehovah, sanctify Israel, when My sanctuary is in their midst forevermore. 37:26-28

The Remnant

"There shall be left in it a Remnant who shall be led out, both sons and daughters; ... they will comfort you when you see their ways and their doings; and you shall know that I have done all which I did not in vain" [14:22]. No matter how much the verdict is deserved, no matter how bad the judgment may get, there never will be a time without promise:

> Son of man, your brothers – your brothers: the men of your redemption [GO'EL] and all the house of Israel –, ... although I have scattered them among the lands, yet I will be as a little sanctuary for them in the lands where they have gone. ... I will gather you from the peoples, ... and I will give you the Land of Israel. ... I will give them one heart, and I will put a new spirit within them; I will take the stony heart out of their flesh, and give them a heart of flesh, that they may walk in My statutes and keep My judgments and do them; and they shall be My People, and I will be their God. 11:15-20

> "As I live," says the Lord Jehovah, "surely with a mighty Hand, with an outstretched Arm, and with fury poured out, I will rule over you. I will bring you out from the peoples and gather you out of the lands among which you are scattered ...
> "I will make you pass under the rod, and I will bring you into the bond of the Covenant; ...
> "I will accept you as a soothing fragrance when I bring you out from the peoples and gather you ... Then you shall know that I am Jehovah, when I bring you into the Land of Israel, to the Land for which I lifted up My Hand to give to your fathers." 20:33-34, 37, 41-42

> Behold, I Myself will search for My Sheep and seek them out.... and deliver them from all the places where they were scattered in a day of cloud and thick darkness. ... and will bring them to their Land; ...

their fold shall be on the high mountains of Israel. ... in rich pasture on all the mountains of Israel they shall feed. I will feed My Sheep, and I will make them lie down. ... I will seek what was lost and bring back the banished, I will bind up the broken and strengthen the afflicted; but I will destroy the fat and the strong, and feed them with judgment. ...

I will raise up one Shepherd over them, and He shall feed them – My servant David. ... I, Jehovah, will be their God, and My servant David a ruler among them; I, Jehovah, have spoken. I will cut a Covenant of peace [*SHALOM*] with them, and make evil 'beasts' to cease from the land; and they will dwell securely in the wilderness and sleep in the forests. I will make them and the places around My hill a blessing; and I will bring down the shower in its season; there shall be showers of blessing. ...

So they shall know that I, Jehovah their God, am with them, and they are My People, ... You, My Sheep, are the Sheep of My pasture; you are men, and I am your God....   34:11-16; 23-26; 30-31

My Holy Name's Sake

"But I worked for My Name's sake, that it should not be disgraced before the nations" [20:9]. The issue is not mere pride, but *honor* – where the Name means something, stands for something, identifies something; that the Name is the shorthand which refers to a background of information (as "Lincoln" might invoke the image of honesty, or "Stalin" that of oppressive treachery). The Name is "Jehovah," the Name which pivots around Covenant, which rises out of God's intimate relationship with Israel.

It is the Name by which "I had made Myself known to them in their sight, by bringing them out of the land of Egypt" [v 9]; a Name which does not signify a wimpy god who caves in to a People who "went after their idols," who "despised My judgments and did not walk in My statutes, but profaned My *Sabbath*s" [v 16, also vv 13, 21], a Name who rather holds them accountable to their Covenant commitment: "Then I said I would pour out My fury on them and fulfill My anger against them in the wilderness" [v 21]. Yet even then "I withdrew My Hand and acted for the sake of My Name, that it should not be profaned in the sight of the nations" [v 22], so that His Name also stands for mercy and grace, even when the direst penalty should be delivered.

Because of "the Blood they had poured out on the Land, and for their idols by which they defiled it, ... I scattered them among the nations, and ... where they went, they profaned My holy Name, [whose inhabitants said] of them, 'These are Jehovah's People, yet they have gone out of His Land'" [36:18-20]. The Gentile observer is confused: Israel's entering into captivity is not because Jehovah is weak, nor does He blindly support His People, nor does He outrightly abandon them: "Thus says the Lord Jehovah: 'Not for your sake do I do this, O house of Israel, but for My holy Name's sake,... I will sanctify My great Name, ... and the nations shall know that I am Jehovah, ... when I am sanctified in you before their eyes'" [22-23].

Yet His Name stands for hope: "goodness, Covenant relationship, grace, and mercy"[190]:

> I will ... gather you ... and bring you into your Land. Then I will sprinkle clean water on you, and you will be clean; from all your defilements and from all your idols I will cleanse you. I will give you a new heart and put a new spirit within you. ... I will put My Spirit within you and make you walk in My statutes, and you will keep My judgments and do them. You will dwell in the Land that I gave to your fathers; you will be My People, and I will be your God. 36:24-28

Chapter 37 follows that pronouncement with an extraordinary declaration of hope: in the vision of the valley of dry bones, a great host emerges as the restored People, a commitment by Jehovah which echoes in the parable of the unifying of the two sticks, the one for "Judah" and the other for "Ephraim, and for all the house of Israel" into "one nation... and one King shall be king over them all," never to be "divided into two kingdoms again" [v 22].

> I will save them out from all their dwelling places in which they have sinned, and will cleanse them. Then they shall be My People, and I will be their God. My Servant David shall be King over them, and

there shall be one Shepherd to all of them; they shall walk in My judgments and keep My statutes, and do them. 37:23-25

Thus says the Lord Jehovah: "Now I will bring back the captives of Jacob, and have mercy on all the house of Israel; and I will be jealous for My holy Name. ... When I have brought them back from the peoples and gathered them out of their enemies' lands, and am sanctified in them in the sight of many nations, then they shall know that I am Jehovah their God, Who made them be exiled among the nations. But I gathered them back to their Land, and left none of them behind. I will not hide My face from them anymore; for I shall have poured out My Spirit on the house of Israel," says the Lord Jehovah. 39:25-29

Recompense to the Nations

Although Jehovah will gather His People, there will be business with the nations of the earth who have delighted in the plight of Israel, such as the Ammonites, who "clapped your hands, stamped your foot, and rejoiced in heart with all your contempt for the Land of Israel" [25:6]; and Edom, who took "vengeance against the house of Judah, and has greatly offended and are avenged on them" [v 12]; as well as the Philistines, who "took vengeance with a spiteful Soul, to destroy because of continuous hatred" [v 15].

Tyre has a special place in God's vengeance, since it enthusiastically declared, "Aha! She is shattered who was the gateway of the peoples; now she is turned over to me; I shall be filled; she is laid waste" [26:2]. But even more, "the prince of Tyre" 's heart is "lifted up,... 'I am a god, I sit in the seat of gods, in the heart of the seas,' yet you are a man, and not a god" [28:2]. However, when "the *king* of Tyre" is addressed, the description of the "Garden of Eden" [28:12] reflects passages where heaven and its occupants are described in crystalline and precious metal terms (Ezekiel 1:16; 10:9; Daniel 10:5-6; Revelation 21). In fact, Satan seems to fit the description far better than a mere man. This suggests that Jehovah's recompense will be in far broader strokes than just dealing with the human kingdoms arrayed against God's People.

To Tyre's close relative, Sidon, "they shall know that I am Jehovah, when I have executed judgments in her and am sanctified by her ..." [28:22]. And then there is Egypt, "O great monster who lies in the midst of his rivers, who has said, 'My River is mine; I have made it'" [29:3]. They also will be scattered, and yet "at the end of forty years I will gather the Egyptians from the peoples in whom they were scattered ... to the land of their origin, and there they shall be a humble kingdom. ... No longer shall it be the confidence of the house of Israel, but will remind [ZECHER] them of the iniquity of their turning to follow them" [13-14, 16].

Seir, the Lord Jehovah would make "a ruin and a waste; ... Because there was a continuous hatred in you, and you poured out [the Blood of] the children of Israel ... at the time of their calamity, when their iniquity came to an end, therefore, as I live," says the Lord Jehovah, "for Blood I will prepare you, and Blood shall pursue you; since Blood you have not hated, so Blood shall pursue you. ... As you rejoiced over the inheritance of the house of Israel because it was desolate, so I will do to you ..." [35:3-6, 15].

It seems, though, that the most profound judgment will be visited upon Magog in chapter 39, when they come to annihilate God's People. Jehovah will rain fire upon them, "I will make known My holy Name in the midst of My People Israel. ... Then the nations shall know that I am Jehovah, the Holy One in Israel" [vv 6-7]. Of such magnitude will be this vengeance that burning the enemy's weapons would last *seven/oath* years, and burying the enemy's dead will last *seven/oath* months. "So the house of Israel shall know that I am Jehovah their God from that day forward. The nations shall know that for their iniquity the house of Israel went into captivity ... because they were trespassed against Me..." [v 23].

> Therefore thus says the Lord Jehovah: "Surely in the fire of My jealousy I have spoken against the rest of the nations and against Edom, all who gave My land to themselves as a possession, with joy of the heart and the scorn of the Soul, to make the open country become its prey." 36:5

Even the Land had a Special Promise

> Prophesy concerning the Land of Israel, and say to the mountains, the hills, the rivers, and the valleys, ... you have borne the shame of the nations. Therefore thus says the Lord Jehovah: I have raised My Hand: surely the nations which surround you shall bear their shame. But you, O mountains of Israel, you shall put out your branches and shall bear your fruit for My People Israel, for they come near to enter. For behold, I am for you, and I will turn to you, and you shall be tilled and sown. I will multiply men upon you, all the house of Israel, all of it; and the cities shall be inhabited and the ruins shall be built. I will multiply upon you man and beast; and they shall increase and bear young; I will make you just as populated as you had been, and I will do better for you than at your beginnings. Then you shall know that I am Jehovah. I will cause men to walk on you, My People Israel; they will possess you, and you will be to them an inheritance; you shall not add to their bereavement. 36:6-12

The New Order

Where one expects rejection, within the new order of the new temple there will be a remarkable act of mercy for those Levites who had betrayed what was entrusted to them and led Israel into sin:

> ... who have gone far from Me ..., who went astray from Me after their idols, they shall bear their iniquity. Yet they shall be ministers in My sanctuary, as overseers at the gates of the house and ministers in the house; they shall slay the *Burnt Offering* and the sacrifice for the People, and they shall stand before them to minister to them ... They shall not come near to Me to serve as priest before Me, nor come near any of My holy things, nor into *the Most Holy Place*; but they shall bear their shame and their abominations which they have done. However, I will make them keepers in charge of the House, for all its work, and for all that shall be done in it. 44:10-14

On the other hand, the sons of Zadok, who remained faithful,

> ... shall enter My sanctuary, and they shall come near My table to serve Me, and they shall keep My charge. ... They shall teach My People the difference between the holy and the common, and cause them to discern the unclean from the clean. ... They shall observe all

> My appointed feasts in My laws and My statutes, and they shall sanctify My *Sabbath*s.... It shall be to them for an inheritance, since I am their Inheritance; you shall not give them a possession in Israel, for I am their Possession. 44:16, 23-24, 28

Like the starting of an engine which had been neglected for a long time, all the worship and sacrificial systems of *the Temple* will be restored. In 46:9, there is the new instruction that worshippers for feasts are not to go backward, but only forward through the city. Although it makes logistical sense, it also has a good spiritual parallel in regard to one's relationship to the LORD. Also new is the commanded role the "Prince" has in preparing the sacrifices at the feasts [45:17]. Only for him would the East Gate be opened, when He makes a voluntary offering [46:12].

But more, there is the image of a river of salvation – a 'Living Water' – which seems small at the start, but then becomes an overflowing flood, a river which heals, which gives Life and abundance to all it touches [47:8-12], and "By the torrent, on its banks, on this side and that, will grow all kinds of trees for food ... They will bear fruit every month, because their waters come out from the sanctuary. Their fruit will be for food and their leaves for healing" [47:12], a picture echoed by John in Revelation 22:2.

And the Name of this "city from that day shall be: 'JEHOVAH IS THERE'" [48:35].

D. *The Minor Prophets*

Daniel

Helpless to Help

The Covenant Name, Jehovah, only occurs in Chapter 9, where Daniel also refers to the Covenant, particularly how it was broken and resulted in the seventy years of captivity [v 4]. Here is a large section in which "I was speaking, praying, and confessing my sin and the sin of my People Israel, and causing my supplication to come before Jehovah my God for the holy mountain of my God" [v 20]. This adds background to the declaration in Ezekiel 14:14, 16-20, as mentioned above, where even "Noah, Daniel, and Job ... would deliver neither sons nor daughters."

Despite being "greatly beloved" [10:11, 19], Daniel is helpless to save anyone else, even his own children – it would take another "Beloved," "My beloved Son, in Whom I am well pleased" [Matthew 3:17; 17:5], Who would be "the atoning Sacrifice for our sins, and not only for ours but also for the sins of the whole world" [I John 2:2].

Seven and the Messiah

Seven/oath and its multiples are referenced a number of times: the furnace for Shadrach, Meshach, and Abednego is heated "*seven/oath* times more than it was usually heated" [3:19]; Nebuchadnezzar is to become like a beast, "let *seven/oath* times pass over him" [4:16, 23, 25, 32]; "the prince of the kingdom of Persia withstood me twenty–one days" (seven times three) [10:13].

It is in chapter 9 where the numbers become more interesting. Seventy is 'Covenant times completion' (*seven/oath* times ten): after the "for the desolations of Jerusalem: seventy years" [9:2], there would be "Seventy weeks ... to finish the transgression, to make an end of sins, to atone [*KAPHAR*] for iniquity, to bring everlasting righteousness, to seal up vision and prophecy, and to anoint the Most Holy" [9:24]. Within that time span, from "the command to restore and to rebuild Jerusalem until Messiah the Prince, there shall be *seven/oath* weeks and sixty–two weeks" [9:25] which adds up to sixty-nine weeks.

In the seventieth week, the Messiah "shall confirm Covenant with many for one week; in the middle of the week He shall make [both] sacrifice and offering cease" [v 27]. Yet it will be at the cost of His Life: "after the sixty–two weeks Messiah shall be cut off, but not for Himself" [v 26]. There is controversy over the rendering of the Hebrew in regard to the last phrase, that it could read, "he shall have nothing." Such an interpretation would fit with such descriptions of the Messiah as Isaiah 53, which regards Him "despised and abandoned by men, a Man of sorrows and acquainted with grief. We hid as it were our faces from Him; ... and we did not value Him" [Isaiah 53:3], or "to the Holy One, the Despised of Soul, to the Hated of the nation, to the Servant of rulers" [Isaiah 49:7].

Still from that same prophesy from Isaiah 53, particularly v 5, "but not for Himself" would also be just as appropriate: "But He was wounded for our transgressions, He was bruised for our iniquities; the chastisement for our peace [*SHALOM*] was upon Him, and by His stripes we are healed." This would mean that if this Messiah does indeed die not for Himself but for others, no wonder the sacrificial system would come to a close – there would be no longer any need for that ineffectual shed-Blood. The New Covenant, that is, the Messiah ("I give You as a Covenant to people" [Isaiah 42:6]) would do the task far more efficiently.

It seems that the argument here is not "either/or," but rather "both/and."

'Epimanes' and Covenant

In chapter 11:21-45, Covenant again becomes a major reference point. The subject of the prophecy is Antiochus IV (175 – 164 BC) – 'Epiphanes' ('Illustrious One') or better 'Epimanes' ('Madman'). He will be the terror of the People of the Covenant in his attempt to 'modernize' them, or 'Hellenize' them (turn them into Greek protégés – or stooges). Jerusalem is renamed 'New Antioch,' the High Priesthood is by bribe, and Antiochus performs the original "'abomination of desolation' standing in the Holy Place spoken of by Daniel the prophet" [Matthew 24:15], when he sacrifices a pig on *the Temple*'s altar, sprinkles a broth from its flesh all around *the Temple*, and allows his soldiers to have orgies in *the Temple*. He forbids the Jews the Scriptures, *Sabbath*, Circumcision, sacrifices, and practices extreme cruelty to those refusing to convert to the Greek pantheon.

"Covenant" as found in "the Prince of Covenant" in v 22 may be a pact with the Egyptian king, Ptolemy Philometor, the king being the "Prince" in question. Others have taken "Prince" to be the High Priest removed because someone else had the better bribe. Yet the following references to Covenant are specifically in regard to the "Holy Covenant" [vv 28, 30]. Since Covenant is used so rarely but specifically in Daniel, it would seem odd that one instance would not refer to the spiritual meaning. Who then would be "the Prince"? Without violating the passage, it might refer simply to the Jews themselves: "With the force of a flood they shall be swept away from before him and be broken, and also the Prince of the Covenant."

In v 28 "moved against the holy Covenant," and v 30 "in rage against the holy Covenant," "holy" Covenant would contrast the wickedness not just of the deeds, but also of Antiochus' spiritual intent: "Evildoers against the Covenant he shall defile with flattery; but the People who know their God shall be strong, and will be active" [v 32]. Ultimately 'the Madman' would "exalt and magnify himself above every god, even against the God of gods shall he speak wonderous things" [v 36].

Hosea

Ignored

"When Israel was a child, I loved him, and out of Egypt I called My son ... I taught Ephraim to walk, holding him by his arms; ... I drew them with human cords, with bands of Love, and I was to them as those who take the yoke from their neck" [11:1-4] – the picture switches from the marriage theme to a gentle parent fondly helping the child, being there in his first steps. But this is brushed aside by Israel; their snub ("sacrificed to the Baals, and burned incense to carved images" [v 2]) is a terrible rejection of such tender steadfast love (*HESED*).

"They did not know that I healed them" [11:3], but this is not merely uninformed ignorance: "My People are destroyed for lack of knowledge: because you rejected knowledge, ... because you have forgotten the teachings [*TORAH*] of your God ... The more they increased, the more they sinned against Me ... They lift up their Soul to their iniquity" [4:6-8]. "My People are bent on backsliding from Me – to the Most High they call, but will not exalt Him at all" [11:7] – perhaps the ancient equivalent to the modern profanity which is fond of using 'God' (for example, 'oh, my god!' where it is now *conveniently* abbreviated 'OMG') and 'Jesus,' without any sense of honor to the Name – although Israel may not have descended to *that* depth of abuse.

"I have written for him the great things of My *TORAH*, but they were considered 'strange'" [8:12] – even today, the judges of Jehovah's Word are the vagrancies of human fascinations: perhaps it is the novelty of an 'exotic' philosophy, perhaps it is where God is not 'nice' enough because of the places where His justice 'should be' deleted, perhaps it is the appeal of 'mental gymnastics' (that is, craving something mentally complex to give the air of superiority, or secret knowledge, or 'superior' mental discipline), or perhaps it is a superficially attractive pagan doctrine which overrides what Jehovah has shown in His *TORAH* (for example, adopting reincarnation), or even the pressure of social fads. "My People seek advice from their wooden idols, and their walking staff/wand enlightens them" [4:12].

"There is no truth or steadfast Love [*HESED*] or knowledge of God in the land: swearing and lying, killing and stealing, and committing adultery increase, as Blood touches Blood" [4:1-2]. This also is surprisingly quite modern – in our world which seeks to take God out of creation (because He is supposedly 'anti-science'), and to take God out of the basis for morality (since we do not want to offend others – or since He is just inconvenient), we too have lost the basis for our lives, giving rise to bigotry, pogroms, 'ethnic cleansings,' and even removing other 'undesirables' from the womb to old age. "Blood touches Blood" – all justified by 'most sophisticated' of arguments.

They insist on doing things according to their own ideas: "... they sacrifice flesh and eat it, but Jehovah does not accept them. ... For Israel has forgotten his Maker, and builds temples [to other gods]..." [8:13-14]. "With their flocks and herds they go to seek Jehovah but will not find Him; He has withdrawn from them. Against Jehovah they have been deceitful, for they have borne foreign children" [5:6-7].

"Their deeds do not allow them to return to their God, for the spirit of adultery is in their midst, and they know not Jehovah" [5:4] – like the addict who thinks he is in control of his addiction, the dismal truth is that the addiction controls him. "Prostitution, wine, and new wine [the root for this Hebrew word carries the idea of being disinherited or impoverished] carry away the heart" [4:11] – many things can hold the addict: the addiction is comfortable or 'fun,' it seems to be empowering, a sense of shame makes him think he has no other options, he believes he cannot survive or cope without it, and so forth.

> Though I redeemed [*PADAH*] them, yet they have spoken lies against Me. They have not cried to Me with their heart when they howled on their beds. ... Though I disciplined, I strengthened their arms, yet they devise evil against Me; they return, but not to the Most High ...
>
> 7:13-16

Ichabod, "The Glory Has Departed From Israel!" [I Samuel 4:21]

"For I desire steadfast Love [*HESED*] and not sacrifice, and the knowledge of God more than burnt offerings; but like men they transgressed Covenant, there they dealt deceitfully with Me" [6:6-7]; "they have transgressed My Covenant and rebelled against My *TORAH*" [8:1]; "they have spoken words, swearing ['*ALAH*] emptiness in cutting Covenant, thus judgment springs up like hemlock in the furrows of the field" [10:4]. Covenant, that precious relationship between two people, the relationship in which Jehovah has given so much of Himself, has been utterly abused.

In Exodus 33 and 34, Jehovah has described His Glory as centered around His goodness, His Covenant relationship, His grace, His mercy and His justice. Originally meant to be "a kingdom of priests and a holy nation" [Exodus 19:6], as the ones through whom the Covenant 'LifeBlood' of God flows, Israel is to be the reflection of Jehovah's Glory on this earth. This is to be their Glory. But although

> To Me Israel will cry, 'My God, we know You!,' [but] Israel has rejected the good ... They set up kings, but not by Me; they made princes, but I do not know [them]. With their silver and gold they made idols for themselves, so that they may be cut off. Your [golden] calf has cast [you] off, O Samaria! My anger is kindled against them ... A craftsman made it – it is not God; and the calf of Samaria shall be broken to pieces. 8:2-6

"I also reject you from being priest for Me; ... I also will forget your children... their glory I will change into shame" [4:6-7] – since the north kingdom will not reflect God's Glory, then all that is left is Justice. This is reflected in the names of Hosea's children: his son "God-Will-Scatter" – Jezreel, the city where Ahab and Jezebel committed murder for Naboth's vineyard [I Kings 21] and where Ahab was 'piously' executed [II Kings 9 and 10] by Jehu, who simply usurped the throne and continued Jereboam's sin of 'alternative worship' [II Kings 10:29, 31] – is symbolic of the kingdom's spiritual treachery; his daughter "No-Mercy"; his second son "No-People"; and Jehovah would be "I-Will-Not-Be-For-You" [1:4, 6, 9].

God's pride is His goodness, Covenant, grace and mercy, while mankind's idea of glory is one's children, but Israel would be stripped of even this pride:

> As for Ephraim, their glory shall fly away like a bird – from birth, from pregnancy, and from conception! Though they bring up their children, yet I will make them barren, without a man. Yes, woe to them when I turn from them! ... O Jehovah – what will You give? Give them a miscarrying womb and dry breasts! ... For the evil of their deeds I will drive them out of My house; I will not love them again. ... Their root is dried up; they shall not bear fruit. Yes, were they to bear [children], I would kill the beloved of their womb. 9:11-12, 14-16

"You have plowed wickedness; you have reaped iniquity. You have eaten the fruit of lies, because you trusted in your way..." [10:13] – Israel is now confronted with the results of what they have nurtured through the centuries, which is not unnoticed: "They do not tell in their hearts that I remember [ZECHER] all their wickedness; now their own deeds have hemmed them in; they are before My face" [7:2]. The final outcome "when he offended through Baal worship, he died" [13:2] and even the Land of Promise would suffer. "Therefore the Land will mourn; and everyone who dwells there will languish with the beasts of the field and the birds of the air; even the fish of the sea will be taken away" [4:3].

"My Heart Reels Within Me" [11:8]

> How can I give you up, Ephraim? How can I hand you over, Israel? ... My heart reels within Me; My compassions are stirred together. I will not execute the heat of My anger; I will turn back from again destroying Ephraim. For I am God, and not man, The Holy One in your midst ...
> 11:8-9

The struggle within Jehovah when it comes to judgment is still evident, therefore hope cannot help but keep surfacing: the Glory will return, the split kingdom will become one, they will be "Sons of the Living God" [1:10]. Although He will "strip her naked and set her out, as in the day when she was born, and make her like a wilderness..." [2:3], there will come a time when, in concepts which would echo the Exodus passages,

> In that day I will cut Covenant for them with the beasts of the field..., to make them lie down securely. I will betroth you to Me forever; yes, I will betroth you to Me in righteousness and justice, in *HESED* and mercy; I will betroth you to Me in faithfulness, and you shall know Jehovah.
> 2:18-20

This will happen because the judgment will indeed jar this People of God into realizing what is truly significant, and finally in repentance they will seek Jehovah:

> "For I will be like a lion ... I, even I, will tear them and prowl ... and no one shall rescue. I will go, returning again to My place until they confess their guilt and will seek My face; in their distress they will earnestly seek Me."
> Come, and let us return to Jehovah; for He has torn, but He will heal us; He has stricken, but He will bind us up. After two days He will revive us; on the third day He will raise us up, that we may live in His sight.
> 5:14-6:2

As Jacob/Israel "by his strength he contended with God... and prevailed; he wept, and sought favor from Him" [12:3-4, Genesis 32:24-30], so also the present Israel is invited to "return to your God; keep steadfast Love [HESED] and justice, and wait on your God continually" [12:6].

> Take words with you, and return to Jehovah. Say to Him, "Take away all iniquity; and receive us in goodness, for we will give the sacrifices of our lips... we will no longer say to the work of our hands, 'You are our gods!' For in You the orphan finds mercy." 14:2-3

"Love a Woman Who is Loved By a Lover"

One of the most powerful images of Covenant commitment can be found in marriage and it shows up early in Hosea in chapter 3 with profound impact.

"Go again, love a woman who is loved by a lover and is committing adultery, just like the love of Jehovah for the children of Israel..." [3:1] – this is indeed an awkward construction, but obviously, if Hosea is to love this woman as the LORD loved Israel, it is no lovers' triangle. Since God is not intruding into Israel's relationship with another god (who does not exist anyway), neither is Hosea *intruding* into another's relationship with this woman, since he is not only husband but also the one who really loves her. It describes how, despite everything, Israel is still beloved. God still sees Himself as intimately connected with them, and will redeem them from their disgrace.

Perhaps worthy of note here, the root of the word for "lover" has elements of shepherding as well as companionship, and may therefore be introducing a 'sub-plot' to the statement – the parallel to how, although the Good Shepherd has been rejected by His sheep (Israel), He still is totally committed to them. Like the Good Shepherd in search of rebellious sheep: "I will heal their backsliding, I will love them freely, for My anger has turned away from him. I will be as the dew to Israel; he shall blossom like the lily, and cast forth his roots like Lebanon" [14:4-5].

Here then is an extraordinary declaration of Jehovah's Covenant commitment to Israel. Not only is He Husband (and Shepherd) of Israel, but He will also be the *GO'EL* Who will ransom them. As He later declares, "I will ransom [*PADAH*] them from the power of Sheol; I will redeem [*GO'EL*] them from death. Where, O Death, are your plagues? Where is your destruction, O Sheol?" [13:14].

There is to be a period of 'celibacy,' or perhaps better (in Israel's case), of spiritual detoxification ("without king or prince, without sacrifice or sacred pillar, without ephod or *TERAPHIM*" [3:4]), after which they will seek/yearn for Jehovah: "Yet I am Jehovah your God ever since the land of Egypt, and you shall know no God but Me; for there is no Savior besides Me" [13:4].

> Sow for yourselves righteousness; reap steadfast Love [*HESED*]; break up your fallow ground, for it is time to seek Jehovah, till He comes and rains righteousness on you.   10:12

> ...there He spoke to us – that is, Jehovah God of hosts – Jehovah is His memorial [*ZECHER*].   12:5

Joel

As had the previous prophets, Joel warns: "Consecrate a fast, ... and cry out to Jehovah. Alas for the day! For the day of Jehovah is at hand; it shall come as destruction from the Almighty" [1:14-15]; "Blow the trumpet in Zion, and raise an alarm in My holy mountain! Let all the inhabitants of the Land tremble; for the day of Jehovah is coming, for it is near" [2:1]. There will be great devastation: "The Land is like the Garden of Eden before them, and behind them a desolate wilderness" [2:3].

Yet in words reminiscent of God's description of His Glory in Exodus 33, again there is the call to repentance:

> "Now, therefore," says Jehovah, "Turn to Me with all your heart, with fasting, with weeping, and with mourning." Rend your heart, and not your clothes; return to Jehovah your God, for He is gracious and merciful, slow to anger, and of great steadfast Love [*HESED*]; He

reverses from doing harm. Who knows if He will turn and relent, and leave a blessing behind Him …? 2:12-14

There is the sure hope of God returning His People to their blessed status, not merely of returned fortunes, but particularly that the essence of Covenant, the very presence of God, will be in their midst once again:

> You shall eat fully and be satisfied, and you shall praise the Name of Jehovah your God, Who has dealt wondrously with you; My People shall not be put to shame any more. Then you shall know that I am in the midst of Israel: I am Jehovah your God and there is no other. My People shall not be put to shame ever again. 2:26-27

But there is a deeper sense, where Jehovah "will pour out My Spirit on all flesh; your sons and your daughters shall prophesy, your old men shall dream dreams, your young men shall see visions; also on My menservants and on My maidservants I will pour out My Spirit in those days" [2:28-29].

Like many other Biblical prophets, Joel declares that a judgment day will come in regard to all the nations "for My People, My heritage Israel, whom they scattered in the nations; they have also divided up My Land" [3:2]. The Promised People and the Promised Land are unmistakably still very precious to Jehovah. The tables will be turned: "You have sold the sons of Judah and the sons of Jerusalem to the Greeks, to remove them from their borders, behold, I will raise them from the place to which you have sold them … I will sell your sons and your daughters into the hand of the sons of Judah" [3:6-8]; "Jehovah will roar from Zion,…the heavens and earth will quake; but Jehovah will be a Refuge for His People, and the strength of the sons of Israel" [3:16].

As Ezekiel similarly described, "A fountain shall flow from the house of Jehovah and water the Valley of Acacias" [3:18] – again a "living water" will flow from God, Who "will cleanse their Blood, which I had not cleansed; for Jehovah dwells in Zion" [v 21].

Amos

Forty years before Israel is carried off into captivity, God prepares a list of the nations which are subject to His judgment: Syria, Gaza, Ammon, and others. However, Judah and Israel cannot gloat since they are on the list [2:4-8] as well. Judah has despised the *TORAH* and commandments, and follows the same lies as their fathers [v4]. Israel has utterly subverted the Glory of Jehovah: "They sold the righteous for silver and the poor for a pair of sandals ... A man and his father go in to the same girl to defile My holy Name" [2:6-7]. "Woe to you who are at ease in Zion ... who lie on beds of ivory ... [who idly sing] ... but are not grieved for the destruction of Joseph!" [6:1, 4-6].

Jehovah has been loyal to His Covenant-partner by removing the Amorites from the Promised Land and bringing Israel home from Egypt [2:9-10]. This is the Creator of the universe: "He made the Pleiades and Orion; He turns the deep shadow into morning and darkens the day into night; He calls for the waters of the sea and pours them out on the face of the earth; Jehovah is His Name!" [5:8]. But already, even in the wilderness they held on to their 'acquired' false gods from Egypt: "Was it to Me that you offered sacrifices and offerings in the wilderness for forty years, O house of Israel? You also carried Sikkuth your king and Chiun, your idols, the star of your gods, which you made for yourselves" [5:25-26].

They abused His special gifts (the prophets and the Nazarites [2:11-12]); therefore weakened spiritually, they now will be weakened physically [vv 14-16; 3:11]. Although they love the religious façade which supposedly balances their rebellion (4:4-5; "I hate, I reject your feast days, and I do not accept your sacred assemblies" [5:21]), they never take the time to realize how their world has eroded [vv 6-10], even to where some have been overthrown [v 11]. "By the sword shall all the sinners of My People die, those who say, 'The calamity shall not come near nor come in front of us'" [9:10]. No matter whether "they dig into hell ... climb up to heaven ... hide themselves on top of Carmel ... hide from My sight at the bottom of the sea ... though they go into captivity before their enemies, ... I will set My eyes on them for evil and not for good" [9:2-4].

Chapter seven opens with Jehovah coaxing Amos into being intercessor by showing possible destructions through locusts and fire, and through Amos' prayer God concedes. Yet the coming judgment will not be escaped, because as the priest Amaziah indicates, no one really wants to hear the tough things Jehovah is saying to Israel [v12-13]. In response, there will be "a famine on the land, not ... of bread, nor ... for water, but of hearing the words of Jehovah ... They shall wander about, seeking the word of Jehovah, but will not find it" [8:11].

"Jehovah has *sworn/seven* by the pride of Jacob: 'I will never forget any of their works – because of this will the Land not tremble and everyone mourn who dwells in it?'" [8:7]. "The end has come to My People Israel; I will not pass over them anymore ... Many will be the corpses in every place, they shall be thrown out in silence" [8:2-3] – the judgment relentlessly will come and the destruction will leave only a paltry few: "As a shepherd takes from the mouth of a lion two legs or a piece of an ear" [3:12]: "The city which goes out by a thousand shall have a hundred left" [5:3].[191] God's judgment will be marked thus: "I will make the sun go down at noon, and I will darken the earth in the daylight" [8:9].[192]

"Seek Me and live!" [5:4, 6] – Covenant is a relationship, not merely a system of rituals, especially when these rituals are the product of man's imagination and not of God's command. But Israel's choice is to ignore all for which Jehovah's Glory stands: "They hate him who rebukes in the gate, and they abhor him who speaks uprightly. ... you trample on the poor and take grain taxes from him – though you have built houses of hewn stone ... oppressing the righteous and taking a bribe; turning away the poor from the [judges'] gate" [v 10-12]. If those who are left really turn away from these things, then there could be hope.

And there is hope – an important hope: the Glory of God will win out, "... I will not utterly destroy the house of Jacob, ... I will sift the house of Israel among all nations, ... yet not a pebble shall fall to the ground. ... On that day I will raise up the tabernacle/tent of David ... I will rebuild it as in the days of old" [9:8-9, 11]. As well, although Esau (Edom) has a sordid role to play in the destruction and captivity of Jacob and will be punished, still the coming Covenant will include "the remnant of Edom," and even beyond that, "'and all the nations who are called by My Name,' says Jehovah Who does this thing" [9:12].

Obadiah

Esau (Edom) and Jacob (Israel) were brothers not only by family but also by being under the Abrahamic Covenant. However when both of these connections are discarded, not only is the misery of Judah increased, Jehovah pronounces condemnation – Covenant-partners cannot escape judgment when they mistreat one another in Covenant:

> For violence against your brother Jacob, shame shall cover you, and you shall be cut off forever. ... But you should not have gawked at your brother in the day of his misfortune; you should not have rejoiced over Judah in the day of their destruction; you should not have opened your mouth so wide in their day of distress ... Indeed, you should not have stared at their evil ..., you should not have stood at the crossroads to cut off those who escaped; nor should you have shut his survivors up in the day of distress. For the day of Jehovah upon all the nations is near; as you have done, it shall be done to you; your recompense shall return upon your head.   1:10-15

"The house of Jacob shall be a fire... but the house of Esau shall be stubble; they shall burn among them and devour them, and there shall be no survivor to the house of Esau" [1:18] – the remnant who survive after this judgment is visited upon them (by the Maccabees) ends up being absorbed into the Jews, and as a separate nation Edom disappears, confirming what Amos had prophesied.

Jonah

Although this book provides an interlude in regard to the judgment on Israel, Jonah does present a contrast in that the heathen respond to the call to repentance while God's own Covenant People refuse to repent.

Jonah himself presents a contrast between the prejudices and hatreds of the human as opposed the *HESED* and Glory of Jehovah (which God has no qualms about showing toward *all* humanity); in words which echo Jehovah's Exodus 33:19; 34:6-7 definition of His Glory, Jonah reluctantly admits: "for I know that You are a gracious and compassionate God, slow to anger of great steadfast Love [*HESED*], One who relents from evil" [4:2].

The LORD sought in Abraham for an intercessor for Sodom and Gomorrah [Genesis 18:17-33] which provided a window to God's conflict when He must act in judgment; now as Jehovah comes seeking an intercessor in Jonah, this prophet is decidedly unAbrahamic – he runs away. But the LORD is persistent in His choice of intercessor.

Much to Jonah's chagrin, the message he preaches works and Nineveh proves more righteous than the People of God. After his song of gratitude from being vomited out by the fish, "But I will sacrifice to You with the voice of thanksgiving; that which I vowed I will fulfill – salvation is of Jehovah" [2:9], one might think he would rejoice over those who also have been saved by God. "But it displeased Jonah and he became angry... 'Therefore now, O Jehovah, please take my Life from me, for my death is better than my life!'" [4:1,3]

Indeed self-centeredly he has more compassion for the plant which has sheltered him than for the lives of the inhabitants of Nineveh. Yet Jehovah (the Covenant Name) cares about those who are spiritually ignorant, "more than one hundred and twenty thousand persons who cannot discern between their right hand and their left" – and even "much livestock" [4:11]. His concern encompasses even more than just the humans involved.

Micah

"Hear, all the peoples! Attend, O earth, and all which is in it! Let the Lord Jehovah be a witness against you, the Lord from His holy temple" [1:2]; "Hear, O mountains, ... for Jehovah has a dispute against His People, and He will challenge Israel: 'O My People, what have I done to you? And how have I wearied you? Answer against Me. For I brought you up from the land of Egypt, I redeemed [*PADAH*] you from the house of slavery'" [6:2-4] – the witnesses to Covenant are called on to judge: Jehovah has followed through on His Covenant, so why has Israel been so intent on sabotaging this relationship?

Again there is the cry against injustice and deceit, "For her rich ones are full of violence, her inhabitants speak lies, and their tongue is deceit in their mouth" [6:12]; "So they oppress a man and his household, a man and his inheritance" [2:2]. 'Trust no one' is the atmosphere of the day:

> The godly man has perished from the earth, and there is no one upright among men. All of them lie in wait for Blood; every man hunts his brother with a net. Evil is upon both palms, to do it well – the prince and the judge seeks a bribe, and the great man speaks according to the lust of his Soul/Life; so they weave it together ... Do not trust a neighbor; do not put confidence in a friend; guard the opening of your mouth from her who lies in your bosom.   7:2-3, 5

They strip "the skin from upon them, and the flesh from their bones;... break their bones and shatter them as for a [soup]pot, like flesh in the [stew]pot" [3:3], "The wives of My People you have driven out..., from their children you have taken away My majesty forever" [2:9], "Yet they lean on Jehovah, and say, 'Is not Jehovah among us? No evil can come upon us'" [3:11].

But judgment will come: "Then they will cry to Jehovah, but He will not answer them; He will hide His face from them at that time..." [3:4]; "Therefore I have made you sick, to strike you, to make you desolate because of your sins" [6:13]. "Therefore, because of you, Zion shall be plowed like a field, Jerusalem shall be ruins, and the mountain of *the Temple* like the high places of the forest" [3:12]; and "I will make Samaria a heap of ruins in the field" because of their spiritual treachery [1:6-7].

Yet, the last word will be 'hope': "Be in pain and deliver, O daughter of Zion, like a woman giving birth. ... you shall come to Babylon, there you shall be delivered; there Jehovah will redeem [*GO'EL*] you from the palm of your enemies" [4:10]. However, redemption merely from this captivity is too small in scope:

> But you, Bethlehem Ephrathah, though you are insignificant among the thousands of Judah, yet out of you shall come forth to Me The One to become Ruler in Israel, Whose comings forth are from of old, from the days of everlasting..., He shall stand and feed [His Sheep] in the strength of Jehovah, in the majesty of the Name of Jehovah His God; and they shall remain, for now He shall be great to the ends of the earth; this One shall be peace [*SHALOM*] ...   5:2, 4-5

At that time, "when [the enemy] comes into our land, and when he treads in our palaces, we will raise against him *seven/oath* shepherds and eight anointed men" [5:5]. Speaking of the time after the Messiah would come, Covenant (*seven*) and renewal (eight) will conquer the one who invades even to the "palaces" of God's People.

Again Jehovah will deal with those who gloat over Israel's distress: "Now many nations gathered against you ... but they did not know the plans of Jehovah, they did not understand His counsel; for He gathered them like sheaves to the threshing floor" [4:11-12]. "The nations watched and were ashamed ... They were licking the dust like a snake; like those which crawl from the earth they were trembling from their holes. They were dreading Jehovah our God, and were afraid because of You" [7:16-17].

Jehovah will also remove that on which Israel had depended: "I will cut off your horses ... and pull down all your strongholds; I will cut off sorceries ... [and] soothsayers; your idols I will cut off ... you shall no more bow down to the work of your hands ... thus I will destroy your enemies" – and it will be that "in anger and in fury I will execute vengeance on the nations which have not heeded" [5:10-15].

So what does the Lord want from His People? Sacrifices? "Will Jehovah be pleased with thousands of rams, ten thousand rivers of oil? Shall I give my firstborn for my transgression, the fruit of my womb for the sin of my Soul/Life?" [6:7] – no, a humbled heart: "He has declared to you, O man, what is good; and what does Jehovah seek from you but to do justly, to love steadfast Love [HESED], and to humbly walk with your God?" [6:8]:

> I will look to Jehovah; I will wait for the God of my salvation; my God will hear me! Do not rejoice over me, my enemy; if I fall, I will arise; if I sit in darkness, Jehovah is a Light to me. I will bear the anger of Jehovah, because I have sinned against Him, until He pleads my case and fulfills my justice. He will bring me out into the light; I will see His righteousness.　　　　　　　　　　　　　　　　　　7:7-9

In response, the guarantee of His Covenant Glory would be:

> Who is a God like You, carrying iniquity away and passing over the transgression of the remnant of His heritage? He does not sustain His anger forever, because He inclines toward steadfast Love [HESED]. He will turn again, He will have compassion on us, and He will bring our iniquities into subjection. You will cast all our sins into the depths of the sea. You will give truth to Jacob and steadfast Love [HESED] to Abraham, as You swore to our fathers from days of old.　　7:18-20

This will extend to all nations: "Many nations shall come and say, 'Come, and let us go … to the house of the God of Jacob; He will teach us His ways, and we shall walk in His paths.' For out of Zion the *TORAH* shall go forth, and the word of Jehovah from Jerusalem" [4:2].

> For all peoples walk each in the name of his god, but we will walk in the Name of Jehovah our God forever and ever.　　　　　　　　4:5

Nahum

Although in Jonah, Nineveh exhibits humility before God, it certainly is no longer the case here. Perhaps the brink of judgment that they teetered on in Jonah's time has become overwhelming, and now "God is jealous, and Jehovah avenges; Jehovah avenges and is the Master of wrath.

Jehovah takes vengeance on His foes, and He keeps it against His enemies" [1:2]. Although His Glory is mercy and grace and slow to anger [Exodus 34:6-7] still He "will not at all acquit (His enemies) ... Who can stand before His fury? Who can rise up against the fierceness of His anger? His rage is poured out like fire" [1:3,6].

What is seen in Nineveh's destruction – is Jehovah simply a destroyer? No, for His Covenant People, "Jehovah is good, a stronghold in the day of distress; and He knows those who trust in Him" [1:7]. Keep holding on to Jehovah because your enemies will be no more: "Behold, upon the mountains the feet of him who bears good news, who proclaims peace [*SHALOM*]! O Judah, celebrate your feasts, fulfill your vows, for the wicked shall not continue to pass through you; he is utterly cut off" [1:15].

Habakkuk

> O LORD, how long have I called, and You have not heard? I have cried out to You, "Violence!" but You have not saved. Why have You shown me iniquity and mischief? Victimizing and injustice are before me; there has been strife, and discord rose up. Therefore the *TORAH* has been helpless, and justice has never gone forth; for the wicked has surrounded the righteous, therefore distorted justice has come forward ... Why have You watched those who deal treacherously, and have kept Silence when the wicked swallows up a person more righteous than he? Why do You make men like fish of the sea, like creeping things which have no ruler over them?   1:2-4, 13-14

So begins the ancient book of Habakkuk, and yet it declares something that is ageless. Why is there injustice even within 'the family,' one's own People? Why do "... the peoples labor only for the fire, and nations weary themselves for emptiness?" [2:13]. Israel is "filled with shame instead of Glory" [2:16] as the bottle is pressed to the neighbor and both act as if there is no Covenant: "You also... [are] exposed as uncircumcised!" "The stone will cry out from the wall, and the beam from the lumber will answer it. Woe to him building a town with Blood and founding a city with iniquity!" [2:11-12].

"I am raising up the Chaldeans...to possess dwelling places which are not theirs" [1: 6] – yet even this instrument of God's judgment will itself fall under condemnation: "Then his spirit oversteps, and he transgresses; he commits offense, attributing this power to his god" [1:11]. How foolish are they that trust in the false gods:

> What profit is the image, for its maker has carved it, the cast image, a teacher of lies, upon which the maker trusts, when he made mute idols? Woe to the one who says to the wood, 'Awake!'; to silent stone, 'Arise! It shall teach!' Behold, it is overlaid with gold and silver, yet there is no breath/spirit in it at all. 2:18-19

Despite what it may seem, "Jehovah is in His holy temple. Let all the earth be silent before Him" [2:20]; "His majesty covered the heavens, and His praise filled the earth. ... He stood and shook the earth; He looked and terrified the nations. The everlasting mountains were scattered, the eternal hills humbled. The ways of eternity are His" [3:3,6].

Indeed, evil will not be overlooked: "The cup of Jehovah's right Hand is turned against you – utter shame is on your glory" [2:16]. Jehovah will ultimately step forward in judgment, "For the vision is yet for an appointed time; and it pants for the end, and it will not lie. Though it seems to hesitate, wait for it; for surely it will come, it will not tarry" [2:3].

"Are You not from everlasting, O Jehovah my God, my Holy One? We shall not die. O Jehovah, You have committed them to judgment; O Rock, You have marked them for rebuke" [1:12]. If Jehovah judges His own People then their enemies will not escape – decisively the Covenant connection will have the last say: "Unsheathed, Your bow was exposed; the oaths [from *oath/seven*] were the arrowshafts of [Your] Word. ... In fury You marched into the Land; in anger You trampled the nations. You went forth for the salvation of Your People, for salvation of Your Anointed. You struck the head from the house of the wicked..." [3:9, 12-13]. And of course, the words for "salvation" in Habakkuk come from the root word that gives us "Yeshua" or "Jesus."

The end result will be: "For the earth will be filled with the knowledge of the Glory [*KABOD*] of Jehovah, as the waters cover the sea" [2:14], and "the just shall live by his faith" [2:4] – the signal declaration that St Paul quotes three times (Romans 1:17; Galatians 3:11; Hebrews 10:38). And though things may not be good right now: "Though the fig tree does not blossom, nor fruit be on the vines; though the product of the olive fails, and the fields grow no food; though the flock be cut off from the fold, and no cattle be in the stalls" [3:17], Habakkuk can finish, confident in Israel's Covenant-partner, "Yet in Jehovah I exult, I rejoice in the God of my salvation. Jehovah God is my strength; He makes my feet like deer's feet, and He makes me walk on my high hills" [3:18-19].

Zephaniah

Right at the beginning, Zephaniah declares strong judgment from Jehovah, "I will utterly terminate everything from the face of the ground ... man and beast... birds of the heavens... fish of the sea... I will cut off man from the face of the ground; I will stretch out My Hand against Judah, and against all the inhabitants of Jerusalem" [1:2-4]. He will remove "the stumbling blocks, even the wicked ... residue of Baal from this place" [1:3-4].

He will deal with those who treat Covenant casually, "who bow down to the host of the heavens..., who bow down and *swear/seven* to Jehovah, yet *swear/seven* by Malcham" [1:5]; whose Covenant relationship is empty, "Those drawing back from following Jehovah, those not seeking Jehovah, and those not inquiring of Him" [v 6]. "I will search Jerusalem with lamps, and will judge the men who are settled on their lees, who say in their heart, 'Jehovah will not do good, nor will He do evil.'" [v 12]. Therefore an encompassing condemnation is declared:

> I said, "'Surely you will fear Me, You will receive discipline" ... but they rose early and corrupted all their doings ... She did not listen to [His] voice, she did not accept discipline, she did not trust in Jehovah, she did not drawn near to her God. Her rulers ... are roaring lions; ...

her prophets are arrogant men of deceit; her priests have defiled the Holy Place, they violate the *TORAH*.　　　　　　　　　　　3:7, 2-4

"Jehovah has prepared a sacrifice; He has consecrated His called ones [the Chaldeans]" [1:7] – as a sword is prepared for its task, so the 'guests' are readied for their coming work. Indeed, "The great day of Jehovah is near; it is near and hurries quickly ... a day of wrath, ... affliction and distress, ... devastation and desolation, ... darkness and gloom, ... I will bring distress to man; they will walk like blind men, because they sinned against Jehovah; their Blood will be poured out like dust" [1:14-17].

None will be exempt from judgment, especially those who have delighted in God's People's misfortune: says Jehovah of hosts, the God of Israel, "... a desolation until forever. ... This they shall have instead of their pride, for they have cursed and become arrogant against the People of Jehovah of hosts'" [2:8-10]. Nineveh, "the jubilant city, dwelling securely, saying in her heart, 'I am, and there is no other' – how has she become a desolation..." [2:15]. "My judgment will gather the nations..., to pour on them My fury, all my burning anger; with the fire of My jealousy all the earth shall be consumed" [3:8].

Hope is available: "Seek Jehovah, all you meek of the Land, who have practiced His justice. Seek righteousness, seek humility. Perhaps you will be hidden in the day of Jehovah's anger" [2:3]. He will be faithful: "Jehovah the Righteous is in her midst, He will do no unrighteousness. Morning by morning He brings His justice to light; He never fails ..." [3:5].

"He will shrivel all the gods of the earth; people will bow to Him, ..." [2:11]; even Babel will be reversed: "For then I will return to the peoples a clear language, to call all of them by the Name of Jehovah, to serve Him with one will" [3:9]. And when He is finished, Jehovah's aspiration will be accomplished:

> I will leave in your midst a humble and poor People, and they shall trust in the Name of Jehovah. The remnant of Israel shall not do unrighteousness nor speak lies... they shall pasture and lie down, and no one shall terrify them. Shout for joy, ... be glad and rejoice with all

the heart, O daughter of Jerusalem! Jehovah has taken away your judgments, He has cast out your enemy. The King of Israel, Jehovah, is in your midst; you shall not observe evil any more. ... Jehovah your God in your midst is mighty, He will save; He will rejoice over you with gaiety, He will [not] hold His peace with His Love, He will rejoice over you with singing. 3:12-17

Haggai

The destruction and captivity are done. Now God's People have returned, but returned to what? "Is it time for you yourselves to dwell in your paneled houses, and this House to lie in ruins?" [1:4]. Their Life is insipid and futile: "he who hires himself sells himself for a bag with holes" [v 6]; "when you brought it home, I blew it away... because of My House which is in ruins" [v 9]; therefore the remedy is to rediscover their sense of purpose in the spiritual: "'build the House, and I will be pleased in it and be glorified [KABOD],' says Jehovah" [v 8].

The People "obeyed the voice of Jehovah their God, and the words of Haggai the prophet" [v 12], and Jehovah responds, "I am with you" [1:13], as He had with Abraham [Genesis 26:24], Jacob [Genesis 28:15], Moses [Exodus 3:12], Joshua [Joshua 1:5], and Gideon [Judges 6:16]. The reassurance is needed to balance the sense of loss, "Who among you is left who saw this House in its former glory? And how do you see it now? Is it in your eyes as if it is nothing?" [2:3]. There is value because, "'I am with you,' says Jehovah of hosts, 'according to the word which I cut with you when you came out of Egypt, so My Spirit remains among you'" [2:4-5].

After all, it is not the physical appearance which fills it with meaning, but rather its content:

For thus says Jehovah of hosts: "Once more (in a little while) I will shake the heavens and the earth, ... and I will shake all the nations, and shall come the Desire of All Nations, and I will fill this House with Glory [KABOD] ... The Glory [KABOD] of this latter House shall be greater than the former ... and in this place I will give peace [SHALOM] ..." 2:6-9

Zechariah

Warning From the Past For the Present

Zechariah speaks warnings which echo the pre-captivity prophets and those generations' rejection:

> "These are the things you shall do: let each man speak truth with his neighbor; in truth, justice, and peace give judgment in your gates; let none of you devise evil in your heart against your neighbor; and do not love a false *oath/seven* – for all these are things which I hate," says Jehovah. 8:16-17

> "Execute true judgment, practice steadfast Love [*HESED*] and mercy each to his brother. Do not oppress the widow, the orphan, the alien or the poor. Let none of you devise evil in his heart against his brother."

> But [your fathers] refused to listen, turned a stubborn shoulder, and stopped their ears from hearing. They made their hearts like flint, lest they hear the *TORAH* and the words which Jehovah of hosts had sent by His Spirit through the former prophets. Thus great wrath has come from Jehovah of hosts. It will be that just as He called and they did not listen, so they called and I would not listen. 7:9-13

> This [scroll] is the curse which goes out over the face of the whole earth: "All who steal ...; and, all who *swear/seven* shall be cut away, ... I will send it out," says the LORD of hosts; "It shall go into the house of the thief and ... of the one who *swears/seven* falsely by My Name ... and consume it ..." 5:3-4

His call to repentance reminds the People what it means to humbly live in the Covenant Land again:

> "Return to Me," says Jehovah of hosts, "and I will turn to you ... Do not be like your fathers, ... they did not listen nor heed Me ... But My words and My statutes, which I commanded My servants the prophets, did they not overtake your fathers?" And they returned and said: "As Jehovah of hosts considered doing to us, according to our ways and according to our deeds, so He has dealt with us." 1:3-6

Hope – for All Nations

In Daniel, the Archangel Michael is named as the Protector of God's People, "the great prince who stands watch over the sons of your People" [Daniel 12:1]; possibly it is he who cries out, "O Jehovah of hosts, how long will You not have compassion on Jerusalem and on the cities of Judah, against which You were enraged these seventy years?" [1:12]. Jehovah of hosts responds: "I am passionate for Jerusalem and for Zion ... I am exceedingly furious at nations which are arrogant; for I was a little enraged, and they helped – for evil" [1:14-15].

Then comes the promise which must have been so welcome to the disenfranchised People: "I have returned to Jerusalem with compassions; My House shall be built in it" [1:16]; "'Jerusalem shall be inhabited without walls for the multitude ... in her midst. For I will be to her,' says Jehovah, 'a wall of fire all around, and I will be the Glory [*KABOD*] in her midst.'... thus says Jehovah of hosts: 'He sent Me for [His] Glory [*KABOD*], ... for he who touches you touches the 'apple' of His eye.'... 'Sing and rejoice, O daughter of Zion! For lo, I come and I will dwell in your midst,' says Jehovah'" [2:4-5, 8, 10], a commitment echoed in 8:2-3: "Thus says Jehovah of hosts: 'I am passionate for Zion with great zeal; with great fervor I am passionate for her. I have returned ... and will dwell in the midst of Jerusalem. Jerusalem shall be called 'City of Truth,' 'The Mountain of Jehovah of Hosts,' 'The Holy Mountain.'' "

> "... as you were a curse among the nations, O house of Judah and house of Israel, so I will save you, and you shall be a blessing. Do not fear, let your hands be strong. ... As I devised to punish you when your fathers provoked Me to wrath," says Jehovah of hosts, "and I would not give in, so again in these days I have devised to do good to Jerusalem and to the house of Judah. Do not fear." 8:13-15

But this will not be an exclusive club: "Many nations will be joined to Jehovah in that day, and they will be My People. I will dwell in your midst, then you will know that Jehovah of hosts has sent Me to you" [2:11].

Joshua

Joshua ("Jehovah saves," the Greek Septuagint translation: "Jesus"), son of Jehozadak ("Jehovah is Righteous"), as the High Priest, wears on his shoulders and over his heart the names of the tribes [Exodus 28:12, 29], over his forehead is "Holy to Jehovah" [v 36], and he would "bear the iniquity of the sacred things" [v 38]. In a dramatic picture of forgiveness, representing the People – and their sin – he stands with filthy garments: "Remove the filthy garments from him. ... See, I have caused your iniquity to pass from you, and I will clothe you with stately robes" [Zechariah 3:4].

Then to Joshua and his "companions," "wondrous" (the word for the "wonders" done in Egypt during the Exodus) men, "behold, I am bringing forth My Servant 'The Branch'" [3:8]. In 6:12, this Joshua is announced as "'The Branch,' He shall sprout up from His place" [6:12]. Isaiah 4:2 also spoke of "'The Branch' ... beautiful and glorious," which would grow from the stem of Jesse [Isaiah 11:1]. Jeremiah 23:5 declares "I will raise to David 'a Branch of Righteousness'; a King shall reign and prosper, and execute judgment and righteousness in the earth," repeated again later in 33:15.

Joshua, "The Branch," "shall bear the majesty, and shall sit and rule on His throne; so He shall be a Priest on His throne, and the counsel of peace shall be between them both" [Zechariah 6:13]. Israel's priests are not of the Jesse/David line, and the throne is promised to David's line, according to II Samuel 7:16 and Psalm 89:28-36, for example. In fact, because they are of different tribes, the Old Testament kings are never to do the priestly duties – some even get into trouble trying to do so [I Samuel 13:8-14; II Chronicles 26:16-23]. Therefore, although Joshua is an actual historical figure at this time, Zechariah must be looking beyond him to an even greater Joshua/Jesus, Who will have *both* priesthood *and* kingship.

"Behold, the Man Whose name is the Branch... shall build *the Temple* of Jehovah" [6:12]. "The Stone which I have laid before Joshua" [3:9] recalls the "precious Cornerstone" of Isaiah 28:16 and the refused Stone which becomes "the Head of the corner" of Psalm 118:22; this Stone is not an object but a Person. "Even those from afar shall come and build *the Temple* of Jehovah" [6:15] – all nations will be involved in this temple, a temple of *people*, as St Peter will admonish: "Come to Him, to that Living Stone... you also as living stones are being built into a spiritual house, to be a holy priesthood, to offer spiritual sacrifices acceptable to God through Jesus Christ" [I Peter 2:4-5].

Regarding "the Stone which has *seven/oath* eyes" [3:9] and the *seven/oath* lamps [4:2; Matthew 6:22: "The lamp of the body is the eye"]: "For these rejoice to see the plumb line in Zerubbabel's hand. These *seven/oath* are Jehovah's eyes, which roam the whole earth" [4:10]. If "I will remove the iniquity of that Land in one day" [3:9], and *"oath/seven"* carries Covenant overtones, these "eyes" which search not just Israel, but the whole earth, seek those who will be part of the coming Covenant – part of this new temple with Jehovah. It will be a temple built "'Not by might nor by power, but by My Spirit,' says Jehovah of hosts" [4:6].

Zerubbabel

Zerubbabel, the *"signet ring*[193] for I have chosen you" [Haggai 2:23], at this return from captivity provides a 'restoration point' – a clear point in time where David's line to the throne of God's People is reestablished and therefore will be an important marker for Jesus' genealogy in Matthew 1:12-13 and Luke 3:27. "The hands of Zerubbabel have founded this house; his hands shall also finish it" [4:9], speak not only of his *hands* and the immediate temple, but also the *hands* of his "Son," "the Capstone with shouts of 'Grace, grace to it!'" [v 7], Who will build the eternal house made up of the People of Jehovah, available to all peoples:

> Thus says Jehovah of hosts: "Peoples will yet come, inhabitants of many cities, ... residents from one city will go to another, saying, 'Let us walk, to go and entreat Jehovah, and to seek out Jehovah of hosts. I also am going.' Many peoples and mighty nations shall come to seek Jehovah of hosts in Jerusalem, and to pray before Jehovah. ... In those days ten men out of all the languages of the nations will grasp and take hold of the sleeve of a Jewish man, saying, 'Let us go with you, for we have heard that God is with you.'" 8:20-23

There is a King coming Who will be humble, Who will have salvation and Who will ultimately rule the world:

> Rejoice greatly, O daughter of Zion! Shout, O daughter of Jerusalem! Behold, your King is coming to you; righteous and victorious is He, humble and riding on a donkey, even a colt, the foal of a donkey. ... He shall speak peace [*SHALOM*] to the nations; His dominion will be from sea to sea, and from the River to the ends of the earth. You also, because of the Blood of your Covenant, I set your prisoners free from the waterless pit.   9:9-11

But we know from history that the physical temple contemporary to Zerubbabel is not the subject of Zechariah's promises, since this temple also is destroyed. For the next five hundred years, there will be no king to sit on Israel's throne which would properly be the king, not merely some designate of a foreign power. In most of that time span there will not even be a prophet.

As is evident in the various outcries of Ezra and Nehemiah, the injustices which had their role in bringing about the captivity still continue afterwards – simply a footnote to how humanity still has selfishness at the core of its nature. No, the promise, "Behold, I will save My People... I will bring them back... they shall be My People and I will be their God, in truth and righteousness" [8:7-8] will not be fulfilled within the next 400 years, at the end of which will come the most marked of all rejections of Jehovah.

Breaking the Covenant – Chapter 11

"Feed the flock for slaughter" [11:4] – not in regard to the Babylonian Captivity as in the previous prophets, since there will yet come another judgment under Rome and the result will be terrible. Who the shepherds are, particularly the three of verse 8, is hard to pin down, other than that their leadership only fits the "flock" for slaughter. The sheep on the other hand unquestioningly and willingly follow, even to the carnage which is coming, for which Jehovah will no longer have pity [v 6] – a carnage which will leave only one out of every ten alive in Jerusalem, and thirty Jews sold as slaves for a penny.

"I took my staff, Kindness/Grace, and cut it in two, that I might break the Covenant which I had cut with all the peoples. So it was broken on that day…" [vv 10-11]. In Romans 3:4, St Paul declares that throughout history, despite the constant breaking of Covenant by humans, Jehovah has always remained faithful to His commitment, "Let God be true and every man be a liar, as it is written, 'That You may be justified in Your words, and prevail when You are judged.'" But now *He* will break Covenant. Although one might have expected it, still, to actually see it happen should leave the observer thunderstruck.

As mentioned in the original discussion in regard to the *GO'EL*, when there is lost Blood to be 'balanced' and one's Life is forfeit, the offended party may allow a ransoming payment instead. When God breaks Covenant, His Life/Blood is forfeit, and, yes, He dies – because He polices Himself according to His own rules: "For when God made a promise to Abraham, since He had no one greater by whom to swear, He swore by Himself" [Hebrews 6:13], thereby making Himself not just Participant, but also Guardian of the Covenant.

When the People, who are 'the offended party'(!), are asked what they see as the value of their Shepherd – both of Him Who breaks the Covenant and of the broken relationship itself – the answer is a complete trivializing of it all: "thirty pieces of silver" [vv 12-13], the price of a slave [Exodus 21:32]. This identifies that the historical context of this breaking of Covenant will be at the death of Jesus, Who is betrayed for thirty pieces of silver which is thrown "into the house of Jehovah for the potter" [Zechariah 11:13, see Matthew 27:5-10].

"Then I cut in two my other staff, Bonds, that I might break the brotherhood between Judah and Israel" [11:14] – if Covenant with Jehovah is distained, then other loyalties cannot be far behind. What is described in this chapter is the disintegration of God's People in every aspect of their Covenant identity.

The final act of judgment will be against spiritual leaders who sabotage the People [11:15-16]: the shepherd who cares nothing for the flock except to satiate his own appetite, the spiritual guide who is more interested in his own stimulation than in reassuring and building up the flock, the expert who follows what appeals to his own sensibilities rather than clearly proclaiming the Word of Jehovah.

Which Covenant?

What is the Covenant which is broken here? Is it the Creation Covenant which reaches all the way back to Adam and Eve's creation? That cannot be, since if "all the peoples" meant all of humanity, then the drive of Jehovah toward restoring that relationship would be broken.

The more likely choice is the Circumcision Covenant with Abraham, because it is not at Sinai, but rather in Circumcision that God's special People receive their unique status – it is the event that *defines* their relationship with Jehovah. Sinai and all other subsequent Covenants only expand on this relationship, just as the subsequent Covenants between David and Jonathan only identify and confirm in more detail what is already present in their original Covenant relationship.

Therefore the breaking of Covenant "with all the Peoples," would speak more toward the nations which Abraham is told will be his offspring [Genesis 17:5-6]: not just Isaac and Jacob's children, but also Ishmael's, Esau's, and Keturah's sons' [Genesis 25:1-4] children, all of whom are circumcised within Abraham's special relationship.

However, affecting more than just his seed, this death will answer the last element in Abraham's call: "all peoples on earth [all humanity] will be blessed through you" [Genesis 12:3]. This Covenant-reckoning will encompass the sins of "the whole world" [I John 2:2], and at the moment of His death, God's and Abraham's Son would 'initiate' a 'New' and "much better" Covenant [Hebrews 7:22; 8:6]. This will *confirm* the Creation Covenant not by adding to that bond, but by providing the vehicle – Jesus – through which all humanity may now participate in this renewed intimacy with Jehovah.

What Does Broken Mean?

> I will establish My Covenant between Me and you and your descendants after you in their generations, for an everlasting Covenant, to be God to you and to your descendants after you.
> Genesis 17:7; also I Chronicles 16:17

Although this Covenant is broken now by both God and man, yet it is "an everlasting Covenant." How could it be said that "an everlasting Covenant" is ended?? What really is broken in the Covenant?

Entrance into the 'Old' Covenant will now cease at the Cross, yet the effects of that Covenant will still be eternal. No longer will subsequent Circumcisions bring about the unity of Jehovah to mankind, yet Abraham will not need to now be baptized under the 'New' Covenant – the relationship established by Jehovah in Genesis will be enough for eternity for those who have been under the 'Old' Covenant. Their connection to Jesus will come (as will be discussed later) in Jesus' Circumcision, which connects Jesus to them by Blood, and therefore also connects them to the Blood of the Cross.

> So all Israel will be saved, as it is written: "From out of Zion will come the Deliverer [Hebrew: *GO'EL*, Isaiah 59:20], and He will turn away ungodliness from Jacob; for this is the Covenant from Me with them, when I take away their sins." In regard to the Gospel [Israel] are enemies to you, but in regard to election they are beloved for the sake of the fathers, *for the free gifts and the call of God are irrevocable.*
> Romans 11:26-29

The 'Old' Covenant ends in favor of the 'New' Covenant, yet Zechariah, as well as the other prophets, indicate that Jehovah's long-term commitment to this Chosen People still holds, a declaration echoed in the New Testament in Romans 9-11, since the "call of God is irrevocable."

God's Love and His Covenants are two different things: the Covenants express the Heart or *HESED* of God, but they do not encompass all which that *HESED* is. It is not from any Covenant obligation that He calls humanity back to Himself; rather, His choice to

Love has moved Him to create the Covenants – they are designed to 'make visible' and to act out this Love. Yet He can work beyond these bonds, beyond even His own deliberate breaking and ending of a Covenant – beyond His death, transcending the boundaries and expired obligations of this pact as even today He continues the special honor and role which He has placed upon this People.

Love and Discipline in Tension

Care must be taken to not descend into 'contract' concepts in terms of Covenant, neither in regard to its origins, nor to its effects. The long-term goals of His *HESED* remain, no matter who breaks Covenant. However, when Jehovah breaks Covenant, it is for something better – when Israel breaks it, it is because of rebellion. The discipline which that calls for is stiff: there will not be the protection, the readiness to help, at the distress of the Covenant-partner:

> For I will not have pity again on the inhabitants of the Land. ... I will deliver each into his neighbor's hand and into his king's hand. They shall destroy the Land, and I will not rescue them from their hand. ... I will not feed you. What is to die, let it die, and what is to be destroyed, let it be destroyed. Let those which are left eat each other, a woman the flesh of her neighbor. 11:6, 9

> Therefore it happened, that just as He proclaimed and they would not hear, so they called out and I would not listen ... But with a storm I drove them among all the nations which they did not know. So the Land is desolate behind them, no one passes through or returns; for they made the precious Land desolate. 7:13-14

Still, because of the *HESED* which will Love even the enemy, a HESED which is greater than Covenant, one can only wonder at how painful it must be for the LORD to visit on Israel what their rebellion requires.

You Prisoners of Hope

> Turn to the stronghold, O prisoners of hope. Even today I declare that I will restore double to you .... Jehovah their God will save them

in that day, as the Sheep of His People; for they are the jewels of a crown, lifted like a banner over His Land.   9:12, 16

This is no trivial hope, but one which rests solidly upon Jehovah's Glory – His goodness, Covenant, grace and mercy. That they will receive double blessings for what they suffer is not true in the four hundred years up to Jesus, therefore the People are entreated to yet look forward:

> I will strengthen the house of Judah, and I will save the house of Joseph. I will bring them back, for I have mercy on them. They shall be as though I had not cast them away; for I am Jehovah their God, and I will answer them. ... For I will redeem [*PADAH*] them ... I will strengthen them in Jehovah, and in His Name they shall walk.
> 10:6, 8, 12

Despite the People not deserving it, despite that in broken Covenant one might expect that He should merely walk away, instead Jehovah protects. He will be *GO'EL* among the nations:

> It will be in that day that I will make Jerusalem a burdensome stone: for all the peoples, all who carry it will be severely gashed, yet all nations of the earth are gathered against it ... In that day Jehovah will defend around the inhabitants of Jerusalem; ... It shall be in that day that I will seek to destroy all nations which come against Jerusalem.
> 12:3, 8-9

And this will be the time of the New Covenant, the new relationship with God in "Me Whom they pierced" [12:10]; but now the realization will hit home hard, since in true Covenant fashion, God's only Son will indeed be their Son as well. They would know the Father's grief, knowing that it is their hands as well as the Father's which held the knife for the sacrifice, just as Abraham must have felt when he was faced with the offering of Isaac.

> I will pour on the house of David and on the inhabitants of Jerusalem the Spirit of grace and earnest prayer; then they will look on Me Whom they pierced, and will mourn for Him as one mourns for an only son, and [grieve] bitterly for Him like the bitterness over a firstborn.
> 12:10

"In that day a fountain shall be opened for the house of David and for the inhabitants of Jerusalem for sin and for impurity" [13:1] – but it has a route to travel before all will be accomplished:

> "O sword, awake against My Shepherd, against the Man who is My Companion," says Jehovah of hosts. "Strike the Shepherd, and the Sheep will be scattered; then I will turn My Hand against the little ones. And it shall be in all the Land, ... that two parts of it shall be cut off and die, but the third shall be left in it: I will bring the third (part) through the fire; I will refine them as silver is refined, and test them as gold is tested. They will call on My Name, and I will answer them. I will say, 'This is My People'; and he will say, 'Jehovah is my God.'"
> 13:7-9

> It shall be in that day that there will not be light ... It shall be one day which shall be known to Jehovah – not day and not night, but it will be at the time of evening that there will be light. It will be in that day that Living Waters shall flow from Jerusalem ... And Jehovah shall be King over all the earth; in that day there shall be one Jehovah and His Name one.
> 14:6-9

This will not be an exclusive club but rather at *the Feast of the Ingathering*, all nations will worship the King:

> It shall be that everyone who is left of all the nations... shall go up from year to year to worship the King, Jehovah of hosts, and to keep *the Feast of Tabernacles* ... In that day on the bells of the horses shall be "HOLY TO JEHOVAH" ...
> 14:16, 20

Malachi

A hundred years later, not much has changed for the People – it definitely is not the ideal relationship to which the New Covenant with Jehovah should lead.

There is suspicion in regard to Jehovah's Love [1:2]; there is no honor or reverence of Him [v 6]; and in contrast to the nations who will respect the Name of Jehovah [v 11], "you sneer at it; ... you bring the stolen, the lame, and the sick" [v 13]. "Cursed be the deceiver ... [who] sacrifices to Jehovah what is blemished" [v 14]. God's People rob Him in their tithes and offerings, thereby depriving themselves of His blessings [3:8-10], and they have turned away from what Jehovah told them He looks for in them [v 7]. Finally, "You have said, 'It is emptiness to serve God; what dishonest gain is there when we keep His charge ...?'" [3:14]

The priests, guardians of the holy, have Levi as their model,

> "My Covenant was with him, one of life and peace [SHALOM], ... so he was reverent toward Me and was in awe before My Name. The law of truth was in his mouth, and iniquity was not found on his lips. In peace [SHALOM] and uprightness he walked with Me and turned many away from iniquity. ... for he is the messenger of Jehovah of hosts. But you have turned from the way; you have made many stumble at the TORAH; you have corrupted the Covenant of Levi," says Jehovah of hosts. 2:5-8

The treachery encompasses the most basic of the Covenants: "to defile the Covenant of our fathers ... that Jehovah has been witness between you and the wife of your youth, whom have dealt deceitfully against, and she is your companion and the wife of your Covenant! But did He not make them one, which has a remnant of the Spirit? Why one? He was seeking offspring for God ..." [2:10, 14-15]. And then is it really any surprise that "you cover the altar of Jehovah with tears, with weeping and groaning, for He does not face the offering, nor receive it with delight from your hands" [2:13].

> "I will draw near you in judgment; I will be a swift witness against sorcerers, adulterers, and those swearing to a lie; against those who extort the wages of the laborers, also of the widows and orphans, and against those who turn away an alien — those who do not fear Me," says Jehovah of hosts. 3:5

The day will come: "Behold, I send My messenger, and he will clear the way before Me ...'Return to Me, and I will return to you,' Says Jehovah of hosts" [3:1, 7]. "Behold, I send you Elijah the prophet before the coming of the great and astonishing day of Jehovah; he will turn the heart of the fathers to the sons, and the heart of the sons to their fathers, lest I come and strike the Land with utter destruction" [4:5-6].

Then "the Lord, Whom you seek, will suddenly come to His temple, even the Messenger of the Covenant, in Whom you delight ..." [3:1]; "to you who fear My Name 'The Sun of Righteousness' shall arise with healing on His wings" [4:2]. The *GO'EL* will come, and will He not vindicate Israel against its – and His – enemies? That indeed will be true, but to set everything back into balance, He will start with the People themselves:

> But who can endure the day of His coming? Who will be standing at His appearing? ... He will sit as a refiner and a purifier of silver; He will purify the sons of Levi, and purge them like gold and silver, that they may bring to Jehovah an offering in righteousness. Then will be pleasing to Jehovah the offering of Judah and Jerusalem ... Then you shall return and distinguish between the righteous and the wicked, between one who serves God and one who does not serve Him.
>
> 3:2-4, 18

The LORD will not give up, not merely because of Covenant, but because His heart has chosen the People: "I am Jehovah, I do not change; therefore you are not consumed, O sons of Jacob" [3:6]. And for those who respect Him, He "listened and heard them; so a book of remembrance [*ZECHER*] was written before Him for those who were reverent before Jehovah and who esteemed His Name. 'They shall be Mine, ... and I will have compassion on them as a man has compassion on his own son who serves him'" [3:16-17].

XIII. The 'New' Covenant of God

A. Two Covenants, One Blood

> I abrogated certain aspects of the Old Testament's form *and substance*. (It is the "and substance" which makes the difference.) ... They should have told me to go back to understanding the Old Covenant before I tackled the New Covenant, and they should have opened my eyes to certain non-negotiable (eternal) traits of the Covenant of Grace which run historically through the entire Bible – those I thought I knew all about, but really swept under the rug.
>
> Dr. C. Matthew McMahon[194]

'The Old Testament is finished, therefore it has nothing the New Testament Christian needs...' Some have tended to mark a bold line between the 'Old' Covenant and the 'New' Covenant, almost as if they were entirely separate theologies. It seems as if 'the God of the Old Covenant' is different from 'the God of the New Covenant' – that is, that the New Testament God is more benevolent, more forgiving, in general just a nicer God.

But then Jesus would have appeared suddenly into history with very little continuity. Who He is would have very limited foundation and there would be disjointedness as to what God would have us understand about Himself. The New Testament Church would only 'after the fact,' based upon what they 'saw' in Him, be able to define His role and mission. Being based primarily on their reaction to Him, their interpretation could be challenged by other 'authorities,' such as: those who do not believe Jesus saw Himself as the Messiah; those who believe He really did not do miracles (that He more or less just practiced 'social and psychological engineering,' as in 'persuading the 5,000 to share their lunches' like the little boy had [Matthew 14:15-21]); and even by such things as the *DaVinci Code* fiction.

Yet the Early Church preaches from the Old Testament; St Paul teaches from Isaiah, Jeremiah, the Books of Moses, not Luke, Matthew and John; the Bereans check Paul out by consulting the written Word that they have, which is the Old Testament. Even Jesus uses these written Scriptures to teach His disciples:

> He said to them, "O foolish ones, and slow in heart to believe on all that the prophets spoke! Was it not necessary for the Christ to have suffered these things and to have entered into His Glory?" And beginning from Moses and from all the prophets, He interpreted to them in all the Scriptures the things concerning Himself.
> Luke 24:25-27

Yes, there are two different Covenants, but the same 'Blood/Life' runs throughout both: the 'Blood' which is there at the creation of Adam, which is there in the Covenant with Abraham, is the 'Blood' which will be praised into eternity by the saints – Jehovah's Blood/Life.

B. What's so New About the 'New' Covenant?

The Old Testament *has* Covenants; in the New Testament, Jesus *is* the Covenant.

Love (*HESED*) *Must* Give Itself

What makes the 'New' Covenant distinctively different from the 'Old' Covenant? Has Jehovah's grace and mercy changed? Has His attitude toward mankind changed? Has His earnest desire for a relationship with humans changed? Has *Jehovah* changed? Or is the difference merely in style or method or focus?

God's attitude and earnest desire do not change. His commitment, indeed, has been total, yet His *HESED* demands more – Covenant has to be taken to a new level. It is useful to repeat the quote used at the beginning of this book:

> What does love always desire? Love does not ask for gifts. Love asks for love. "I don't want your gifts" says the maid to the lover, "I want you." Why this? Because love must always give itself to and for the beloved. If love were to give anything else but love, it would not be

real love. Now this little baby in Bethlehem is God. It is love, it is God giving Himself.
... When we realize that God is Love, Bethlehem *must* follow....
Because God is Love, Love had to give itself. It did give itself. The Child in Bethlehem was born because God loved the world.

Berthold von Schenk[195]

This is the framework which stands behind Covenant, both the 'Old' *and* the 'New': God *must give Himself.* However in the 'New' Covenant, the dramatic difference is that Jehovah breaks the barrier between God and human, between Creator and creature. The precious Birth in Bethlehem is the reality, the fulfillment, the inevitable conclusion of HESED/Love giving Itself, the crowning point of Covenant itself.

Actually 'Really Real'?

Blood Covenant between people (like Jonathan and David's) throughout the world is never 'really real' – one Life/Blood never does *actually* flow between them. If a person gives a 'pint' of Blood at the local Blood bank, his Covenant-partner does not experience a loss of half a 'pint,' nor any other effects from that donation. Although the *concept* is powerful and meaningful enough, it still is only figurative – they are indeed *in* Covenant, however they in reality are still very separate people – their Bloods do not in fact become a single entity.

Even in regard to God's Covenant, throughout the Old Testament He does not have Blood to share – He is (as best as our words can describe Him) a Spirit Being. Every Covenant in the Old Testament could only be by proxy, by the Blood of *sacrifices* sprinkled on the altar and then sprinkled upon the People [Exodus 24:6, 8]. Even in His Covenant with Abraham, there seems to be a sense that if only He could just take that one step further through some sort of *physical* personal commitment, He would have. Of course, spiritually the Covenant connection is powerfully real, as the intercession in regard to Sodom and Gomorrah indicates. Yet Covenant just seems to always have a limp.

That is, until Jesus: "because in Him dwells all the fullness of the Godhead *bodily*" [Colossians 2:9].

In Jesus, the unity of Covenant is no longer merely a strong concept, now it is a fully tangible reality, an absolute reality, a reality in a Person: *in one Body* is found two Persons (God and Man), and *the same Life/Blood actually flows in both.* If Jesus bleeds, Man bleeds and God bleeds. Everything that is Man's is now God's, and vice versa, in a total sharing with nothing held back. This is a Covenant impossible to divide, impossible to break – which has been one of its main (theoretical) hallmarks all along. He is the 'really real' of the prophesy: *"I will ... give You as a Covenant* to people, as a Light to nations" [Isaiah 42:6, also 49:8] – in other words, '*You* are the Covenant,' the "one Mediator between God and men, the Man Christ Jesus" [I Timothy 2:5].

As a corollary to this discussion, the Gospels describe that the veil in *the Temple* is torn apart at the death of Jesus [for example, Matthew 27:51]. The veil, preventing access to Jehovah, is again the evidence that the 'Old' Covenant unity is not a full-fledged unity – it demonstrates a separation between God and human. When Jesus dies, officially ending the 'Old' Covenant and cutting the 'New,' that separation no longer exists and the veil no longer has a place, not because man compels his way into God's presence, but rather because God joins Himself to Man *as* the 'New' Covenant: "a new [Greek: freshly slaughtered] and living way which He consecrated for us, through the veil, that is, His Flesh" [Hebrews 10:20].

The "I Am" Statements

Once 'Jesus *is* the New Covenant' is realized, it falls into place alongside the "I Am" statements in the Gospel of John. The significance of these statements might be identified by looking at His declaration to Martha, "I am the Resurrection and the Life" [John 11:25], in the account of the raising of Lazarus.

Jesus does not say, 'I bring...' or 'I give...' or 'I demonstrate...' or 'I empower...' or 'I initiate...' the resurrection. He says simply, *"I am* the

Resurrection" – in other words, He is *identical* to the Resurrection, He is interchangeable with the Resurrection. In place of the Resurrection, insert His Name – and vice versa. In light of His promise "For where two or three are gathered in My Name, there am I in the midst of them" [Matthew 18:20], the Resurrection Himself with nail-printed hands and a spear cut in His side stands in every group of disciples' midst just as He does that first Easter evening [Luke 24:36] (a wonderful concept at a Christian funeral).

And just as powerful in that John 11 verse is the "*I am* ... the Life ..." [see also John 14:6] – it is not that He '*has*' Life, but rather *He is Life*. In Covenant context, since Life and Blood are synonymous, in Holy Communion it is not that Jesus would give us Life/Blood as if it were some accessory to Himself. It is His very self.

When this writer's father was asked to speak about First Communion as an earlier event to Confirmation, the inevitable question was raised, "Do children really understand Holy Communion?" His answer was to turn the question around: "Do *you*? What do *you* understand?" He found that the replies he received usually spoke of Holy Communion as "receiving IT." He commented that "we will never really begin to understand this Sacrament until we learn to say 'HIM' – *for we receive the Lord Jesus Christ.*" It must be 'HIM' – *Jesus* – *Life* – that flows through us in Covenant.

> At that day you will know that I am in My Father, and you in Me, and I in you. John 14:20

According to Isaiah, it would not have been outlandish for Jesus to also declare, 'I am the Covenant.' He does not merely represent, nor bring, nor initiate the Covenant with us. Just as to have the Resurrection means you had to have Jesus, and to have Life you have to have Jesus, so also to have this 'New' Covenant means that you have to have Jesus – because He is the Resurrection and the Life, *and He is the Covenant.*

Covenant's New Name is: Jesus!

Aside from the book of Hebrews, the Greek word for Covenant [*DIATHEKE*] only appears fifteen times in the New Testament – does that mean that the New Testament has lost interest in this great theme? Not in the least! The Name of the New Covenant is '*JESUS,*' since He is the exquisite description and personification of everything that Covenant has taught throughout the Old Testament – indeed, throughout the world. Everything to be said about the 'New' Covenant must be found *in Jesus*, or as St Paul is fond to put it: *"in Christ."* That is why Jesus can say without arrogance, "No one comes to the Father except through Me" [John 14:6].

C. Circumcision

The New Bond of Blood

GOD HAS BLOOD!

> When the eight days were completed in order to circumcise Him, His Name was called 'Jesus,' the Name given by the angel before He was conceived in the womb.
> Luke 2:21

It almost seems like a 'throw-away line,' an 'oh, yeah, by the way...,' but in Covenant-terms, it should have rocked the universe. Now after thousands of years and perhaps a hundred generations, for the first time in all of the universe's history, instead of by proxy and by symbolism, *Jehovah's own Blood* flows, and it flows in Circumcision – God has, so to speak, become the equal of man in Covenant. Extending *HESED*'s demand for self-giving in the Birth in Bethlehem, such a *personal* involvement by Jehovah has never before been seen.

Jesus' Circumcision is unique: throughout history, Circumcision has been a human becoming one Blood *with God*, one human at a time; but in this one, God becomes one Blood *with mankind.* No mere mechanical/dutiful ritual, the effect of that action races from generation to generation, like the rapid expansion of an explosion, enveloping *every* godly

Circumcision throughout the history of Covenant. All Circumcisions throughout all the generations suddenly connect – with Jesus, and in Jesus, to God.

The Blood Flows Both Ways

From this point the significance of the Person of Jesus is not just in having a human nature, but now in being connected to MANKIND. The genealogies of Matthew 1 and Luke 3 are not merely the ANCESTRY, but also the HISTORY of Jesus. By the oneness of Covenant Blood, Jesus is the murderer, the poet, the traitor, the hero of faith. It is not Adam, but Jesus; not Abraham, but Jesus; not David, but Jesus; not King Jehoram, who "died to no one's regret" [II Chronicles 21:19-20], but Jesus; not King Ahaz, who "became even more faithless to Jehovah" [II Chronicles 28:22], but Jesus; not Judas Iscariot, but Jesus. This all now becomes JESUS' history.

Jesus' shed Blood also points forward, not just to the Cross, but to Holy Communion, "the Blood of the New Covenant" [Luke 22:20]. Here again, Jesus 'connects': the Blood of the 'New' Covenant reaches down through thousands of years and perhaps fifty generations to make OUR history also become His, OUR Life become His.

'Old' *and* 'New' – all Covenant participants' history becomes Jesus' – BUT Jesus' history also becomes theirs: His Life becomes theirs, His death becomes theirs, His resurrection becomes theirs, His ascension becomes theirs, His eternity becomes theirs – all who enter Covenant through faith now share in all this, because there is one Life/Blood poured out as a never-ending stream, entering, filling, flowing between Jesus and His Covenant-partners, they in Him and He in them.

And as Holy Communion graphically portrays, all actually become "partakers of the Divine Nature" [2 Peter 1:4]. In this Sacrament, the Life/Blood of Jesus, which feeds and nourishes, which upbuilds and strengthens the Body of Christ, is constantly renewed in us. Truly, so real is this connection that indeed we are that Body of Christ [I Corinthians

12:27], indeed One Spirit is between us [Ephesians 4:4], indeed we share in all that Jesus is and has.

The Enduring Relationship of the Heart

> In Whom also you were circumcised with a Circumcision made without hands, by putting off the body of flesh, in the Circumcision of Christ, and you were buried with Him in Baptism...
> Colossians 2:11-12

Even in the 'Old' Covenant, Circumcision is never meant merely as a cutting away of a piece of skin, but the cutting away of that which prevents the "one Blood" from flowing between God and His People, that is, sin. The focus has never been on a dead ritual but on a relationship of the heart between God and His People:

> *Jehovah your God will circumcise your heart and the heart of your offspring,* [so that you will] love Jehovah your God with all your heart and with all your Soul, that you may live.
> Deuteronomy 30:6; cf. 10:16; 30:6; Leviticus 26:41; Jeremiah 4:4

The heart is the fountain of Blood, the fountain of Life, the fountain of Love. The real environment of Covenant is not to be a relationship which would merely "scab over" – become a memory – as a cut on the body would close the wound and just leave a scar, rather it is meant to be a flowing relationship throughout each day, in every moment – with every beat of the heart – in a literal oneness with God. Ever since the creation of *ADAM* (from *DAM*, Blood), who is the 'blood-image' (*DAMAH*) of God, created in Life/Blood (*ADAMAH* – the Blood soil) and given Life ("Blood") by God's Breath, Jehovah has not been looking for *man's* Life/Blood ("you have no Life in you" [John 6:53]), He seeks *His* Life/Blood flowing into and through His People.

"We are the [real] Circumcision, those who by the Spirit of God worship and glory/boast in Christ Jesus" [Philippians 3:3] – so Circumcision has never really been abolished – it is still around! But it is right where it ought to be, where Jehovah had originally indicated it had to be: in a heart filled with God's Life/Blood, with the blockage of sin cut away.

The Foundation of All 'Circumcision' is Still Grace

In Genesis, Circumcision does not speak of law and judgment (which actually come almost 600 years[196] later at Mount Sinai) but rather that *Jehovah yearns* for an extraordinary relationship with a human (Abraham) – and with all who are willing to join His People – going so far as to commit Himself to Covenant twelve years before Abraham's part in Circumcision. Jehovah's Glory – goodness, Covenant, grace and mercy – is the center of this Covenant action.

In *HESED* and grace He demands that even the eight-day-old child and the slave be equally included in this bond. In fact, within the Family of God's People, Circumcision is never to be by human permission at all, but by Jehovah's heartfelt command for this act of relationship. The "babies in arms" of Luke 18:15 would have *already* been personally 'in Covenant' with Jehovah by Circumcision; and when Jesus insists that they "come to Me" [Matthew 19:14; Mark 10:14; Luke 18:16], God's deepest longing for this personal relationship begun in the eight-day-old's Circumcision does not change.

> What if some did not believe? Will their unbelief make worthless God's faithfulness? By no means! Let God be true and every man a liar, as it is written, "That You will be justified in Your words, and will overcome when You are judged."   Romans 3:3-4

Paul's argument is significant: Jehovah would be faithful to His earnest desire. Grace WOULD NOT be withdrawn. It WOULD NOT be modified. That "some [of the Circumcised] did not believe" has never and could never compel the LORD to alter the very roots of His deep yearning, which come not from human initiative, but from the heart of Jehovah. Although God will never back away from His commitment, as always, only those having faith will experience "the breadth and length and height and depth, and to know the Love of Christ" [Ephesians 3:18-19], while those rejecting this relationship experience the sad conclusion of "no Life in you."

Circumcision and St Paul

Law and Paul

The Two Layers to the Old Testament

> Brothers, I speak in human terms, even a Covenant ratified between men cannot be set aside or added to. Now to Abraham and his Seed were given the promises. It does not say, "and to the seeds," as of many, but as of one, "and to your Seed," Who is Christ. This I say: a Covenant previously established by God cannot be annulled four hundred and thirty years later when the Law comes into being, as if to abolish the promise. Galatians 3:15-17

St Paul declares that even between men, a Covenant cannot be broken or changed. His point is that when the Law does come into play many generations later, it cannot change what is sealed by the Covenant, in a Promise which, in the end, is actually made to Christ. There are two layers to the Old Testament, the one being the Covenant (Circumcision), which is *Promise*, and the other is the *TORAH* from Sinai (as opposed to the *whole* Law) [Galatians 4:22-28].

Promise and Law are not synonymous: the Promise is a gift upon which faith is based, whereas Law is a righteousness which one must not fail to accomplish. Nor are they two avenues to the same end, since the Law's conclusion is a curse: "Cursed is everyone who does not continue in all things which have been written in the book of the Law, to do them" [Galatians 3:10], "that every mouth may be stopped, and all the world may come under judgment before God" [Romans 3:19]. On the other hand, the Covenant Promise results in blessing, "that to the nations might come the blessing of Abraham in Christ Jesus, that we might receive the Promise of the Spirit through faith" [Galatians 3:14].

So in Galatians 3:19 comes the natural question, "Why then the Law?" Paul argues that the Law comes in to lend order to our existence until the Promise should come; it is the guard and tutor [v 23-24] which is to direct our attention to Christ, making the People yearn – or better, desperately reach out – for the better solution which is found in the 'New' Covenant, "to bring us to Christ, that we might be justified by faith" [v 24]. For its part, the Law is not wrong, just helpless. It does indeed declare what holiness should be about, but it cannot give that holiness.

Blameless??

When Paul recounts what humans would normally regard as his credentials, he makes an intriguing statement: "as to the righteousness which is in the Law, blameless" [Philippians 3:6; so also are Zacharias and Elizabeth described as "blameless" – Luke 1:5-6]. How could anyone be "blameless" under the Law, and if so, why is that not enough – why would Paul "count [this] as garbage, that I may gain Christ" [Philippians 3:8]?

Martin Luther touches on this in his explanations to the Ten Commandments in his *Small Catechism*. Indeed, one may keep, for instance, the command "Thou shalt not kill,'" perhaps even, if it were possible, to the extent that Jesus defines it, as to never get angry, nor curse, nor ridicule one's brother [Matthew 5:22]. The problem is that one might do so by literally having nothing to do with the brother. The priest and the Levite in the parable of the Good Samaritan [Luke 10:30-37] indeed do not break that commandment as they see what is perhaps a man who by his dying touch (Law: 'unclean' [Leviticus 21:1-4; Numbers 19:11]) would prevent them from 'doing their jobs.' So they simply ignore him.

Although the Law does, at least within the circle of the nation of Israel, admonish "love your neighbor as yourself" [Leviticus 19:18], still with the proper loopholes, one might indeed end up "blameless" (Paul did) – and yet not holy. However, when Jesus restates the command to "love one another *as I have loved you*" [John 13:34], the true will of God is that we reach out in love to another's – even an enemy's – need as *He* does (as also in the rest of the Good Samaritan parable). Therefore, in his explanation, Luther goes beyond simply "not hurt nor harm our neighbor in his body," but also includes "help and befriend him in every bodily need." In the fulfilling of the Law, it is no longer enough to do nothing.

What the Law Really Means

> But who of you, who has a slave plowing or keeping sheep, which on coming in from the field, you say to him, "Come at once and recline at table"? Will you not rather say to him, "Prepare what I might eat, and having girded yourself, serve me, till I eat and drink; and after this you may eat and drink"? Do you thank the slave because he did what was commanded? Of course, not! *So also you, when you do all that is commanded of you, say, "We are useless servants; we have merely done what was our duty."* Luke 17:7-10 (italics added)

The frustration of the Law, especially as redefined by Jesus' Love, is that even when one has literally done all, there is no room for boasting. However, if even one small part of the Law is broken, the penalty of broken Law is demanded [James 2:10]. How could one do more than to "love the Lord your God with all your heart, and with all your Soul, and with all your mind, and with all your strength" [Mark 12:30] and your neighbor *"as I have loved you"*? How could one go beyond that for 'extra credit' to make up for even one small breaking of the Law?

The more we know about ourselves, the more we are aware that our problem is not merely one small breaking of the Law. Indeed, "A brother cannot at all redeem [*PADAH*] a man, nor give to God an atonement/ransom [*KAPHAR*] for him – for costly is the redemption [*PADAH*] of their Soul/Life which ceases forever – how can he live forever? How can he not see corruption?" [Psalm 49:7-9]. That's why Paul speaks not of the hope of the Law, but of the curse of the Law.

Circumcision's Place

The Privilege

Paul emphasizes that the "real Circumcision is of the heart — of the spiritual and not of the letter" [Romans 2:29], yet he does not disparage the Covenant of Circumcision — there is and would always be a specialness in God's choice for this intimate relationship. The Jews are marvelously privileged:

> What advantage then has the Jew, or what is the profit of Circumcision? Much in every way! Chiefly because they were entrusted with the oracles of God..., who are Israelites, to whom is the adoption, the Glory, the Covenants, the giving of the law, the service [of God], and the promises; of whom are the fathers and from whom is Christ, according to the flesh, He being over all, blessed God throughout the ages. Amen.   Romans 3:1-2; 9:4-5

Circumcision is the SIGN/seal of Abraham's righteousness *by faith* [Romans 4:11], meant to represent a unity of Life/Blood, not a mechanical obligation; it is a unity of the heart, not a religious façade; it is the great gift of grace, not lifeless action. As "the *'OTH* (SIGN) you do, only it is *God's* SIGN," it is done *to you*, not by your choice, but *by Jehovah's choice*, done by the demand of *Jehovah's heart*.

The Promise and the Environment of Faith

However, there is more to this picture: "Now to Abraham and his Seed were the promises made ... 'and to [Abraham's] Seed,' Who is Christ" [Galatians 3:16]. Paul indicates that the Promise in which all the nations would be blessed [from Genesis 22:18; 26:4]) hints toward the New Testament: it would be not to scattered individuals, but rather to Him Who is the 'New' Covenant. Circumcision points to the grand climax to be found in Jesus Himself: in Him "all nations would be blessed," in Him the 'Old' Circumcision Covenant completes, and in Him the 'New' Covenant begins. "The adoption, the Glory, the Covenants" and the rest all now describe what is to be found "in Christ."

In other words, physical Circumcision is simply an anticipation for a more confident hope rather than an end in itself, a temporary SIGN rather than the accomplishment; it is faith looking forward rather than basking in a status. It has a finishing point, yet its foundation would be carried forward because it originates in God's grace and Abraham's faith, therefore in the 'New' Covenant, "those who are of faith, these are sons of Abraham ... if you are Christ's, then you are Abraham's seed, [heirs] according to the promise" [Galatians 3:7, 29].

Physical vs Spiritual

God's intent behind *spiritual* Circumcision of the heart has never changed throughout the ages, but, alas, physical Circumcision has became the focus rather than the SIGNpost – it is now the 'poster child' of self-righteous obedience to the Law. No longer is it the union with Jehovah springing from His *HESED*, by His invitation, received by faith (as with Abraham); now it is the attempt to storm heaven by the magnificence of accomplishments. To this attitude, Paul scornfully declares:

> Look, I, Paul, tell you that if you become circumcised, Christ does not benefit you. I testify again to every man being circumcised that he is a debtor to all which the law tells him to do. You are severed from Christ, you who are made righteous by the Law; you have fallen from grace. For we, in the Spirit, await the hope of righteousness by faith. For in Christ Jesus neither Circumcision nor uncircumcision amounts to anything, but faith working through Love. Galatians 5:2-6

The New Creation

> For neither Circumcision nor uncircumcision is anything, but a new creation. Galatians 6:15

"If anyone is in Christ, [he is] a new creation; old things have passed away; behold, they have become new" [II Corinthians 5:17] – ultimately, though, any debate concerning Circumcision can miss the fantastic implications of the 'New' Covenant: not only is the form totally new, that is, in one Person (Jesus) is the reality of oneness which the 'Old' Covenant could only hint at; but even those who enter into *this* Covenant themselves become 'new,' "new creations" with new perspectives, new values, and new purpose ("living no longer for themselves, but will live for Him Who died and rose again on their behalf" [v 15]). Such a newness requires a new birth.

D. The Blood and the Water

Covenant Incongruity

From the opening chapters of humanity, *God Himself* lays the foundations and pattern for Covenant: the co-mingled Blood which flows through both participants. However, in the 'Old' Covenant, God only symbolically enters the relationship – after all, He has no Blood to shed – yet His participation is total; on the other hand, man enters by shedding *his* Blood (physical Circumcision) – probably we best not dwell on *his* half-hearted participation; and the renewal of Covenant is by the proxy of the Sacrifices.

This all changes with Bethlehem. Now Jehovah has Blood and He enters into the 'New' Covenant by that Blood. One would think that, within the framework of Covenant, some sort of shedding of Blood for the human should also continue. *But human Blood is now already joined to God's Blood in Jesus!* This is sufficient; there is nothing that a subsequent human action could do to increase or enhance this fact. This design reflects and perhaps is predicted in Genesis 15 when Jehovah *alone* had committed Himself in Covenant [two chapters prior to Abraham's part in Circumcision] in a relationship totally by grace.

From Jesus' Heart

> One of the soldiers pierced His side with a spear, and immediately there came out Blood and Water. John 19:34

Since the Roman Empire probably met every method to sabotage death by crucifixion, they had developed an effective method to guarantee the results when Jesus appears dead: a spear thrust up into the heart decides the matter once for all. John places great significance in the result, and so he should, because this is the evidence that the death for broken Covenant is indeed fully paid: like both halves of the split animals at Jehovah's Covenant with Abram/Abraham [Genesis 15], *both God and Man* (in the single Jesus) have paid the full price.

But something else is *initiated*: the Water and the Blood also speak of a powerful depth and direction as the 'New' Covenant has now been cut. No longer does Jehovah stop at the brink of Blood-involvement – the barrier is broken and God is involved in Covenant in a whole new way, and it specifically is *from His heart*.

Witnesses

The Three Witnesses

> This is He who came through Water and Blood – Jesus Christ; not by the Water only, but by the Water and the Blood. And the Spirit is the one bearing witness, because the Spirit is truth. For there are three bearing witness in heaven: the Father, the Word, and the Holy Spirit; and these three are one. There are three bearing witness on earth: the Spirit, and the Water, and the Blood; and these three agree as one. If we receive the witness of men, God's witness is greater; for this is God's witness by which He testified of His Son.   I John 5:6-9

In the Old Testament, Blood Covenant always has a 'witness' – some enduring sign or *'OTH* which serves as a declaration and confirmation that this relationship exists. Like Circumcision or a scar from a human Covenant, it may have been something irremovable on the body, or a stone monument of sorts [Genesis 28:20-22; Joshua 24:27], or some other way to proclaim this unique and intimate relationship.

But what of the New Testament? St John indicates that there are three significant earthly witnesses: The Spirit, the Water, and the Blood – but witnesses of what? After John records that out of Jesus' side came Blood and Water [John 19:34], in the next verse, he says, "The one having seen [this] has witnessed, and his witness is true; and he knows that he speaks the truth, *so that you may believe.*"

"Witness(ed)" – although the Greek word is later adopted as "Martyr," it actually is not an unusual word, especially for St Paul, to simply describe verifying something [for example, Romans 9:1; II Corinthians 1:23; Galatians 4:15]. However, John uses this word group 45 times in his Gospel, 14 in his letters, 11 in Revelation – 70 times out of the 116 in the New Testament. It is an important word for him, and often it is in regard to vital spiritual foundations (for example, John 1:7-8, 34; 5:31-39; 15:26-27). So also, in both I John 5 and John 19, the "witnesses" of Blood, Water, and Spirit are defined as essential for faith in God's Son, very much in keeping with a Covenant *'OTH*, since they announce the intimate and personal flow of Life: "*This is the witness*: that God has given eternal Life to us, and this Life is in His Son" [I John 5:11].

Water and Blood

"This is He who came through Water and Blood – Jesus Christ; not by the Water only, but by the Water and the Blood" [I John 5:6] – as often with John, a variety of images can be packed into a simple statement. One such example is when John the Baptist proclaims: "Behold the Lamb of God, Who takes away the sin of the world!" [John 1:29]. No Old Testament passage exactly fits this, however it contains a multitude of images, from Isaac's question of where the sacrificial lamb is [Genesis 22:7-8], to the *Passover* lamb [Exodus 12], to the ordinary morning and evening sacrificial lambs [Exodus 29:38-41], to the lamb of the *Sin Offering* [Leviticus 4:32; 5:6], as well as others.

At first glance, "the Water" might symbolize Jesus' human birth in the water of the womb, while "the Blood" would refer to His death, thereby encompassing His Life and work on earth. But John's is the most sacrament-conscious of the Gospels – he has much greater detail in regard to Baptism (becoming God's Children born by His will [John 1:12-13], of being born again [3:1-8], and of "the rivers of Living Water" from the heart [4:14; 7:38]); he then spends a chapter focused on Jesus' declaration that he who "eats My Flesh and drinks My Blood has eternal Life" [6:48-58]. It is more likely that by "the Water and the Blood," he is identifying the direct Source for the daily life power of the two Sacraments of Baptism and Holy Communion.

These two "witnesses" complement each other: "the Water" or rather *"the Living Water"* alludes to the flowing, building stream of Ezekiel 47 and to the *'River of Living Water'* in John's Revelation 22. And it recalls the Red Heifer Sacrifice mixed with "Living Water," which cleanses from death's touch [Numbers 19] and from living death (leprosy [Leviticus 14]), that here in the *seventh* and final Red Heifer (Jesus), Life will not be intimidated by death nor can sin staunch the flow of Life. And, of course, "the Blood" has always been synonymous to 'Life' – both, therefore, are an embodiment of Jesus' "I am ... the Life'" [John 11:25; 14:6] and "I am come that they might have Life ... more abundantly" [John 10:10].

When just prior to the passage quoted above from I John 5, John again speaks of being born of God, it is not a far leap to see the faith-grounding "witnesses" of Water and Blood tied in to the very physical sacraments of Baptism and Holy Communion, both extraordinary earthly 'witnesses' of our relationship to Jehovah.

The Witness of the Spirit

"... [When] *we* cry 'Abba, Father,' *the Spirit Himself witnesses* with our spirit that we are God's children," (Romans 8:15-16) – as discussed earlier in section "IV. The Covenant Mosaic," this is one of those *'OTHs* which *you* do, yet it is *God's* SIGN' events. Although *we* pray, it actually is *the Holy Spirit's "witness,"* His confirmation of what Baptism proclaims to us – our prayer is the bursting forth of the Holy Spirit's work within us. A similar idea, although not quite on the same level, might be the Cross which hangs on our wall: it is not *our* sign to God, but rather it is *His 'OTH (sign)* or *"witness" to us* of His salvation, even though our hands may have put it together.

Pentecost is another 'witness,' SIGN or *'OTH* of the Holy Spirit. As the pillar of fire at the Exodus from Egypt had, so also the "sound as if borne of a violent wind, and ... divided tongues, as of fire" [Acts 2:2-3] demonstrates the presence of God: a comfort to His Covenant-partners and the announcement to all others that Jehovah is at work for His People's blessing. But there is a more subtle 'witness': "The ones therefore welcoming his word were baptized; and there were added [to them] about three thousand Souls that day" [Acts 2:41]. Since "no one can say 'LORD JESUS' except by the Holy Spirit" [I Corinthians 12:3], the 'witness' is not merely splash but that hearts were actually turned to the Lord.

This is also why the Spirit makes a dramatic appearance – *witness* – whenever the Church enters each stage of outreach which Jesus defines in Acts 1:8: "you shall receive power when the Holy Spirit has come upon you; and you shall be *witnesses* of Me both in Jerusalem, and in all Judea and Samaria, and to the end of the earth." So Pentecost begins the outreach in Jerusalem. Then when what the Jews had considered the spiritual, cultural 'no-counts,' the 'lost house of Israel,' Samaria, are approached [Acts 8:14-17], the Seal and Guarantee ("He has both put His Seal upon us and given us His Spirit in our hearts as an Earnest[197]/Guarantee" [II Corinthians 1:22]) is placed even upon them; so also when the enormous shift of cultural thinking is required when "those of the Circumcision who believed were astonished ... because on the nations also had the gift of the Holy Spirit been poured out" [Acts 10:45]. In fact, the revision of thinking in this last case is so profound that the incident is recounted three times in Acts [chapters 10, 11, 15].

Especially in the 'New' Covenant, "witness" is more than merely a sterile signpost, but, as the *'OTH*s of the plagues in Egypt had been active demonstrations of Covenant at work, so also the Holy Spirit is not merely a bystander but the active Creator and Confirmer of faith.

The Witness of the Water

From His Heart to Ours

'Living Water'

> ... Jesus stood and cried out, "If anyone thirsts, let him come to Me and drink. He who believes in Me, as the Scripture has said, "out of his heart will flow rivers of *Living Water*." But this He said about the Spirit, Whom those believing in Him were about to receive ...
> John 7:37-39

> Jesus answered her, "If you knew the Gift of God, and Who He is Who is saying to you, 'Give Me a drink,' you would have asked Him, and He would have given you *Living Water* ...a fountain of *Water springing up to eternal Life.*"
> John 4:10, 14

Jesus is *"the Life"* [John 14:6] – that is, identical with Life – and the Holy Spirit is associated with the *"rivers of Living Water,"* which speak of God's total involvement in Covenant, Life pouring from Jesus' heart and fountaining in our hearts through the Holy Spirit. This is exactly the intimacy which Covenant has proclaimed all along: the oneness of heart / Soul / Life which Jehovah Himself yearns for and commands from the beginning, but now is actually happening.

Born of the Water – Baptism

> Jesus answered, "Very truly I tell to you, unless one is born of Water and Spirit, he cannot enter God's Kingdom." John 3:5

St John's emphasis on "three bearing witness on earth: the Spirit, and the Water, and the Blood; and these three agree as one" [I John 5:8] is needed here. The "Water and Spirit" – these are not separate stages of salvation (for example, 'Water Baptism' vs 'Spirit Baptism')[198], since that would not make sense with Covenant. World-wide, Blood Covenant always involves the total person right from the beginning, and since Jesus *is* the 'New' Covenant, either one is in Him or not – talking 'stages' makes no sense.

However, combine John's point that the "witnesses" form the grounding of faith, together with Deuteronomy 19:15: "by the mouth of two or three *witnesses* the matter shall be established"[199] along with "the Water and the Blood" as the "witnesses" which flow from the Covenant event of the Cross. In Baptism, then, "the Water and Spirit" take us to the death of Jesus and to the cutting of the 'New' Covenant, confirming this new Birth just as powerfully as when the 'witness' of Circumcision confirms the children of Abraham in the 'Old' Covenant relationship.

"How Can These Things Be?" – John 3:9

When Jesus told Nicodemus that he must be born of water and the Spirit, he was bewildered. What can be missed is that Jesus' answer to him is two-fold: on one hand is the significance of the serpent in the wilderness, "As Moses lifted up the serpent in the wilderness, even so it is necessary that the Son of Man be lifted up, *that all who believe in Him should not perish but have Life (Jesus) eternal*" [John 3:14-15]; and on the other is the familiar John 3:16.

What saves the Israelite in that Numbers 21 incident [see page 143] is an amazingly uncomplicated strategy: just simply look to the promise attached to God's solution. All the Israelite needs to do is to look at the bronze serpent when he is bitten by a snake. He does not need to study it, draw a picture of it, describe it, do spiritual calisthenics (nor physical ones), improve his life, pray harder nor anything like that. In fact, if he is at the fringe of the camp, all he may see is the glint in the sun. And he is saved.

In other words, Jesus says that the New Birth in Baptism is that simple and that easy. It just requires that we look to the promise attached to God's solution hanging on the cross, and that is enough to end the plague of death, it is enough to transfer us into the Kingdom of God, it is enough to cause us to be born again.

Like Nicodemus, we still question "How can this be?" and Jesus' continued response is "For God so loved the world that He gave His only begotten Son, *that all who believe in Him should not perish but have Life (Jesus) eternal*" [John 3:16]. What is italicized here in many (English, Greek, Latin and German) versions is identical to verse 15 (above) – the two concepts are linked together. How then can these things be? It is because of an extraordinary Love which would make the Covenant-Partner sacrifice His own Son in order that we might live. It is not our faith, but the power of astonishing Love which has always been at the root of God's Covenant.

"Who were born, not of Blood, nor of the will of the flesh, nor of the will of man, but of God" [John 1:13] – even though we do the action, Jehovah is the One Who accomplishes it. It is not our decision, but rather His command, His deliberate act, His earnest desire – His delight [Isaiah 62:4; Malachi 3:1]. *He* incorporates us into His Covenant ("for God is working in you, both to *will* and to work for [His] delight" [Philippians 2:13]), His act of grace reaches out to those He would have as His People:

> ... as Christ also loved the Church and gave up Himself for her, that *He* might sanctify and cleanse her by the washing of Water in the Word, that *He* might present to Himself the glorious Church, not having spot or wrinkle or any such thing, but that she should be holy and without blemish.   Ephesians 5:25-27

A Word about Faith and Baptism

What Faith Is

Often people have the impression that spiritual faith must be unique – but exactly how are we to think of it? How should it be described so that an 'outsider' would understand what is required?

Actually faith is quite simple. One may be surprised at how much of our lives involves faith. In the assisted living facility where this writer worked, at the meal times, the residents go to the tables in the dining room. There is no second thought, they just expect to be fed – they are responding to a promise that their meals will be provided. If they were asked to describe where in their lives they use faith, this kind of very common incident would probably never even cross their minds, yet it is faith nonetheless.

They call the doctor to make an appointment and are told "Next Wednesday at 1 o'clock." They hang up and their life is changed: transportation must be arranged, they may bathe beforehand, appropriate clothes are chosen, the kitchen may be asked to prepare their meal a little early – in a variety of ways life is altered simply because a voice on the telephone *made a promise*. A green light at an intersection, merchandise in a store, even the TV guide – all have implied promises which we depend on in faith, all the time. This is what St James [2:17-18] speaks of when he says, "... faith by itself, if it does not have works, is dead. ... I will show you my faith by my works": choices are made, courses of action are determined, Life – and living – is altered because of a promise.

What Makes Spiritual Faith Different

> ... no one can say "LORD JESUS" except by the Holy Spirit.
> I Corinthians 12:3

When ordinary faith is so easy, why is spiritual faith so difficult? Because sinful humans from Adam and Eve down to you and me *expect* Jehovah to be untrustworthy. That is why the Holy Spirit is necessary, as only through Him can we count on God as not only able but also willing to keep the promises which spring from His *HESED*. Such faith is His gift to us:

> If you would be saved, you must begin with the faith of the sacraments, without any works whatever. The works will follow faith, but do not think too lightly of faith, for it is the most excellent and difficult of all works. Through it alone you will be saved, even if you should be compelled to do without any other works. For [spiritual] faith is a work of God, not of man, as Paul teaches [Eph 2:8]. The other works he works through us and with our help, but this one alone he works in us and without our help.   Martin Luther[200]

> Given these strong motifs all throughout the New Testament, we can see that it is no more possible for an adult to receive faith than it is for an infant. As the disciples asked Jesus in Matt. 19:25: "Who then can be saved?" Jesus answers in v. 26: "For mortals this is impossible, but

for God all things are possible.'" What seems humanly impossible is possible only for GOD. Andrew Das[201]

Faith Does Not Initiate the Promise

> So shall My Word be that goes out of My mouth; it shall not return to Me empty, but it will do that which I please, and it shall prosper in that which I sent it. Isaiah 55:11

> If a man is to deal with God and receive anything from him, it must happen thus: Not that man begins and lays the first stone, but that God alone – without any entreaty or desire of man – must first come and give him a promise. ... God must anticipate all [of man's] works and thoughts, and make a promise clearly expressed in words, which man then takes and keeps in a good firm faith. Martin Luther[202]

Faith does not create the promise: the assisted living facility will provide the meals whether or not the residents decide to come; the doctor's office will have everything waiting whether the patient shows up or not (although they may charge for a no-show because the patient has broken *his* promise to be there). Equally so, it is the promise which made the difference with Noah – 'faith' without a promise would be empty and useless, no matter how sincere and energetic it may be. But when Jehovah makes a promise, it will be accomplished and those who with faith remain inside the promise are blessed. This is the background to Martin Luther's words in regard to Baptism:

> Further, we say that we are not so much concerned to know whether the person baptized believes or not; for on that account Baptism does not become invalid; but everything depends upon the Word and command of God. ... Baptism is nothing else than water and the Word of God in and with each other, that is, when the Word is added to the water, Baptism is valid, even though faith be wanting. For my faith does not make Baptism, but receives it. Now, Baptism does not become invalid even though it be wrongly received or employed; since it is not bound (as stated) to our faith, but to the Word.
>
> Martin Luther[203]

The Covenant principle, of two persons in one Life, and of Human and God in one Jesus, is reflected here: the physical (Water) and the spiritual (the Word) are joined in one Baptism, not by human ability, but by the working of Jehovah Himself.

The Problem of Which Comes First

Although we acknowledge that the promise must come first, sometimes our practice can 'muddy the waters' a bit. A favorite question this writer often asks in Bible studies is, 'Which comes first, repentance or forgiveness.' Since our normal practice, for instance in worship services, is that we repent and then forgiveness is pronounced over us, there seems to be an implied assumption that our repentance causes forgiveness.

The truth is really the opposite: our repentance is an act of faith based upon Jehovah's forgiveness. Without the security of this promise, we would be terrified of seeing the depth of our sin – we would be faced with the potential of utter despair with no answer. When Judas Iscariot realizes the extent of what he did by betraying Jesus, when he turns to the only place where forgiveness is supposed to be found, the priests reply, "What is that to us? See to it yourself!" [Matthew 27:4]. Since Jesus is out of the picture (in his mind), there is no other God-commanded place for him to turn. Suicide is his conclusion to his utter despair.

Therefore forgiveness has to be a secure option: "If You, Jehovah, should mark iniquities, O Lord, who shall stand? But there is forgiveness with You, that You may be feared" [Psalm 130:3-4]. St John reminds us that this forgiveness is an already accomplished fact for everyone in the world [I John 2:1-2]. The promise has indeed come first and only now we respond by repenting, handing over this hindrance in our relationship with our Lord, that He may "cast all [our] sins behind [His] back" [Isaiah 38:17] and "[our] sins [He] will not remember again" [Jeremiah 31:34].

Covenant is no different – it is a promise which places the person into the security of the relationship. The person now responds: either by using this security to confront his way of life as God's person, or to regard the relationship as if it has no value. In the Old Testament, the People generally reacted as if this extraordinary connection did not matter all that much. The wonderful privilege was ignored, and they brought upon themselves the curses of broken Covenant.

Baptism is no different. Sometimes we try to set up stringent regulations to prevent its abuse, seemingly to protect God from failed Covenant (Baptisms) – but the Lord does not need our protection. Or we want to protect people from apparently becoming more damned than otherwise.[204] However Jehovah, in His *HESED*, chooses to rather bring people into the security of His promises than to leave them outside until they measure up (to what often is a human-made standard). His promise is concrete inclusion, and only now will come the person's reaction in faith.

The Promise's Center is the *HESED* of Jehovah

> ...when I first encountered the Reformed doctrine of infant baptism, I was immediately put off by the concept because I misunderstood the radically God-centered, unconditional character of this "everlasting covenant." While others may dissent from this view for other reasons, my problem was that I viewed baptism as my own "sacrament," my own act of obedience in which I declared my resolve to follow Jesus. How could a child acknowledge, "I have decided to follow Jesus"? and make this public profession before the whole church? What jarred my confidence in this position, however, was the testimony of the Scriptures as to the nature of this covenant. Just as the rainbow was a sacrament of divine, not human, resolve, and the ceremony of the halved animals was a sacrament of God's commitment to the covenant, baptism is God's announcement of his intentions to bring me into his dynasty of faith. Faith was necessary, but faith was promised by God in the covenant through Word and Sacrament.
>
> Dr. Michael S. Horton[205]

Jehovah never made a mistake in the 'Old' Covenant which now has to be corrected by a 'New' Covenant. It is not that we are demanded to be better believers than Abraham, David, or Daniel; nor that we are to walk closer to God than Enoch or Elijah; nor that we are to be more committed than Moses or King Josiah. Rather, because of His birth in Bethlehem, *He* enters Covenant with a whole new depth, with an even greater personal involvement in this relationship: Jesus *is* the Covenant, He will "pour out

[His] Spirit on all flesh" [Joel 2:28], and ultimately "the Lord Jehovah will wipe away tears from all faces" [Isaiah 25:8].

Jehovah acts because He chooses to, He wants to, He said He would. Our confession of faith may be defective, our fervency may be for all the wrong reasons, our understanding may be limited, our commitment may wax and wane over the years, our emotions may even run contrary to our faith – or be lacking at the moment, if not today, then perhaps tomorrow. But entrance into God's Covenant is not by negotiation – if it depends on us, indeed, "Who then can be saved?" The 'New' Covenant is not based upon a change in *mankind's* involvement or commitment, but in *Jehovah's* involvement: *HE is the 'New' Covenant, HE is the Promise.*

Concerning Infants Placed Within the Promise

> For the Promise is to you and to your children, and to all who are afar off, as many as the Lord our God will call.   Acts 2:39

What of the infant, once by Circumcision set within the 'Old' Covenant, but now by Baptism is placed within the 'New' Covenant? When Abraham first enters into Covenant, it is by *God's* commitment – this defines Jehovah's attitude by which every subsequent eight-day-old child is also equally connected to Jehovah. It is not enough to dismiss this as simply 'Old' Covenant but rather to see how this relationship stems from Jehovah's definition of His Glory – His mercy, grace and Love/ HESED – in a relationship which He has intensely desired, even when it would cost Him the Life of Jesus. That intensity has never changed.

It is in the 'Old' Covenant where the fundamental specialness which God Himself has always placed upon His People is forcefully revealed. Circumcision is not a failure; rather it accomplishes exactly what God has intended from the beginning, an intimate relationship with humans, just as Adam and Eve are placed into such an intimate relationship with Himself by His hand in Creation. It is true that the Covenant is broken and abused by the humans, but so is every Covenant with Jehovah. This is why the

'New' Covenant's difference is not based on mankind's participation as if we are now better people, but on the change in God's participation.

Now, with Jesus *being* the 'New' Covenant, no longer do the People need to cut their flesh, but by the Water and the Spirit – the *'OTH*s, the witnesses – each is brought into those singular Covenant events of the Cross and the Resurrection [Romans 6:4] and thereby included into the 'New' Covenant (Christ), just as much as Abraham and the eight-day-old infant are included in the 'Old' Covenant by Circumcision.

Meanwhile the 'Old' Covenant – His activity of the past – is the window which shows what God will do within His commitment and the intimacy of this relationship. It is fully in character, for example, to find in the promises of Exodus 6:6-8 a description of what God still does for His People of today, young and old, as indicated in the following excerpt from this writer's sermon, at the Baptism of baby Elise:

> So also, here in Baptism, Jehovah of the Covenant, Yahweh God, comes and says to a small individual, also in great need, in the words of the Exodus text:
>
> > "I AM JEHOVAH! I will bring Elise out from under the yoke ...; I will free Elise from being a slave ...; I will redeem Elise with an outstretched arm and with mighty acts of judgment; I will take Elise as My own People; and I will be Elise's God. Then she will know that I AM JEHOVAH her God, Who brought her out from under the yoke ... I will bring Elise to the land I swore with uplifted hand to give ...; I will give it to Elise as a possession. I AM JEHOVAH, the Lord."
>
> What a series of promises is made to her and to each one of us! ... In Baptism, Elise is taken out from being under the yoke of Satan; she no longer is to be a slave to natural desires; she has been redeemed with God's outstretched arm and mighty act of judgment to be found on the Cross and in the resurrection; He will bring her to His Land, the heavenly Jerusalem; here, God takes Elise as His very own person – she now becomes not just His creature, but His very own child; and He becomes not merely some benevolent "fate" – "providence" –, but her eternal Father.   James Lindemann[206]

Indeed, "once you were no people but now you are God's People; once you had not received mercy but now you have received mercy" [I

Peter 2:10]. It is in the Old Testament that one can see God's constant commitment to His Covenant promises and willing response to any and all who turn to Him, despite even centuries of abuse. And when He finally does break Covenant it is only so that He can initiate a better one.

Baptism and Faith in Colossians

> In Him you were also circumcised with the Circumcision made without hands, by putting off the body of the flesh, by the Circumcision of Christ, buried with Him in Baptism, in which you also were raised with Him through faith in the working of God, Who raised Him from the dead.   Colossians 2:11-12

What is intriguing is that St Paul does not mention "faith" in regard to Circumcision, nor in regard to "buried with Him in Baptism," but only as he speaks of being "raised with Him" is it now brought in. Remember that Circumcision is a passive event – the infant does not, could not do it to himself. Baptism is also a passive event. It is never 'I baptize myself,' but rather 'I am baptized' by the hand of another: "I need to *be baptized*" [Matthew 3:14]; "you shall *be baptized*" [Acts 1:5]; "Arise and *be baptized*" [Acts 22:16].

In the passage above, "you were ... circumcised ... *by the Circumcision of Christ*," "you were ... buried," "you also were raised" are all passive and even when faith shows up, it is "faith *in the working of God*, Who raised Him from the dead." It certainly does not sound as though faith makes all this happen, but rather it receives what has been done by God, it is holding on to the Promise found in God's raising Christ from the dead. It drives us back to the definition of the Glory of God found in Exodus 33:19, as Paul emphasized to the Romans:

> For he says to Moses, "I will have mercy on whom I have mercy, and I will have compassion on whom I have compassion." So therefore, it depends not on the one who is resolved, nor on the one exerting himself, but on the one who has God's mercy. [9:15-16]

The Role of Faith in Infant Baptism

But is not one required to believe and then be baptized? How then can an infant meet such a prerequisite? The crux of such a question lies in the source of 'faith' – is it a gift or is it from one's own nature?

> The proof text for this objection is Mark 16:16: "He that believeth and is baptized, shall be saved; but he that believeth not, shall be damned."
> If the first part of the verse excludes infant baptism, because infants cannot believe, the second part denies infant salvation for the same reason. ... But why interpret one half of a verse one way and refuse to take the other half the same way? ...
> Rev. John Scott Johnson[207]

Trained over a thousand years and every generation, the Covenant People had never asked about faith in the infant – they automatically included their eight-day-old son under Covenant – *because that's what Jehovah wanted and He would see to it that what is required would be given, since there is no other way anyone could have it.*

> A faithful, God-fearing heart does this: it asks first whether it is God's Word. When it hears that it is, it smothers with hands and feet the question why it is useful or necessary. For it says with fear and humility, "My dear God, I am blind; truly I know not what is useful or necessary for me, nor do I wish to know, but I believe and trust that Thou dost know best and dost intend the best in Thy divine goodness and wisdom. I am satisfied and happy to hear Thy simple Word and perceive Thy will."
> Martin Luther[208]

When Peter proclaims, "For the promise is unto you and to your children" [Acts 2:39], it is a totally natural reaction for his Jewish listeners to place their children under the 'New' Covenant – hence no need to command what is already so familiar.[209] With the inclusion of their infant children being so ingrained over so many generations, if such is supposed to cease, there would need to be many discussions in the Bible as to why infants specifically are now excluded – should *not* be baptized. However there is not a word, nor are there any regarding a substitute practice, nor even in regard to what would be an appropriate age for Baptism to consequently be administered[210] – a very important question since, really, who has the capacity to judge another person's faith level, especially when *young children* are given as the model for what adult faith ought to be like [Mark 10:15; Luke 18:17]?

No, as always, it is the Glory of God to have mercy, grace, goodness *and* Covenant, Whose heart's desire does not change because of a Covenant change – if anything, if possible, it has only heightened.

"The Right to Become Children of God" [John 1:12]

> Faith has its place and it is essential, but only to grasp, hold, and receive the wonders that grace offers. The blessings of grace are for all, but only he who believes receives them. By grace then in Holy Baptism God opens His treasure-store and invites us to enjoy it by taking Him at His Word. So then God makes us His children, members of the Body of Christ, the Holy Church, royal priests, possessors of the divine nature, saints, righteous ones, members of the new creation. Robert Lindemann[211]

Birth of Privileged Ones

> Jesus answered, "Very truly I tell to you, unless one is born of Water and Spirit, he cannot enter God's Kingdom. That which is born of the flesh is flesh, and that which is born of the Spirit is spirit."
>
> John 3:5-6

> Created originally in the image of God, redeemed humanity has been elevated by means of a *divinely conceived genetic process* known as the new birth to the highest rank of all created beings ... Thus, through the new birth – and I speak reverently – we become the "next of kin" to the Trinity, a kind of "extension" of the Godhead ... Here is a completely new, unique, and exclusive order of beings which may be called a "new species." *There is nothing like it in all the kingdoms of infinity* ... But from all eternity God purposed to have a family circle of His *very own*, not only created but *also generated* by His own life, incorporating His own seed ... or heredity ... While we recognize the infinite distinction between the Eternal Son and the "many sons" born into the family, yet such is their heredity as the result of the new birth that He recognizes them as bona-fide blood-brothers. Paul E. Billheimer[212]

"One came running, knelt before Him, and asked Him, 'Good Teacher, what shall I *do* that I may *inherit* eternal Life?'" [Mark 10:17] – this is a most odd question: after all, one does not inherit by one's own deeds, but rather by being a child, through birth or through adoption, by the will and choice of the benefactor. It results in the same frame of answer as Nicodemus encountered in the John 3 quote above. St Paul rejoices that

> ... in Love He destined us to the adoption of sons to Himself through Jesus Christ, according to the delight of His will, to the praise of the Glory of His grace in which He gave us grace in the Beloved – in Him we have redemption through His Blood, the forgiveness of trespasses, according to the riches of His grace which He *lavished* upon us ...
>
> Ephesians 1:4-8

How extraordinary is the concept of "lavished"! It speaks of enthusiasm, of energy, of an unstoppable fountain of goodness – it is as if a dam burst and what had been pent up finally is released in a wondrous flood "of the riches of His grace" – released not because of better human cooperation, but because of Jehovah's unique participation in the 'New' Covenant.

"Baptized Into Christ Have Put On Christ" [Galatians 3:27]

Becoming a Child of God through Baptism is a worthwhile doctrine, but what does it have to do with Covenant? As we look at various facets of what comes to us through the witnesses of the Water, the Blood, and the Spirit, since Jesus does not bring us the 'New' Covenant, but rather *is* this Covenant, then to be in Covenant means we must be placed into Jesus. Being, for example, a 'Child of God' means that when we are in Jesus, *then* we experience *His* relationship of beloved Son with the Father. We cannot be God's Children outside of being in Jesus.

However, now in the 'New' Covenant, we are placed within a new 'household' specifically because of His Love: we become children of Jehovah, and "if children, then heirs – heirs of God and joint heirs with Christ" [Romans 8:17] – what an astonishing position this is! The imagery is profound: we are co-heirs, not with angels, but with God the Son Himself; recipients of that relationship which the Son enjoys with the Father, equal in status as to that Beloved Son [Matthew 3:17; 17:5].

"Adoption as Sons"

> But when the fullness of the time had come, God sent forth His Son, made of a woman, made under the law, so that He could redeem those who were under the law, so that we might receive the adoption as sons. And because you are sons, God has sent forth the Spirit of His Son into our hearts, calling, "Abba, Father!" So no more are you a slave but a son, and if a son, also an heir of God through Christ.
> Galatians 4:4-7

"He destined us for adoption as His children through Jesus Christ" [Ephesians 1:5]. Within the subject of 'God's Children' comes a powerful word picture, that of 'adoption.' This method of becoming a 'child of the Father' contributes some profound additional elements which directly relate to Covenant.

The atmosphere of adoption is the atmosphere of Love, *HESED*, if you will. Just as Jehovah chose Abraham for His Covenant, so also our adoption occurs because of *choice*: "He *chose* us in Him before the foundation of the world" [Ephesians 1:4] – *His* choice. In the culture of the day, by law the adopted child could never be disowned, the inheritance could never be withdrawn – the adopting parent is 'stuck' with the child, unless the child himself turns away from the relationship. Would Jehovah's steadfastness in Covenant have said it any differently?

Like Covenant, adoption is entered into because He insists: He commands it [Matthew 20:28]; He requires it [John 3:5]; it is His will [John 1:12-13]. There is no hesitation on HIS part: there is no provision, for example, for achievements to first be made; there is no preliminary foster program – His desire is 'to go for broke.' As adoption is the parents' proof to their child of his belongingness from this 'new birth,'[213] so in Covenant, Jehovah's desire is for us to *unmistakably* know *for certain* that we are indeed

His. It is His solemn guarantee that He will never back out on us. He will never stop lavishing the riches of His grace upon His children.

My Father

> For you did not receive a spirit of slavery in order to fear again, but you have received the Spirit of sonship. [When] we cry 'Abba, Father,' the Spirit Himself witnesses with our spirit that we are God's children, and if children, then heirs, God's heirs and fellow heirs with Christ ...
>
> Romans 8:15-16

> This is extraordinary! *"Abba!"* – a child's version of *"ABBAS"* (Father), "Daddy" – is a term of familiarity and endearment. We run to the arms of the Almighty God of the whole wide Universe, He Who is above every angel and power and principality, He Whose Word creates and cannot be thwarted, He Who judges the world in righteousness and holiness – we call HIM, "Daddy"?? Yes!!   James Lindemann[214]

What boldness, what audacity, what comfort! We can "with confidence draw near to the throne of grace" [Hebrews 4:16]; with "confidence to enter the sanctuary by the Blood of Jesus" [Hebrews 10:19]; "this is the confidence which we have in Him, that if we ask anything according to His will He hears us" [I John 5:14]. How is such a thing possible? Only because we have entered the 'New' Covenant, that is, into Jesus Himself. We have the right of access 'in Him' [Ephesians 3:12], and when the Father turns to us His response is "My Son, My Beloved!" [Matthew 3:17; 17:5] because *we are 'in Christ.'*

Same Ol' Me?

> Nicodemus said to Him, "How can a man, already old, be born? Can he enter a second time into his mother's womb and be born?"
>
> John 3:4

Actually, the question is reasonable and is still a struggle to comprehend. We can go on and on in glowing terms about the new birth, but what is hard is to really identify what happens. Obviously, for such a change there is no physical evidence or *'OTH* (sign) as Circumcision had been, and we do not even reenter the womb. If now 'in Christ,' the 'New' Covenant Life/Blood flows in us, how can we tell?

True, for some, a change in Life is so pronounced that it can make us say, 'Aha, there it is!', but this kind of experience does not happen as much as we would like. For the most part, it is only over time that we begin to note differences in attitude, manner, speech, and actions which demonstrate that we have been infected by a new nature:

> But the fruit of the Spirit is Love, joy, peace, longsuffering, kindness, goodness, faithfulness, gentleness, self–control... Galatians 5:22-23

In fact, the ability to believe Jehovah's Word at all demonstrates the presence of the Holy Spirit, the Earnest/Guarantee[215] [II Corinthians 1:22, 5:5; Ephesians 1:14] Who confirms our Covenant relationship with Him. Also, as has been mentioned previously, prayer has a significant role as a spiritual *'OTH*; although we think we are doing the speaking with Jehovah, He meanwhile is confirming our New Birth: "it is the Spirit Himself bearing witness ... that we are children of God" [Romans 8:16].

Still, how often we share St Paul's frustration in Romans 7:14-25, in which we seem to be a battleground between the Old Me and the New Me (or better, between my old nature and 'Christ in Me' [Galatians 2:20]). What is worse are the verses in I John 3: "All who are abiding in Him do not sin; all who are sinning have not seen Him nor known Him... all who have been begotten of God do not sin; for God's nature abides in each one, and he cannot sin because he is born of God" [verses 6, 9]. Realizing that in spite of any progress we have made in "the fruit of the Spirit," as we wrestle with John's claims, Paul's cry escapes from our lips as well: "O wretched man am I! Who will deliver me from this body of this death?" [Romans 7:24].

Because our sensitivities have been raised, we are well aware that sinlessness is beyond our grasp. But John also has more to say: how easily our hearts can condemn us, but "God is greater than our hearts" [John 3:19-20] and "if we confess our sins, He is faithful and righteous, so that

He will forgive us [those] sins and cleanse us from all unrighteousness" [I John 1:9], therefore "Beloved, since our hearts no longer have any basis to condemn us, we have confidence before God" [John 3:19-21 paraphrased]. It is the same conclusion to which Paul comes as he begins his great Romans 8 chapter: "There is therefore now no condemnation to those who are in Christ Jesus..."

> [The salvation through Noah's Ark] was a prototype of Baptism, which now saves you, not as a putting away of the filth of the flesh but the answer of a clear conscience to God, through the resurrection of Jesus Christ, ...
> I Peter 3:21

The key evidence of the New Birth, in the 'New' Covenant, is that we can take such promises of forgiveness and hold tightly to them, even in the face of our own self-condemnation; it is the ability to cling to the truth of "in this is Love, not that we loved God but that He loved us and sent His Son to be the atonement (ransom) for our sins" [I John 4:10]. And now as faith takes hold of such forgiveness, our perception of Life is altered and the fruit of the Spirit begins to grow.

The Witness of the Blood

In Baptism, the Water and the Spirit have taken us to the Cross, there to encounter the third "witness," the Life/Blood. Baptism, as the New Covenant Circumcision, places us into this wonderful relationship with Jehovah, but now comes the sustenance that revitalizes who we are, what we are, and what we are about.

God's Purchased People

The People

> But you are a chosen generation, a royal priesthood, a holy nation, a People purchased [by God], that you may proclaim the praises of Him Who called you out of darkness into His marvelous light.
> I Peter 2:9

Covenant is always about relationships – not 'business' relationships, but rather the intimacy which links hearts into a common Life. Circumcision is not just a relationship with Jehovah but it also places an individual inside the 'Old' Covenant's 'People of Jehovah.' So also the 'New' Covenant places each of us into a new People and because of the intimacy of God's own Blood, it is a Living People, a Living 'Body of Christ.' But to make such a wonderful relationship happen, the cost has been high – we are a *purchased* People.

The *GO'EL*

> A brother cannot at all redeem [*PADAH*] a man, nor give to God an atonement/ransom [*KOPHER*] for him – for costly is the redemption [*PADAH*] of their Soul/Life which ceases forever – how can he live forever? How can he not see corruption?   Psalm 49:7-9

As with all broken Covenants, there is a price to be paid. Life/Blood has to be brought back into balance. Although the 'Old' and 'New' Covenants focus mostly on the People of God, yet there is an even greater Covenant which has to be dealt with: the Creation Covenant first broken by Adam and Eve, where the spilled Covenant Life/Blood of God involves *all* mankind. A *GO'EL* is required, but no minor one, since this broken Covenant has *cosmic* effects:

> For in earnest expectation, creation is anxiously waiting for the sons of God to be revealed. For creation was subjected to aimlessness and frailty, not willingly, but because of Him Who subjected it in hope; because the creation itself also will be delivered from the slavery of corruption into the freedom of the Glory of the children of God.
> Romans 8:19-21

There is One Who is both Participant *and* Overseer of Covenant; there is One Who is both Creator *and* Creature in one Person; there is One Who as God broke Covenant and as Man bears all broken Covenant; there is One Who as *GO'EL* would take upon Himself His own judgment and use His own Life/Blood to recreate Covenant: Jesus! – 'Jehovah Saves' (Joshua).

It is the "Name which is above every name" earned the hard way: "He humbled Himself, becoming obedient unto death – the death of a Cross" [Philippians 2:8]; the spilled Blood of broken Covenant is balanced with *His own* [Hebrews 12:24], bringing forgiveness [Hebrews 9:22], cleansing [I John 1:7], justification [Romans 5:9] and redemption – "In Him we have redemption through His Blood, the forgiveness of sins, according to the riches of His grace" [Ephesians 1:7; see Colossians 1:14]; "being justified freely by His grace through the redemption which is in Christ Jesus, Whom God set forth as a satisfaction for sin[216] by His Blood" [Romans 3:24-25].

The redemption which no other human being could bring about has now happened because of God's personal involvement. It takes a perfect sinless Human, Who does not deserve death, to pay the penalty of death He does not deserve (otherwise, had He committed even one sin, one break in the Covenant, He would Himself need saving). But since a creature can only have one creature's value, He must also be God, Whose worth is infinite; therefore His Blood can ransom any and every person and still not be diminished.

> They sing a new song, saying: "You are worthy to take the scroll, and to open its seals; for You were slain, and, by Your Blood, have redeemed us to God out of every tribe and tongue and people and nation." Revelation 5:9

In the Name of Jesus

> Peter said to them, "Repent, and be baptized every one of you in the Name of Jesus Christ for the forgiveness of your sins; and you shall receive the gift of the Holy Spirit." Acts 2:38

> The formula *eiv to onoma* [into the name] seems rather to have been a tech[nical] term in Hellenistic commerce ("to the account of"). In both cases the use of the phrase is understandable, since the account bears the name of the one who owns it, and in baptism the name of Christ is pronounced, invoked and confessed by the one who baptizes or the one baptized (Ac. 22:16) or both. *TDNT*[217]

"This goes on His account" – the *GO'EL* does not delegate but rather uses His own 'account': the forgiveness He 'owns' because He paid the penalty, the Life which He 'possesses' in His own nature, the relationship with the Father which He has embraced from eternity. The Name on the account is highly unique – because of His humility and obedience even to the death on the cross,

> therefore God also highly exalted Him and gave Him the Name which is above every name, that at the Name of Jesus every knee should bow, of those in heaven, and of those on earth, and of those under the earth, and that every tongue should confess that Jesus Christ is Lord, to the Glory of God the Father. Philippians 2:9-11

Because of what this *GO'EL* has accomplished, "there is no salvation in any other [source], for there is no other name under heaven given among men in which we must be saved" [Acts 4:12], therefore "you were washed, you were sanctified, you were justified in the Name of the Lord Jesus Christ and in the Spirit of our God" [I Corinthians 6:11].

In the Covenantal flow of the Life/Blood through us, "whatever you do, in word or work, do all things in the Name of the Lord Jesus, giving thanks to God the Father through Him" [Colossians 3:17] – what we do 'goes to His account,' not because we presume to contribute our own flawed righteousness, but because "we are His handiwork, created in Christ Jesus for good works, which God prepared previously that we should walk in them" [Ephesians 2:10].

All the Life of God in One Sip

> A happy Christian met an Irish peddler and exclaimed, "It's a grand thing to be saved!"
> "Aye," said the peddler, "It is, but I know something better than that."
> "Better than being saved?" asked the other. "What can you in your position possibly know what is better than that?"
> Came the unexpected reply, "The companionship of the Man Who saved me." unknown

It may come as a surprise to discover that redemption is not enough, or at least what we often consider as redemption. Shifting the image a bit, redemption or forgiveness could be treated like patching together the broken carcass of Covenant. Consider the valley of dry bones in Ezekiel 37:8: "I watched, and behold, upon them came the sinews and the flesh, and the skin spread over them; but there was no breath in them." The bodies were in perfect condition – restored! – but there was no Life.

Just as with those bodies, even after 'redemption' we have a dire need for Life, but it has to be a Life which is "perfect" [Matthew 5:48] and "holy" [Leviticus 19:2]. Only one Source's Life/Blood meets those requirements – He Who said "*I am the Life*," Jesus:

> Jesus said to them, "Very truly, I say to you, unless you eat the Flesh of the Son of Man and drink His Blood, you have no Life in you. Whoever eats My Flesh and drinks My Blood has Life eternal, and I will raise him up at the Last Day. … He who eats My Flesh and drinks My Blood abides in Me, and I in him." John 6:53-54, 56

As we approach the Table of the Lord, in the Life/Blood of Jesus is found all the Life of God in one sip – yet *He* is not content with just one sip! Rather, Communion needs to be thought of as the pulsing, the heartbeat, of God's Life in our veins, and through the "witnesses" of this Life/Blood and of the Spirit, "having raised Christ from the dead, He will also give Life to your mortal bodies through His Spirit dwelling in you" [Romans 8:11].

This is a Sacrament of Love

> A new commandment I give you, that you love one another; as I have loved you, that you also love one another. By this all people will know that you are My disciples, if you have Love for one another.
> John 13:34-35

When Jesus gives us His Body and Blood in Communion, it comes from a framework that has always been built upon Love. This 'pulsing' of Jehovah's Life/Blood in us is not merely a rite or a doctrine, nor is it merely that *we* have Communion with Him – it is that *Jesus* is having Communion *with us*, it is *His design* to share *His personal Life* with us, it is His "earnest desire" [Luke 22:15] to have this meal with us. There are no limits set, there is no place where *Jesus* has ever complained about having Communion too often!

Our response also reflects this Love. For example, when Jesus says, "Do this, as often as you drink it, in remembrance of Me" [I Corinthians 11:25], the "often" is defined by Love. If you see someone once a year and that is too often; if you see someone once a month and that is often enough; if you see someone every day and that is not often enough, these all declare something about how much you love these persons. From a different angle, Jesus spoke of "those who hunger and thirst for righteousness, for they shall be filled" [Matthew 5:6] – how often has Holy Communion been approached as a ritual, a duty, and on the other hand, how often could the motivation be described as a "hunger and thirst" for the pulsing of God's Life in us?

But also this is not a closed little group of two in the corner:

> Here your heart must go out in love and learn that this is a sacrament of love. As love and support are given to you, you in turn render love and support to Christ in His needy ones. Some gladly share the profits but not the costs – they like to hear that in this sacrament the help, fellowship, support of all the saints are promised and given to them. But they are unwilling in turn to give themselves into this fellowship – they won't help the poor, suffer with the suffering, put up with sinners, intercede for others, care for the sorrowing, defend the truth, and at risk of their own life, property, and honor seek the betterment of the Church and of all Christians ... They are self-seeking, and this sacrament does not benefit them! Martin Luther[218]

Indeed, if we are to "love one another as I have loved you ... By this all people will know that you are My disciples," this is never something 'between God and me and no one else.' Jesus states that the 'OTH, the SIGN, the 'scar,' the mark of His People is the Love that cannot but be visible to all.

The Calling Continues from 'Old' to 'New'

In the 'Old' Covenant, Jehovah desires His People to have a unique role in His creation: "You shall be to Me a Kingdom of Priests and a holy Nation" [Exodus 19:6]; "a holy People to Jehovah your God..., a special treasure above all the peoples who are on the face of the earth" [Deuteronomy 14:2] – they are to be the reflection/"Image" of God to this world as Adam and Eve were originally created to be, and a nation of priests to encourage the worship of God by all creation.

Indeed, Israel demonstrates this identity – whenever faith in Jehovah is in the center of their existence, they represent Him before the nations (they have had their moments, occasionally). However, all too often they are poor examples of the privilege and honor that they hold.

Looking at Moses' prophecies, it is evident that the Lord knows what is in store, yet that does not discourage Him from seeking a return to 'the Image of God' in the 'Old' Covenant, the same honor He still provides in the 'New.' Unfortunately, looking over Christian history, we do not have the best record either. However, Jehovah never backs away from His goal; and the fulfillment of His dream and His prophesy will come when all has been completed, when, according to Revelation: "He has made us kings and priests to His God and Father" [1:6, 5:10].

What of Israel, Now that Jehovah Broke the Old Covenant?

St Paul presents an interesting aspect to the 'Old' Covenant in Romans, chapters 9 through 11. Four hundred years before Jesus, Hezekiah prophesies the breaking of the 'Old' Covenant within the context of the Cross, the very place where the 'New' Covenant would take effect. One would expect that as Jehovah finishes the 'Old' Covenant, He should now dust off His hands and walk away from the People who have given Him such heartache for so many centuries.

Perhaps so, if Covenant were only a contract. But as when Jonathan cut Covenant with David, this relationship comes from the depths of the heart. Although the 'Old' Covenant is fulfilled and finished [Matthew

5:17], Jehovah still has a heart for Israel, "concerning [God's] choice, they are beloved because of 'the fathers,' for the gifts and the calling of God are irrevocable" [Romans 11:28-29]. When a second child is born into a family, the parents' love is not transferred from the first child as if there were a finite amount of Love available. So also, although the nations are now included under Covenant, God's Love has never diminished for His firstborn (as Jehovah refers to them in Exodus).

> Jehovah determined to love your fathers and chose their descendants after them, you out of all peoples, as at this day. Deuteronomy 10:15

Throughout the 'Old' Covenant, even when things seem at their worst, Jehovah always preserves a remnant of His special People. Now in the 'New' Covenant Paul can confidently say in Romans 9:27, "The remnant will be saved" and will indeed join the nations within the wonderful privilege of being God's 'New' People in Jesus (note how Jehovah's description of His Glory, "I will have mercy on whom I will have mercy" [Exodus 33:19] enters in here):

> So all Israel will be saved, as it is written: 'The Deliverer [GO'EL – Isaiah 59:20] will come out of Zion, and He will turn away ungodliness from Jacob; for this is My Covenant with them, when I take away their sins. ... For as you once disobeyed God but have now obtained mercy through their disobedience, so they also have disobeyed, so that now by the mercy shown you they also may obtain mercy. For God has bound all of us over to disobedience, so that He might have mercy on all. Romans 11:26-27, 30-32

The Body of Christ – Covenant, New Testament Style

One Body

> For by one Spirit we were all baptized into one Body...and all were given to drink of one Spirit. I Corinthians 12:13

"In that day you will know that I am in My Father, and you in Me, and I in you" [John 14:20] – Jesus is the Covenant: 'in Him' is that perfect connection between Jehovah and humans, and we must be 'in Him' to have this relationship with God. By Baptism, we enter into one of St Paul's most powerful word images, "the Body of Christ":

> "Body of Christ" is an extraordinary expression. It is without parallel even in the Old Testament. Seneca, to be sure, was quite ready to refer to the citizens of Rome as a body politic. We are quite familiar with terms "student body" or "church body." To speak of church members as a body of Christians creates no particular excitement. However, that is not what the apostle chose to write. He spoke of Christians as the "body of Christ." That is to say, in some mysterious sense the church is an extension of the incarnation of our Lord. It does His work. It is His instrument within history to carry on Christ's mission of gathering all things under His lordship.
>
> Dr Martin H Scharlemann[219]

Using the example of the human body with its diversity of members, yet a single body, in I Corinthians 12:12, Paul concludes, "so it is with Christ." He does not say, 'so it is with Christ and the Church,' or 'Christ and believers,' but rather, simply "Christ" – Jesus and His entire Body will always be a seamless whole.

> Consequently, the word "in" in the Colossians [2:9, 10] passage means far more than being in the same place as Christ, or being near Him, or He being near us. It means more than a partnership with Christ or Christ being a partner with us. It means that out of the two of us there is one new man. Christ is that man and I am in Christ to be that man.
> Theodore H. Epp[220]

That's what Covenant has been saying all along!

"Participation"

The Body of Christ is a dramatic step toward fulfilling the Creation Covenant's objective that God's People would be "in the Image of God." This is so much more than a merely reflected image, or some badge to be carried about. This is 'participation':

> ... have been baptized into Christ Jesus ... buried therefore with Him by baptism into death, so that as Christ was raised..., we too might walk in newness of Life (Jesus). Romans 6:3-4

In section "IV. The Covenant Mosaic," the Hebrew *ZIKARON* and the Greek *ANAMNESIS* are discussed because they involve so much more than merely 'remembrance.' In very real terms, these are a *participation* in a past event, where one considers himself *in that event*, even if it were only "in the loins of his forefather" (as when Levi "paid tithes through Abraham, for he is still in the loins of his ancestor" [Hebrews 7:9-10]; or the modern Jew is there at the first Passover 'in the loins of his ancestor'). As the Romans 6 passage points out, because we are His Body, we cannot help but be affected – no, included – in all that Jesus is about. Saying it differently but still with the same message is St Peter:

> *His divine power has granted to us* all things which belong to Life (Jesus) and godliness, through the knowledge of Him Who called us to His own Glory and excellence, through which He has given to us His precious and very great promises …, and [we] *become participants of the Divine Nature …* II Peter 1:3-4

'Jesus is the Covenant' is essential in understanding Peter, since only as we enter into *this* Covenant can we be actual "participants of the Divine Nature."

> Therefore, at the Altar we touch Calvary. The same Body which was offered then is present at the Altar; and every time I communicate I show forth His death, the same death. I link myself to it, and Calvary becomes a reality. At Communion we are actually on the mount called Calvary. We see it all. Some of us stand, as did John, in mystified wonder; others, like Mary, in love and tears; some, like the soldiers; and others, still, like the Centurion, and say: "Surely, this is the Son of God." The Lord's Supper is not the symbol of the death of Christ, but it is the personal appropriation [taking in] of the person of Christ in His death. The Communicant takes the crucified Savior into Himself as the bread and wine serve as carriers … Here I find the secret whereby I can touch my God, the secret whereby divine love can also be born in me and thus radiate through me into the lives of my fellow-men. Berthold von Schenk[221]

KOINONIA

"Participant" is from the Greek "*KOINONIA*" word group, which word group the New Testament Church uses to describe our partnership within the ongoing, intimate 'New' Covenant connection:

> The Cup of Blessing which we bless, is it not the participation of the Blood of Christ? The bread which we break, is it not the participation of the Body of Christ? I Corinthians 10:16

Holy Communion is where the vibrancy of Covenant should be recognized – this is no occasional event, but rather this participation is the pulsing, the heartbeat, of the Life/Blood of Jesus throughout His Body (which is the Church – Colossians 1:18, 24; Ephesians 5:23]). It is the "participation of the Holy Spirit" [II Corinthians 13:14, see Philippians 2:1], the "participation of the mystery, which from the beginning of the ages has been hidden in God" [Ephesians 3:9]. It joins all who are in Covenant: "so that you also may have participation with us; as indeed our participation is with the Father and with His Son Jesus ... we have participation with one another, and the Blood of Jesus Christ His Son cleanses us from all sin" [I John 1:3, 7].

> For He is our peace, who has made [Jew and Gentile] both one ..., so that from the two He would create in Himself one new man, thus making peace, that He might reconcile them both to God in one Body through the Cross ... because through Him we both have access by one Spirit to the Father. Ephesians 2:14-16, 18

This is no sterile theoretical participation; it is to be fully immersed into the 'New' Covenant, "to know Him and the power of His resurrection and the participation of His sufferings..." [Philippians 3:10, also II Corinthians 1:7]. This true sharing of the single Covenant Self echoes throughout the New Testament: "...our old man was *crucified with* Him... if we *died with* Christ, ...we shall also *live with* Him... we were *buried with* Him through baptism into death, that just as Christ was raised..., *even so we also*..." [Romans 6:4, 6, 8]; "... *joint heirs with* Christ, if indeed we *suffer with* Him, that we may also be *glorified together*" [Romans 8:17].

The Blood which flows brings Life, it is the Blood of "the Divine Nature": "it is no longer I who live, but Christ lives in me" [Galatians 2:20]; and because Jesus is the 'New' Covenant, the participant finds himself at a most extraordinary level and privilege: "...made us *alive together with* Christ..., and *raised us up together,* and made *us sit together* in the heavenly places in Christ Jesus" [Ephesians 2:5-6], "If then you were *raised with* Christ, seek the things which are above, where Christ is, sitting at the right hand of God" [Colossians 3:1]. All of this comes to us in the instant we enter into Covenant – because Jesus occupies all of them at this same moment.

"A *Living* Sacrifice"

> I beseech you therefore, brethren, by the compassions of God, that you present your bodies as a living sacrifice, holy, well-pleasing to God, which is your logical service. ... For as in one body we have many members ... so we, the many, are one Body in Christ, and each one, members of one another.   Romans 12:1, 4-5

Paul instructs us to be a *living* sacrifice, however not the sacrifice for sin, since only One can and has done that. Ours is the *Whole Burnt Offering,* the dedication of oneself wholly to the Lord, and it is Bloodless since it is not our Life/Blood which God seeks, but Jesus' in us. Like the *Grain Offering* which could never stand alone, but had to be thrown on top of an animal sacrifice [See "IX. Time with Jehovah – The Worship of Israel – B. The Sacrifices"], our sacrifice is only effective when we are in the Body of Christ, participant in *His* "Offering and Sacrifice to God for a sweet-smelling aroma" [Ephesians 5:2[222]] – outside of Him there is no righteousness before God [see the discussion "Outgrowing Jesus" below]:

> He has reconciled [you] in the Body of His flesh through death, to present you holy, and blameless, and without accusation in His sight.
>   Colossians 1:22; see also Ephesians 2:16 above

> To be sure this sacrifice of prayer, praise, and thanksgiving, and of ourselves as well, we are not to present before God in our own person. But we are to lay it upon Christ and let him present it for us ... We

> learn that we do not offer Christ as a sacrifice, but that Christ offers us.
> Martin Luther[223]

What shape will these sacrifices take? "A broken spirit, a broken and a contrite heart" [Psalm 51:17]; "through all things, a sacrifice of praise to God, this is the fruit of lips which together confess His Name; to do good and to share also do not neglect" [Hebrews 13:15-16]; "To love Him with all the heart, with all the intellect, with all the Soul, and with all the strength, and to love one's neighbor as oneself, is more than all the *Whole Burnt Offerings* and sacrifices" [Mark 12:33].

However, Paul declares that this body which we offer cannot also be used, for example, at the altar of sexual immorality. After all, being joined in the sexual act is as uniting as cutting Covenant and "sins against his own body" [I Corinthians 6:18]. In today's world, this type of sin is very powerful (for instance, 'sex sells'). Perhaps that is why Paul uses a strong Covenant contrast, "he who is joined to the Lord is one spirit with Him" [v 17], to remind us of the greater power we have in Jesus: "the body is... for the Lord, and the Lord for the body; and God both raised up the Lord and will raise us up by His power" [vv 13-14, 19].

Although Paul emphasizes how the body, the flesh, is indeed the frustrating repository of sin [Romans 7:24], and that he must "pommel my body and subdue it" [I Corinthians 9:27], still he reminds us that we are "bought at a price," that the "body is the temple of the Holy Spirit Who is in you, Whom you have from God – you are not your own", and therefore we are to Glorify God both in the spirit *and in the body* [I Corinthians 6:19-20].

"With ... All the Company" (from the Liturgy's "Preface")

> Two or three believers, huddled behind locked doors, or in some concentration camp, are suddenly thrust into the midst of this great host. They are not alone.
> Those who are addicted seeking to be free from this stranglehold on their Life come to the Table, there to find many hands lifting them in prayer, many scarred by the same bonds. They are not alone.

The lonely, the downtrodden, the bewildered, the grieving, all find that they are welcome, all have a home. They are not alone.

A famous actress, who in later life received an important award, remarked afterwards that she was struck by melancholy because, "I have no one to share the good news with." But not so at this Table! There is a great shout of praise and joy when good things happen to each other. They are not alone.

We are not just this little group. We are not just this little church. We are not just this little denomination. We are ... God's own holy, chosen People. ...

In Jesus, time and space collapse into the moment of eternity. We are in the midst of a great throng of His People throughout the world and throughout history as Jesus reaches out to all whom He has so powerfully loved in this world.   James Lindemann[224]

At the Altar the faithful believer is in fellowship and in union with his Lord. And as the believer receives at the Altar he is not only in fellowship with his Lord, but through that Communion he is in fellowship with all Christians who kneel at the Christian Altars, and who with him are receiving the true body and the true blood of Christ. The Communion may be celebrated at thousands of Altars, yet it is only one Communion. ... In the Holy Communion we have the basis for true Church unity and union. It transcends all denominational lines.   Berthold von Schenk[225]

As pointed out before, sometimes we think that 'my faith is between God and me, and nobody else's business.' The interconnectedness of Covenant does not allow that. When we stop to think about it, it truly is wonderful that it is not that way. In the oneness of the Body of Christ, His People do not have to go far to find Him – His beloved voice speaks through one person, His caring help comes through another, His loving comfort through another, and so forth – He not only is in our midst but also He is found *in us*. In I Corinthians 12, St Paul gathers "gifts, ... ministries, ... activities" under the unity of the Spirit Who manifests "to each one for the profit of all" [vv 4-7], "the members of that one body, being many, are one body, so also is Christ ... you are the Body of Christ, and members individually of it" [vv 12, 27].

The tendency to isolate oneself can be very strong in fallen human nature (after all, 'gods' – à la Adam and Eve – should be self-sufficient). That is why, in I Corinthians 11, starting from verse 17, St Paul takes the congregation to task. What should be a unifying 'fellowship meal' is used as a subtle put-down of the 'have-nots,' especially since the meal is to culminate in the Holy Communion, which really is about Holy *Community*. As Paul repeats Jesus' blessing of the sacrament [vv 23-25], it is a powerful reminder of the Source of this Communion/Covenant-Community and of its Life/Blood ("you proclaim the Lord's death till He comes" [v 26]).

What is the "unworthy manner" [vv 27, 29] of participating in Holy Communion/Community? It is the neglect of realizing what this *Community* is about, that is, "not discerning the Lord's *Body*" [v 29]. Wherever Paul uses only "the Body" in I Corinthians, it is in reference to the People of Christ; however when it is paired with "the Cup" then it becomes a specific reference to the act of Holy Communion. It is their neglect of who they are as Christ's Body which brings judgment: weakness, sickness, and even death [vv 29-30]. On the other hand, the Love/*AGAPE* chapter 13 follows both of these chapters as the "more excellent way" [12:31], and such Covenant-unity "causes growth of the Body for the building up of itself in Love" [Ephesians 4:16].

"With ... All the Company *of Heaven*" (from the "Preface")

When Paul's vision of the Church as the reality of the Body of Christ is understood, it is indeed a doctrine of powerful comfort and help. However, remember that the Covenant connection is with the eternal Jehovah: "not the God of the dead but of the living, for all live to Him" [Luke 20:38] and the resurrected Jesus. The Covenant unity of the Body of Christ is far greater than an individual congregation, greater than even the present world-wide Church:

> We cannot divide the Body of Christ. The Church militant [on earth] and the Church triumphant [in heaven] form one Church. Nothing can separate the members of the Church, neither life nor death, nor power, nor principalities. At the Altar we have fellowship with our

risen and ascended Lord. But there is also a fellowship with all the members of the Church. At the Altar we join hands not only with the great saints in Heaven, but also with all our loved ones who have passed within the veil, our faithful departed. ...

The Church tells her children that there is a Communication possible; that there is a medium between our departed ones and ourselves, and only one, – it is our Blessed Lord Himself ... To countless Christians the reality of the Communion of Saints has been an unfailing source of love and joy in the face of otherwise heartbreaking bereavement. ...

The living Christ creates and guarantees this joyful fact. It is Christ, and not just our wishful hoping, Who assures us that nothing can pluck out of His hand those who loved Him and trusted Him. ... It is found in these words, "Because I live, ye shall live also."...

... We must come to a sense of the continuing presence of our loved ones, and we can do this if we realize the presence of our Living Lord. As we seek and find our Risen Lord we shall find our dear departed. They are with Him, and we find the reality of their continued life through Him. ...

... How pathetic it is to see men and women going out to the cemetery, kneeling at the mound, placing little sprays of flowers and wiping their tears from their eyes, and knowing nothing else. How hopeless they look. Oh, that we could take them by the hand, away from the grave, out through the cemetery gate, in through the door of the church, and up the nave to the very Altar itself, and there put them in touch, not with the dead body of their loved one, but with the living soul who is with Christ at the Altar. Our human nature needs more than the assurance that some day and in some way we shall again meet our loved ones "in heaven." ...

My loved one has just left me ... But I am in touch with her. I know that there is a place where we can meet. It is at the Altar. How it thrills me when I hear the words of the Liturgy, "Therefore with angels and archangels and all the company of Heaven," for I know that she is there with that company of Heaven, the Communion of Saints, with the Lord. The nearer I come to my Lord in Holy Communion, the nearer I come to the saints, to my own loved ones. I am a member of the Body of Christ, I am a living cell in that spiritual organism, partaking of the life of the other cells, and sharing in the Body of Christ Himself.   Berthold von Schenk[226]

The Living Bread

From Living Water to Living Bread

In counterpoint to the 'Living Water' of the Holy Spirit, St John includes the discourse on the 'Living Bread':

> *I am* the Bread of Life ... *I am* the Living Bread which came down from heaven. If anyone eats of this Bread, he will live forever; indeed the Bread which I shall give is My Flesh for the Life of the world. ... He who eats My Flesh and drinks My Blood has Life eternal, and I will raise him up at the last day... This is the Bread which has come down from heaven – not as the fathers ate [the manna] and died. He who eats this Bread will live forever. John 6:48, 51, 54, 58

Again, in his economy of images, John confronts us with a variety of thoughts: As Jesus talks about His Flesh, His audience is looking at Him – His Flesh, His Body – standing before them [John 6:52]. Here is a concrete reality, but its significance surfaces particularly at His Resurrection, where all are called to faith [John 20:29] because *His risen Body* is tangible proof [John 20:20, 25, 27] that Jesus can indeed raise Himself from the dead [John 2:19-22].

There is also 'the Body of Christ,' the favorite theme of St Paul mentioned above, which describes more than an assembled group of believers, but rather the living extension of Jesus in this world, those who *participate* in His Life, death, resurrection and gifts forever. To be 'in Christ' means that we are placed within this "one Bread ... one Body" [I Corinthians 10:17] to reflect Him and to bring others into a 'living relationship' with this Savior.

Jesus' 'Flesh' stands in stark contrast to the rest of mankind's: theirs is corrupted, useless before God – "the flesh profits nothing" [John 6:63]; but when "the Word became Flesh and dwelt among us" [John 1:14], here is a 'Flesh' which is sinless and intimately connected to Jehovah Himself. Jesus claims that we must have participation in it – "eats My Flesh" – we must become "participants of the Divine Nature" is the way St Peter put it [II Peter 1:4].

It is impossible to not connect this discussion with Holy Communion. Although John does not describe the Communion event itself, with his emphasis on the Water and the Blood being essential Witnesses, along with sections on Baptism and Water (in chapters 3 and 4), he here includes a theology for Communion. The concept of food is quite useful; the Bread, for example, once digested enters the Bloodstream, and then is brought to cells which need energy and building up – it sustains Life. The physical aspect of Communion also gives us an actual point in time when we can know for sure we have an intimate encounter by faith with our Lord and Savior Himself.

Changing the 'eat' to 'consume' (where one is so focused on something that one 'forgets himself') brings to mind, "Zeal for Your house [dwelling place] has consumed Me" [John 2:17]. Since I Peter describes us as "*living stones…* being built up as a spiritual house" [2:5], and St Paul identifies us as "*the temple* of God and that the Spirit of God dwells in you" [I Corinthians 3:16; also 6:19], we are God's house or dwelling place. In light of His "you in Me, and I in you" [John 14:20; Psalm 69:9], one might say that Holy Communion is an extraordinary act of Covenant intimacy in which we are 'consumed' by each other. Jesus puts aside His royalty to be found among us sinners, and we put aside our self-centeredness to be filled with all the promises of Jesus.

Outgrowing Jesus?

One may find oneself struggling with a vague perception: how easily the thought comes that once Jesus has saved us, then it is done. The task is finished. And on the Last Day, when broken Covenant will be gone forever; when we no longer will wrestle with sin and will have bodies to match Jesus' resurrected body; when, as children of God, we will have a seemingly godlike status (equal to Jesus as God's child) – when we no longer have need to be saved by Jesus, will we have outgrown Him? Just how *essential* will Jesus be then?

The answer to such a question must turn to Covenant and the reason why Jesus does not merely *bring* the Covenant, but *is* the 'New' Covenant. All of these benefits come not because He gives to us a 'package' of salvation (although we often think of it that way), but rather, because *only He* is the perfect relationship between God and man – this 'New' Covenant is *an eternal state of being* in Jesus.

Therefore, on earth, and even in heaven, the moment one steps outside of Jesus *there is no relationship* – "there is no salvation in any other [source], for there is no other name under heaven given among men in which we must be saved" [Acts 4:12]. The whole conversation about "participation" (above), of "participating in the Divine Nature," *cannot be had outside of Jesus*.

That is why we are warned that the relationship can be lost. Although there is always room for the returned prodigal son [Luke 15:11-32], deliberately stepping outside of the 'New' Covenant is most dangerous:

> For those who once were enlightened, who tasted the heavenly Gift, who became partakers in the Holy Spirit, who tasted the goodness of God's Word, of the power and of the age to come, and who then fall away, it is impossible to restore them to repentance, since they crucify again for themselves the Son of God and hold Him up to contempt.
> Hebrews 6:4-6 (see also II Peter 2:20-21)

Note that it does not say that God has irrevocably condemned them and will not forgive them, but rather how it is "impossible ... to return them again *to repentance*" – they refuse to repent: it is a self-condemnation, not Jehovah's verdict. Yet there are passages which declare that God can do the impossible [Matthew 19:26; Mark 10:27; Luke 1:37; 18:27] – we therefore never have the authorization to dismiss someone as a lost cause. After all, "perhaps God may grant them repentance into a full discernment of the truth, that they regain their senses and escape the snare of the devil" [II Timothy 2:25-26]. There are many examples where God has done just that.

No, we never outgrow our need for Jesus. He is as indispensable to us in eternity as He is here

All that I Am

The Bridegroom and His Bride

In section "VI. The Old Testament – THE Foundational Covenant," it is discussed how in Marriage the two (man and woman) are intended to form a unified "Image of God" through this Covenant. However, throughout the Old Testament, Marriage sadly all too often is the metaphor which describes the Husband (Jehovah) betrayed by an unfaithful wife (Israel). Yet there are allusions to something more wonderful coming:

> For as a young man marries a virgin, so shall your sons marry you, and as a bridegroom rejoices over the bride, so shall your God rejoice over you. Isaiah 62:5

Now in the New Testament, the picture switches to the excitement, the anticipation and the joy of *newlyweds*: Jesus is the Bridegroom and the Church is His Bride [Revelation 21:2, 9; 22:17]. In parables, the marriage feast has a prominent place [Matthew 22:2; 25:10; Luke 12:36] and the "beginning of signs," when Jesus begins His ministry – if you will, the wooing of His Bride – takes place at a wedding [John 2:1-11]. Since Covenant can easily degenerate into an almost staid clinical doctrine, the concept of newlyweds, with its freshness and energy provides a very welcome contrast.

Covenant within Covenant, Demonstrating the Image of God

The original Marriage Covenant with Adam and Eve is indeed a bond with each other, but it also has a special role within the greater Creation Covenant. In that first great Covenant, mankind is to be "the Image of God," demonstrating not just Jehovah's governance, but particularly also the Glory of God [II Corinthians 3:18] – His goodness, Covenant, grace, mercy, Love and justice. Within that Covenant, in Marriage, they are to be that Image to each other.

In Ephesians 5:25-33, St Paul declares that Genesis 2:23-24 is really the description of the newlyweds of Jesus and His Bride:

> Husbands, love your wives, just as Christ also loved the Church and gave Himself on (her) behalf, that He might sanctify and cleanse (her) by the washing of water in the Word ... because we are members of His Body, of His flesh and of His bones. "For this reason a man shall leave his father and mother and shall cleave to his wife, and the two shall become one flesh" – *the mystery of this is great, and I speak concerning Christ and the Church.*

Jesus is the 'New' Covenant; yet, since our relationship with Him is expressed in terms of a Marriage (as had been declared in regard to Adam and Eve), He and we have a joint Covenant connection to God. It is startling to contemplate how we are as necessary to Jesus as Eve is to Adam, in order for Jesus to fulfill His task of being "the Image of God" to creation – and forever as we occupy heaven "in Him" [Ephesians 2:4-6]. Obviously Jesus does not *need* it to be this way, yet this is His *design*.

The Unbreakable One

"The two shall become one flesh" [Genesis 2:24] describes the Covenant ideal. By faith, through Baptism, as "one Flesh" or "one Person" with Jesus, we receive everything – all He is, all He has – and He receives everything – all we are, all we have. There is no holding back on anything – it is no longer 'yours and mine,' but 'ours.' So He shares with us His power, His Love and His Life; and then receives our love, our living – and shoulders our sins.

Christmas tangibly demonstrates the Bridegroom's commitment to this oneness ('withness' – or "Immanuel," that is, "God with us" [Matthew 1:23]). He personally enters into His Bride's Life where we live, experiencing it just as we do. He will be with us "always" [Matthew 28:20], "never fail you nor forsake you" [Hebrews 13:5], never "leave you desolate; I will come to you" [John 14:18]. The familiar form of the traditional wedding vow echoes Paul's confidence in this union:

For better and for worse, for richer and for poorer, in sickness and in health, to have and to hold from this day forward until death do us part.

For I have been persuaded that neither death, nor Life …, nor things present, nor things to come …, nor any other creation, will be able to separate us from the Love of God in Christ Jesus our Lord.
Romans 8:38-39

Maintaining the Unity

But how can the Bridegroom keep reassuring His Bride – a Bride which covers the earth – that He still is part of our Life, that He Himself is with us in every locale simultaneously? With the intensity of a Bridegroom He eagerly awaits [Luke 22:15] the Covenant meal, where He again withholds nothing, not His Life/Blood, not His Body – where He once more earnestly, delightedly, boldly, actually gives Himself 'heart and Soul,' giving literally everything of Himself to His Bride – this is His desire, His choice, His extravagant relationship of Love, His joy – His Glory:

Now Glorify Me, O Father, with Yourself, with the Glory which I had with You before the world was created. … The Glory which You gave Me I have given them, that they may be one just as We are one.
John 17:5, 22

All the different concepts of our unity in Him: Blood-redeemed People of God, the Body of Christ, in the oneness of the Bridegroom with His Bride are all drawn together as Jesus says to each one of us, "This is My Body, this is My Life/Blood – for you."

XIV. The New Testament and the 'New' Covenant

A. The Synoptic Gospels, John and Acts

In the following, '*' indicates that there are parallel accounts in the other Gospels.

The Synoptics

'Syn-optic' means that Matthew, Mark and Luke see with the same eye or point of view. Many of their stories are similar; they simply accent certain aspects in order to fit their audiences as well as their purpose in writing. So, despite their common accounts, Matthew, writing to the Jews, has many references and tie-ins to the Old Testament, while Mark has the direct simplicity which the Roman would appreciate, while Luke reminds his readers that the Gospel and the Book of Acts take place in a historical setting and culture.

Luke's Prologue to the New Testament

Luke's first chapter – or rather his prologue to his Gospel – through the mouth of Mary [vv 46-55], and particularly through Zechariah's prophecy [vv 67-79] defines what the Gospel, that is, Jesus, would be all about. Mary rejoices in the mercy (Glory) of the God Who will 'turn the world on its ear': "He has pulled down the powerful from their thrones, and exalted the lowly. He has filled the hungering[227] with good things, and the rich He has sent away destitute" [vv 52-53]. Her song reaches its high point by emphasizing the fulfillment of the 'Old' Covenant, "As He spoke to our fathers, to Abraham and to his seed forever" [v 55].

But Zechariah marks out the territory which will be covered: "He has visited and ransomed ... raised up a horn of salvation ... saved from our enemies ... the mercy promised to our fathers and to remember His holy

Covenant, the Oath which He swore to our Father Abraham ... to give knowledge of salvation ... by the forgiveness of their sins, through the tender mercy of our God" [vv 68-77].

Covenant's Invisible Presence

It would make our task easier if only the Synoptic Gospel writers had been more obvious about Covenant, but a society which is as disadvantaged in regard to Covenant-awareness as we are, would probably miss it anyway. So, although there are some mentions of Covenant (particularly in regard to Holy Communion), the writers simply choose to identify, as St Paul puts it, "that God was in Christ, reconciling the world unto Himself" [II Corinthians 5:19], that is, Covenant's new Name is *Jesus*.

The evidence is presented: Although Jesus is a real, born-human being, He redefines the God-dictated Ten Commandments and *Sabbath* [Luke 6:5]; He has authority over creation (stilling of the sea and multiplying bread and fish to feed a multitude); and even death cannot resist Him – all indicating that God is indeed come to earth in Christ. However, for some it is not easy to see God in this human – even His hometown struggled with accepting this [Mark 6:1-6*].

But for us who are beginning to grasp what Covenant is about, we become aware of the atmosphere in which the Gospel accounts are set. So, for instance, the temptations of Jesus [Matthew 4, Luke 4] are Satan's attempt to split into two the unified Covenant that Jesus is, to separate the 'emptied' "Son of God" [Philippians 2:6-8] from the finite human side. Even in His humble state, it is the 'New' Covenant, united to the Father's will [John 5:36], Who touches an 'untouchable' leper [Matthew 8:3*], and children [Mark 10:13*]; Who heals [Matthew 11:5*], and raises people from the dead [Mark 5:35-42*; Luke 7:11-16].

It is the compassion of God's Glory which reaches out to feed the 5,000 from five loaves with twelve baskets left over [Matthew 14:14-21*], and the 4,000 from *seven* loaves with *seven* baskets left over [Matthew 15:32-38*]. It is the majesty of the Covenant One Who rebukes the storm [Mark

4:37-41*], before Whom demons kneel [Mark 5:6*] and Who casts them out "with a word" [Matthew 8:16]. It is Love which underlies the 'New' Covenant from which forgiveness is declared [Luke 5:17-26], which comes not "to destroy men's lives but to save them" [Luke 9:56] and from which Life is given [John 6:63]. It is the upraised mighty Hand of Covenant which is nailed to the Cross, yet is proof of the Resurrection [Luke 24:39] and is the very Hand of Blessing [Luke 24:50-51] at the Ascension.

The Kingdom of God

Although Luke refers to "the Kingdom of God" far more than anyone else, it is still a frequent term throughout the New Testament. This Kingdom/Rule of God – "the Kingdom of the Son of His Love" [Colossians 1:13] – is bound up very much in Jesus, Who has "all things put under His feet" [Ephesians 1:22; Hebrews 2:8]; it is a Kingdom of "righteousness and peace and joy in the Holy Spirit" [Romans 14:17]. It is the message of the Gospel [Luke 4:43; 8:1] and when it is described as something you enter [3:28-29; 18:24-25] and which enters you ("within you" [17:21]), it is of the same frame of concept as "Jesus is the Covenant," echoing John 14:20: "I am in My Father, and you in Me, and I in you"; and John 17:21: "that they all may be one, as You, Father, are in Me, and I in You; that they also may be one in Us."

The Transfiguration

> As He prayed, the appearance of His face was different, and His clothing became white and glistening. Behold, two men talked with Him, who were Moses and Elijah, who appeared in Glory and spoke of His exodus which He was about to accomplish at Jerusalem.
>
> Luke 9:29-31

Why do Moses and Elijah appear during the Transfiguration? On the one hand, Moses represents 'the Law,' or more accurately, 'the Torah.' As mentioned previously, the Torah contains not just the Law, but also, for instance, the book of Genesis, which came '430 years' before the Law [Galatians 3:17]. It is the story of Jehovah establishing His Covenants and also initiating His plan of salvation which will culminate in the Cross and on the Last Day. Although the Law does speak of our need for a Savior, it would seem that Jesus and Moses would have even more to talk about if one included Genesis in the discussion.

Luke uses an unusual word as he tells us that Moses and Elijah talk with Jesus about "His *exodus*." This word, appearing only three times in the New Testament [see Hebrews 11:22, II Peter 1:18] would likely recall to his reader (or hearer) the second book of the *Septuagint* (the Greek translation the Old Testament made around 200 BC), titled "Exodus." This book opens with the story of Jehovah's promised Covenant-rescue of His People from slavery, accomplished through the Blood of the *Passover* Lamb and accompanied by Covenant-affirming SIGNS.

As counterpoint to Moses we hear the prophets, such as Isaiah and Zechariah, who prophesy of the Messiah and what He will mean as the 'New' Covenant. However, *Elijah* is the one who appears on this occasion. Why him?? He is not the first major prophet – which would be Samuel [See Jeremiah 15:1]. Elijah prophesies about the future of Israel and of its Messiah, like Isaiah does. He doesn't even have a book of his own, as do other prophets. But there is a uniqueness to Elijah – he never died, but ascended directly into heaven [II Kings 2:11]; we may assume that he is in the presence of Jehovah Himself, and therefore is in eternal Life already.

So Moses and 'the prophets' speak with Jesus about His 'exodus' or rescue and salvation in the 'New' *Passover*. There is also death (Moses died) and eternal Life (Elijah) involved in this discussion. And there is the Glory which, in Exodus, Jehovah declares is His goodness, Covenant, mercy and grace [33:18-23], as well as His *HESED*/Love and justice [34:6-7], equally fitting topics as they discuss what will take place shortly on the Cross.

John's Covenant Setting

John, except for one instance in referring to *"the Ark of the Covenant"* in Revelation [11:19], never uses the word 'Covenant' and surprisingly omits such a 'New' Covenant-significant item as the consecration of Holy

Communion. Yet he also seems the most sacramentally oriented of the Gospel writers and at the very beginning of his Gospel account he makes it unmistakable that "the Word," Who "was God ... became flesh and dwelt among us, and we beheld His Glory, the Glory as of the only begotten of the Father, full of grace and truth" [John 1:1, 14] – in other words, he ends up right in the middle of the 'New' Covenant (that is, Jesus).

Along with "witness" (which is discussed previously), John also uses "SIGN" (sometimes translated as 'miracles') as it is used in the Old Testament, by which Jesus "manifest[s] His Glory" [John 2:11], which demonstrates the presence of God [3:2], and which challenges people to either believe in Him [2:23; 12:18; 20:30-31] or to reject Him [11:47]. It is the logic of the SIGN through which the man born blind (who has not yet seen Jesus) recognizes Who He is [9:25, 30-33] and which makes the rejection of the Pharisees the more pathetic [v 34]. This usage of SIGNS seems to be commonly understood in the New Testament, for example in the dual Luke-Acts books, especially in Acts, where they also challenge people to recognize God's involvement, leading either to faith or to rejection of Who and What Jesus is [for example, Acts 2:22; 4:16, 30; 14:3].

"We beheld His Glory ... full of grace and truth" [John 1:14]; "this beginning of SIGNs Jesus does in Cana of Galilee, and manifested His Glory" [2:11] – although 'Glory' is used in different settings throughout the New Testament, it is useful to have in mind the definitions of Glory from Exodus as mentioned above to see how these add a different perspective to the places where 'Glory' appears.

B. St Paul's Writings

(These are in addition to many of his concepts already discussed.)

With Covenant being the environment, for one familiar with God's Glory (as the source for Covenant), along with this relationship's *GO'EL*, Life/Blood, and the rest, then such statements as "having now been justified by His Blood" [Romans 5:9] have a richer meaning.

Then connecting "the promises made to the fathers" to the fact that "Jesus Christ has become a servant to the Circumcision [that is, Israel]" [Romans 15:8], Paul sets the groundwork for Jesus' salvation upon the Covenant made with Abraham and son (Isaac), extending back as far as Adam and Eve. Using these as our vantage point, we also recognize "As God is faithful, ... for as many are the promises of God, in Him [they] are 'Yes!', and through Him 'Amen!' to God for [His] Glory through us" [II Corinthians 1:18, 20].

The Glory

> ... God chose you from the beginning for salvation through sanctification by the Spirit and faith in the truth, to which He called you by our Gospel, as a 'purchased possession'[228] in the Glory of our Lord Jesus Christ. II Thessalonians 2:13-14

In II Corinthians 3, Paul contrasts the Glory of the Law with the Glory of God's unstoppable Love: 'For if the ministry of condemnation has Glory, much more does the ministry of righteousness [of the New Covenant – v 6] abound in Glory" [v 9] – in fact, the Glory of the Law, which fades away [vv 11,13], really is no Glory [v 10] in comparison to "the ministry of righteousness."

Moses uses a veil over his face, so that the fleeting Glory of the Law is will not be noticed [v 13]; so even today, because of that veil, there appears to be more splendor than is really there [v 14-15]. The real Glory as defined in Exodus 33 and 34 overwhelms the Law, and it does not fade. Rather by the Spirit it shines increasingly more forcefully each day in our faces [v 18], and "in our hearts ... with the light of the knowledge of the Glory of God in the face of Jesus Christ" [II Corinthians 4:6]. Therefore,

> that, according to the riches of His Glory, He would make you become strong with power ["made powerful by the strength of His Glory" – Colossians 1:11] through His Spirit in the inner man, that Christ may dwell through faith in your hearts; that you, being rooted and founded in Love, may have full capacity to comprehend with all the saints what is the width, length, depth and height, and to know with transcending

> knowledge the Love of Christ; that you may be filled with all the fullness of God. Now to Him who is able to do exceedingly abundantly above all that we ask or think, according to the power that works in us, to Him be the Glory in the Church by Christ Jesus to all generations, forever and ever. Amen. Ephesians 3:16-21

GO'EL

> For in Him all the fullness [of God] was pleased to dwell, and through Him to reconcile all things to Himself, having made peace through the Blood of His cross – through Him whether things on earth or things in heaven. And you, previously alienated and enemies in your mind by evil works, now He has reconciled in the Body of His Flesh through death, to present you holy, and blameless, and without accusation in His sight ... Colossians 1:19-22

"Now all things are of God, having reconciled us to Himself through Jesus Christ" [II Corinthians 5:18], "He made Him Who knew no sin be sin for us, so that we might become the righteousness of God in Him" [v 21]. He is the "one Mediator ['intercessor'] between God and men, the Man Christ Jesus, Who gave Himself as a ransom for all" [I Timothy 2:5-6]. What a strange way to resolve broken Covenant, that the agent to 'balance the Blood' for the offended party would Himself personally pay the penalty.

The work of this *GO'EL* has an even broader task, that of uniting Jew (Israel) and non-Jew ('the nations') "so as to create in Himself *one new Man* from the two" by breaking down "the middle wall of separation, ... the enmity, that is, the Law of commandments ... that He might reconcile them both to God *in one Body* through the Cross" [Ephesians 2:14-16]. This vividly expresses the prophesy "I will ... give *You as a Covenant* to people" [Isaiah 42:6], as all this takes place *in and through Jesus*.

The Riches of the Mystery in the 'New' Covenant

> Without debate, great is the Mystery of godliness: God was manifested in flesh, justified in Spirit, seen by angels, proclaimed in the nations, believed on in the world, taken up in Glory. I Timothy 3:16

What is Paul's "Mystery"? Although 'Jesus *is* the Covenant' ("God manifested in the flesh") would be the primary foundation, he goes on to say that the Mystery particularly is that the promise of salvation is not merely limited to a small favored few, but extends worldwide: "that the nations should be joint-heirs and a 'joint-Body,' and 'joint-sharers' of His promise in Christ through the Gospel," "in the nations the unsearchable riches of Christ, ... the participation [*KOINONIA*] of the Mystery" [Ephesians 3:3-6, 8-9].

He comes back to the topic of Glory: "God's wisdom in the mystery, once hidden, which God predetermined before the ages for our Glory" [I Corinthians 2:7]; "the riches of the Glory of this Mystery among the nations: which is Christ in you, the hope of Glory" [Colossians 1:27]. This of course is not our personal glory, but rather the Glory which is transforming us [II Corinthians 3:18], the Glory according to the meaning Jehovah gave it in Exodus 33 and 34. It gives substance to the word "riches," that is, 'abundant treasures,' even 'raw materials,' having such a wealth that one would be hard-pressed, if it were possible, to exhaust this resource. In Jesus, the 'New' Covenant,

> *In Him* we have redemption through His Blood, the forgiveness of trespasses, according to the riches of His grace that He lavished on us. With all wisdom and insight, making known to us the mystery of His will, according to His good pleasure, ... to gather all things under one Head *in Him*, things in heaven and things on earth...
>
> God, Who is rich in mercy, through His great Love with which He loved us, even when we were dead in trespasses, made us alive *with Christ* – by grace you have been saved – and "jointly raised up" and "jointly seated" us in the heavenly places *in Christ Jesus*, so that in the coming ages He might show the surpassing riches of His grace in kindness toward us *in Christ Jesus*. Ephesians 1:7-10, 2:4-7

> ... that their hearts may be encouraged, being joined together in Love, and for all the riches of the full assurance of understanding, to the discerning of the Mystery of God, both of the Father and of Christ, in Whom are hidden all the wealth of wisdom and knowledge.
> Colossians 2:2-3

"Riches" means that if we stop to contemplate this Mystery, we should be overwhelmed by the abundance of God's Glory in Christ Jesus. And God will be as fully committed to this 'New' Covenant as He has been to the 'Old':

> [Our Lord Jesus Christ,] Who will also confirm you to the end, to be blameless in the day of our Lord Jesus Christ. God is faithful, by Whom you were called into the participation [KOINONIA] of His Son, Jesus Christ our Lord.   I Corinthians 1:8-9

C. Hebrews

The Will and the Way

> Therefore by this He is the Mediator of a New Covenant*, since a death occurred under the First Covenant* for the redemption of the transgressions, so that those who are called may receive the promise of the eternal inheritance.
>
> Because where a Testament* is brought forth, the death of the testator is necessary – for a Testament* is only in force after men are dead, since it never has power while the testator lives.
>
> On this account, not even the First Covenant* was established without Blood. For when Moses had spoken every precept to all the people according to the law, he took the Blood of calves and goats, with water, scarlet wool, and hyssop, and sprinkled both the book itself and all the people, saying, "This is the Blood of the Covenant* which God has commanded you."   9:15-20 [* = DIATHEKE]

The task of a translator is never easy, and this is one example. In Hebrews 9, in many translations, both "Covenant" and "Testament" (as in 'Last Will and Testament') are used for the same Greek word (*DIATHEKE). 'Will' or 'Testament' is a legitimate interpretation, since that is a normal usage of the time. However when the Hebrew ('Old') Testament is translated into the Greek two hundred years before Jesus, DIATHEKE is also chosen to be the equivalent to 'Covenant,' and therefore it takes on this new dimension.

But 'Will' is the dispersal of assets *after* the death of the testator, while 'Covenant' is a unity in force *before* someone dies – the concepts are really not interchangeable. Therefore, although using *both* 'Covenant' and 'Will/Testament' in translating this Hebrews passage may initially make better sense of the wording, it is admittedly awkward since the Greek original uses *only DIATHEKE* to talk about *both* concepts. Indeed, there is a lot of opportunity for confusion: under the 'New' Covenant, "Testament" is understandable in the sense that Jesus' death does 'will' to us a multitude of 'assets' – forgiveness, salvation, Life, and the rest. But in "the first Covenant" – or "the first Testament" – the Testator, Who is Jehovah, does not die at Sinai, so how can the idea of the dispersal of assets work in that Covenant/Will's context?

Actually, the "first Testament" has an unusual twist to it. Normally, the death must happen before the 'Will' can take effect, but not so here – in the 'Old' Covenant, the dispersal of benefits throughout thousands of years takes place *before* the death. Just as the effect of Jesus' Circumcision races backward in time, connecting to every faithful circumcision in the past, so also the death of the Testator, Jehovah/Jesus, at the *end* of the Covenant races backward in time dispersing the benefits to the earlier beneficiaries of this 'Will.' Under the 'Old' Covenant, the People first receive the benefits 'in hope,' and then when Jesus dies, those benefits become 'real' – otherwise, how could they have received the forgiveness of their sins?

Thus, in Jesus' death the Sinai Covenant is fulfilled, so also is the Circumcision Covenant closed, meanwhile simultaneously the 'New' Covenant is initiated. In one death truly *all* is 'finished,' and therefore "He sat down" [1:3; 10:12].

The Need for a Better Covenant

> The previous commandment was rejected because it was feeble and useless, for the Law made nothing perfect ... For if that first [Covenant] had been faultless, then there would be no need to require a second. 7:18; 8:7

That is pretty strong language, but it is true. Although this specifically points to the Sinai Covenant, the Circumcision Covenant is also included. The Sinai Covenant is ineffective because it centers on the Law, which tells people what they ought to be like, but it has no power other than by threat to make them do it. As all Law does, it requires a system of penalties to compel people to do what is 'right, necessary, and safe' – and also a police force. Just look at the resistance to the speeding or the seat-belt legislation of today.

However even the Circumcision Covenant is under the same condemnation, not because it is founded on Law (it is founded on grace and Abraham's faith), but because it speaks of a connection with God which could only anticipate a more full relationship. Yes, Abraham does have a real connection with Jehovah, as we have seen, and yet it is not the true oneness which that Covenant could describe only as an ideal. Although we are not in heaven yet, still, with the Spirit living in us, with our being joined to Jesus as a Body is joined to the Head, with our adoption (both Jew and non-Jew) as Children of God, with a right of access not available before [10:19], and with forgiveness as a completed fact [8:12], the 'New' Covenant is "a better Covenant, which is established on better promises" [8:6].

The Better High Priest/ *GO'EL*

Even the 'Old' Covenant priesthood stands under the condemnation of being weak and useless, not because the priests were not dedicated, but because by their fallen humanity, they were part of the problem: "there were many priests, because they were hindered by death from continuing ... those high priests, daily offer up sacrifices, first for [their] own sins and then for the people's" [7:23, 27].

So a more effective High Priest is needed: "because He continues forever, He has an unchangeable priesthood ... since He always lives to intercede for them ... holy, innocent, undefiled, separate from sinners, and exalted above the heavens" [7:24-26]. This High Priest steps in like

Melchizedek who had appeared suddenly, "without father nor mother nor genealogy nor beginning of days nor end of life, but made like the Son of God he remains a priest continually" [7:3]. Unlike the 'Old' Covenant's priests who assumed office simply by their family birth, this High Priest is personally, specifically and permanently authorized by God, Whose "word of the oath, sworn after the Law, appoints the Son Who has been consecrated forever" [7:28, see vv 20-21].

Yet, as a High Priest must be, He cannot be so remote that He is out of touch with humanity:

> Since the children participate [KOINONIA] in flesh and blood, He Himself likewise shared the same things, that through death He might nullify him who had the power of death, that is, the devil, ... Therefore, in everything He had to be made like His brethren, that He might be a merciful and faithful High Priest before God, to atone for the sins of the People. For in that He Himself has suffered, being tempted, He is able to help those who are tempted. 2:14-18

And therefore He is approachable:

> Since then we have a great High Priest Who has passed through the heavens, Jesus, the Son of God, let us hold fast the confession. For we have not a High Priest Who is unable to sympathize with our weaknesses, but One Who in every respect has been tempted like we are, yet without sin. Let us therefore with confidence draw near to the throne of grace, that we may receive mercy and find grace to help in time of need. 4:14-16

And this High Priest goes right to the top: "Who has sat down at the right hand of the throne of the Majesty in the heavens" [8:1]; "For Christ has not entered the Holies made with hands – copies of the true – , but into heaven itself, now to appear in God's presence for us" [9:24].

The Better Sacrifice

"Almost everything is cleansed by Blood according to the law, and without the shedding of Blood there is no forgiveness" [9:22] – there is a certain bewilderment here: on the one hand, the ritual structure to deal with sin is Jehovah-designed, yet on the other hand is its foundational ineffectiveness:

> Every priest stands day by day ministering and often offering the same sacrifices, which can never take away sins... For the Law ... with these same sacrifices, which they offer continually year by year, can never make those who approach perfect... But in [those sacrifices] is a reminder of sins year by year. For it is impossible for the Blood of bulls and goats to take away sins. . 10:11, 1, 3-4

But then, there is no normal Blood on earth which could do the task. It would take a remarkable sacrifice, a sacrifice so complete which once done, all would be finished, rather than an endlessly repeating cycle from "since the foundation of the world" [9:26]. It would take One "Who through the eternal Spirit offered Himself without spot to God" [9:14], Who "with His own Blood entered the Holies once for all, having obtained eternal redemption" [9:12], Who "sanctified through the sacrifice of the Body of Jesus Christ once for all" [10:10] – "For by one sacrifice He has perfected forever those who are being sanctified" [10:14].

It would take the Blood of God as well as Man to accomplish this task; it would take the Body of the 'New' Covenant Himself to be the perfect sacrifice. Because He has come, "by so much more Jesus has become the Guarantee of a better Covenant" [7:22], "the Mediator of the new Covenant" [12:24]. Having this concrete pledge in hand,

> having boldness to enter the Holies by the Blood of Jesus, (where) He consecrated for us a new and living way through the veil, which is His Flesh, and having a High Priest over the House of God, let us approach with a true heart in full assurance of faith, having our hearts sprinkled from an evil conscience and our bodies washed with clean Water. 10:19-22

D. The Minor Letters

James

St James touches on Covenant, but really does not say that much directly. There are a couple of items, though, that are of side interest: "Mercy triumphs over judgment" [2:13] can call to mind the dialogue between Jehovah and Abraham in regard to Sodom and Gomorrah, where 'justice' bent over backwards in favor of 'mercy', as well as the Cross, where justice is turned inside out for the sake of mercy (those who deserve punishment receive the reward, He Who deserves the reward receives the punishment).

Also his concern about partiality [2:8-9] and the arrogance of the rich [4:1-6] echoes many of the prophets, and in Covenant terms these things tearing apart the oneness in Covenant which his readers have, breaking the Old Law [2:10] but also the 'New' Commandment of Jesus ("as I have loved you").

His concern that works are necessary [2:14-20; "by works faith was made perfect" v 22] does not earn high marks with Martin Luther, who strongly emphasized "He who through faith [alone] is righteous shall live" [Romans 1:17]. However James' point is a truism: faith that does not affect Life ('works') is really no faith at all – faith is always in response to a promise, and if one operates as if the promise and God's plan do not exist, then the faith is merely lip service. Jesus would concur: "Not everyone who says to Me, 'Lord, Lord,' shall enter the Kingdom of Heaven, but he who does the will of My Father in heaven" [Matthew 7:21].

Peter

St Peter also does not specifically refer to Covenant, although he does emphasize key 'New' Covenant concepts, for example, "[God] has called us by Glory and virtue," and given "His very great and precious Promises," through which we "participate (*KOINONIA*) in the Divine Nature" [II,1:3-4]. In this we are "begotten into a living hope through the resurrection of Jesus Christ" [I,1:3], "baptism ... also now saves us ... through the resurrection of Jesus Christ, Who is at God's right hand" [I, 3:21-22]; "begotten, not of perishable seed, but of imperishable, through the living and enduring Word of God" [I,1:23].

We have been chosen "according to the foreknowledge of God the Father, in the sanctification of the Spirit, into obedience and the sprinkling of the Blood of Jesus Christ" [I,1:2]; redeemed not with gold or silver, "but with the precious Blood of Christ, as of a Lamb without blemish or defect. He was predestined before the creation of the world, but was revealed in these last times for your sake" [I,1:18-20]. Echoing John the Baptist's multi-concept "Lamb of God Who takes away the sin of the world" [John 1:29], the "Lamb" seems to especially hint of the *Passover* Lamb, which is chosen, then kept for four days, and whose Blood literally redeemed the firstborn from death [Exodus 12].

He "died for sins once for all, the righteous for the unrighteous, to bring you to God" [I,3:18], so

> Come to Him, to that Living Stone rejected by men but in God's sight chosen and precious; and you also as living stones be built into a spiritual house, to be a holy priesthood, to offer spiritual sacrifices acceptable to God through Jesus Christ.   I,2:4-5

John's Letters

> That Which was from the beginning, Which we have heard, Which we have seen with our eyes, Which we have looked upon, and our hands have handled, concerning the Word of Life – the Life was manifested, and we have seen, and bear witness, and proclaim to you that Life Eternal which was with the Father and was manifested to us – that Which we have seen and heard we declare to you, that you also may have fellowship [*KOINONIA*] with us; and indeed our fellowship [*KOINONIA*] is with the Father and with His Son Jesus Christ. These things we write to you that your joy may be full.   I,1:1-4

Here is a powerful emphasis on Jesus (the 'New' Covenant)'s tangible reality – this is no "cleverly devised myth" [II Peter 1:16]! In the emphasis on Life, which in the Old Testament is 'Blood/Soul,' there is a continuity of thought between the Covenants (especially of Him Who is Life Himself [John 11:25; 14:6]) and in the "Advocate with the Father, Jesus Christ the Righteous – He Himself is the atoning Sacrifice for our sins, and not only for ours but also for the sins of the whole world" [I,2:1-2], "the Blood of Jesus Christ His Son cleanses us from all sin" [I, 1:7], the *GO'EL* has been at work for our sakes.

Again the concrete "we have seen and testify": "the Father has sent the Son as Savior of the world" [I, 4:14], and "God gave us eternal Life, and this Life is in His Son – whoever has the Son has Life" [I, 5:11-12]. This solid evidence means that "you who believe in the Name of the Son of God, ... you can know that you have eternal Life" [I, 5:13] – which means, "God abides in [you], and [you] in God" [I, 4:15].

"We have known and believed the Love [*AGAPE*] which God has for us. God is Love [*AGAPE*], and he who abides in Love [*AGAPE*] abides in God, and God in him" [I, 4:16]; "We know Love [*AGAPE*], because He laid down His Life for us" [I,3:16] – throughout his letters, exclusively using the word which is reshaped by the Christian community, *AGAPE*, John echoes Exodus 34:6, where Jehovah includes in His definition of His Glory, "abounding in *HESED*," the 'Old' Covenant's powerfully encompassing word for Love. This is that dependable, steadfast, faithful, enduring Love which is constantly demonstrated even when Israel is so consistently rebellious.

If the unity of the Life/Blood indeed circulates through us, then like Abraham in regard to Sodom and Gomorrah, God's Love in us must escape beyond us: "Beloved [*AGAPE*], let us Love [*AGAPE*] one another, for Love [*AGAPE*] is of God; and everyone who Loves [*AGAPE*] is born of God and knows God" [I, 4:7]. It is a unique and precious confirmation of what has happened within us: "We know that we have passed from death to Life, because we Love [*AGAPE*] the brethren" [I,3:14]. This Covenant flow is empowered because "we know that we abide in Him, and He in us, because He has given us of His Spirit" [I,3:13].

Jude

St Jude does not appear to have anything unique in regard to Covenant.

E. Revelation

Numbers

There are fifty-four instances of *'seven'* in Revelation, six in 1:20. In the Greek there is no dual meaning to the number as there is in the Hebrew, but if John's audience is immersed in the Old Testament culture, it is likely that the number would have flagged their attention anyway, that here could be a signal to remind them that Covenant is at work (as the repetition of *seven* at the fall of Jericho may have done [Joshua 6:2-8]). It is of interest that *seven* is even connected to the "great red dragon" and the "beast" [12:3; 13:1], which may indicate that there is a Satanic counterfeit to Covenant, which of course will ultimately fail, but not without first causing a lot of distress to those within Jehovah's Covenant.

This raises the question as to whether the numbers in Revelation are symbolic or literal. For instance, the "one hundred and forty-four thousand" redeemed [7:4; 14:1, 3] could be broken figuratively to twelve times twelve, times ten to the third power. 'Twelve' not only reflects the twelve tribes of Abraham's descendants, but here it also is the symbol of God's faithful ones; 'ten' is the symbol of completion, and in Hebrew, something repeated three times often ascends the scale to comparative then to superlative (for example, "Holy, Holy, Holy" = "Holy, Holier, Holiest" [4:8; Isaiah 6:3]).

So rather than supplying a precise number, God may be indicating that absolutely completely, *all* God's faithful People in each tribe (twelve thousand [7:5-8]) will be sealed and saved – none lost, none forgotten, none overlooked. When the host "which no man could number" [7:9] is then referred to, it echoes St Paul's distinction between "the Jew first and also the Greek (non-Jew)" [Acts 13:46; Romans 1:16; 2:9-10] and Jesus' instruction when He sends the disciples out in Matthew 10:5-6, "Go nowhere among the nations, and enter no town of the Samaritans, but go rather to the lost sheep of the house of Israel" – there is an eternal special uniqueness to God's "Firstborn," Israel [Exodus 4:22], yet not to the exclusion of the nations (non-Jews).

Life/Blood and Judgment

In the ten plagues (SIGNs) in Egypt at the Exodus, Blood figures prominently in terms both of salvation (for the follower of Jehovah) and of judgment (for those who rebel against His will). There, the water turned to Blood may have been, among other things, a symbol of the Blood of God's People shed under Pharaoh's persecution, the Blood crying for justice as Abel's had [Genesis 4:10] – reassurance to the suffering Israelite, and judgment against the oppressor. That pattern seems to be repeated here.

In Revelation when the first two of the *seven* angels with the *seven* trumpets sound their instruments: "hail and fire followed, mingled with Blood, ... and a third of the sea became Blood" [8:7-8]; when the great winepress of the wrath of God is "trampled ... Blood came out of the winepress, up to the horses' bridles, for one thousand six hundred furlongs" [14:19-20]; when the angels with the bowls of God's wrath poured out the second and third bowls, "the sea ... became Blood as of a dead man ... the rivers and springs of water ... became Blood" [16:3-4]. Here it is stated as to why, "they have shed the Blood of saints and prophets, and You have given them Blood to drink – it is what they deserve" [16:6].

The woman, "Babylon the Great," is "drunk from the Blood of the saints and from the Blood of the martyrs of Jesus" [17:6], "in her was found the Blood of prophets and saints, and of all who were slain on the earth" [18:24], but then the great multitude in heaven cries out, because the *GO'EL* has stepped in, "Alleluia! Salvation and glory and honor and power be to the Lord our God! For true and righteous are His judgments, because He has judged the great prostitute who corrupted the earth with her fornication; and He has avenged the Blood of His servants at her hand" [19:1-2].

Life/Blood and Salvation

I saw ... a Lamb standing as though it had been slain, ... He came and took the scroll out of the right hand of Him Who is sitting on the throne. ... And they sang a new song, saying: "You are worthy...; because You were slain, and have redeemed us to God by Your Blood out of every tribe and tongue and people and nation, and have made us kings and priests to our God" 5:6-7, 9-10

... from Jesus Christ, the faithful Witness, the Firstborn from the dead, and the Ruler over the kings of the earth. To the One loving us and having washed us from our sins in His Blood, and has made us kings and priests to His God and Father, to Him be Glory and dominion forever and ever. Amen. 1:5-6; also 7:13-14

I heard a loud voice saying in heaven, "Now has come the salvation, the power, and the Kingdom of our God, and the authority of His Christ, because the accuser of our brothers, who accused them before our God day and night, has been thrown down. They overcame him by the Blood of the Lamb and by the word of their witness, and they did not love their Souls/lives even to death." 12:10-11

I saw heaven opened, and behold, a white horse, and He Who sat on it was called Faithful and True ... He was clothed with a robe dipped in Blood, and His Name is called The Word of God. 19:11, 13

The Living Waters and Salvation

The culmination of the 'Living Waters' is in the heavenly city: "the Lamb in the midst of the throne will shepherd them and lead them to Living Fountains of Waters" [7:17]; "to him who thirsts I will freely give of the Fountain of the Water of Life" [21:6]; "He showed me a pure river of the Water of Life, clear as crystal, coming out from the throne of God and of the Lamb. In the midst of its street, and on either side of the river, was the Tree of Life ... The leaves of the Tree were for the healing of the nations" [22:1-2].

John in his Gospel [7:38-39] ties "out of his heart shall flow rivers of Living Water" to the gift of the Holy Spirit, and in Revelation, the context of this 'Living Water' describes the culmination of Covenant as a personal companionship and oneness with Jehovah forever:

> They are before God's throne, and serve Him day and night in His temple. He who sits on the throne will dwell among them. They shall hunger no more nor thirst anymore; the sun shall not strike them, nor any heat; the Lamb ... will lead them to Living Fountains of Waters and God will wipe away every tear from their eyes.　　　　7:15-17

> Behold, God's dwelling is with men: He will dwell with them, and they shall be His People; God Himself will be with them and be their God. God will wipe away every tear from their eyes; death shall be no more, nor grief, nor crying, nor pain any longer, for the former things have passed away... To the thirsty I will freely give from the Fountain of the Water of Life. He who overcomes shall inherit all things, and I will be his God and he shall be My son.　　　　21:3-4, 7

XV. Epilogue

This is no conclusion, because all which can be said about God's Covenant has not been said. This is no summation, because there is so much of Covenant yet to be learned. Epilogue, however, is "A short addition or concluding section at the end of a literary work, often dealing with the future of its characters."[229] Covenant lives on forever, and if this book sparks further dialogue and discovery, then perhaps 'Epilogue' is indeed a fitting title to this section.

The Panorama of Blood-Covenant

Our western culture has very little familiarity with Covenant. We do have an accumulation of various bits of information, although one must ask whether everything which has called itself Covenant is indeed that relationship, or whether it has only borrowed from Covenant, hoping to tap into its power.

Covenant encompasses humanity. It is there at the Creation of mankind; it is there between Jehovah and Abraham, earning the man the unique title, "the Friend of God"; it is there between Jonathan and David, because of Love "as his own Soul"; it is there when Covenant itself walked in Human Flesh in Jesus; and it is the crown for all believers on the Last Day. It is found in cultures around the world. It is a most profound relationship, unmatched by normal friendships, even by familial ties.

Covenant is precious. It speaks of utter commitment to the Covenant-partner, of utter dependability, and of the oneness of the Life/Blood which flows between the participants of Covenant. It speaks of comfort, hope, strength, protection and self-giving. It speaks of Glory: goodness, grace, mercy, *HESED*, faithfulness, forgiveness and justice.

Covenant is serious. It declares the horror of the culture when even human-to-human Covenant is broken; of death and of the Life/Blood poured out, as in the gutter at the Altar of Sacrifice under the 'Old' Covenant'; and of what happens when Jehovah Himself breaks Covenant.

Covenant is eternal. It does not cease on the Last Day. Jesus, the 'New' Covenant, does not become obsolete in the age to come, but rather He will always be the point of unity which we have with Jehovah forever.

The Tension over Covenant

Perhaps the tension in regard to interpreting Covenant may be (over-)simplified in this way: is Covenant merely a collection of duties, or is it a personal relationship of deep Love within which there is duty? If it is the first alternative, then Covenant is just another name for 'contract,' 'treaty,' or 'transaction' – benefit given and benefit taken. This requires no real personal involvement, no core-of-being involvement. Although it may mean well, and may actually be done for the welfare of the other, one does not really have to deeply Love the other – it is merely a business deal of some sort, perhaps with a bit more 'teeth' to it.

If, on the other hand, Covenant is a personal relationship of deep Love within which there is duty, the main focus of Covenant is the bond between two who are intent on making concrete this relationship. The (legal) stipulations are simply the tool of *Love, self-imposed* to indicate the degree to which one will go for the sake of the other, much on the same lines as the traditional marriage vow. However, using marriage as the example, should the relationship degrade to simply the legal aspect, it is commonly recognized that 'that's not what marriage is supposed to be about' – there is an important aspect which has been lost, since the relationship is supposed to be centrally about Love.

One can see the drift into such a situation. The Torah includes so much more than just commandment since it describes the beginnings of Covenant as well as Jehovah's focus concerning his Glory, yet it has gradually lost the aspect of the loving bond which God seeks with His creature (first indicated by His coming "at the cool of the day" to Adam and Eve; articulated in His Covenant with Abraham; and which will finally be fully demonstrated in His dwelling among His People "after those days").

Instead, the commandment of the Law has taken over. It is of interest to note how often Jesus refuses to accept the Law as the governing principle of man's relationship to Jehovah, as particularly demonstrated in His refusal to follow the *Sabbath* 'laws' or, rather, the rabbinical redefinitions of the Law, in favor of genuine concern for another person – "as I have loved you." Paul also spends a lot of time in his letters, particularly in Galatians, identifying that the Law is not the pivot around which God wants our relationship to turn.

Yes, duty has its place as the tool of Love, but not to hijack the purpose of Covenant. This is no business deal! Covenant is an expression of Jehovah's heart, a deep and *vulnerable* yearning to have oneness with His creature, the goal of which will be achieved, finally, on the Last Day – that is the motivation and the end product of Covenant. He deliberately constructs Covenant to make Himself vulnerable even to the point of His own death; and throughout the centuries with Israel, He never turns His back on Covenant, always keeping a remnant even during the darkest hours, never walking away from His Promises. Then when He finally from His side does break Covenant, it is only to initiate a 'New' and 'better' Covenant – even though, by His own rules, He dies. Yet He will never leave a gap which is not covered by Covenant, so that in the very moment of breaking the 'Old' Covenant, He initiates the 'New.'

When Jehovah must act because of Israel's breaking of Covenant, although the punishments may need to be severe, still His hand is shackled because of *His* keeping of Covenant. Despite what the rebellions of Israel demand (and what some extremists may think really should have been done), He deflects the deserved complete annihilation. As terrible as the captivities are, as terrible as the persecutions through the centuries are, Israel survives, the remnant has been kept.

This is no contract basis; this is a relationship which springs from Jehovah's heart, powerfully described in the argument between Him (His justice) and Abraham (God's Love) over Sodom and Gomorrah – the willingness of God to bend justice almost to the breaking point for the sake of His Love, despite the rampant rebellion surrounding the situation. Jehovah's Covenant must and does fall within this context of such Love even for enemies (as St Paul identifies so powerfully in Romans 5) – Covenant is about Love, or better, Covenant is about the Glory of God.

What's in Your *Veins?*

The point of the Bible is not to be merely a history book, whether the history of God's People, or the history of the concept of Covenant. The purpose and goal are to invite us, its readers, into this Covenant which has been so vividly displayed. It calls us into the flow of Life which has only been intensified in the 'New' Covenant by the indwelling of the Holy Spirit and by the unity Jesus gives us in sharing His own Body and Blood with us. It summons us to recognize and to experience the Glory of God: His goodness, grace, mercy and *HESED* within the heartbeat of a unique relationship. It warns us to take this relationship with utmost seriousness because God does. It bids us to grab hold of this bond designed from before the beginning of the world and which will remain even when this world is no more – a bond which can only mean Life and the companionship of Jehovah forever.

> Now the God of peace Who, by the Blood of the eternal Covenant, brought from the dead the great Shepherd of the sheep, our Lord Jesus, equip you in every good work in order that you may do His will, doing in you what is pleasing in His sight, through Jesus Christ; to Whom be Glory for ever and ever. Amen.   Hebrews 13:20-21

Endnotes

[1] Fred Handschumacher, "Why The Blood Covenant Has Lost Its Meaning," Rock of Offense "Foundational Topic" [http://www.rockofoffence.com/myst6.html]:

> Revival Among the African Zulus
> Recently, I was listening to a seminar given by Malcolm Smith, author of the book, "Blood Brothers in Christ." ... I recognized that he was speaking on the subject of the blood covenant and decided to stop and listen. Malcolm told of an experience he had while in Africa. He had traveled to Africa to do some evangelistic work. Apparently, someone ask [sic] him to speak to a tribe of Zulus, but time would not allow him to do so. Instead of speaking to the Zulus directly, Malcolm made a cassette tape on the subject of the gospel of Jesus Christ, teaching it within the framework of the blood covenant. Being an African tribe, the Zulus were very familiar with the blood covenant since it was part of their culture. When these tribes got hold of the Gospel and understood it as a blood covenant, revival began to break out. On a return trip at a later date, much to his surprise, Malcolm learned that as a result of this cassette tape, whole Zulu tribes in some areas had received the gospel and accepted Jesus Christ. What made the difference in this situation? Other missionaries had preached the Gospel to the Zulus with little success. Conveying the Gospel in the framework of the blood covenant was the reason Malcolm had been successful when other missionaries before had failed. It made all the difference. The Gospel of Christ cannot be fully understood apart from a blood covenant mentality. The whole message of the Gospel is firmly grounded in blood covenant terminology. In this area, the Zulus have a big advantage over the church in modern America.

[2] Berthold von Schenk, *The Presence* (New York: Ernst Kaufman, Inc., 1945), 41.

[3] H. Clay Trumbull, THE BLOOD COVENANT: *A Primitive Rite and Its Bearing on Scripture* (Reprint Publisher: Kirkwood, Mo.: Impact Christian Books, 1975); First Edition Preface dated August 14, 1885; Second Edition Preface dated January 30, 1893.

[4] Walter R. Roehrs, "Divine Covenants: Their Structure and Function," *Concordia Journal* 1/1988, 12.

[5] Do we really know what can be 'seen' spiritually? Perhaps what we call 'qualities,' especially when it comes to God, rather than depending on history to make them visible, in the heavenly sphere may indeed have 'visible' forms of their own. Even Jehovah, although an undefinable spirit in this universe, manifests Himself in a concrete way a number of times throughout the Old Testament.

In Proverbs, particularly chapter 8, is wisdom merely personified or is there actually a spiritual concreteness to its existence? Just what are the "seven spirits" before the throne of the Lamb in Revelation 1:4; 3:1;

> From the throne proceeded lightnings, thunderings, and voices. Seven lamps of fire were burning before the throne, which are the seven Spirits of God.   4:5

> I looked, and behold, in the midst of the throne ... stood a Lamb as though it had been slain, having seven horns and seven eyes, which are the seven Spirits of God sent out into all the earth.   5:6

Yet in Exodus 33, the Lord describes first His goodness, which is basically the same word which reverberates throughout Genesis 1. Blood Covenant seems to be in the background of the creation of Adam, and is in evidence in the sacrifice of the animal which covers the sin of this fallen man in Genesis 3:21. Grace and mercy make their first appearance in man's creation, as well as immediately following the fall into sin, in the choosing of Abraham, and in the circumcision of the helpless (the infant and the slave). The match between God's description of His Glory and His activity throughout the first book of the Bible is profound.

Obviously the "qualities," whether spiritually visible entities or not, cannot be separate from how Jehovah acts – similar to how "faith without works is dead" [James 2:17]. It would seem a false dichotomy to separate them. For humanity, one cannot divorce the 'qualities' from how they are 'fleshed out' in this world, the greatest example being Jesus Himself, where "we have seen His Glory, the Glory of the only begotten of the Father, full of grace and truth" [John 1: 17] – not as a static display, but as the dynamic interaction of the Creator with His creatures.

[6] Martin Luther, "The Treatise on the New Testament, that is, the Holy Mass" (1520), in *Luther's Works*, Vol 35 (*Word and Sacrament I*), gen. ed. Helmut T. Lehmann, (Philadelphia: Muhlenberg Press, 1960), 82.

[7] Genesis 2:7 ... and man became a living *soul* [NEPHESH].
Genesis 9:4 You shall not eat flesh with its *life* [NEPHESH], that is, its Blood.
Genesis 23:8 ... If it be your *mind* [NEPHESH] that I should bury my dead ...
Exodus 15:9 The enemy said, '... My *desire* [NEPHESH] shall be satisfied ...'
Exodus 23:9 ... you know the *heart* [NEPHESH] of a stranger, you were strangers ...
Numbers 6:6 ... he shall not go near a dead *body* [NEPHESH].
Numbers 30:6 ... by which she bound *herself* [NEPHESH]
Judges 18:25 ... lest *angry* [NEPHESH – "soul-ish"? perhaps in the New Testament negative sense of "the Flesh"?] men fall upon you, and you lose your *life* [NEPHESH], with the *lives* [NEPHESH] of your household!

[8] Gary Piltingsrud. A friend's succinct description.

[9] Trumbull, 38.

[10] Therefore the variety of handshake symbolisms in our culture, from the "unbreakable" deal to the common greeting, to the expression of solidarity, as Trumbull points out, p 340:

> So simple a matter as the clasping of hands in token of covenant fidelity, is explicable, in its universality, only as a vestige of the primitive custom of joining pierced hands in the covenant of blood-friendship.... But, even where hand clasping is unknown in salutation, it is recognized as a symbol of the closest friendship. Thus, for example, among tribes of North American Indians where nose-rubbing is the mode of salutation, there is, in their widely diffused sign language, the sign of clasped, or inter-locked, hands, as indicative of friendship and union....In the Society Islands, the clasping of hands marks the marriage union, and marks a loving union between two brothers in arms; although it has no place in ordinary greetings...

[11] Trumbull, 235, footnote.

[12] *Ibid*, 38.

[13] *Ibid*, 11f.

[14] *Ibid*, 77, 194-196.

[15] *Ibid*, 191-192, 197.

[16] See "IV. The Covenant Mosaic, A. The Oath-To 'Seven' Oneself."

[17] *Numbers*, in *The Pulpit Commentary*, ed. H.D.M. Spence and Joseph S. Exell, (NY, NY: Funk & Wagnalls Company, 1950), 240.

[18] Note Hebrews 9:13-14:

> For if the Blood of bulls and goats and the ashes of a heifer, sprinkling the unclean, sanctifies for the purifying of the flesh, how much more shall the Blood of Christ, Who through the eternal Spirit offered Himself without spot to God, cleanse your conscience from dead works to serve the living God?

[19] Gerhard Kittel and Gerhard Friedrich, ed., *Theological Dictionary of the New Testament*, volume II (Grand Rapids, MI: Wm. B. Eerdmans Publishing Co., 1966), 106-134.

[20] *Ibid*, 112.

[21] Trumbull, 56.

[22] *Concordia Self-Study Bible (New International Version)*, Robert Hoerber, gen. ed. (St. Louis: Concordia Publishing House, 1986).

[23] See Trumbull, 25-26, 28; also 36-37. The chief is Itsi, later Ngalyema.

[24] James Lindemann, unpublished sermon, "The Circumcision and Name Day of Jesus," January 1, 1995.

[25] Trumbull, 270:

> From that hour the hearts of David and Jonathan were as one. Jonathan could turn away from father and mother, and could repress all personal ambition, and all purely selfish longings, in proof of his loving fidelity to him who was dear to him as his own blood. His love for David was "wonderful, passing the love of women."

[26] *Ibid*, 10.

[27] *Ibid*, 46.

[28] Lori Macintosh, a friend who has Native American background; the story was related in personal conversation.

[29] Trumbull, 10, 56.

[30] *Ibid*, 56.

[31] *Ibid*, 6.

[32] *Ibid*, 27-28.

[33] *Ibid*, 314.

[34] *Ibid*, 334-335.

35 R. Scott Clark, "A Contemporary Reformed Defense of Infant Baptism."

36 *Joshua,* in *The Pulpit Commentary,* ed. H.D.M. Spence and Joseph S. Exell, (NY, NY: Funk & Wagnalls Company, 1950), 98.

37 R Laird Harris, *Theological Wordbook of the Old Testament,* vol II (Chicago: Moody Press, 1981), 899-900.

38 In 1957, market researcher James Vicary claimed that quickly flashing messages on a movie screen, in Fort Lee, New Jersey, had influenced people to purchase more food and drinks. Vicary coined the term *subliminal advertising* and formed the Subliminal Projection Company based on a six-week test. Vicary claimed that during the presentation of the movie *Picnic* he used a tachistoscope to project the words "Drink Coca-Cola" and "Hungry? Eat popcorn" for 1/3000 of a second at five-second intervals. Vicary asserted that during the test, sales of popcorn and Coke in that New Jersey theater increased 57.8 percent and 18.1 percent respectively. [http://en.wikipedia.org/wiki/Subliminal_message#_ref-5].

39 Circumcision was 1 year old when Isaac was circumcised on the eighth day;
    Isaac was 60 at the birth of Jacob (Genesis 25:26);
    Jacob was 130 upon entering Egypt (Genesis 47:9);
    Israel would be "enslaved and mistreated four hundred years" in Egypt (Genesis 15:13; Acts 7:6);
    = just shy of 600 years
Galatians 3:16-17 seems to indicate 430 years from Abraham whereas Exodus 12:40-41 speaks of 430 years in Egypt (which probably included Joseph's thirty years; see endnote 94).

40 Trumbull, 63-65.

41 Jean-Jacques Von Allmen, *The Lord's Supper, Ecumenical Studies in Worship* No. 19 (Richmond, Virginia: John Knox Press, 1969), 23-24.

42 Trumbull, 235-236.

43 Harris, *Wordbook,* vol I, 363-364.

44 A primitive root: to tie, physically (gird, confine, compact) or mentally (in love, league); Harris, *Wordbook,* vol II, 818:

> Basically this root denotes binding or tying something to something. Its synonyms are `anad` 'bind' (occurs only twice, see Pr 6:21), `asar` 'bind, tie up with a rope or thicker object,' *habash* 'to wrap with a wide object.' Synonyms to the secondary meaning (conspire) are *nabal* 'to show oneself deceitful,' and *karat berit* 'to make a pact.' Our root (with the derivatives listed) occurs sixty times.

45 Trumbull, 6-7,232-234, 237; also 236:

> The Egyptian amulet of blood-friendship was red, as representing the blood of the gods. The Egyptian word for "red," sometimes stood for "blood." The sacred directions in the Book of the Dead were written in red, hence follows our word "rubrics." The Rabbis say that, when persecution forbade the wearing of the phylacteries with safety, a red thread might be substituted for this token of the covenant with the Lord. It was a red thread which Joshua [sic] gave to Rahab as a

token of her covenant relations with the people of the Lord. The red thread, in China, to-day, as has been already shown, binds the double cup, from which the bride and bridegroom drink their covenant draught of "wedding wine"; as if in symbolism of the covenant of blood. And it is a red thread which in India...is used to bind a sacred amulet around the arm or the neck.

[46] *Ibid*, 232.

[47] *Ibid*, 65ff; from this same section:

> ... [I]n India, where blood-shedding is peculiarly objectionable, the gift and acceptance of a bracelet is an ancient covenant-tie, seemingly akin to blood-brotherhood. Of this custom, an Indian authority says: "Amongst the rajput races of India the women adopt a brother by the gift of a bracelet.... The adopted brother may hazard his life in his adopted sister's cause, and yet never receive a mite in reward; for he cannot even see the fair object, who, as brother of her adoption, has constituted him her defender."...
>
> In the Norseland, an oath of fidelity was taken on a ring, or a bracelet, kept in the temple of the gods; and the gift and acceptance of a bracelet, or a ring, was a common symbol of a covenant of fidelity....
>
> It would...seem, that from this root-idea of the binding force of an endless covenant, symbolized in that form, ...of the bracelet, the armlet, the ring, -- there has come down to us the use of the wedding-ring, or the wedding-bracelet, and of the signet-ring as the seal of the most sacred covenants. The signet-ring appears in earliest history. When Pharaoh would exalt Joseph..., "Pharaoh took off his ring from his hand, and put it on Joseph's hand.".... ...
>
> That a ring, or a circlet, worn around a thumb, or a finger, or an arm, in token of an endless covenant between its giver and receiver, has been looked upon, in all ages, as the symbol of an inter-union of the lives thereby brought together, is unmistakable; whether the covenanting life-blood be drawn for such intercommingling, directly from the member so encircled, or not.
>
> It is not improbable, indeed, that the armlets, or bracelets, which were found on the arms of Oriental kings, and of Oriental divinities as well, were intended to indicate, or to symbolize, the personal inter-union claimed to exist between those kings and divinities. Thus the armlet worn by Thotmes III...bears the cartouche of the King, having on it his sacred name, with its reference to his inter-union with his god. It was much the same in Nineveh....

Further, in regard to the נזם [*NEZEM* - nose-ring], pp 165-166:

> An Oriental scholar has called attention to the origin of the nose-ring, so commonly worn in India, as described in the Hindoo Paga-Vatham. The story runs, that at the incarnation of Vishnoo as Krishna, the holy child's life was sought, and his mother exchanged her infant for the child of another woman, in order for his protection. In doing so, she "bored a hole in the nose of her infant, and put a ring into it as an impediment and a sign. The blood which came from the wound was as a sacrifice to prevent him from falling into the hand of his enemies." And, to this day, the nose-ring has two names, indicative of its two-fold purpose. "The first [name] is *nate-kaddan*, which signifies 'the obligation or debt a person is under by a vow'; the second [name] is *mooka-taddi*, literally 'nose-

impediment or hindrance,' that is, to sickness or death". The child's blood is given in covenant obligation to the gods, and the nose-ring is the token of the covenant-obligation, and a pledge of protected life. When a Hindoo youth who has worn a nose-ring would remove it, on the occasion of his marriage, he must do so with formal ceremonies at the temple, and by the use of a liquid "which represents blood," composed of saffron, of lime, and of water.

[48] *Ibid*, 238.

[49] *1 Samuel*, in *The Pulpit Commentary*, ed. H.D.M. Spence and Joseph S. Exell, (NY, NY: Funk & Wagnalls Company, 1950), 99.

[50] It is curious, though, that as the fictional Vampire legend was formulated, where Blood would be so pivotal, the Cross – essentially the Blood of Jesus – would strike such terror in the Vampire.

[51] Trumbull, 355.

[52] *Ibid*, 340.

[53] *Ibid*, 335.

[54] The source for this information has been lost.

[55] Harris, *Wordbook*, vol II, 930-932.

[56] James Lindemann, *Living Waters – Baptism: From His Heart through Ours* (Lethbridge, Alberta: RFLindemann & Son, 2013), 138-39.

[57] Trumbull, 303-305.

[58] Harris, *Wordbook*, vol I, 426-427, on -כבד - [*KABED*].

[59] Also Exodus 29:22; Leviticus 3:4,10,15; 4:9; 7:4; 8:16,25; 9:10,19.

[60] Harris, *Wordbook*, vol II, 813.

[61] *Ibid*, vol I, 440-441:

> ... perhaps because of their density and color they were associated with the blood ...
>
> The remaining nine references all use kidneys as a symbol of the innermost being. ... In this usage it is frequently paralleled with heart (as it is at least once in Ugaritic). Jeremiah seems to be emphasizing this innermost idea when he says that the religion of the wicked is superficial, on their lips, but far from their kidneys (12:2). The idea that the wicked would prosper grieves the heart and kidneys of the psalmist (73:21), but they rejoice in the writer of Proverbs when his son speaks right (23:16). Five times in Jeremiah and Psalms the importance of inner religion is stressed when it is said that God tries the heart and the kidneys (Jer 11:20; etc.).

With the kidney's direct line off the Aorta, because of its appearance (noted above), and its production of urine, it obviously has a significant role the elimination of what is bad in the Blood. The smell of urine can be affected by dehydration, infections, foods, medicines, or problems in the body, and therefore it is sensitive to its world. And as anyone who has experienced a kidney stone can attest, like a conscience, it can create a terrible discomfort in a person.

[62] Dr. C. Matthew McMahon, "My Retraction: A 15 Year Reformed Baptist Turns Paedo-Baptist" (September, 2002), http://www.apuritansmind.com/Baptism/MyRetraction.htm.

[63] Dr. Greg L. Bahnsen, "Baptism: Its Meaning and Purpose"; http://www.cmfnow.com/articles/pt069.htm.

[64] George Kraus, "The Concept of Blood in the Holy Scriptures", unpublished paper dated "X Trinity 1973," 4.

[65] "Glory be to Jesus", Hymn, Translator, Edward Caswall.

[66] Trumbull, 259-263.

[67] Harris, *Wordbook*, vol I, 452-53.

[68] On the tenth (completion) day of the *seventh/oath* month is *the Day of Atonement*; on the '*seventh'/oath* month* later (the first month) on the tenth day the lambs for *the Passover* (on the fourteenth) are chosen – every 'seventh' month has a major celebration in regard to Israel's Covenant relationship with Jehovah and of His rescue of His People. Consider Hebrews 10:14.

*Note that when the Hebrew counts time, the current unit of time is considered the 'first' unit. So to the Hebrew, this month is the first month and the 'seventh' month from today is what we would call the 'sixth month.' So also a week from today we would call the seventh day, but the Hebrew would say it is the eighth day.

[69] ימ הכפרימ –*YOM HA-KIPPURIYM* – actually "*Day of the Atonements.*"

[70] *Leviticus*, Vol 2 in *The Pulpit Commentary*, ed. H.D.M. Spence and Joseph S. Exell, (NY, NY: Funk & Wagnalls Company, 1950), 3:

> The aspect under which atonement is presented here and elsewhere in the Old Testament is that of covering. But it is not the sin that is covered, but the sinner.... No longer being the object of wrath, he becomes at once an object of benevolence and mercy.

[71] זתזל- *Ibid*, 240:

> *Azazel* is a word softened (according to a not unusual custom) from *azalzel*, ...derived ultimately from *azal* (connected with the Arabic word *azala*, and meaning "removed"), but more immediately from the reduplicate form of that verb, *azazel*. The reduplication of the consonants...give the force of repetition, so that while *azal* means "removed", *azalzel* means "removed by a repetition of acts." *Azalzel*, or *azazel*, therefore, means "one who removes by a series of acts."

Since, although a different goat, it was the SAME Sin Offering as the goat that shed its Blood, this was the second "act" in the series of Atonement, as the Covenant with Abraham had had two parts.

[72] The Scapegoat was NOT given to Satan because he had nothing to do with Atonement; just like when the LORD talked about "ransom" and "redeem", it was not

from Satan, but from His Justice that held us in the prison of the penalty for our sins. Besides, the sacrifices were dedicated to Jehovah, never to Satan.

73 Harris, *Wordbook*, vol I, 716-717.

74 *Ibid*, 19:

> The NIV renders "fool" in Prov 1:7 with the footnote: "The Hebrew words rendered *fool* in Proverbs, and often elsewhere in the OT denote one who is morally deficient." Such a person is lacking in sense and is generally corrupt....
>
> As indicated, *'ewil* primarily refers to moral perversion of insolence, to what is sinful rather than to mental stupidity. This kind of a fool despises wisdom and is impatient with discipline. He who does not fear God is a fool and will be unable to grasp wisdom or benefit from godly discipline (Prov 1:7)....
>
> This moral perversion is seen in the statement, "Fools mock at guilt: (Prov 14:9). The word for guilt can also mean the trespass offering (Lev 5). Thus the fool scorns and despises restitution for the injuries and sins he commits (NIV, "Mock at making amends for sin"). He flouts his responsibility to the community as a responsible person...

75 *Ibid*, 192 (English is substituted for the Hebrew).

76 This subject is discussed in more detail in the author's book, *In the Image of God: Male and Female He Created Them*.

77 Fr. John S. Romanides, "Original Sin According to St. Paul" in *St. Vladimir's Seminary Quarterly* Vol. IV, Nos. 1 and 2, 1955-6. See the author's website at http://www.romanity.org.

78 To further the image, if another diver attached his own lifeline to the first diver, the second would die by giving his life to the first. That is exactly what Jesus did for us.

79 "*keep* the Garden" [Genesis 2:15]; "I ... will *keep* you in all the places where you go" [Genesis 28:15]; "feed and *keep* your flock" [Genesis 30:31]; "*keep* the feast of unleavened bread" [Exodus 12:17]; "*keep* my statutes and judgments" [Leviticus 18:5].

80 Trumbull, 110-12:

> For example, in an inscription from the Egyptian monuments, the original of which dates back to the early days of Moses, there is a reference to a then ancient legend of the rebellion of mankind against the gods; of an edict of destruction against the human race, and of a divine interposition for the rescue of the doomed peoples. In that legend, a prominent part is given to human blood, mingled with the juice of mandrakes – instead of wine – prepared as a drink of the gods, and afterwards poured out again to overflow and revivify all the earth. And the ancient text which records this legend, affirms that it was in conjunction with these events that there was the beginning of sacrifices in the world.
>
> An early American legend has points of remarkable correspondence with this one from ancient Egypt. It relates, as does that, to a pre-historic destruction of the race, and to its re-creation, or its re-vivifying, by means of transferred blood. Every Mexican province told this story in its own way, says a historian; but the main features of it are alike in all its versions....

An ancient Chaldean legend, as recorded by Berosus, ascribes a new creation of mankind to the mixture, by the gods, of the dust of the earth with the blood that flowed from the severed head of the god Belus. "On this account it is that men are rational, and partake of divine knowledge," says Berosus. The blood of the god gives them the life and the nature of a god.

[81] Derek Kidner, *Genesis: An Introduction And Commentary* (Downers Grove, Illinois: Inter-Varsity Press, 1975), 89.

[82] *Concordia Self-Study Bible*, 16, in regard to Genesis 8:1:

> The Hebrew word translated 'Spirit' in 1:2 is here rendered 'wind' and introduces a series of parallels between the events of chs. 8-9 and those of ch. 1 in their literary order: Compare 8:2 with 1:7; 8:5 with 1:9; 8:7 with 1:20; 8:17 with 1:25; 9:1 with 1:28a; 9:2 with 1:28b; 9:3 with 1:30. Ch. 1 describes the original beginning, while chs. 8-9 describe a new beginning after the flood.

[83] Admittedly the concept of Covenant that is presented in chapter 9 does not fit comfortably with the concept presented in this study – for instance, God's Covenant with every living creature and His Covenant with the earth [vv 9-10, 12-13] is awkward in regard to the idea of the common Blood/Life between God and His Covenant-partner (here the animals and the earth itself). On the other hand, neither is there any alternate definition of Covenant that this writer is aware of that adequately answers this puzzle. This just demonstrates that the last word on Covenant has not yet been spoken.

[84] The mention of "waters above the firmament" [Genesis 1:7], as well as 40 days of rain (just a half inch an hour would yield 40 feet of water which had to come from somewhere), there is strong possibility that originally earth had a vapor canopy which collapsed during the flood. If so, with sunlight no longer diffused by the canopy, this would have been the first time mankind ever saw the rainbow.

[85] Kidner, *Genesis*, 102.

[86] Robert F Lindemann, from an unpublished paper.

[87] On Melchizedek, "King of Righteousness", note Jeremiah 23:6; 33:15-16; on King of Salem, "King of Peace", note Isaiah 9:6-7; also Isaiah 32:17. These concepts (righteousness and peace) lie at the center of two of the three major sacrifices, the "*Sin Offering*" and the "*Peace/Fellowship Offering*."

[88] Harris, *Wordbook*, vol I, 51-52:

> האמין [*HEEMIN* – he believed] from אמן [*AMAN*]
>
> At the heart of the meaning of the root is the idea of certainty. And this is borne out by the NT definition of faith found in Heb 11:1.... [it] is used in the sense of the strong arms of the parent supporting the helpless infant.... In this sense the word ...shows that biblical faith is an assurance, a certainty, in contrast with modern concepts of faith as something possible, hopefully true, but not certain. ... The various derivatives reflect the same concept of certainty and dependability. The derivative '*amen "verily"* is carried over into the New Testament in the word *amen*... Jesus used the word frequently (Mt 5:18,26, etc.) to stress the certainty of a matter. The Hebrew and Greek forms come at the end of prayers and hymns of

⁸⁹ The first time that צְדָקָה [TSEDAQAH – "righteousness"] appears; only the third time any from the family of the root צדק [TSEDEQ – righteous, just] appears. The other places are Genesis 6:9 and 7:1 in regard to Noah. Note Romans 4:1-5; Galatians 3:6-9.

⁹⁰ R. Scott Clark, "A Contemporary Reformed Defense of Infant Baptism," http://www.seeking4truth.com/a_contemporary_reformed_defense.htm (accessed Oct 23, 2005).

⁹¹ See endnote 38.

⁹² Trumbull, 217.

⁹³ Verse 26 does say, "If I find in Sodom fifty righteous *within the city*," however, since both Sodom and Gomorrah have been named as to be destroyed, and Zoar of the five kingdoms of 14:2 is spared by Lot's plea [19:18-23], this writer is assuming that the acceptable righteous would not necessarily have to be just in Sodom. If any righteous were found on the rest of "all the plain" [19:25], then Abraham's concern for sparing the righteous would seem a bit on the hollow side if he is not concerned about all who stand under judgment.

⁹⁴ *Ibid*, 224-230.

⁹⁵ The parallels to Jesus' sacrifice on the cross are remarkable – the unsung hero, perhaps twelve-year-old Isaac, was obedient to his father (elderly Abraham), potentially even to death ("like a lamb which is led to the slaughter" [Isaiah 53:7; Acts 8:32]); even to the indignity of carrying *the wood* meant for his own death.

⁹⁶ 41:46 (30 years old) - 37:2(17 years old); 39:1-41:2; after at least 9-10 more years (7+7, minus 5 years to come [45:11], Israel came down to Egypt. This would account for 23 or more years of the "30" for the 430 years which Israel was in Egypt [Exodus 12:40-41].

⁹⁷ Jehovah had turned the world in upheaval (the famine) in order to move Israel to Egypt according to promise. Millennia later, the world would be turned in upheaval (Caesar Augustus' census) in order to move a single couple to Bethlehem, that a birth would happen according to promise.

⁹⁸ *Concordia Self-Study Bible*, 88:

> 2:10 ... Throughout this early part of Exodus, all the pharaoh's efforts to suppress Israel were thwarted by women: the midwives (1:17), the Israelite mothers (1:19), Moses' mother and sister (v. 3-4, 7-9), the pharaoh's daughter (here). The pharaoh's impotence to destroy the people of God is thus ironically exposed.

⁹⁹ *Concordia Self-Study Commentary*, ed., Walter R. Roehrs and Martin H Franzmann, (St Louis: Concordia Publishing House, 1979), 63:

> For every evasive objection He supplied an assuring answer: (a)"Who am I...?" – answer: 3:12; (b)"Who are You?"– answer: 3:14; (c)"They will not believe" –

answer: 4:3-4; (d)"I am not eloquent" – answer: 4:12; (e)"Send...some other person" – answer: 4:14; (f)"I am of uncircumcised lips" – answer: 7:1f... The prophets too had to learn not "to confer with flesh and blood" when God claimed them for His service. (Jer 1:6-10; Is 6:1-8; Am 7:14-15; Gal 1:16).

R. Alan Cole, *Exodus: An Introduction and Commentary* (Downers Grove, Illinois: Inter-Varsity Press, 1973), 68:

> *Who am I?* This is not an existential question, but an expression of disbelief (*cf.* Jdg 6:15). Moses, unlike his early days in Egypt, has learnt to distrust himself so thoroughly that he will incur God's anger (Ex 4:14). Self-distrust is good, but only if it leads to trust in God. Otherwise it ends as spiritual paralysis, inability and unwillingness to undertake any course of action. Moses, like Elijah (I Ki 19), is a picture of a man who has had a 'nervous breakdown', and is now unwilling to work for God at all.

[100] *Ibid*, 70:

> Perhaps the easiest way to understand what the name YHWH meant to the Jews is to see what it came to mean, as their history of salvation slowly unrolled. It ultimately meant to them what the name Jesus has come to mean to Christians, a 'shorthand' for all God's dealings of grace.

[101] Trumbull, 222f.

[102] Moses begins his career with water turned to Blood; Jesus begins His career with water turned to wine [John 2:1-11], and at the other end of John, the wine of the Last Supper is His Blood.

[103] This writer's father once remarked that when St Paul wrote: "that at Jesus' Name every knee should bend, in heaven and on earth and under the earth, and every tongue confess that Jesus Christ is Lord, to the glory of God the Father" [Philippians 2:10-11] – on the Last Day that will indeed happen, either willingly or unwillingly.

[104] *Concordia Commentary*, 68, which later adds:

> Because [Christ] was a sacrifice, "a lamb without blemish," His blood "cleanses us from all sin" (1 Co 5:7; 1 Ptr 1:19; 1 Jn 1:7; Jn 1:29; 19:36; Heb 7:26; 9:13-14,26,28). He who eats His flesh and drinks His blood "has eternal life" (Jn 6:54). Rejoicing in their deliverance "from the dominion of darkness" (Cl 1:13), His redeemed community gathers to "celebrate the festival" in order to "proclaim the LORD's death until he comes" (1 Co 11:23-26).

[105] Leaven – no sacrifice by fire included it [Leviticus 2:11; 6:17], no Blood was offered with it [Exodus 23:18; 34:25], no grain offering contained yeast [Leviticus 2:11]; only a thank offering [Leviticus 7:13] and a First Fruits offering [Leviticus 23:17] allowed it.

[106] Cole, *Exodus*, 120. Note II Chronicles 20:17; Joshua 10, up to verse 14; II Samuel 5, particularly around verse 24; also Isaiah 30:15.

[107] The Hebrew for "wall" [14:22] specifically means a wall of protection, [e.g., Joshua 2:15; 6:5,20]. Therefore the "walls" of water on each side were like stockade walls preventing attack.

[108] *Exodus*, in *The Pulpit Commentary*, ed. H.D.M. Spence and Joseph S. Exell, (NY, NY: Funk & Wagnalls Company, 1950), 341.

[109] Note the New Covenant description, 1 Peter 2:5; Revelation 1:6; 5:10. Cole, *Exodus*, 145:

> It is the universal priestly status of Israel to which attention is called.... Presumably the basic thought is of a group set apart peculiarly for God's possession and service, with free access to His presence. The thought of acting as God's representative for, and to the other nations of the world cannot be ruled out. Whether realized... or not, this was to be the mission of Israel (*cf.* the ultimate promise to Abraham in Gn. 12:3).

[110] See Judges 7:16, 20; 15:4, 5; Job 12:5; 41:19; Isaiah 62:1; Ezekiel 1:13; Daniel 10:6; Nahum 2:4; Zec 12:6

[111] Cole, *Exodus*, 216. Jehovah loved to mock the gods created by their own worshippers (see Isaiah 44:13-20).

[112] *Ibid*, 217.

[113] *Ibid*, 225.

[114] David Plotz, *The Good Book* (New York: Harper Collins Publishers, 2010), 2.

[115] Harris, *Wordbook*, 786-789.

[116] Note Galatians 3:13, where even THE Lawgiver, God (Jesus), is not exempt, where He is cursed by hanging on a tree, and that is not even by His own hand!

[117] Harris, *Wordbook*, vol II, 571:

> As the object of faith resembled the curse in the case of the "snakes," so Jesus resembled the cursed in that he took the form of a servant and was made in the likeness of man (Phil 2:7).

Note II Corinthians 5: 21. Consider Mark 16:15-18 – what a picture of the Christian's boldness even to death, because the "Serpent" (Satan)'s bite has become meaningless – dust. Yet within such a wonderful salvation, consider the danger that was later fallen into, II Kings 18:4. Can the same type of superstition happen in regard to Jesus' crucifixion?

[118] Perhaps the first Oktoberfest, although 'Beer' actually just means 'well/oasis of water.'

[119] This is not a nomadic tribe: Israel is literally a landless country – not a horde out to enlarge their borders, but a nation going to a specific target – not an established state moving from one local to another, but a nation which literally came out of nowhere (slavery).

[120] Consider the extraordinary uniqueness of Israel, which Balak probably could not understand: Israel had no physical king. Moses, leader though he was, was not a king but a prophet; Aaron was only High Priest; there was no human king, president, premier. No other nation has ever been run that way. One day it shall be that way again.

[121] Martin Luther, "The Babylonian Captivity of the Church," in *Luther's Works*, Vol 36 (*Word and Sacrament II*), gen. ed. Helmut T. Lehmann, (Philadelphia: Muhlenberg Press, 1960), 112-113.

[122] C S Lewis once remarked (perhaps in regard to some sort of attempt at world peace), "The besetting sin of such endeavors is that they seek to give what Christ offers, yet without Him."

[123] also Isaiah 42:8; 45:6, 14, 18, 21, 22; 46:9.

אחד [*ECHOD* – unified one – sometimes contrasted against יחד [*YACHAD* – unit, solitary one]]; Harris, *Wordbook*, vol I, 60:

> It stresses unity while recognizing diversity within that oneness....In the famous Shema of Deut 6:4, "Hear, O Israel...the Lord is one," the question of diversity within unity has theological implications. Some scholars have felt that... the word allows for the doctrine of the Trinity. While it is true that the doctrine is foreshadowed in the OT, the verse concentrates on... one God and that Israel owes its exclusive loyalty to him (Deut 5:9; 6:5)....
>
> ...The option "The LORD is our God the LORD alone" has in its favor both the broad context of the book and the immediate context. Deuteronomy 6:4 serves as an introduction to motivate Israel to keep the command "to love (the Lord)" (v. 5). The notion that the Lord is Israel's only God suits this command admirably (cf. Song 6:8f). Moreover, these two notions, the LORD's unique relation to Israel and Israel's obligation to love him, are central to the concern of Moses' addresses in the book (cf. Deut 5:9f.; 7:9; 10:14ff., 20f, 13:6; 30:20; 32:12). Finally Zechariah... applies it universally with reference to the eschaton: "The Lord will be king over all the earth; in that day the Lord will be (the only) one, and His name (the only) one" (14:9 NASB).

[124] After 1500 years, wrath exploded: "as Jehovah rejoiced over you to do you good and to multiply you, so Jehovah shall rejoice over you to destroy you, and to lay you waste" [28:63]. Vv 48-57 describe a terrifying siege, with Israel driven to cannibalism; its emphasis on iron and the eagle may not predict so much the Babylonian Captivity, as the destruction of Jerusalem in 70 AD by Rome – a siege so horrible that only ONE out of every 10 SURVIVED. Moved to great anger, the Romans' destruction of Jerusalem and the enslaving of the people (a penny bought 10 slaves) were extraordinary. Israel was scattered, as Cain was, as restless wanderers throughout the world, as unwanted slaves [vv 64-68].

[125] In the forty years in the wilderness, Israel learned that Jehovah was indeed God Almighty. In the 70 years of the Babylonian Captivity, Israel learned that there are no other gods. In the 2,000 years of the dispersion after the fall of Jerusalem, what is Israel to learn now?

[126] *Deuteronomy*, in *The Pulpit Commentary*, ed. H.D.M. Spence and Joseph S. Exell, (NY, NY: Funk & Wagnalls Company, 1950), 304:

> ...as a succession of priests, of judges, and of kings was contemplated in this part of the Mosaic legislation, the presumption is that a succession also of prophets was contemplated. At the same time, the use of the singular here is remarkable,

for nowhere else is the singular, *nabhi* [נביא], employed to designate more than one individual; and this suggests that the reference here may be to some individual in whom not only was the succession to culminate as in its crown and eminence, but whose spirit was to pervade the whole succession, -- that each member of it should exercise his functions only as that Spirit which was in them did signify (1 Pet. i. 11). It is possible, also as O. von Gerlach has suggested, that "Prophet" here may be used as "seed" is in Gen. iii.15, and that this is a prediction of Christ as the True Prophet, just as the assurance to Eve was a prediction of the messiah, who, as the Head and Crown of the "godly seed," should end the conflict with the serpent and his seed by a crushing victory.

[127] *Exodus, Pulpit Commentary*, 291:

> Imperfection attaches to everything that man does; and even the sacrifices that the people offered to God required to be atoned for and purified. It was granted to the high priest in his official capacity to make the necessary atonement, and so render the people's gifts acceptable.

Concordia Commentary, 82:

> *Holy to the Lord.* This inscription epitomized the significance of his office. God, as it were, laid His hand on his forehead as if to declare him a sacrificial offering to the Lord (cf. 29:10; Lv 4:4). Furthermore *any guilt* incurred in the holy offering ... rested on his head. But functioning as a divinely appointed mediator, he nevertheless bore before his eyes the constant assurance that through his mediation the people's offering was *accepted before the Lord.* The High Priest who actualized what Aaron's tiara symbolized wore as His headdress a crown of thorns. (Mt 27:29)

[128] *Leviticus, Pulpit Commentary*, 238:

> Dr. Thomson, in 'The Land and the Book,' tells us that it is a habit still common among the Bedawin, and probably coming from the remotest times, for host and guest to eat together. This is said to be *bread and salt* between them, and constitutes a pledge of protection, support, and fidelity even to death.

[129] Called BAPTISM by the Jews, but also a picture of Christian Baptism preparing us for our "royal priesthood" [I Peter 2:9]. Note St Paul parallel in Ephesians 5:25-27.

[130] Note Romans 6:23.

[131] The seat of emotion and affection.

[132] "This is a lasting ordinance for the generations to come, wherever you live: You must not eat any fat or any Blood." [Leviticus 3:17]; see IV. The Covenant Mosaic - G. The Live-r of Glory - The Appendage of the Liver

[133] The English "holy," cousin to "hale" and "heal," was derived from an Old English word meaning "whole," reflecting that in becoming holy, one became "whole" -- healthy, complete. In re-establishing his dependence on/submission to Jehovah, re-affirming he was creature (not god) to the Creator, this sacrifice returned to man his original state: he would become "whole" – spiritually "healthy."

[134] Harris, *Wordbook*, Vol II, 666-668:

The key appears to be that alone among the Israelite sacrifices the *'ola* is wholly burned, rather than partially burned and eaten by the worshipers and/or the priest. Thus, the whole animal is brought up to the altar and the whole is offered as a gift (*minha*, q.v.) in homage to Yahweh. Whole offering would be a better rendering in English to convey the theology of the *'ola*. It is indeed burned, but the burning is essentially secondary to the giving of the whole creature to Yahweh....

...Normally the act of sacrifice was performed by the priest, but for the *'ola*, only the birds were slaughtered by the priest.... It was essential that the blood be put on the altar. A bull, sheep, or goat was killed by the worshiper himself beside the altar (Lev 1:5,11,15), after which the priest poured the blood against or upon the altar. Only after the worshiper had skinned and cut up the animal and washed the parts in water was the whole animal conveyed to the priest. He then took it to the altar and arranged it there where it was wholly burned up....

...Evidence from Ugarit antedating the OT and from the Phoenician texts postdating the OT gives evidence of rites that parallel the Hebrew *'ola*. But, missing from all of these is the one essential element in the Hebrew structure – the offering of the blood and the contact of the blood with the altar. The offering of the life (cf. Lev 17:11, the blood is life) to the God of life makes the difference between a simple slaughter and an acceptable sacrificial gift.

[135] ריח- [*REYAH* - aroma - Gen 8:21; Ex 29:18,25,41; Lev 1:9,13,17; 2:2,9,12; 3:5,16] comes from - רוח- [*RUAH* - breath, wind - the word for "spirit" in the Hebrew]. The sacrifice's pleasing aroma was the sacrificer's pleasing "spirit."

[136] The work of Jesus (redemption; justification) is mixed together with the work of the Holy Spirit (sanctification) and both are bestowed upon those who will do Jehovah's work [Hebrews 10:22; 12:24].

[137] *Concordia Self-Study Bible*, 147.

[138] The writer's book, *Creation's Ballet for Jesus*, details some of the Jewish traditions involved in these festivals.

[139] Rarely occurring, "the Lord Jehovah" ("*YHWH Adonai*" – NIV: "Sovereign LORD") indicated that this was "THE Master, THE Owner, THE Superior" speaking; perhaps a not-so-gentle reminder that the men were accountable to something greater than themselves -- their worship identified that the real Lordship of their lives was Jehovah's.

[140] Christians still celebrate the three feasts, although with far greater meaning because of their fulfillment in Jesus - except for Thanksgiving Day. Thanksgiving Day is not often viewed with a "Last Day" Harvest significance, and is therefore not often considered as part of the great Salvation drama of the Church Year.

The Harvest Festival, also called "*the Festival of Booths*", is a reminder of Israel's wandering in the wilderness and the complete dependence they had on Jehovah, as well as the fact that during this time in their history, Israel was homeless - "strangers and pilgrims." This also is not part of the *modern* Thanksgiving Day celebration.

See the author's *Creation's Ballet for Jesus* for other connections to these festivals.

¹⁴¹ Poverty is no excuse. *The Meal Offering* of Leviticus 5 is for the poor person who cannot afford even two pigeons. The LORD permits him to take a handful of flour or grain and throw it on someone else's sacrifice.

¹⁴² Note how the "image of God" must treat even the animals: Exodus 23:5,12; Leviticus 22:28.

¹⁴³ James Lindemann, *Creation's Ballet for Jesus*, 110-111

¹⁴⁴ *Concordia Self-Study Bible*, 119:

> In later Judaism it came to commemorate the giving of the law on Mount Sinai, though there is no evidence of this significance in the OT. In NT times it was called "(the day of) Pentecost" (Ac 2:1; 20:16; I Co 16:8), which means "50."

¹⁴⁵ This writer's book, *Creation's Ballet for Jesus*, details some of the many traditions surrounding this occasion; for example, this is the anniversary of creation, the pre-anniversary of when God the King begins His reign and therefore of Judgment Day.

¹⁴⁶ *KIPPUR* is the same word as *KAPHAR* with vowel and other normal vocal changes.

¹⁴⁷ Some interesting traditions for this festival are identified in *Creation's Ballet for Jesus*, notably that in Genesis 33:17, Jacob builds for his animals stables – *SUKKOTH*! – and Jesus was born in a stable; also as part of the tradition, the family in their *SUKKOTH* are visited by the *seven* shepherds of Israel: Abraham, Isaac, Jacob, Moses, Aaron, Joseph and David.

¹⁴⁸ It is interesting that *two* sets of "a ram and *seven/oath* lambs" are involved, perhaps indicating two major Covenants are celebrated, the Circumcision and the coming "New Covenant"?

¹⁴⁹ In modern warfare, when soldiers go out on patrol, often they fan out behind a "point man". His job is to set the pace and direction, and should they run into the enemy, he is usually the first to get shot at.

¹⁵⁰ This writer's father told of classmates at the Seminary who were assigned to foreign mission work, who had to be circumcised before they went. Whenever they went to urinate, another person had to go with them because some would faint from the pain.

¹⁵¹ The surrounding peoples, especially those in Canaan, watched Israel very closely – a fact made obvious when Rahab rehearsed to the spies the great things Jehovah had done [2:10]. What do you think would have been the chances for victory if the Allies had done the same on D-Day in World War II?

¹⁵² חרם- [*HARAM* – devote utterly]. Harris, *Wordbook*, vol I, 324-325:

> The basic meaning is the exclusion of an object from the use or abuse of man and its irrevocable surrender to God. The word is related to an Arabic root meaning "to prohibit, especially to ordinary use." The word "harem," meaning the special quarters for Muslim wives, comes from it...
> The idea of devoting an object for service to God appears in Lev 27:28. Whatever is devoted to the Lord, whether man, animal, or property, is considered most holy by God and is therefore not to be sold or redeemed.... According to

Num 18:14 and Ezk 44:29, all such objects are to be given to the priests for the support of the religious ceremonies. The gold, silver, bronze, and iron from Jericho, for instance, were so designated (Josh 6:19, *qodesh layhwh*).

Usually *haram* means a ban for utter destruction, the compulsory dedication of something which impedes or resists God's work, which is considered accursed before God... This word is used regarding almost all the cities which Joshua's troops destroyed (e.g. Jericho, Josh 6:21; Ai, Josh 8:26; Makkedah, Josh 10:28; Hazor, Josh 11:11), thus indicating the rationale for their destruction. In Deut 7:2-6, the command for this manner of destruction is given, with the explanation following that, otherwise, these cities would lure the Israelites away from the Lord (cf. Deut 20:17-18). Any Israelite city that harbored idolaters was to be "utterly destroyed" (Deut 13:12-15; cf. Ex 22:19).

[153] The idea of *blasphemy* does not necessarily mean something spoken, as the *Concordia Self-Study Bible*, 1535 (on Mark 14:64) put it:

The sin of blasphemy not only involved reviling the name of God (see Lev 24:10-16) but also included any affront to his majesty or authority (see Mk 2:7; 3:28-29; Jn 5:18; 10:33). Jesus' claim to be the Messiah and, in fact, to *have* majesty and authority belonging only to God was therefore regarded by Caiaphas as blasphemy, for which the Mosaic law prescribed death by stoning (Lev 24:16).

Consider the "blasphemy" in John 10:33; also in James 2:6-7.

[154] "cut" -כרת- [*KARATH*] -- the normal word for cutting a Covenant, a very strong idea of cutting off or cutting apart

"statute" --הקק- [*HOQ*] -- Harris, *Wordbook*, Vol I, 316:

"*haqaq* ... has the primary meaning of cutting in or engraving in stone as hewing a tomb in the rock (Isa 22:16) and as drawing a picture on a brick (Ezk 4:1) or a wall (Ezk 23:14). It may also describe writing on the palm of one's hand (Isa 49:16) or in a book (Isa 30:8; Job 19:23).

Perhaps here it might suggest the "scar" of Covenant.

[155] *Judges*, in *The Pulpit Commentary*, ed. H.D.M. Spence and Joseph S. Exell, (NY, NY: Funk & Wagnalls Company, 1950), 65:

The sentiment expressed by Gideon [was not] a general one, but peculiar to the Israelites. The Greek knew not this fear, because his conception of the nature of the gods was different. They were but as men, only more glorious and powerful. To the Israelite God was Supreme in holiness and authority. Reverence for the character of God deepened into fear, because of the tradition that a visitation as he now received meant death, either immediate or at hand, because of the sense of sin. No man could see God and live....the remnant and echoes of this belief [are] still among us, in the fear of supernatural appearances.... It is the dread of the simple, absolute holiness and goodness of God, deepened by our sense of sinfulness.

[156] נדר [*NEDER* - vow]. Harris, *Wordbook*, vol II, 557-558:

neder occurs in the lists of sacrifices (e.g. Deut 12:6,11) as a species of peace offering (Lev 7:16). A closer description occurs in Num 30:3 [H 4] where to *nadar* a *neder* is to swear to God with an oath (*hishshaba' sh^ebu'a*; cf. Ps 132:2) and to bind one's self with what proceeds from one's mouth. A *neder* is something promised to God verbally (Num 30:4 [H 5]). If one so promises he is obliged to fulfill/do his promise (Deut 23:22). In most cases, the context shows that the vow implies a promised gift for sacrifice, not merely a course of action as is implied in the English word "vow".... A *neder* is a species of thank offering ... vowed (Ps 116:14,18) in return for God's favor (Num 21:1-3) or as an expression of godly zeal and devotion and in praise for answered prayer (Ps 22:25 [H 26]). Happiness results when a vow is properly fulfilled (Job 22:27).

...A person can even vow himself to service, or be vowed to service, and can be redeemed (or redeem himself) thus giving to God a value equal in worth to his actual service, but being free to pursue his own life (Lev 27:2ff)...

There are at least two noteworthy special vows: the Nazirite (Num 6:13ff; *nazar*,. q.v.) and the *herem* (Num 21:2; *hrm*, q.v.). Absalom begged leave of David's court to fulfill a vow (II Sam 15:7-8). The depth of his deceit is shown by both his having lied and having lied respecting divine ordinances. Elkanah on the other hand, both conscientiously fulfilled his own vows (I Sam 1:21) and concurred with Hannah's (I Sam 1:11,22-23; Cf. Num 30). Jephthah's rash promise ... was tempered when he dedicated his only daughter to lifelong service in the tabernacle, as seems at least possible (Jud 11:30,39; cf. KD).

[157] Knowing Jehovah's revulsion at the innocent Blood of child-sacrifice, as well as Jephthah's commitment to the LORD's will, it would seem unlikely that she was sacrificed, but rather entered a sort of monastic commitment, perhaps on the order of Anna in Luke 2:36-37 (I Samuel 2:22, although in a different context, spoke of "the women who served at *the Tent of Meeting's* door").

[158] "Why do you ask my name, since it is *Wonderful?*... and he did *wonderfully*" [13:18,19] פלא [*PALA'* – wonderful]. Harris, *Wordbook*, vol II, 723:

> The basic meaning of the verb is "to be wonderful" and in the Hiphil "to cause a wonderful thing to happen." In the Piel, however, it means "to fulfill (a vow)," Lev 22:21; Num 15:3, 8, though this nuance is also present in two instances of pala' in the Hiphil (Lev 27:2; Num 6:2).
>
> Preponderantly both the verb and substantive refer to the acts of God, designating either cosmic wonders or historical achievements on behalf of Israel. That is, in the Bible the root *pl'* refers to things that are unusual, beyond human capabilities. As such, it awakens astonishment (*pl'*) in man....
>
> It is of interest to note that the function of God's wonders is ultimately to make mercy available to the recipient or reciter, and not just to make a demonstration of power. Thus, in Ps 107:8,15,21,31 *nipla'ot* is parallel with *hesed* "loving kindness, mercy." God performs 'marvels of love,' Ps 31:21 (H 22), *hipli hasdo*.

Because of the above "nuance" of fulfilling a vow, this "name" may be appropriate for this angel on this occasion.

[159] נזר- [*NAZAR* -- separate]. Harris, *Wordbook*, vol II, 567-568:

The basic meaning of *nazar* is "to separate." ... The verb is used in the sense of separation in Lev 22:2 where Aaron and his sons were commanded through Moses to keep away from the holy offerings that were presented to the Lord... they could not use them as long as they were ritually unclean (v 3). The word is used in the same construction in the sense of separating from idols (Ezk 14:7). It bears the meaning "abstain from" when used with *min* in the Hiphil in Num 6:3 where it occurs in connection with the Nazirite vow of abstinence. The idea of separation is inherent in the use of the word without min in Lev 15:31 where the Israelites were to be separated from uncleanness incurred as a result of certain physical discharges....

The specialized sense of the word, "Nazirites," refers to those who took a special vow of abstention as an act of devotion to God. The specific aspects of the vow of separation are recorded in Num 6:1-21, where the Nazirite is described as abstaining from grapes and various products of the grape, refraining from cutting the hair, and avoiding the ceremonial defilement incurred when one touched a dead body.

[160] Why such power in regard to the hair? Perhaps it was not so much the hair as the *head*:

"All the days of his vow of separation no razor shall come upon his *head*; until the time is completed for which he separates himself to Jehovah, he shall be holy; he shall let the locks of hair of his *head* grow long... because his separation to God is upon his *head*. All the days of his separation he is holy to Jehovah...[If] he defiles his consecrated *head*, then he shall shave his *head* on the day of his cleansing... He shall consecrate his *head* that same day, and separate himself to Jehovah for the days of his separation...The Nazirite shall shave his consecrated *head* at the door of *the Tent of Meeting*, and shall take the hair from his consecrated *head* and put it on the fire..." [Numbers 6:5,7,9,11-12,18]

The High Priest's head was not to be uncovered [Leviticus 21:10] and shaving the head was a sign of mourning and death (Ezra 9:3; Job 1:20; Jeremiah 7:29 -- contact with death negated the vow and caused it to be restarted [Numbers 6:11-12]). Isaiah 1:5 spoke of "the whole head is sick", it was the place of guilt [Joshua 2:19; Ezekiel 9:10;17:19]. The New Testament idea of "head" often revolved around authority [I Corinthians 11:3-10; Ephesians 5:23; Colossians 1:18, 2:10,19].

Perhaps this vow was therefore a symbolic declaration of submission to Jehovah's will and authority in regard to a specific part of life. It represented what Samson's life should have been and later what *Samuel's* life was.

[161] [v 9] The word "whole" is added to the name for "*whole burnt offering*" – this combination appears in only one other place, Psalm 51:19. Consider this Psalm and why this combination of words could be important.

[162] Things don't change over the millennia: a man goes out looking for jackasses and comes back a politician...

[163] נחם - [*NACHAM*]; Harris, *Wordbook*, Vol II, 579-580:

The origin of the root seems to reflect the idea of "breathing deeply," hence the physical display of one's feelings, usually sorrow, compassion, or comfort....

...The majority of these instances refer to God's repentance, not man's. The word most frequently employed for man's repentance is *shub* (q.v.), meaning "to turn" (from sin to God)... [The] Scriptures inform us that God repents (Gen 6:6-7; Ex 32:14; Jud 2:18; 1 Sam 15:11 et al.), i.e. he relents or changes his dealings with men according to his sovereign purposes. On the surface, such language seems inconsistent, if not contradictory, with passages which affirm God's immutability: "God is not a man ... that he should repent" (I Sam 15:29 contra v. 11).... From man's limited, earthly, finite perspective it only appears that God's purposes have changed.... Certainly Jer 18:7-10 is a striking reminder that from God's perspective, most prophecy (excluding messianic predictions) is conditional upon the response of men. In this regard, A.J. Heschel (*The Prophets*, p. 194) has said, "No word is God's final word. Judgment, far from being absolute, is conditional. A change in man's conduct brings about a change in God's judgment."

The second primary meaning of nacham is "to comfort"...or "to be comforted".... This Hebrew word was well known to every pious Jew living in exile as he recalled the opening words of Isaiah's "Book of Consolation," *nachamu nachamu 'ammi* "Comfort ye, comfort ye my people" (Isa 40:1).

164 נֶצַח - [*NETSACH*] as in "the *Strength* of Israel"; Harris, *Wordbook*, Vol II, 593:

netsach denotes both "brilliance" (yielding the connotations "preeminence, surpassing glory, victory, leadership") and "endurance" (supplying "longlasting, perpetual")....

Returning to the noun form for the moment, then, one can grasp the difficulty of choice between "strength" or "glory" (the problem being in the English distinctives, since the Hebrew obviously embraces both at once) in references to divine attribute or Person, as in I Sam 15:29.....

165 "An evil spirit from Jehovah terrified him"–by Jehovah's permission,Satan used his expertise as "the Accuser"(note Romans 2:15). We all do some really stupid things, but what does Jehovah promise when we repent? (Isaiah 43:25) If HE forgets them, how come they keep popping up in our minds to be re-lived and re-agonized all over again? Consider Satan's characteristic goal in John 8:44 and our defense in Hebrews 9:14; 10:19-22; I Peter 3:21.

166 "and you shall bring their pledge/token [עֲרֻבָּה – '*ARUBBAH*]" [I,17:18]; Harris (*Wordbook*, Vol II, 593) points out that this can carry a meaning of "to strike the hands in agreement." What this means in this context may have many guesses as to why this possible Covenant concept was chosen.

167 This was not a valid Blood-balancing within the office of *GO'EL*, since the death of Joab's brother was in battle and in self-defense (see II, 2:18-24).

168 "David divided to all the people..., to man, even to woman, a cake [loaf - I Chronicles 16:3] of bread, ..."[II,6:19] The next item in Hebrew cannot be interpreted accurately. The King James decided for "a good piece [of flesh]". For the following word, although the King James renders it "a flagon [of wine]", modern translators vote for "raisin cake"; it appears to be derived from a root meaning "to press".

Since both II Samuel AND its parallel in I Chronicles emphasize "even the women" as an apparently unusual occurrence, and since this follows immediately after references of whole burnt and peace/fellowship sacrifices, it would seem as though these two words might relate to the sacrificial action.

On that basis, perhaps the King James has a point, where the second word might relate to the fellowship sacrifice, where "even the women" participated in eating the meat – highly unusual! The following word may also have been a euphemism for wine, like "fruit of the vine" or "blood of the grape" – as a meaning that passed in and out of fad in that era. If this is true, it would present an interesting link to the New Testament Covenant's Holy Communion. But presently these words only lend themselves to conjecture.

169 If Jehovah could be so "grieved" over these dead, imagine His grief over His Son on the cross, where there would be no "Enough!"

170 שלם - (SHALOM - peaceful, whole, perfect).

171 שמ - (SHEMA - listen, hear, harken, obey) This is the same word which begins the great Jewish creed, the "Shema, Israel" (Deuteronomy 6:4). Although supposedly unrelated, the word for "name" as in "the Name of God" is SHEM.

172 And points forward to the New Name of the New Covenant: Philippians 2:9-11.

173 "sign" in verses 3,5 is not the "'OTH" of Covenant, but a word which means "wonder" or "portent."

174 Was this an accurate number or a symbolic one? Did Jehovah stand with a clicker counting out exactly the number; or is it a symbolic 7,000 – 7 x 10^3; ten (completion) to the third power (superlative, absolute) times *seven/oath* – not one believer will be missed, but God will honor His promises to absolute fulfillment?

175 "Is your heart true to my heart as mine is to yours?" [II,10:15]. Would this be a Covenant, or a pact with borrowed imagery from Covenant?

176 [II Kings 11:15] "Do not let her be killed in the house of Jehovah" – Women were not allowed in *the Temple* anyway! Besides murdering, she apparently didn't even keep the visible formalities of worship of Jehovah.

177 As the North returned with captives, the prophet Oded warned them from enslaving their own brothers against God's command, and the warning was heeded [vv 9-14]. It is almost surprising that the North would care that much about God's will, yet there still remained an ingrained awareness of God and His will.

178 The "uncleanness" from *the Temple* (however Ahaz had desecrated it) was dumped into the brook Kidron – the brook Jesus passed over on His way to Gesthemane.

179 dumped into the brook Kidron again.

180 "I shall defend this city for My own sake, for My servant David's sake" [v 6].

181 See the author's book, *Creation's Ballet for Jesus*, which also discusses the religion of Persia at the time.

182 Harris, *Wordbook*, Vol I, 404.

183 This is the same word used in the Sabbath day command for when God "rested" from his work of Creation [Exodus 20:11].

184 Trumbull, 341.

185 *KABAD* related to *KABOD*, "Glory."

186 Galatians 3:29 And if you are Christ's, then you are Abraham's offspring, heirs according to promise.

187 Harris, *Wordbook*, Vol II, 605:

> This noun, when used in reference to man, generally signifies the breath of life. It is frequently found in combination with *rûah* 'spirit' and seems synonymous with *nepesh* (q.v.). In KJV it is twice translated 'spirit'. {Job 26:4 Pr 20:27} For Pr 20:27 some feel the mind or intellect is denoted. In Isa 2:22 the reference to man, whose 'breath is in his nostrils,' is a figure of man's frailty. Life itself is a fragile existence. The 'breath of God' may refer to his creative activity (as in Ge 2:7), but it can also be a hot wind which kindles flame, {Isa 30:33} a destructive wind (2Sa 22:16 = Ps 18:15 [H 16]; Job 4:9), or even a wind cold enough to produce ice. {Job 37:10}
>
> The fact that precise translation of this noun must fluctuate in accordance with its contextual usage is aptly demonstrated by the following instances. In the poetic expression of 2Sa 22:16 (paralleled by Ps 18:15 [H 16]) *nishmat rûah* signifies 'blast of his breath,' while in Ge 7:22 *nishmat rûah hayîm* means 'the breath of life,' breath here expressed by the combination 'breathing of breath.' The concrete concept 'breathing (that is, living) beings' is expressed by *neshamâ* in either the singular from (as in Jos 10:40) or the plural. {Isa 57:16}

188 In *Biblia Hebraica* [Rudolf Kittel, ed (Stuttgart: Württembergische Bibelanstalt, 1966), 841-842] this is verses 8-10.

189 *Ibid*, 843; this is verses 28-29, 36-37.

190 Exodus 33:19.

191 At the end of the Roman siege in 70 AD, only 1 in 10 are left alive.

192 As Jesus dies, the sun is unexplainably darkened from noon to 3 PM.

193 See "IV. Covenant Mosaic – B. The SIGN of Covenant – 'A Sign on Your Hand…' – The Ring."

194 McMahon, "My Retraction"

195 von Schenk, 41.

196 See endnote 38.

197 This old world term was used during the time when down payments were not as common a practice as today. If you could not at that particular occasion buy an item which you strongly desired, you would put down some money to show that you were 'in earnest' about buying it – hence the term, 'earnest money' or simply 'earnest.'

198 Andrew Das, "The Holy Spirit and Water Baptism in Acts," www.issuesetc.org

> This entire Pentecost phenomenon began with the work of the Holy Spirit. The Spirit had come down upon the apostles and given them the gift of foreign languages. When Peter addresses the amazed onlookers, he explains that that day was the fulfillment of Joel's prophecy that the Spirit would be poured out.

There's another very similar prophecy that I think sheds light on Acts 2. Ezekiel 36:24-27 prophesies a future day when the Lord would sprinkle water upon His people and cleanse them from their impurities, their sin, and put a new Spirit in them. As in Ezekiel, the forgiveness of sins and the gift of the Spirit are connected and related to water, in this case water baptism. And did you notice how the Spirit is simply promised to all who are baptized. There are no conditions attached. It's simply a promise of God. There is no second or subsequent stage in the Christian life. Christians are all to be granted the Holy Spirit. There's no such thing as a "have-not" Christian.

Acts provides ample evidence that the people DO receive the gift of the Spirit. Luke does not narrate a mass phenomenon of 3,000 people speaking in tongues. Rather, what Luke describes is a Spirit-filled community that came together for the breaking of bread, the apostles' teaching, fellowship and prayer. The early believers held all things in common. Actually, all throughout Luke's Gospel and Acts, how you use your possessions is a sign of your inner condition and status before God.

[199] See Matthew 18:16; John 8:17; II Corinthians 13:1; Hebrews 10:28.

[200] Martin Luther, "The Babylonian Captivity," 62.

[201] Das, "Water Baptism."

[202] Martin Luther, "The Treatise … the Holy Mass," 82.

[203] Martin Luther, *Large Catechism*, in *Triglot Concordia: The Symbolical Books of the Evangelical Lutheran Church*, trans. F. Bente and W.H.T. Dau (St. Louis: Concordia Publishing House, 1921), 565-773.

[204] Dr. Michael S. Horton, "God's Grandchildren: The Biblical Basis for Infant Baptism," in *Modern Reformation Magazine* (1995), http://www.scionofzion.com/infantbap.htm (accessed Nov 20, 2005):

> To be sure, there are dangers in the paedobaptist position. Nevertheless, there are also dangers in the Baptist view. First, it is just as easy for men and women to place their faith in the extrabiblical rite of "making a decision" or responding to the invitation during an "altar call." Human nature is forever looking for ladders to climb into God's presence and favor, and unbiblical "sacraments" are no less prone to this use than are biblical ones. At the end of the day, abuses must never be allowed to cloud our vision of the biblical data and to that data we must ultimately submit, regardless of the practical consequences.

[205] *Ibid.*

[206] From an unpublished sermon by the author.

[207] Rev. John Scott Johnson, "In Defense of Infant Baptism," http://www.mountainretreatorg.net/apologetics/baptism3.html.

[208] Martin Luther, "That These Words of Christ, 'This Is My Body,' etc., Still Stand Firm Against the Fanatics" (1527), in *Luther's Works*, Vol 37 (*Word and Sacrament III*), gen. ed. Helmut T. Lehmann, (Philadelphia: Muhlenberg Press, 1960), 127.

[209] Robert F. Lindemann, unpublished papers:

To this day a Jew, even a not-so-good one, diligently circumcises his sons on the eighth day, because of the Covenant-command. It is so ingrained that it explains why the early Church was silent about infant-baptism. Originally the Church consisted entirely of Jews who accepted Jesus as the Messiah ("*Yeshuah Hammasheach*") and who would naturally see baptizing their infants as entering them into the New Covenant. As membership became non-Jewish, distanced from Jewish thinking, the question grew, "Can an infant believe?"

For the Jew, this was immaterial, since *Yahweh El Shaddai*, Jehovah the Almighty God, reached down to include him into Covenant. Whether his infant understood made little difference – Jehovah did it. As his son grew, then it was necessary to teach him what being under Covenant meant. Surely, many "circumcised" did not live worthy of Covenant, but broke it. Many prophets pleaded with this unique People (Israel) to have "a Circumcision of the heart" – a spiritual participation and entering into Covenant, beyond the physical marking. But that still did not make God change His mind and later require only adults to become circumcised. Rather, whenever there was faith, the LORD poured out the fullness of Covenant; whenever Covenant was defied, He separated himself from the man or people.

Bahnsen, "Baptism":

Since baptism is the New Covenant equivalent of circumcision, and since circumcision taught that the children of believers are included under God's covenant, and since our covenant-keeping God does not change His principles (Ps. 89:34; Matt. 4:4; 5:18; Rom. 15:4; Jas. 1:17), we would fully expect that baptism should be applied – as was circumcision – to believers and their seed or households. This theological inference is inescapable...

McMahon, "My Retraction":

I should have said it like this: the Apostles had no need of a positive sanction in order to continue the inclusion of infants in the covenant because they have always been included in every covenant through the history of redemption. This is a different statement altogether and does not allow for looking up baptism Scriptures in the New Testament as a remedy or answer to the question of Infant Baptism... Furthermore, there is not one "reference" to Infant Baptism in the New Testament. The Baptist argues that the reason for this is because Jesus or the Apostles did not teach it. The Paedo-Baptist argues that the Jews had a very good idea of infant inclusion in the covenant since every covenant and every dealing with those infants of believing households up until this time did include infants. They would not have needed another lesson on that again – their lessons concerning covenant theology have lasted as long as men have walked the earth... Instead, what we find is the New Testament, everywhere, mentioning covenant theology in terms like "households." This is very strange language for the Baptist to deal with since "household" is a covenant term the Jews would have certainly understood, and the New Testament church would have required, as Jews, entire households to become part of the church. This is not Baptist Theology at all. In fact, of all the treatises I have read on Baptistic theology in this area, none make good mention, or any at all, on why the term "household" is even used by the Holy Sprit all through the book of Acts if "individualism" (single converts coming to faith apart from familial relations) is now the norm (especially with the Greek forms surrounding this word).

210 Francis A. Schaeffer, "Baptism," http://www.spiritone.com/~wing/fs_bapt.htm:

> These questions would be further aggravated by what this saved Jew himself would have heard taught in the New Testament time. For example, he would have heard Peter in his sermon on the Day of Pentecost, Acts 2: 38, 39: "Then Peter said unto them, 'Repent, and be baptized every one of you in the name of Jesus Christ for the remission of sins, and ye shall receive the gift of the Holy Ghost. For the promise is unto you and to your children, and to all that are afar off, even as many as the LORD our God shall call.'" Remember, Peter said this to Jews, Jews who were used to having the outward sign of their faith applied to their children.
>
> With all these things in his mind, he would expect his child to be baptized. If it were refused, what would you have done in his place? You would have asked the Apostles the reason why. So would the thousands of Christian Jews in that day. The question would have been asked in a hundred meetings; and Peter, John, Paul, and the others would have sat down and written in their Epistles to clear up the matter, just as they answered other questions that arose. The New Testament would have contained the clear answer as to why in the Old Testament the Covenant sign was applied to the infants of believers, but in the New Testament it was to be withheld from them.
>
> The only reason possible for the New Testament not dealing with this problem is that the problem did not exist. The only possible reason that there was no problem in the Jews' minds was that the believing Jews did apply the covenant sign to their children. They baptized their babies as they had circumcised them in the Old Testament dispensation.

211 Robert F Lindemann, "Reflections Upon Holy Baptism," unpublished paper.

212 Paul E. Billheimer, *Destined For The Throne* (Fort Washington, PA: Christian Literature Crusade:, 1976), 33,35-37.

213 When this writer and his wife adopted two children, the children were issued new birth certificates with our names as their parents. In a very real sense, it was a new birth.

214 This writer's book, *Celebration – Communion: A Love Story*, scheduled to be published.

215 See endnote 194.

216 The Greek word used here is used in the Septuagint (the Greek translation of the Old Testament) for *the Atonement Cover* ("Mercy Seat") over *the Ark of the Covenant* [for example, Exodus 25:17-22. See Kittel, ed., *Theological Dictionary*, Vol III, 318-323.

217 Kittel, ed., *Theological Dictionary*, Vol I, 539-540.

218 Martin Luther, *Luther's Works*, Vol 35, 57.

219 Dr Martin H Scharlemann, *The Secret of God's Plan: Studies in Ephesians*, (Saint Louis: Concordia Publishing House, 1970), 20.

[220] Theodore H. Epp, "Praying With Authority," Back to the Bible Broadcast (1965), 69-70.

[221] von Schenk, 90-91.

[222] See endnote 133.

[223] Martin Luther, "A Treatise... the Holy Mass," 99.

[224] Lindemann, *Celebration!*

[225] von Schenk, 157.

[226] *Ibid*, 128-131.

[227] Same word and form as in Matthew 5:6: "hungering and thirsting for righteousness" and Luke 6:21: "Blessed are those who are hungering now ..."

[228] Same word as used for "'purchased' People" in I Peter 2:9.

[229] *The American Heritage Dictionary of the English Language*, Fourth Edition (Houghton Mifflin Company, 2000), http://www.houghtonmifflinbooks.com/epub/ahd4.shtml

www.ingramcontent.com/pod-product-compliance
Lightning Source LLC
Chambersburg PA
CBHW030330240426
43661CB00052B/1589